An Introduction to Foreign Language Learning and Teaching

An Introduction to Foreign Language Learning and Teaching provides an engaging, student-friendly guide to the field of foreign language learning and teaching. Aimed at students with no background in the area and taking a task-based approach, this book:

- introduces the theoretical and practical aspects of both learning and teaching;
- provides discussion and workshop activities throughout each chapter of the book, along with further reading and reflection tasks;
- deals with classroom- and task-based teaching, and covers lesson planning and testing, making the book suitable for use on practical training courses;
- analyses different learning styles and suggests strategies to improve language acquisition;
- includes examples from foreign language learning in Russian, French, and German, as well as English;
- is accompanied by a brand new companion website at www.routledge.com/cw/johnson, which contains additional material, exercises, and weblinks.

Written by an experienced teacher and author, *An Introduction to Foreign Language Learning and Teaching* is essential reading for students beginning their study in the area, as well as teachers in training and those already working in the field.

Keith Johnson is Emeritus Professor of Linguistics and Language Education in the Department of Linguistics and English Language, University of Lancaster, UK.

LEARNING ABOUT LANGUAGE

Series Editors:
Mick Short, Lancaster University, UK; **Brian Walker**, Huddersfield University, UK; **Willem Hollmann**, Lancaster University, UK; and the late **Geoffrey Leech**, Lancaster University, UK

Further titles in this series can be found online at www.routledge.com/series/PEALAL

An Introduction to Foreign Language Learning and Teaching

Revised Third Edition

KEITH JOHNSON

Routledge
Taylor & Francis Group

LONDON AND NEW YORK

Revised third edition published 2018
by Routledge
2 Park Square, Milton Park, Abingdon, Oxon OX14 4RN

and by Routledge
711 Third Avenue, New York, NY 10017

Routledge is an imprint of the Taylor & Francis Group, an informa business

First edition published by Pearson Education Limited 2001
Third edition published by Routledge 2017

British Library Cataloguing-in-Publication Data
A catalogue record for this book is available from the British Library

Library of Congress Cataloguing-in-Publication Data
Names: Johnson, Keith, 1944– author.
Title: An introduction to foreign language learning and teaching /
Keith Johnson. Description: Revised third Edition. |
Milton Park, Abingdon, Oxon ; New York, NY :
Routledge, [2017] | Includes bibliographical references and index.
Identifiers: LCCN 2016030349 | ISBN 9780815380160 (hardback) |
ISBN 9780815380177 (pbk.) | ISBN 9781351213868 (ebook)
Subjects: LCSH: Language and languages–Study and teaching. |
Language acquisition.
Classification: LCC P51 .J55 2017 | DDC 418.0071–dc23
LC record available at https://lccn.loc.gov/2016030349

ISBN: 978-0-815-38016-0 (hbk)
ISBN: 978-0-815-38017-7 (pbk)
ISBN: 978-1-351-21386-8 (ebk)

Typeset in Sabon
by Out of House Publishing

Visit the companion website: www.routledge.com/cw/johnson

For Helen and Hugh

Contents

Author's acknowledgements

Books often carry just one name on their cover, but are the product of many people's efforts. This book is no exception, and I have many people to thank. The series editors, Mick Short and the late Geoffrey Leech, were conscientiously supportive in the early days, and Mick has continued to be so as the book goes into its third edition. My former colleague Alan Waters has been generous with advice and insights, and I am very grateful to Phil Benson, Pauline Foster, Qiuping Gao and Huw Jarvis for their suggestions on the shape and direction of this third edition.

Thanks also to all at Routledge, particularly Nadia Seemungal and Helen Tredget for their valuable help in the production of this edition; and to Heidi Cormode and Alex Higson for their very useful work.

Most thanks of all to my wife, Helen, for her support as constructive critic and spouse. It is no mean feat to be able to combine these roles and at the same time maintain good humour in the way that she does. From edition to edition.

Publisher's acknowledgements

The author and publishers would like to thank the copyright holders for their permission to reproduce the following material:

> Box 2.5 from Watt, T. S. (1954) 'Hints on Pronunciation for Foreigners' in *The Guardian*, © Guardian News and Media Limited 1954
>
> Box 10.4 from Stern, H. H. (1983) *Fundamental Concepts of Language Teaching*, Oxford University Press
>
> Chapter 11 figure from Dudley-Evans, T. and St John, M. J. (1998) *Developments in English for Specific Purposes: A Multi-Disciplinary Approach*, Cambridge University Press
>
> Chapter 12 image from GRAPHIC NEWS, reproduced with kind permission
>
> Box 12.9 from Broughton, G. (1968) *Success with English: Coursebook 1*, Penguin Books. Reproduced by permission of Penguin Books Ltd
>
> Chapter 13 figure from White, R. V. and Arndt, V. (1991) *Process Writing*, Longman Group UK Ltd, published by permission of Pearson Education Limited.

Every effort has been made to contact copyright holders. Please advise the publisher of any errors or omissions, and these will be corrected in subsequent editions.

Abbreviations and acronyms

ACTFL	American Council on the Teaching of Foreign Languages (organization which sets up language proficiency guidelines)
AL	audiolingualism; audiolingual
ARELS	Association of Recognised English Language Schools
ASTP	Army Specialized Training Program
BICS	basic interpersonal communicative skills
CA	contrastive analysis
CALL	computer-assisted language learning
CANAL-FT	Cognitive Ability for Novelty in Acquisition of Language – Foreign Language Test
CBI	content-based instruction
CDS	child-directed speech
CEELT	Cambridge Examination in English for Language Teachers
CLT	communicative language teaching
CM	communicative methodology
CNP	Communicative Needs Processor
C-Test	a type of 'Cloze' test in which the second half of every second word is deleted
DEC	declarative knowledge; the provision of declarative knowledge; the learning model in which just declarative knowledge is provided
DECPRO	the learning model in which declarative knowledge is taught and then converted into procedural knowledge
EA	error analysis
EAP	English for academic purposes
EC	error correction
EGRUL	sequence in (inductive) learning where examples are given before rules
EIL	English as an International Language
ELF	English as a *lingua franca*
ESL	English as a second language
ESP	English for specific purposes
EST	English for Science and Technology
FCE	First Certificate of English

FL	foreign language
GG	generative grammar
i+1	language which is at a level slightly higher than the acquirer's present level of competence (i)
IELTS	International English Language Testing System
IQ	intelligence quotient
IT	information transfer (exercises)
L1	first language; mother tongue
L2	second language; some people use this term to include all languages except for the L1 (i.e. including 'foreign' languages)
LAB	Language Aptitude Battery
LAD	language acquisition device
LAP	languages for academic purposes
LOP	languages for occupational purposes
LP	lesson planning
LSA	Learning Situation Analysis
LSP	languages for specific purposes
MALU	mobile-assisted language use
MLAT	Modern Language Aptitude Test
n/f	notional/functional
NEST	native English-speaker teacher
NfM	negotiation for meaning
NNS	non-native speaker
Non-NEST	non-native English-speaker teacher
NS	native speaker
OCC	oral communication course
PPP	the sequence of presentation → practice → production
PRO	procedural knowledge; the provision of procedural knowledge; the learning/acquisition model in which just procedural knowledge is provided
PRODEC	the learning/acquisition model in which procedural knowledge is taught/acquired and then converted into declarative knowledge
RULEG	sequence in (deductive) learning where rules are given before examples
SC	sentence combining (exercises)
SLA	second-language acquisition
S-R-R	the sequence of stimulus → response → reinforcement
TBT	task-based teaching
TEEP	Test of English for Educational Purposes
TEFL	teaching English as a foreign language
TENOR	teaching English for no obvious reason
TESL	teaching English as a second language
TESOL	teaching English to speakers of other languages

T-Level	the Threshold Level
TOEFL	Test of English as a Foreign Language
TPR	Total Physical Response
TSA	Target Situation Analysis
UCH	Unitary Competence Hypothesis
UCLES	University of Cambridge Local Examination Syndicate
UG	Universal Grammar

Introduction

One of the original aims of *An Introduction to Foreign Language Learning and Teaching* was to provide an account of the field which was up to date but at the same time gave a historical perspective, showing where current ideas and developments have come from. This perspective, I still believe, is important if we are to understand where we are and even where we may be going.

Water has flowed under the applied linguistic bridge since the second edition, and a main aim of the third edition has been to update. Another aim has been to make the text itself a little shorter, following feedback from users that the earlier editions went beyond being an introductory text. The hope is that the book will now be better suited to use on short introductory courses.

Although the text itself has been shortened, almost no material at all has been lost. What is not now in the text has been put onto the book's 'Companion Website.' The letters CW in the text direct you to a website entry. For example, in Chapter 2, there is a section dealing with English sounds and pronunciation. Associated with this is a website entry dealing with the 'weak' vowel /ə/, sometimes called 'schwa.' This vowel often causes problems for learners of English, so it deserves some special treatment. Because it is the second entry related to Chapter 2, this is marked in the text as 'CW2.2 (*A very troublesome vowel*)', with the CW logo in the margin. There are 90 CW entries in all, and the expectation is that you may not want to look at all of them. But they are there for those who want to go beyond the 'bare essentials' on any topic.

The third edition continues to be full of activities and suggestions for discussion. I have added, at the end of each chapter, a section called 'Issues to think or write about.' This contains suggestions for extended treatment, through class discussion or written work. I hope you like the fact that the book is full of questions. Reading is important; so too is thinking about what you read.

Earlier editions have enjoyed some success among those preparing to become teachers, following degree or training courses at tertiary institutions. The book is not, nor cannot be, a fully fledged teacher training course. But I have tried, at the very least, to sensitize teachers to important practical language-teaching skills. I hope this effort will be apparent throughout the book, even in the more theoretical parts. I want my book to help you become a knowledgeable, but also a reflective, language teacher.

Keith Johnson

Part I
Background

1 Five learners and five methods

1.1 Introduction

B1.1 Boxes, boxes, boxes

This book is full of boxes, so perhaps it should start with one. The boxes often contain points to think about, or activities to do. Here are some things to think about before you start to read the book.

In Chapter 13 (Sections 13.3.3 and 13.3.4) we will see that tapping a person's expectations before they read something is a useful technique for improving reading skills. To experience this process, you are invited to think about the content of this book before you read it. Look first of all just at the book's title (*not* the contents page). What areas do you expect the book to cover? What is it going to be about? Then look at the contents page and see whether your expectations seem correct.

Is it clear from the contents page how the book is organized? And do the chapter titles clearly indicate what each chapter is about? If not, try to guess, and check whether your guess is right by skimming through the chapter itself.

Now consider what you already know about the subjects of this book – language learning and teaching. Look at each chapter title and consider the same thing – what you already know about it. Finally, what parts of the book do you expect to be particularly interesting for you? And less interesting? Why?

Now read on …

According to one estimate[1] there are about a billion people in the world today learning English as a foreign language. A billion is a thousand million – a phenomenally large number of people! If you add to this the number of individuals who are learning foreign languages other than English – Chinese, Japanese, Spanish, Italian, German, French, and many others – then you realize just how many people on the planet are engaged in the process of foreign language learning.

Why the quite phenomenal expenditure of human energy in this direction? Why on earth do people bother to learn foreign languages on such a grand scale? In this chapter we shall think about some of the reasons why they do it, how successful they are at it, and some of the ways in which they may be taught. A major theme of the chapter will be *variety*. There are, we shall find, many different reasons for learning, many different degrees of success, and many different ways of teaching.

1.2 Why do people learn foreign languages?

B1.2 Reasons for learning

Before we look at other people, try to answer the *Why Question* for yourself and for friends. First consider your own language learning experiences, and ask yourself what your motives for learning were. Make a list of these. If you were obliged to learn, think what the motives of those who obliged you were. When you have thought about yourself, consider other people you know.

Think finally about the world beyond your immediate environment. Write a list of what you imagine to be the main motives for people worldwide learning foreign languages. As you read on, note how many of the reasons on your list are discussed below.

In order to answer the *Why Question*, and to appreciate the variety of answers it may receive, we will focus on five individuals involved in foreign language learning. They have been chosen to reveal some of the common motivations learners have.

Learner number one is Lilian Rivera. She lives in Santiago, the capital city of Chile. She has a bachelor's degree in business studies from a local university, and she wants to do a master's degree overseas. She has applied to universities in Britain, the United States and Australia, and there is the chance that she may receive some scholarship money. But all the universities require her to take an internationally recognized English test before she is offered a place, and her score on the test must be very high.[2] It is now January, and Lilian's test is in June. She does not enjoy language learning at all, but her situation explains very well why so very many of her daily waking hours are spent in the (for her) tedious business of improving her English.

Mike is an Australian, and his reason for learning Japanese could not be more different from Lilian's reason for learning English. Mike has just got married to Junko, a Japanese girl he met in Sydney, where she was, among other things, following an English language course – yet more language learning! Mike has never been to Japan and does not speak Japanese at the moment. But both these things must change. In the summer the two of them plan to visit Junko's parents in Kyoto, and neither of her parents speaks English. Hence Mike is at present as intensely engaged in foreign language learning as Lilian is.

Learner number three is an Indian girl whose name is Jasmine. She lives in Chennai (formerly Madras), the capital city of the Indian state of Tamil Nadu. Her native language is Tamil. The foreign language she is learning is another Indian language, though a very different one from Tamil. It is Hindi, considered a national language of India. In India many diverse, mutually unintelligible languages are spoken, and there is the need for one tongue to be spoken by all; the phrase *lingua franca* describes such a language, used as a means of communication between speakers of other languages. Jasmine wants to continue living and working in Chennai, but the job she has in mind will involve communication with Indians throughout the subcontinent. This is why she is learning Hindi.

Wai Mun Ching is from Hong Kong and her first language is Cantonese. Since Hong Kong was returned to China in 1997, she (like many other Hong Kong citizens) has wanted to learn Standard Mandarin Chinese (called Putonghua), spoken as a *lingua franca* throughout China. The reason she wants to learn this language is so that she will feel more integrated with the country she is now a part of. Though some people refer to Cantonese and Mandarin as 'dialects' of the same language, they are in fact very different, and Wai Mun does not find learning Mandarin easy at all. But this does not bother her; she is very well motivated, and can indeed get quite lyrical on the topic – she really does regard Mandarin as opening a window onto a somewhat new and very meaningful culture for her.

Anna Vecsey is a scientist who works for a research institute attached to a university in Budapest, Hungary. She studied English at school, but her English is poor, and she is constantly made aware of her need to improve it. This awareness is particularly strong at the moment because her institute is about to host an international conference. The delegates will come from all over the world, and the language of communication will be English. Papers at the conference will be delivered in English, chat over coffee will be in English, and there is unlikely to be any respite even over dinner, where English will be spoken. English, English, English. As a consequence, Anna Vecsey has signed up for a language improvement course at a local private language school.

These five characters illustrate some of the many reasons why people take time to learn a foreign language in today's world. The reasons are indeed various. Lilian is learning English in Chile for study purposes. Mike is busy with Japanese in Australia to integrate himself within his wife's culture, while Wai Mun in Hong Kong is learning Mandarin to strengthen her own cultural identity. Jasmine learns Hindi in India for purposes of *intranational* communication (that is, with people from within her country), and Anna in Hungary learns English to facilitate *international* communication (with people from other countries).

1.3 The multilingual world

It is not in fact difficult to understand the importance of foreign language learning in today's world. As the planet becomes smaller, and the means for moving round it easier, so it has become more multicultural and multilingual. Not so long ago we used to be able to talk of nation states which could be associated with single languages – in France they spoke French, in Germany German, and so on. But it is no longer like that. Take a country like Australia. Clyne (1991) plots the immigration patterns into Australia since the Second World War. In the 1950s came the Latvians, Lithuanians, Estonians, Czechs, Poles, Hungarians, Croats, Slovenians and Ukrainians. Then there were Germans from Eastern Europe, and refugees from Greece in 1967, from Hungary following the Soviet intervention in Hungary in 1956 and from Czechoslovakia in 1968. The list really could be expanded very considerably, still talking about the same period – British, Maltese, Cypriots, Dutch, Germans, Italians, Yugoslavs, Lebanese, Turks, Chinese, Vietnamese, Cambodians. Clyne (1991) gives some revealing details of various censuses on language use in Australia. The 1986 Census, for example, looks at languages used in the home, state by state. No fewer than 63 languages are listed, and in fact some of these are language families ('Aboriginal languages' are grouped together, for example). All this means that a stroll down a main street in any major Australian city is likely to be an informal introduction to the languages of the world. You are certainly not going to hear just English, the one language traditionally associated with Australia. The same is true of the United States, another country where it is a common perception that just English is spoken. But the United States, like Australia and much of the rest of the world, is far from monolingual. Today's world is truly multilingual.

B1.3 Multilingual places and people

Perhaps you live in a place where many different languages are spoken. Or if not, perhaps you have visited such a place. If so, list the languages that are spoken, and where possible explain how they have come to be used there. Perhaps there have been many recent immigrants? Or have different ethnic groups always lived in the place? Or are there many tourists from specific countries?

Do you know any individuals who regularly use more than one language in everyday life? What languages do they use? When, and why?

In a multilingual world, it is natural to find large numbers of people who speak (and have therefore learned) more than one language. In many countries there are many more than two languages in operation, and it is not difficult to find examples where large numbers of languages are spoken on a daily basis. According to Crystal (2003), in many African countries as much as 90 per cent of the population regularly uses more than one language. The oft-cited champions in the language learning stakes are the Vaupes River Indians, a tribe of around ten thousand Indians living in what is today Colombia. They have some dozen mutually unintelligible languages. Indeed, it seems to be the custom to find a marriage partner who speaks another language. This means that children have to start off by learning Mum's language, Dad's language, and a language common to the tribe. Many more languages may be added through an individual's life (especially if one were to become engaged to marry several times!).

The Vaupes Indians may be an extreme case, but multilingualism in the world is a hard fact, and with it comes the need to develop common languages for communication. It is indeed becoming the model for people to have one language to speak at home and another to communicate with some group of people outside. It is important for those of us who live with one language only to understand that we are the exception rather than the rule. Learning a foreign language may nowadays be regarded as a normal, almost everyday, activity.

1.4   Individual learning differences

We have seen that people learn foreign languages for a great variety of reasons. Another dimension on which we find great variety is in the degree of success foreign language learners enjoy. This is one way in which <u>first language learning</u> (learning your mother tongue as a child) and foreign language learning differ. Though there are many ways in which the following statements need to be qualified, it is broadly true that all children, whatever their 'talent' for language learning, whatever their social background, whatever their level of educational achievement, learn to speak their native or first language by a very early age. Some will take slightly longer than others, but they all get there.

A similar statement could not be made about foreign language learning. It is unfortunately very far from the case that everyone who attempts to learn a foreign language 'succeeds.' Indeed, the figures for successful school learning of a foreign language are in some countries (such as England) depressingly, even shamefully, low. With foreign language learning, individual differences seem to make themselves felt. Some people do it very well. Sir Richard Burton (not the actor, but the nineteenth-century explorer who translated the *Kama Sutra*) appears to have spoken more than 40 languages, and according to Edwards (1994: 34) one Giuseppe Mezzofanti, the chief curator of the Vatican Library at the beginning of the nineteenth century, reportedly spoke 60 languages fluently and could translate more than 150 languages and dialects. You may well be able to think of individuals in your own experience who seem to have a special talent for language learning. Others are hopeless; they may be well-intentioned, but they are simply dreadful, quite unable to put a sentence together in a foreign tongue, and incapable of modifying their native language accent in any way. You may be able to find examples of public figures in your own country who come into this category. An example from Britain is Edward Heath, prime minister from 1970 to 1974. As a supporter of what became the European Union, he was brave enough to make speeches in French. It was horrible.

B1.4 Differences in people you know

Consider some examples of successful and unsuccessful learners among those you know – people perhaps who at school have come top and bottom of the language learning class. Why were they successful or unsuccessful? Can you account for their performance in any way?

Your answers could contribute towards a solution to the puzzle of what makes people good or bad at language learning.

Most of us fall somewhere between Richard Burton and Edward Heath. We manage to get by in a foreign language, though we mostly never approach the level of the native speaker. At some point along the way we <u>fossilize</u> – that is, our foreign language stops moving forwards, and 'sticks.' First language learners do not fossilize in this way.

How can we account for these individual differences? We shall consider this question in some detail in Chapters 7 and 8. Meanwhile, Box 1.5 offers a 'taster' of some of the fascinating findings that research in the 'individual differences' area suggests.

B1.5 Individual learning differences. A 'taster' (of some issues discussed at length in Chapters 7 and 8)

- You do not have to be intelligent to learn a foreign language, but you do have to be intelligent to follow some methods.
- There are some people with a talent for foreign language learning, but apparently not much else. Smith and Tsimpli (1995) devote a 240-page book to discussion of a boy called Christopher who suffers from brain damage, and who has to live in an institution because of his inability to handle life outside. Yet in one area, Christopher excels – he can speak 16 foreign languages.
- Attitudes towards the native speakers of the foreign language you wish to learn may sometimes be very important. Some people would argue that if for some reason you intensely dislike the native speakers of a particular language, you are wasting your time trying to learn that language.
- Parental support is very important for children. If mother and father want a child to do well at learning a foreign language, this will help the process a good deal. As we shall see later, some parents regard language learning as a 'girlish' activity, so they support girls' learning but encourage boys in other directions.

- Factors like those just considered can 'trade each other off.' For example, you may find a learner who is highly motivated, loves language learning and puts a lot of effort into it. Yet they may not do very well, simply because they lack something – talent (or aptitude) perhaps. Just such a case is reported in Chapter 7's Box 7.18.

1.5 Language teaching: a variety of methods

We've noted great variety both in the reasons why individuals learn foreign languages and in their success at doing so. We also find variety when we turn to the other subject of this book: language teaching. It would be an understatement to say that there is no consensus of opinion as to what is the best way to teach a foreign language. To illustrate the point, consider the five language teaching classrooms below. They are very different from one another.

B1.6 Methods you have experienced

Before looking at the five methods, reflect on the language learning methods you yourself have experienced. Describe them in as much detail as possible. What were their main characteristics? Did you have to know a lot of grammatical terms to be able to use them? Was there a lot of parrot-like repetition involved? Did they concentrate on reading and writing more than listening and speaking? What did you find to be their strengths and weaknesses?

Classroom 1 is in Abu Dhabi, in the United Arab Emirates, and the language being taught is Arabic. The pupils are children, the sons and daughters of business people and diplomats living in the Emirate. Their native language is English, but this is hard to believe as you listen to what goes on during the school day. From the time they arrive till the time they leave, the pupils are spoken to almost entirely in Arabic. They are greeted by their teacher in Arabic, their lessons are conducted in Arabic, teachers speak to them in the playground and the dinner hall in Arabic, and they say goodbye to them at the end of the day in Arabic. When the pupils started at this school, they themselves replied to the teachers in English (that is, the teachers spoke Arabic and the pupils responded naturally in English), but over time this has changed, and now the pupils themselves are increasingly using Arabic. This mode of teaching is commonly referred to as <u>immersion</u> (because the learners are being 'immersed' in the language). It is based on the idea that learners can 'pick up' a foreign language in much the same way as children 'pick up' their native language.

In **Classroom 2,** the teenage English pupils are learning Italian. The book they are using is full of extremely complicated grammar rules, explained in English. The teacher spends some 20 minutes of the lesson explaining the grammar point of the day, in English, using diagrams on the blackboard and plenty of grammatical terms (talking of 'tenses', 'nouns', 'adverbs' and the like). The learners are then given a series of translation exercises to do, both from English into Italian and vice versa. One glaring characteristic of the sentences the learners are given to translate is that one can never imagine anyone ever saying them. They are sentences clearly concocted to practise grammar points – Dobson *et al.*'s (1981) example of a typical sentence from this method is *The flowers of my grandmother are in the garden of the Dutchman.* When did you, or anyone else, last say that? This method is called grammar-translation, and although its heyday is really now past, it is still used in many parts of the world today, to teach many languages.

Classroom 3 is in Seoul, South Korea. The students are Americans learning Korean, and the method being used is called Total Physical Response (TPR). Even though the learners are truly beginners – in their first month of learning – Korean is the only language used throughout the lesson. At this stage it is only really the teacher who talks, and what they say in Korean is easy for the learners to understand, because all sentences are instructions for action – *Stand up*, *Walk over there*, *Stop*, *Turn round*, *Sit down*. The teachers first demonstrate these actions themselves; then they choose members of the class to do them. It will be a while before the learners themselves are asked to speak, but when they do, it will be in the foreign language and to ask other members of the class to follow similar action sequences. As with the immersion approach, part of the rationale for TPR lies in a parallel with first language learning, in which a close relationship between words and actions is developed.

Classroom 4 uses a version of a method which will be familiar to many of you. It is known as audiolingualism. The lesson (in this case teaching French in the African state of Cameroon) focuses on a grammar point, but unlike in Classroom 2 there is no explanation whatsoever, and the learners' native language is hardly used at all. The grammar point is made clear in the textbook by the use of example sentences, accompanied by pictures which help make meanings obvious. The time spent on exemplifying the grammatical point is quite short, and it is not very far into the lesson before the learners are given a series of rapid-fire exercises (or drills) to practise the grammar point. One of audiolingualism's central tenets is that learning a language is largely a question of habit formation, and for this reason a good part of the lesson is spent on drills, in an attempt to make using the grammar point an automatic habit.

Classroom 5 is in Beijing. In their English lesson, the learners are put together into pairs. They are told that they are friends, planning to go on a week's holiday together. They can go – they are told – either to Hong Kong or to Macau. Details of each holiday are given to them – information about the hotel and its location, sights for them to see, activities for them to do. They have to decide which holiday to take. The teacher plans to give them just ten minutes to make up their minds, but he is soon surprised at the amount of heated controversy the task generates, so much so that he has to keep very alert to ensure that English and not Mandarin is used all the time – many learners tend to revert to their mother tongue when they have a real urge to say something. The teacher had planned, as the next stage of the lesson, to get the pairs to phone up a travel agent (a role played by another class member), to make the holiday booking. But the initial discussion takes so long that there is no class time left for this. The lesson is an example of <u>task-based teaching</u> (TBT). It is a method that is very popular today.

In this chapter we have looked at five different learners and five different teaching methods. It would of course be an exaggeration to say that there are as many methods of teaching a foreign language as there are learners. But there are, clearly, very many ways of skinning the language-learning cat. Chapter 9 provides a detailed survey of recent language teaching methods.

1.6   Plan of the book

Part 1 of this book deals with background issues. In Chapter 2 we ask: what does learning a language involve? What exactly needs to be learned, and what can be taught? We seek answers to these questions by analysing language in its component parts and considering which of those component parts need attention from the learner, and which from the teacher. In Chapter 3 we deal with some key ideas about language and language learning that have had particular influence in the field.

Then, in Part 2, we focus on language learning. In Chapters 4 to 6 we survey some of the theories that have been prominent in recent times. Chapters 7 and 8 look at some of the factors that have been associated with success in language learning. Several of these have already been mentioned in Box 1.5.

In Part 3 our attention turns to language teaching. Chapter 9 gives a brief recent history of teaching approaches, talking in more detail about some of the methods seen in the five classrooms above, and others besides. In Chapter 10 we look at issues related to the planning of language teaching within a social and even political context (teaching a foreign language can be a very political act indeed!). Chapter 11 also deals with planning, but of specific programmes. It is largely about syllabus design. Chapters 12 and 13 look at what actually happens in classrooms – the nuts and bolts of how to teach a language. Chapter 14 is about testing. Chapter 15, the final chapter, is entitled *When all has been said*. It is useful for a teacher to know about all the areas covered in the first 14 chapters. But knowledge isn't everything and, 'when all has been said', a teacher needs to have skills as well as knowledge. Chapter 15 deals with some of these skills, including lesson planning, correcting learner errors and aspects of classroom management (such as the highly practical question of how to do groupwork in class).

This book has a companion website. Its resources are integral to the book; they are more than 'add-on extras.' You are always directed to these resources by a specific mention in the text, signaled by the letters CW. Each chapter also has a section near the end called 'Issues to think or write about.' This is exactly what it says. The issues raised are complex ones, worthy of extended treatment (in an assignment, for example).

Few people read books in a linear fashion, starting at the beginning and working through page by page until the end. This book does try to 'tell a story' about language learning and teaching, and it is true that you may miss the unfolding of this 'story' if you do not read from beginning to end. But it may well be that certain parts of the book talk about things which you already know or which are of little interest to you. If so, it is expected that you will pick and choose what you read, and in what order. An attempt has been made to put lots of 'signposts' in the book, connecting ideas by referring backwards and forwards. This should help you to follow what you read even if you have not read every word that comes before it. Hopefully, the combination of your knowledge plus what you read will tell the same 'story' you would get if you read every word.

1.7 Some terminology and some conventions

Terminology plagues the language learning and teaching worlds. One website, www.tesol.org, has a useful list of the more common terms. For many people ESP stands for 'extra-sensory perception', but to language teachers it means 'English for specific purposes' (teaching English, for example, for business studies, or to airline pilots). Associated with ESP are EST (English for science and technology) and EAP (English for academic purposes). Then there is TESOL (teaching English to speakers of other languages), TEFL (teaching English as a foreign language) and even TENOR (teaching English for no obvious reason – the opposite, perhaps, of ESP).

To help you through the jungle of terminology, in the prelims you will find a list of the abbreviations and acronyms used in this book. But some pieces of terminology need attention at the very beginning. TEFL has already been mentioned, but there is also TESL – teaching English as a second language. What is the difference between a foreign and a second language? For some, a second language is one that is used (probably as a *lingua franca*) in the learner's home country – French for people in ex-French colonies, for example – while a foreign language is one without that special status. But nowadays many do not make this distinction, and it has become the case that 'second language learning' often refers to the learning of any language other than the mother tongue. It is perhaps lamentable that the word 'second' as opposed to 'foreign' has taken on this general meaning, because 'foreign' is the more general word. We shall accordingly use the word 'foreign' throughout this book.

Another way of saying 'foreign language' is 'FL', and we shall often use phrases like 'FL acquisition', and speak of a learner's 'FL.' We shall also refer to a learner's mother tongue as their 'L1'; so the phrase 'an L1 Cantonese speaker' would mean a person whose native language is Cantonese. A 'target language' is the one being learned.

A further term that needs explanation is 'applied linguist.' Anyone who applies the findings of linguistics to some area is an applied linguist. So for example, a speech therapist who uses linguistics to help in the understanding and treatment of speech defects is an applied linguist. One major application of linguistics is in the areas of foreign language learning and teaching. In this book we shall often speak of applied linguists, referring to those interested specifically in the FL learning and teaching fields.

Some conventions: first, when new pieces of terminology are introduced, they are often first expressed in everyday terms, with the 'technical' term being underlined and put in brackets afterwards. An example is the way the word *drill* is introduced in discussion of Classroom 4 above.

Second, in recognition of the fact that this book covers a great deal of ground, sometimes with little space for detailed discussion, each chapter gives suggestions for further reading. On occasions (both in the further reading and in the text itself) websites are referred to. All websites were accessed and found to be available in 2016.

Third, to help you make links between ideas, the book is full of references forwards and backwards to previous or following sections which discuss relevant ideas. The first number of a section is the same as the chapter's number. So 'in 3.2.6' is a shorthand way of saying 'in Chapter 3's section 2.6.' The same convention is used to refer to boxes. Thus Box 3.7 is in Chapter 3, Box 9.5 in Chapter 9.

Talking of boxes, the book is indeed full of them. As you have already gathered, many of them suggest points to think about or activities to do. You should not, of course, feel obliged to spend time on all of them. The assumption is that you will pick and choose.

Notes

1. The source is the 1997 British Council/British Tourist Authority advice pack entitled *Marketing English Language Courses*. I am indebted to David Crystal for making this information available. His own estimate is for a lower number.
2. There are a number of internationally recognized tests for people who plan to study or work where English is the language of communication. The best-known are IELTS (for International English Language Testing System, a British test) and TOEFL (Test of English as a Foreign Language, an American test). Take a look forward to 14.8 (Chapter 14, section 8) which lists some important tests.

Issues to think or write about

1. How important are methods? One point of view is that a good learner will learn – and a bad learner will fail to learn – whatever method is used. Another point of view is that the method used is crucial to whether or not success will be the outcome. Argue these two points of view, and give your own opinion.
2. What makes a good method? Think about your own situation (or one that you know well). What characteristics should a method have to make it 'good' in that situation? Make your answer as specific and concrete as you can.

Further reading

Edwards, J. 1994 *Multilingualism* London: Routledge
If you want to know more about multilingualism, this book will give you an interesting account of the growth of multiculturalism in the modern world.

Crystal, D. 2003 *English as a Global Language* 2nd edn Cambridge: Cambridge University Press
This highly readable book shows how increasing globalization has created the need for a global *lingua franca*, a role which English is at the moment fulfilling.

Skehan, P. 1989 *Individual Differences in Second-Language Learning* London: Edward Arnold
Individual learner differences will be discussed at length in Chapters 7 and 8 of the present volume. This book is key reading on the topic.

Dörnyei, Z. 2005 *The Psychology of the Language Learner: Individual Differences in Second Language Acquisition* London: Lawrence Erlbaum Associates
A more recent account of individual differences.

Richards, J. C., and Rodgers, T. S. 2001 *Approaches and Methods in Language Teaching* 2nd edn Cambridge: Cambridge University Press
Chapter 9 of the present volume will concentrate on language teaching methods. This book provides a useful survey.

2 What is there to learn?

2.1 Introduction

B2.1 FL troubles

Think – before you start on this long chapter – about your own FL learning experiences. Identify some of the areas in the FL that you found particularly difficult to master – sounds you had trouble pronouncing, grammatical structures that you never got right. Is spelling in the FL a problem for you, and what about learning its vocabulary? Can you come up with reasons that explain the difficulty of the areas you identify?

What exactly is involved in learning a foreign language? What kinds of 'knowledge' and 'skill' need to be mastered? If you are asked questions like this, your initial response is likely to involve words like 'pronunciation', 'vocabulary' and 'grammar.' These are the questions we shall ask in this chapter. One intended outcome is to lead you to realize how complex an operation learning a foreign language is. There is indeed an immense amount to be mastered.

Questions like the ones above need to be approached in two stages. First, we will identify what different types of knowledge and skill are involved in *using* a language: the skills and knowledge that the competent language user possesses. This will involve the areas already mentioned – like pronunciation, vocabulary and grammar – as well as some less obvious ones. The result of this stage of enquiry will be a list of all the levels on which a language can be analysed; the levels which the discipline of linguistics is concerned with.

But describing these different levels of knowledge and skill will only half answer our questions. This is because not everything involved in using a language needs to be learned afresh by the learner. A rather extreme example will clarify this. One of the things that the speakers of all languages do is to produce sounds by pushing air from the lungs, through the vocal cords and up into the mouth. We may legitimately say that this skill is part of what is involved in speaking a foreign language. But the learner has already mastered this skill in relation to L1 learning. It does not have to be either learned or taught. So the second stage of enquiry asks the extent to which mastery of the levels which we identify involves new learning.

To develop some feel for the complexities of the 'what is involved in learning a foreign language' question, we may add to the extreme example of breathing a more modest and more revealing one. Part of the English grammatical system involves use of 'articles': the words *the*, *a* and *an*. We may legitimately say that in order to use English properly, this article system has to be mastered. But this will entail very different amounts of learning for speakers of different languages. For some learners, there will be a rather small amount of learning involved, because their own L1 has a comparable system. So L1 speakers of German, for example, will have relatively few problems with the English articles (which are in many respects much simpler than the German ones). But the situation will be dramatically different for the speakers of L1s which do not have a comparable article system, or indeed any article system at all. So for Japanese or Russian speakers, the operation involves very much more than learning the words *the*, *a* and *an*. With these learners, the whole issue of what an article is, what it 'means', and – most difficult of all – when each is used, has to be tackled. A pause for thought may make you realize what a phenomenally difficult issue this is likely to be.

We shall see in 4.2 that one way of finding out what a particular learner will find easy or difficult in the FL is to undertake a comparison of FL and L1 in order to identify similarities and differences. Similar areas should lead to ease of learning, and where there are differences we should expect learning difficulties. This suggests correctly that the answer to our question 'what exactly is involved in learning a foreign language?' is not just complex but will also differ from learner to learner depending on what L1 they speak.

2.2 Categorizing knowledge and skill

How does one begin to categorize the levels of knowledge and skill involved in language use? One possible 'way in' is to look at, and categorize, the mistakes that a learner makes. Box 2.2 gives you an example of learner language to think about in this way:

B2.2 'Cats' – useless domestic animals

Below is an essay produced by a foreign language learner on the topic of 'Cats.' The essay is full of mistakes and inadequacies of various kinds. Identify as many different categories of error as you can. For example, the essay contains a number of spelling mistakes, so one category for your list would be 'spelling.' Note that all the crossing out in the essay was done by the student, not a teacher.

By identifying categories of error you are in fact identifying categories of knowledge and skill involved in FL use.

The cats are useless

The cats is useless as domesic animal.
Specially in cities there is no problem of
rates and mices. In my life, I haven't kept a cat
in the house. I think, this decision come from that
my life is full of hard work. Perhaps, you might
say: It is a nice thing to find a game (cat) for
your childern, as demostic aniual. I reply; OK.
for I life like this thing one time a week while
I don't leave my children to play with useless
game. My brother has a son, and this he had
his a cat. Later on, the cat was died. However
the boy was in deep sorrow and still of this
feeling for a long hime.

We shall now consider how others have attempted to categorize linguistic levels. A number of frameworks have been put forward,[1] but we will focus on the one developed by Canale and Swain (1980) to describe what they (and many others) call 'communicative competence.' This phrase is worth a moment's thought. 'Competence' is the term linguists use to describe roughly what we have so far rather ponderously been calling knowledge and skill, and this section's heading might therefore have read 'categorizing the levels of competence involved in language use.' The use of the word 'communicative' allows us to avoid a more restricted term like 'grammatical' – worth avoiding because, as we shall see, there is much more to using a language than grammar.

In fact, Canale and Swain's (1980) model of communicative competence identifies three levels of analysis: what they call grammatical, sociolinguistic and strategic. We shall introduce one change in terminology, using the word 'systemic', which we define below, for their first level. Otherwise our framework is identical to theirs. We shall deal with each of the levels of analysis in turn. For each, we have two aims: to clarify just what is associated with the category; then to develop, in relation to each, some feel for what needs to be learned by (and taught to) the FL learner. The final result will be to give us some sense of what, in general terms, is involved in learning a foreign language.

2.3   Systemic competence

The word 'systemic' means 'as a system', and the term <u>systemic competence</u> therefore covers knowledge and skill related to the way the language works as a system. This involves many different levels, the main ones being 'sounds' (<u>phonetics</u> and <u>phonology</u>), 'grammar' (<u>morphology</u> and <u>syntax</u>), and <u>lexis</u> ('words', 'vocabulary'). Also under this category come other skills which will have made an appearance in your response to Box 2.2, like handwriting, spelling and punctuation. We may be tempted to call these 'mechanical' skills, though a moment's thought will indicate that often they are very far from being purely mechanical – try for example to explain the difference in use between a comma and a semi-colon. Not so easy!

The following sections give examples of some important areas of systemic competence, and nearly all the examples relate to the English language. This chapter cannot hope to provide anything like full coverage of these areas, and the 'Further reading' section at the end of the chapter will help you in this respect. But the chapter is still quite a long one. As it proceeds, you may find yourself exclaiming – with some feeling – 'do I *really* have to know so much about English?' Native speakers of the language may want to add 'I learned the language as a child. I can speak it instinctively. Why do I have to learn about rules?' If you are an aspiring language teacher, you need to come to terms with this issue early on. The truth of the matter (as many would see it, at least) is that yes, you have to know how the language works if you are to teach it properly. It does not necessarily follow that you will want to give your students lengthy and abstract grammatical rules to learn. But if you do not know yourself what these rules are, you have perhaps little chance of teaching them well. Knowing how the language works will also help you to understand and manage the errors your learners make. Of course, if you already have a good knowledge of how English works, you may wish to pass over some of the boxed examples and exercises in these sections.

We start with an area which will not have occurred in your consideration of Box 2.1, because that is an example of written, not spoken, English.

2.3.1 Sounds: the pronunciation iceberg

You will probably have no trouble in accepting the general notion that pronunciation causes FL speakers all kinds of difficulties. You have doubtless noticed that immigrants may spend very many years indeed in the target language country and still fail even to approximate native language pronunciation. Such individuals will, perhaps for all their lives, maintain their foreign pronunciation. Sound habits die very hard indeed.

Sometimes the problem is that a learner finds it very difficult to pronounce a particular sound, or perhaps even to perceive the difference between two sounds. It is well recognized, for example, that speakers of some oriental languages have problems with the English /l/ and /r/ sounds, so that sometimes a word like *rice* comes to be pronounced like *lice*, and *like* may be *rike*. The reason is that in these languages /l/ and /r/ are simply not distinctive sounds – there are no word pairs, like English *rice* and *lice*, where the /l/–/r/ difference is crucial to distinguish words. They are not, in linguistic parlance, <u>phonemes</u>: the name linguists use for sounds which distinguish words. Because these two sounds are not important in this way, speakers of these languages are not attuned to 'hearing' the difference and hence have difficulty producing the two sounds.

Readers who are native speakers of English may appreciate these sorts of difficulties more strongly with the realization – obvious if you think about it – that native speakers of English will experience similar types of difficulty learning an FL. An oft-cited and clear example relates to the learning of Russian. In both English and Russian there are two rather different ways of pronouncing the sound /l/. In the English word 'like', for example, the tongue touches the gums behind the top teeth, and the front part of the tongue is raised upwards. The resulting sound is what is called the 'clear /l/.' The so-called 'dark /l/' is found in a word like 'real.' Here the tongue again touches the gums behind the top teeth, but the part of the tongue that is raised is much further back.

English, then, uses both the clear and dark /l/ sounds. But a native English speaker might find it difficult without any phonetic training even to hear the difference between the two sounds, and to identify one from the other. This is because in English the difference is not crucially important, in the sense that there are no words which differ only because a clear or dark /l/ is used (a linguist might say that the clear/dark /l/ distinction is not <u>phonemic</u> in English). But this is not true in Russian, where the distinction does actually differentiate words. So, for example, there are two different Russian words roughly written in Latin script as 'lyk', which means 'the hatch (of a ship)' when the /l/ is clear, and 'onion' when the /l/ is dark – an important distinction, especially if you are a sailor about to dine. It will help you to understand the problem oriental learners of English have with /l/–/r/ to realize that it is exactly the same as the problem English learners of Russian have with the clear–dark /l/ distinction.

But pronouncing individual sounds is only the start of the learner's difficulties, just the tip of the pronunciation iceberg. Lurking under the surface are tricky rules governing when one or another sound can be used. It comes as a surprise to many that there are definite 'rules' which govern how we pronounce our native language. Box 2.3 illustrates a pronunciation rule of English associated with a very simple grammatical area indeed – how we form the plurals of regular nouns in English. We do this, of course, by adding an 's': *one book, two books*. But think now about pronunciation, about how the plural is *said*, not *written*. There are in fact three different ways in which the final 's' may be pronounced. Before reading what these are, look at Box 2.3 and try to identify them for yourself:

B2.3 The plural 's.' It couldn't be simpler – or could it?

Below are three English nouns with their plural forms. Say the words, both singular and plural, to yourself and try to isolate how the 's' is pronounced or said. It is different in each of the three cases. Then think about what is controlling how the 's' is pronounced. Unless you know it already, it is unlikely that you will be able to work out exactly how the rule works, but you may be able to guess what kind of factor is controlling it.

1. book   books
2. rug   rugs
3. horse   horses

The explanation that follows uses slanted brackets //. These conventionally denote a distinctive sound (a 'phoneme', to use the term introduced earlier). So /s/ is not the letter 's', but the sound /s/. Often, of course, the sound /s/ is represented in writing with the letter 's.' But this is not always the case. The word 'bounce' for example contains the /s/ sound, but it is written as 'ce.' If you have not done it before, it is quite difficult to think in terms of sounds, not spellings. As you read the following lines, you will perhaps need to remind yourself constantly to 'think sound.' Here is the explanation: in Box 2.3, plural (1) is pronounced as /s/. Plural (2) is pronounced more like the first sound of the word *zoo*, and we represent this as /z/. Plural (3) is pronounced /iz/. So the three ways of pronouncing the plural 's' are /s/, /z/ and /iz/. The factor that controls which is used is the sound that comes immediately before it. In (1), a /k/ comes just before the 's', and we pronounce the final letter as /s/. Because /g/ comes before the 's' in (2), we pronounce it /z/. Because the sound /s/ comes before 's' in (3) we pronounce it /iz/. With this final example it is particularly important to 'think sound' not spelling: the spelled word 'horse' ends with a 'e', but this 'e' is not pronounced at all.

All native speakers of English 'know' the rules that are exemplified here, from an early age. Take a look at CW2.1 (*Wugs*) for description of a linguistic experiment showing that children at the tender age of six have already mastered these 'plural pronunciation rules.' Six-year-olds would not of course be able to express them in the way that linguists would. The latter would speak about whether the preceding sound were <u>unvoiced</u> (no vocal cord vibration) or <u>voiced</u> (vocal cord vibration). /k/ is unvoiced, so it is followed by unvoiced /s/, while /g/ is voiced, so it is followed by voiced /z/. Incidentally, the 'plural pronunciation rules' provide a good example of how linguistic knowledge will be useful to the teacher. Few teachers would stand up and give a lecture to explain the difference between voiced and unvoiced sounds (showing pictures of vocal cords vibrating, perhaps). But you can probably imagine that knowing the rules about pronouncing the plural 's' would help you to teach plural forms – and to correct the mistakes your learners might make.

The 'plural pronunciation rules' are about how sounds behave when they join together into larger units (words, in this case). These 'joining together' rules are a large part of the pronunciation iceberg. CW2.2 (*A very troublesome vowel*) gives another example of an associated area which causes learners difficulty.

More difficulties related to joining sounds together are associated with stress and intonation. Box 2.4 gives examples of the kinds of issues faced there.

B2.4 Blackbirds and swimmers

1. Consider the word 'blackbird' and the phrase 'black bird.' The first refers to a specific type of bird; the second, to any bird that is coloured black. How would you use stress to make it clear which you were referring to? For example, if you said 'I saw a blackbird in my garden yesterday', how would it differ from 'I saw a black bird in my garden yesterday.' Be as explicit as you can about the difference.

2. The sentence 'John can't swim, can he?' can mean at least two things. To see how, imagine John is a small baby. In (a) below you are seeking confirmation of the fact that John can't swim, and the sentence might be paraphrased as 'It's true that John can't swim, isn't it?':

(a) Let's not go swimming tomorrow. John can't swim, can he?

But in (b) the sentence might be paraphrased as 'It's not true that John can swim, is it?':

(b) You want to go swimming tomorrow? Good heavens! John can't swim, can he?

> Say the sentences (a) and (b) over to yourself several times. You probably use different intonation for 'John can't swim, can he?' in (a) and (b). Try to describe what this difference is.

'Blackbird' is a noun, and the main stress is on the first syllable (which is often, but not always, true in English); it is 'BLACKbird.' 'Black bird' is an adjective plus a noun, and the stress goes on the noun; it is 'black BIRD.' You probably decided that in Box 2.4's sentence 2(a) the speaker's voice falls at the end, while in sentence (b) it rises. These rising and falling intonation patterns are but two of those found in English. Gimson and Cruttenden (2001) in fact identify no fewer than five basic patterns (what they call nuclear tones). Just for the record, the list is: *falling, rising, falling-rising, rising-falling* and *level*. To complicate matters, each of these main nuclear tone types can be divided into sub-categories. The details of when these tones are used cannot be covered here, but the list suggests just how complex this one area of language is; not straightforward at all! All the more astonishing then to realize that the rules exemplified in Box 2.4 are (just like those in Box 2.3) ones which native speakers know instinctively, and which they use as part of their repertoire of rules of the language.

But are such rules not instinctive to all humans? Do intonation patterns really need to be learned by students of English as a foreign language? In fact, intonation is notoriously likely to cause problems to the learner whose L1 is not English, because it is associated so often with strong feelings. I remember an occasion when a courteous and friendly Italian student was asked to leave her British host family, apparently largely because of her intonation patterns. When she asked for help, for example, her intonation would fall at the end, making it sound as if she were giving an order – *Please would you help me carry this bag!* The family thought, quite wrongly, that she was being rude and brusque; in fact all she was doing was using Italian intonation patterns in English. One celebrated language teacher and linguist from the past, H. E. Palmer, has this to say about intonation problems:

> I often have occasion to say to my foreign students: 'I quite understand your sentence, as a sentence, but excuse me, I cannot see what you wish to convey. Was your sentence an assertion, a comment, an exclamation, a contradiction, a corroboration, or a question?'
>
> (Palmer 1922: 4)

One further area which you may have considered in relation to the 'Cats' essay in Box 2.2 is spelling and its relationship to pronunciation. English seems to employ eccentric and bewildering ways of connecting sounds with spellings. There are a number of reasons for this. One has already been mentioned: that some words have more than one pronunciation. This means, if you come to think of it, that on some occasions they are almost certain to be pronounced differently from how they are written! Eccentricities in the sound–spelling relationship understandably always cause great problems for the learner. Box 2.5 is a humorous poetic reflection on this ubiquitously fascinating topic. To appreciate the poem fully, pause over words that are spelt similarly (like those in line 2) and relish the differences in their pronunciation.

B2.5 Hints on pronunciation for foreigners

I take it you already know
Of tough and bough and cough and dough?
Others may stumble but not you,
On hiccough, thorough, laugh and through,
Well done! And now you wish, perhaps,
To learn of less familiar traps?

Beware of heard, a dreadful word
That looks like beard and sounds like bird,
And dead: it's said like bed, not bead –
For goodness' sake don't call it 'deed'!
Watch out for meat and great and threat
(They rhyme with suite and straight and debt).

A moth is not the moth in mother
Nor both in bother, broth in brother,
And here is not a match for there
Nor dear and fear for bear and pear,
And then there's dose and rose and lose –
Just look them up – and goose and choose,
And cork and work and card and ward,
And font and front and word and sword,
And do and go and thwart and cart –
Come, come, I've hardly made a start!
A dreadful language? Man alive
I'd mastered it when I was five.

T. S. Watt
(From a letter published in the *Manchester Guardian*, 21 June 1954.[2]
Copyright *Guardian News & Media Limited* 1954)

The moral of all this is that the pronunciation iceberg is one on which many learners founder. There is a good deal to learn, particularly when we also consider sound–spelling relationships. Exactly how much, and exactly what, will of course depend on the learners' L1. But we have said enough here to establish the importance of the area. There is certainly also a moral for language teaching (as well as language learning); as Abercrombie (1949: 115) is moved to claim: 'the language teacher … will inevitably be a phonetician.'

2.3.2 Grammar: morphemes …

A second level on which a native speaker displays knowledge is that of the morpheme. A morpheme is often defined (in Richards *et al.* 1985, for example) as 'the smallest meaningful unit in a language.' Morphemes are the building blocks of words. Box 2.6 illustrates:

B2.6 Identifying and analysing morphemes

Consider the word 'unbelievable.' This is made up of three morphemes, or 'building blocks.' Identify what they are. Try to say what each 'means.'

The 'core' of Box 2.6's word is the unit 'believ(e).' To this has been added the morpheme 'able', which attaches to verbs and changes them into adjectives, and means something like 'capable of.' 'un' is another morpheme, which is often put on the front of an adjective to mean 'not.' That all native speakers know this is evidenced by the fact that they will often coin new words using the 'able' morpheme. In my notes on a draft of this chapter, I used the word 'relatable' (in the context of saying that two points I was making were 'relatable' to each other). My word processor's spelling check denied the existence of this word 'relatable.' But neither you nor I have any problem working out what it means; we know what the constituent parts signify, so we can easily work out what the whole means.

We all have minor problems with the morphemes of our own language on occasions. Native speakers of English may pause, embarrassed, when they want to express the notion of 'not authentic', being uncertain as to whether the correct word is *inauthentic* or *unauthentic*. But someone learning a foreign language has to master all kinds of morphemic rules which are right there in the centre of how the language works. A learner of English, for example, has to know that '-*ed*' is the morpheme used to express (simple) past time (turning present *I walk* into past *I walked*), and that certain sorts of present time are expressed through use of the verb ending -*ing* (as in *He is walking*). They have to know that the -*s* morpheme we considered in Box 2.3 marks plurality in nouns, as well as possessiveness (in this latter sense it is accompanied by an apostrophe when written – *the doctor's* and *the doctors'*). Even to express the simplest of propositions involves a whole 'mass of morphology.'

As with pronunciation, you will probably have no trouble with the notion that morphological difficulties can be huge for the foreign learner. Where the language being learned is one in which there is a complex and rich morphology, these difficulties will be particularly daunting. Think about the morpheme 'endings' to nouns and adjectives, for example. In English the rules are very simple. We have already seen that there is a morpheme which indicates plurality, a final -s in the case of regular nouns. We have also seen that a final -s marks possessiveness (the possessive <u>case</u> as it is called by some linguists). These are the main grammatical morphemes that can be added to the end of nouns. Adjectives in English are even simpler; their form does not change at all according to what noun follows them. Those of you who have learned French will know that the rules are more complex in this respect. French nouns have different genders, masculine and feminine, and the form of the adjective will depend on the noun's gender (*le petit homme – the small man* versus *la petite femme – the small woman*). But Russian is in quite a different league of complexity! For starters, there are *three* genders (masculine, feminine and neuter), not two. Within these genders there are different noun types which take slightly different endings. Next, there are *six* cases which are marked with different endings. The possessive which we have discussed in relation to English would be one of them, but there would be others to mark whether a noun was the subject of a sentence, its object, its indirect object, and so on. Singular and plural are also marked. Then there is the fact that adjectives as well as nouns have endings, and that the noun/adjective endings are often different from each other. If you want an illustration of just how complicated it all is, take a look at CW2.3 (*A mass of Russian morphology*) which looks at some of the endings associated with Russian nouns and adjectives. This should give you an idea of the challenges that some learners of Russian as a foreign language face in the morphology department (yet native speaker Russian children learning their L1 seem to cope very well – more on that in the next chapter).

Another characteristic of morphology is that even if it is 'simple' (as English morphology tends to be), this does not appear to mean that it will be easily learned. An oft-cited example of this is the final -s morpheme in English marking the third person singular of a verb in the simple present tense (*He likes* in contrast to *I like*). On many levels this -s morpheme really is rather easy – after all, there are not many morpheme endings to remember in English, and the form of this one could not be simpler. Yet various studies (including Dulay and Burt 1973 and others we shall mention in 4.4) show that learners acquire this form rather late. Indeed, if you live in an English-speaking country which has an immigrant population, you may be able to think of immigrants who have lived there for years and yet still forget this final -s – saying for example *He like it very much* instead of *He likes it very much* (a star * in front of a sentence means it is not acceptable in English). Why, do you think, is such a seemingly simple piece of morphology apparently so difficult to learn?[3] As another example of the actual difficulty of apparently 'easy' morphemes, research done by Lightbown (1987) on French-speaking learners of English found that accuracy for the basic -ing morpheme (as in *He is working*) went from 69 per cent in Year 1, to only 39 per cent in Year 2, though it went back up to above 60 per cent in Year 3.

2.3.3 ... and syntax

Monsieur Jourdain, a character in Molière's 1678 play *Le Bourgeois Gentilhomme* (Act II, Scene IV), does not know what the word 'prose' means, and he is filled with astonishment when he is told that he has been speaking it all his life (*Good Heavens! For more than forty years I have been speaking prose without knowing it*). A similar astonishment is sometimes expressed when native speakers (of English, or any other language) find out that their own language has a <u>syntax</u>, defined by Swan (2005a) as the 'rules governing the ways in which words are assembled into structures.' They know that foreign languages have syntactic rules that can be learned. But because they have acquired their native language in a seemingly unconscious way as a child, they are unaware that their own language has rules and are usually unable to articulate what those rules are. They have been speaking with syntax all their lives without knowing it!

Box 2.7 invites you to explore part of the syntax of a reasonably simple area of grammar, related to how we form <u>interrogative</u> sentences in English. A major use of interrogatives is to ask questions.

B2.7 Forming English interrogatives

(a) below illustrates a sentence together with its interrogative form. State as precisely as you can what 'operations' are performed on the statement to change it into an interrogative.

(a) John is playing tennis   →   Is John playing tennis?

Now form the interrogative equivalents of (b) and (c), and again explain how you do it. Try to explain it in such a way as to clarify the similarities of interrogative formation in (a), (b) and (c).

(b) John can play tennis   →
(c) John should play tennis   →

Now look at (d). What happens to the statement here to form an interrogative? How is it different from the other examples?

(d) John plays tennis   →   Does John play tennis?

Form interrogatives out of (e) and (f):

(e) John and Mary play tennis   →
(f) John played tennis   →

Is it possible to devise a general rule that will explain how all the interrogatives you have seen – (a) to (f) – are formed? This is discussed in Note 4.

If your L1 is not English, or you have studied or speak any language other than English, you might like to think how the English way of forming interrogatives differs from how it is done in the other language. English in fact has a rather unusual way of interrogative formation, particularly where some form of the verb 'do' is used. This is the reason why these forms cause problems for many learners of EFL. A common mistake is for learners to produce *Plays John tennis?* or *Played John tennis?* Why do you think they do this?

As with the other linguistic areas we are dealing with in this chapter, we have here done no more than touch upon the huge problems which syntax may give the EFL learner (remembering always that degree of difficulty will depend on similarities and differences between English and the learner's L1). One area we have said nothing explicit about is to do with the *meaning* of syntactic patterns. As an example, think for a moment about what language teachers call the present perfect tense in English.[5] In this tense, the present tense of the verb *have* (*I have*, *he has*, etc.) is followed by the past participle of a verb (*seen*, *lived*, etc.), to form phrases like *I have seen*, *He has lived*. This is how the tense is formed. But what about its meaning? How, for example, does it differ in meaning from another tense, the simple past, as in *I saw*, *I lived*. Compare these sentences taken from Swan (2005b):

(a) Have you seen *Romeo and Juliet*?
(b) Did you see *Romeo and Juliet*?

What is the difference in meaning between them? Why is the present perfect tense used in (a), and the simple past in (b)? Note 6 explains.

Many languages, like French, German and Italian, have equivalents to the present perfect tense. But these are often used in slightly different ways from the English tense, and these differences often lead FL speakers to make mistakes with the tense. Consider for example another sentence from Swan (2005b):

(c) *I have seen Lucy yesterday.

Why is this wrong? Again, Note 6 will clarify. This one small example illustrates that students will indeed have to learn not just how to *form* syntactic patterns but also what they *mean*. CW2.4 (*More areas of syntactic difficulty*) provides a few further examples of the types of difficulties EFL learners have to deal with in relation to syntax.

2.3.4 Lexis

Towards the end of the previous section we discussed the meaning of syntactic structures like the present perfect. The area of linguistics which deals with meaning is <u>semantics</u>. In this section we will look at semantics, not of syntactic structures but of individual words, or lexis.

Words are very important in language learning. When asked what advice he would give to someone wishing to become a successful language learner, one well-known applied linguist identified learning words as being one of the main strategies – 'Try and deliberately build up a large vocabulary', he said.[7] Grammar is of course important, and so is pronunciation. But you have to use words when you speak, and the more words you know, the more likely you are to be able to say what you want in a foreign language.

But what's in a word? This question – like most we are asking in this chapter – is more complex than it may at first seem. Box 2.8 focuses on one of the complexities associated with knowing what a word 'means':

B2.8 Fat or well-built, small or petite?

Learners of English as a foreign language may often find it relatively easy to learn what a word <u>denotes</u> – what it describes in some 'factual', 'basic' way. The word *house*, for example, refers to a building in which people live. This is the word's <u>denotation</u>. But <u>connotations</u> – what words <u>connote</u> – are sometimes much more difficult to learn. Connotations are the 'emotional' associations a word carries with it. The word *home* may, for example, have a similar denotation to *house*; it is the place where you live. But *home* can carry many connotations which *house* does not have – the place where your loved-ones are situated, where you can relax and be yourself, a refuge from the troubles of the world ('Home', as Robert Frost said in his poem 'The Death of the Hired Man', 'is the place where … They have to take you in'). A learner must come to grips with connotations. You must know that to describe a man as *well-built* is complimentary, while to say he is *fat* is not (though the two words may denote roughly the same thing). Similarly, a girl may be flattered to be called *petite*, but probably not if you call her *small* or *tiny*.

You may like to consider the following pairs of words or phrases which have similar denotations but rather different connotations (in each case one of the pair has rather negative associations). For each pair, say what the 'basic' denotation is and how the connotations differ. You might invent some sentences which clarify these differences.

costly – expensive	*vagrant – homeless person*
freedom fighter – guerrilla	*skinny – slim*
single-minded – obstinate	*a spinster – an unmarried lady*

But, alas, knowing a word means more than knowing its denotation and connotations. It also means knowing something about the company it keeps.

This relates to the area of <u>collocation</u>, the way that words are conventionally used together. To illustrate this, consider the following example taken from McCarthy (1990: 12). He looks at four adjectives: *large*, *great*, *big* and *major*. These are very close, though not identical, in meaning. So it is very often a question of convention, rather than precise meaning, that decides when one rather than another can be used. Box 2.9 below shows whether these adjectives co-occur with the four nouns that appear across the top of the table. A tick means that collocation occurs, a cross that it does not, and a question mark that there is a degree of uncertainty. These collocations, by the way, hold for British English, and there are doubtless differences for English as spoken in other parts of the world.

B2.9 Some English collocations

	problem	amount	shame	man
large	?	✓	✗	✓
great	✓	✓	✓	✓
big	✓	✓	✗	✓
major	✓	?	✗	✗

(McCarthy (1990))

Box 2.9 shows among other things that in British English we say something is *a great shame*, but not *a big shame* or *a large shame*. You can well imagine that FL learners will find these conventions very difficult to master. Because they are usually simply convention, it is often just exposure to the language that is needed, though help is also at hand in the shape of the many usage guides and learner dictionaries currently available – such as Swan (2005b), Cobuild (1992), and Greenbaum and Whitcut (1989). Take a look at CW2.5 (*'Head' in French*) for an associated problem with lexis that learners have to cope with.

It is easy to find amusing examples of unusual collocations made by learners. The student who came up to me at the end of a lesson and complimented me on my *delicious lesson* was making a mistake of collocation. 'Delicious' does carry the general meaning of 'very good' that (I assume!) he intended, but it is used for food, not lessons.

Remaining with the topic of food, consider the following list of menu mistakes from around the world:[8]

B2.10 Would *you* eat these dishes?

Stuffed nun	(Indian restaurant)
Smoked Solomon	(Jakarta)
Turdy delight	(Israel)
Pig in the family way	(West Germany)
Terminal soup	(Istanbul airport)
Steamed dick with vegetables	(Chinese restaurant)
Quick Lorraine	(London)
Roast Headlamp	(Greece)
Squits with source	(Alpes-Maritimes)
Boiled god in parsley	(London)
Calve's dong	(Athens)
Fish Rotty and spaghetti Bolograse	(North Yemen)
Battered soul	(Switzerland)
Hard-boiled eggs, filled with a delicate curried mouse	(Manchester)

Investigators who try to pin down rules about how things work invariably have to develop systems for classifying and categorizing the things they are studying. This is what linguists studying lexis do; <u>word classes</u> are created in order to capture regularities in the way words behave. The most common classification of words is into <u>parts of speech</u> – nouns, verbs, adjectives and adverbs being the biggest divisions. But within each of these classes there are sub-divisions which behave in particular ways and follow their own rules. Many of these can be problematical for learners whose own languages may work rather differently. We shall illustrate this by looking at a class of verbs called 'phrasal' verbs. These are made up of a verb plus a <u>particle</u> – a word like *up*, *in* or *off* (some of which are also prepositions). Examples of phrasal verbs are *look up*, *put off*. Sometimes these verbs have a literal meaning, which learners can easily work out. Hence in (a), the meaning of 'look up' is quite clear – it is the meaning of 'look' plus the meaning of 'up':

(a) Mary looked up the chimney and saw a bird's nest there.

But these verbs often have a meaning that cannot be worked out by combining together the meanings of the constituent parts. Hence the meaning in (b) is not so easy to guess if you do not happen to know it:

(b) Mary looked up the word.   (i.e. in her dictionary)

The meanings of these verbs are difficult for learners. They also follow word order rules which are even more unfriendly. Hence you can put *up* after the noun *word* in (c), but not after *chimney* in (d):

(c) Mary looked the word up
(d) *Mary looked the chimney up

As for 'look up', so for 'put off.' If you take the meaning of 'put' and add it to the meaning of 'off', you do not arrive at the sense of 'postpone' which is one of the verb's meanings. All very bewildering. You may like to think of some other verbs like this, where there is a literal meaning that is the 'sum of the parts', as well as one that cannot be so easily guessed. CW2.6 (*Giving bad advices*) looks at another problematic word class, this time a sub-division of nouns.

In this treatment of systemic competence we have left many stones unturned. Some of these you will have come across in Box 2.2 where you considered the 'Cats' essay, and it may now be of interest to you to revisit your categorization of errors in that essay, to see how many of your categories you feel fit under the title of systemic competence.

The picture which should be emerging as this chapter progresses is of the complexity of learning a foreign language. It is indeed a complex and multifaceted process. This will become increasingly apparent as we turn to Canale and Swain's second area …

2.4 Sociolinguistic competence

2.4.1 Rules of use

Though most of you will have some idea of what Canale and Swain's first category entails, it may well be that the other two will be less familiar. Canale and Swain divide their <u>sociolinguistic competence</u> into two categories. The first they call (sociocultural) 'rules of use.'[9] A slightly modified example of theirs: imagine a man and a woman go into a restaurant and are approached by the waiter, whom they have never seen before. If the waiter were to address them by saying *OK chump, what are you and this broad going to eat?*, then they would doubtless be shocked and bewildered, perhaps even enough to beat a hasty retreat towards the door. Notice that the rude waiter is not breaking any rule of grammar – as he would have done if he had said **What are you and this broad going to eating?* for example. He is instead offending against a 'rule of use' – one which deals with how it is appropriate to address customers in a restaurant. The example illustrates that it is possible to be rude (or in general to break rules of use) in a perfectly grammatical way.

Rules of use are often less easy to state than rules of grammar, and sometimes need careful thought before they can be articulated clearly. Box 2.11 invites you to think about rules of use:

B2.11 Thinking about rules of use

Here are some questions to stimulate you into thinking about rules of use in your L1:

1. In many languages there is a conventional greeting question that people ask when they meet a friend or acquaintance. In some English-speaking

areas, the question is something like *How are you?* What is the conventional greeting question in the area where you live (whether English-speaking or not)? What is the expected reply?

Think of two ways of greeting someone, one extremely informal and one very formal. Give examples of concrete situations in which you would use one, then the other. Imagine what the reaction would be if the informal greeting were used in a very formal situation, and vice versa.

What do you say when you are introduced to someone for the very first time? Is it different from a normal greeting?

2. Imagine that you are in a railway carriage. It is very hot, and you'd like the window opened. Before opening it, you want to check that everyone else in the compartment is happy for you to do this. How would you ask? Think also of two other ways – one that you feel would be excessively polite, another that would be too direct.

Language groups often differ in terms of how polite you are expected to be when asking someone a favour, for example. In some language groups you are expected to be very polite and indirect. In others it is considered normal to be forthright, making your meaning straightforward and clear. You might be able to think of a language group which in your mind is associated with being very polite when asking favours. And one associated with directness?

3. Imagine you are walking along the street and you want to know the time. You stop someone and say *Excuse me, do you have a watch?* They reply *Yes I do, thanks*, and walk off. What would your reaction be? Try and say in what way the person has violated a rule of use.

Does sociolinguistic competence need learning? Surely, you might think, the same rules apply universally. Here is an anecdote illustrating that this is not at all the case. One of them is associated with the area of greeting. My first teaching job abroad was in the country now called Croatia, where I was fortunate to spend time in a small, almost deserted village on one of the beautiful Adriatic islands. Each day as I left the house, I was approached by the very elderly lady who lived next door. She always said the same thing, *Where are you going?*, to which I would reply *To the shop* or *Down to the sea*, or whatever. I must confess to becoming a little irritated over time with the lady's question. 'Why doesn't she mind her own business?' I would silently complain; 'you can't even leave the house without her wanting to know where you're going!' It was only some years later, when I had travelled a little more widely, that I realized what had been happening here. Her question was exactly equivalent to the British English *How are you?* said as a conventional greeting. The question *Where are you going?* is just a way of saying 'hello', and the expected response might be *Out*. This response performs the same function as the English *Fine* in response to the question *How are you?* What would be completely incorrect would be for either of these questions to be taken at face value as serious requests for information. If you were to reply to *How are you?* with a list of ailments, your interlocutor would be justifiably bewildered. A 'rule of use' about the way we greet would have been broken. CW2.7 (*Mistaking a greeting for a request for information*) illustrates just this situation.

The point is that in some countries of the world the conventional question asked on meeting is not *How are you?* but *Where are you going?* and the expected response in such situations is not a true statement of one's movements, but a simple formulaic phrase. In other parts of the world the greeting question is *Have you eaten?* The moral is simple: since greeting questions differ from culture to culture, a language learner from a different culture needs to learn them. Many rules of use need to be learned. CW2.8 (*How to obtain sweet potatoes*) has another anecdote illustrating the same thing.

In a fascinating article dealing in detail with what she calls 'pragmatic failure', Thomas (1983) considers the sorts of things that go wrong when people try to communicate messages. She begins her paper with the following quotation from Miller (1974) which seems to imply that rules of use should occupy a central position in foreign language learning:

> most of our misunderstandings of other people are not due to any ability to hear them or to parse their sentences or to understand their words ... a far more important source of difficulty in communication is that we so often fail to understand a speaker's intention.

This is really the point that, as we saw earlier in this chapter, H. E. Palmer was making to his foreign students. There are different sorts of pragmatic failure; one common one occurs when the rules of use differ in native and target language.[10] One of Thomas's examples deals with the phrase *Would you like to*. This is very often used in English as a polite command, as for example when a teacher says to a pupil in class *Would you like to read*. The teacher saying this is not really giving the pupil any option – it is truly intended as a command. Thomas, working as a teacher of English in Russia, would sometimes say this to her pupils. On a number of occasions the reply came back: *No, I wouldn't*. The pupils replying in this way were not being cheeky or rude – they genuinely thought their preferences were being consulted. CW2.9 (*Some differences in English and Russian rules of use*) contains various other illustrations of pragmatic failure from Thomas (1983), again related to her Russian experiences.

Are there any rules of use in your L1 that you have noticed cause problems for foreign learners? What about rules of use you have found difficult in a language you have learned?

2.4.2 Rules of discourse

Canale and Swain's second category of sociolinguistic competence concerns what they call 'rules of discourse.' The word discourse is used to refer to the way that pieces of speech or writing are joined together to form stretches (sometimes involving one or more participants, as in spoken conversations for example). 'Rules of discourse' are essentially 'joining together rules.' Box 2.12 invites you to consider two different types of discourse rules:

B2.12 Two ways of breaking discourse rules

Here are two short 'texts.' Both are a little odd as regards 'rules of discourse.' Say as precisely as you can what makes each text odd:

(a) John saw a man in the park. The man's name was Jack. The man was wearing a coat. The man had a hat on. The man was carrying a stick.

(b) (spoken in a street, between two strangers):

    X: Excuse me, can you tell me the way to the bus station?
    Y: The clouds in the East are gathering, and war may ensue.

Try to express the way in which the rules being broken in (a) and (b) are different.

Notice first that, as with the rude waiter's 'rules of use' example, these sentences do not contain grammatical mistakes. What is odd is how they are joined together. In (a) it is a little strange how the words 'the man' are repeated. It is clearly the same man who is being referred to in each sentence, and we are even told his name (Jack). So why, in sentence 3, do we not read *Jack* or *he*, instead of *the man*? Probably you would also expect sentences 3 and 4, and perhaps 5, to be joined together to form a longer sentence – *He was wearing a coat and hat, and was carrying a stick* perhaps. As well as being grammatical, the sentences in (a) make perfect sense. But the grammatical means of joining sentences together are a little strange, though not actually wrong. The sentences are <u>cohesive</u> (linguistically joined together, that is); they do show <u>cohesion</u> of sorts. But the cohesion is rather unusual.

The problem with (b) is to do with <u>coherence</u>, not cohesion. It lies on the level of 'making sense unity.' Indeed, in the circumstances, Speaker X could be forgiven for smiling wanly and walking briskly away from Speaker Y. Y's response clearly breaks the rules of discourse which require a response to have some relevance to the question asked. The result is that X probably wonders whether Y is mentally unhinged, or drunk, or otherwise incapacitated (though again, we note, in a linguistically well-formed way – it is possible to be mentally unhinged but grammatical). It is also possible that disobeying rules of discourse can lead to being considered mad.

Notice in this context that sentences may seem on the surface to be entirely unconnected, yet may in fact be perfectly coherent. A much-quoted instance (cited in Brown and Yule 1983: 196) is:

A: There's the doorbell.

B: I'm in the bath.

Though the sentences in this example may seem as unconnected as those in Box 2.12's example (b), you will find it easy to imagine the context in which they hang well together.

Do rules of discourse need learning? As with rules of use, one's first reaction might be that the same rules apply universally. But, again, this is not the case. Look back to the 'Cats' essay, in Box 2.2. Notice in general how difficult it is to understand the writer's line of argument – to make a 'sense-unity' out of what they say. Look also at the use of the word *however* in the last sentence. You will probably conclude that it is not the right word to link the penultimate and the last sentences together. Perhaps *thus* would be better? (You might like to take a moment to consider the difference in meaning between *however* and *thus*.) The 'Cats' essay shows that FL speakers do indeed make errors of cohesion and coherence. But, you may wonder, are these errors based in language or culture, or just to do with the fact that the learner is writing in a slapdash fashion?

Though slapdash writing will of course result in poor cohesion and coherence, these can also be caused by language-related differences. Particularly vivid examples of this are found in the work of Kaplan and in the area of study called 'contrastive rhetoric', where the writing styles of different language groups are observed. Kaplan (1966) reports on the analysis of some seven hundred compositions written by students from different language groups. He plots differences in writing styles associated with the different language groups. Here is one paragraph from a composition written by an Arabic-speaking student. Does anything strike you about the way sentences are joined together?

> At that time of the year I was not studying enough to pass my courses in school. And all the time I was asking my cousin to let me ride the bicycle, but he wouldn't let me. But after two weeks, noticing that I was so much interested in the bicycle, he promised me that if I pass my courses in school for that year he would give it to me as a present. So I began to study hard. And I studying eight hours a day instead of two.

Kaplan notes that 80 per cent of these sentences begin with a co-ordinating element (a word like *and* or *but*), and that there is also an absence of subordination – both trends which continue throughout the whole essay. He associates these characteristics with Arabic, and perhaps all Semitic languages.

The fact that using rules of discourse in a non-standard way can be blamed on slapdashness makes them particularly serious in some contexts. In Johnson (1977), I report on the reactions of university tutors to 'errors' occurring in overseas students' writing. Grammatical mistakes are often simply ignored, but non-standard discourse – particularly when it results in incoherence – is often treated very severely. This is because it is often automatically associated with slovenly, slapdash writing. Rules of discourse, like rules of use, often need to be learned.

2.5 Strategic competence

Canale and Swain (1980: 30) describe their third area – <u>strategic competence</u> – as 'verbal and non-verbal communication strategies that may be called into action to compensate for breakdowns in communication.' This is a very important type of competence for the learner to develop, because they will inevitably face many breakdowns in communication when struggling to use the foreign language with their restricted linguistic resources.

Communication strategies have been much studied, and different ways of classifying them have been developed. Box 2.13 gives some examples of the way learners cope with communication breakdowns when using a foreign language.

B2.13 Person worms?!?

Bialystok (1990) gives some examples of the communication strategies used by 9-year-old English-speaking children learning French. One major strategy-type is described as *paraphrase*. For example, the learner who wishes to express the notion of 'playpen', but who does not have the French word, says *On peut mettre un bébé dedans. Il y a comme un trou* (*You put a baby in it. It's like a hole*).

Tarone (1977), whose classification Bialystok uses for her data, gives an example of paraphrase which involves 'word coinage.' An example: the learner wants to describe an animated caterpillar, and they call it a 'person worm.'

On other occasions, the learner will simply use the native language for an unknown item. One learner trying to define what a 'swing' is, said *C'est une sorte de, tu peux dire, chaise que quand tu 'move'* (*It's a kind of, you could say, chair for when you move*).

Some of the strategies learners use involve non-linguistic means such as mime. Tarone's example of mime is the learner who claps hands to indicate the word 'applause.'

Think of your own language learning experiences. Can you identify any other communication strategies that you yourself have used?

Does strategic competence need to be learned? Several things need to be said about this issue. First, it is certainly true that many traditional teaching methods not only ignore strategic competence but may actually hinder its development. These are methods which never involve the learners in taking any risks. The only speaking or writing they are asked to do involves reproducing material that has recently been practised, while their listening and reading classes entail going through texts word by word so that 'total comprehension' is achieved (we discuss this approach in 9.7, where we refer to it as the '100 per cent comprehension' school). But the communicative situations the learner will experience when using a foreign language outside class will commonly involve risk-taking. The learner will regularly want to say and write things which have not been recently practised, and they will need to understand messages when they do not understand nearly every word contained in that message. If they have not learned to do so, they will become silent, tongue-tied, when they are asked to say something they have not practised saying. Nor will they be able to understand something containing words they have not met before. They will have hardly any strategic competence.

But the question of how best to facilitate the development of strategic competence is a difficult one. Some believe that there is benefit in drawing learners' attention to the different types of strategy, like the ones in Box 2.13. Others believe that we should put learners into simulated communicative situations where they have to take risks, so as to facilitate the development of communication strategies. There is some evidence that strategic competence will develop by itself, as long as the learner is exposed to communicative situations. Schmidt (1983) discusses the fascinating case of a learner called Wes. He was a 32-year-old Japanese artist spending time in Honolulu. His language development was followed over a three-year period. By the end of this time, Schmidt says, 'Wes's grammatical control of English had hardly improved at all' (p. 144). But his strategic competence had improved a lot. Schmidt again:

> Since Wes clearly has a very limited command of the grammatical aspects of English, communication breakdowns do occur when he is talking to native speakers. Yet Wes is almost always able to repair these breakdowns, and it seems that his confidence, his willingness to communicate, and especially his persistence in communicating what he has in his mind and understanding what his interlocutors have in their minds go a long way towards compensating for his grammatical inaccuracies. (p. 161)

One might almost say that Wes's English improved little over the period, but what he could do with it improved greatly.

The tale of Wes points up a dilemma associated with the development of strategic competence. It is natural that we should want our learners to develop the means of 'getting by' with imperfect language resources. But we do not want to develop this so effectively that the language resources themselves never become developed. Learning how to paraphrase is indeed a useful skill, but better still is knowing the correct words themselves, making paraphrase unnecessary.

2.6 Conclusion

In this chapter we have looked at some (though not nearly all) of the skills involved in using a foreign language, and we have considered whether these skills need to be learned. Quite a lot of ground has been covered, and you may on occasions have felt a little lost among the trees, wishing that you could see what the wood overall looks like. You might like to draw up a 'map of the wood' for yourself, in the form of a chapter summary. Alternatively, use the 'map' in Box 2.14. Go through the list of areas mentioned there, and recall what the examples given for each were (adding perhaps some examples from your own language learning experience).

B2.14 A map of the wood

Systemic competence

Sounds

Pronunciation of specific sounds
'Joining together' rules
Stress
Intonation
Sound/spelling relationships

Grammar

Morphemes
Syntax (form and meaning)

Lexis

Denotation and connotation
Collocation
Lexical fields
Word classes (and associated rules)

Sociolinguistic competence

Rules of use

Pragmatics (remind yourself about what this word means by looking at
    Note 9)

Rules of discourse

Cohesion
Coherence

Strategic competence

Communication strategies

Perhaps this chapter leaves you shocked by the sheer amount that there is to master, and leaves you wondering how on earth anyone ever manages the task. 'How people learn foreign languages' will be the subject of Part 2 of this book. Underlying the various theories of FL learning we shall consider there, as well as the views of FL teaching we shall meet in Part 3, are a small group of key ideas which it will be useful to discuss at the outset. We shall do this in Chapter 3.

Notes

1. Bagarić and Djigunović (2007) is a useful review paper, providing an overview of different frameworks.
2. There has been much discussion concerning the source of this poem (see for example http://linguistlist.org/issues/13/13–3353.html), but T. S. Watt in the *Manchester Guardian* seems to be the most likely. I am indebted to Maria Sifianou for drawing my attention to the poem.
3. Part of the problem is doubtless the comparative communicative redundancy of the form; if a learner says *He like* instead of *He likes*, the chances are that they will be understood; the message will be conveyed.
4. In (a) the <u>auxiliary</u> part of the verb (*is*) is put before the subject noun (*John*). Sentences (b) and (c) contain modals (*can* and *should*). In some ways these act like auxiliaries – as here where they are put before the subject noun to form interrogatives (*Can John play tennis?* and *Should John play tennis?*). Sentences (a), (b) and (c) all have two verb forms – an auxiliary or modal and the main verb (*play*). But in (d)–(f) there is just a main verb. In English you need an auxiliary or modal to form the interrogative, and where there is not one present, the verb *do* is brought in to fulfil this purpose. So in (d) to (f) the interrogatives begin with a part of *do*. All the interrogatives in the box have the same order of elements: auxiliary (or modal) + subject noun + main verb. The interrogative of (f) highlights another aspect of the system, that it is the auxiliary or modal which shows the tense. (d) is in the simple present tense, and (f) in the simple past. This is indicated by *do* in (d) and *did* in (f). Notice that in the non-interrogative sentences (d) and (f), tense is indicated by the form of the main verb (*plays* is simple present, *played* simple past).
5. Strictly speaking, 'perfect' is an <u>aspect</u> – a term used to refer to concepts like completion and duration rather than time (which is <u>tense</u>). We should really talk about the 'present/past tense with perfect aspect' rather than the 'present/past perfect tense.' But referring to these tenses is so widespread in the language teaching literature that we will use these names. The same is true of <u>continuous</u>, which is also an aspect. We should speak of the 'present/past tense with continuous aspect', but the terms 'present/past continuous tense' are common, and are used in this book (in CW2.4, for example).
6. One of the 'meanings' of the present perfect in British English is to signify any time up to the present. So a possible paraphrase of question (a) might be *Have you seen* Romeo and Juliet *at any time up to the present?*, or *Have you ever seen* Romeo and Juliet? The simple past tense (in British English again) often refers to a specific point in the past. So question (b) would refer to a particular performance of the play, perhaps one that was on television yesterday. When a word like *yesterday* is used, specifying a particular point in the past, you would expect the simple past – not *I have seen Lucy yesterday*, but *I saw Lucy yesterday*.
7. Paul Meara in the BBC television programme *Lingo! How to Learn a Language*, 1991.
8. I am indebted to Maria Sifianou for providing the list of menu mistakes.

9. The word <u>pragmatics</u> has come to be used in relation to Canale and Swain's sociocultural rules of use. Cook (1998a: 249) defines pragmatics as 'the study of how language is interpreted by its users in its linguistic and non-linguistic context.'
10. Thomas (1983) identifies two sorts of pragmatic failure. The examples in Box 2.12 are of what she calls <u>pragmalinguistic failure</u>. This can occur when a language user assumes that a rule of use in their L1 is the same in the FL. <u>Sociopragmatic failure</u> is primarily to do with cultural rather than linguistic differences. An area where this type of failure occurs relates to taboo subjects. A subject that is talked about normally in one culture may be almost taboo in another.

Issues to think or write about

1. In this chapter, some English tenses have been mentioned, including a version of the present using the ending -*ing* and one of the past using -*ed*. Find out something about the English tense system as a whole. What tenses are there? What are their names? How are they formed? How are they used? Think about some of the problems FL learners of English might have with these (including yourself if you are a non-native English speaker). You might also (if you have a lot of time available!) compare the English tense system with another one you know – your own language's if that is not English.
2. In 2.3.4 the term 'parts of speech' is used, and some examples are given. What are the main parts of speech? Say something about the functions and forms of all or some of these (being precise and accurate about this is not at all easy). If you have knowledge of a language other than English, you might also like to consider the forms of some of these. What, for example, do nouns look like in the language? What about adjectives?

Further reading

Canale, M., and Swain, M. 1980 'Theoretical bases of communicative approaches to second language teaching and testing' *Applied Linguistics* 1: 1–47
This paper may make challenging reading for someone new to the field, but it is a worthwhile challenge.

Widdowson, H. G. 1996 *Linguistics* Oxford: Oxford University Press
A useful book for someone who wants a general overview of the field of linguistics.

Thornbury, S. 1997a *About Language: Tasks for Teachers of English* Cambridge: Cambridge University Press
This teacher-friendly book looks at many areas of English, from pronunciation to discourse. It provides brief explanations, together with many tasks to help the reader develop an understanding of how English 'works.'

Ballard, K. 2001 *The Frameworks of English* Basingstoke: Palgrave
One of a number of books providing an overview description of English.

Parrot, M. 2000 *Grammar for English Language Teachers* Cambridge: Cambridge
    University Press
Intended for language teachers, this is an excellent background book for syntax/
grammar. It will give you an overall knowledge and understanding of English grammar,
as well as providing a quick source of reference in planning lessons or clarifying
learners' problems.

3 Some views of language and language learning

3.1 Introduction

As perhaps in all areas of human knowledge, in the field of applied linguistics nothing ever happens in a vacuum. New ideas do not just spring out of thin air; they often come out of old ideas, and from ideas in other areas of knowledge. In this chapter we shall look into the background of two sets of ideas which have had a great deal of influence on the direction of foreign-language learning and teaching studies. These ideas are not easy ones to grasp, and for this reason you may find this chapter the most challenging of the book. But understanding the ideas and where they come from really will enrich your insight into the field.

3.2 A central conflict: empiricism and mentalism

There is a conflict that continually rears its head throughout this book. This is what Diller (1971: 5) says about it: 'the great theoretical division between linguists – the empiricists versus the rationalists – also divides the language teaching methodologies.' Not just teaching methodologies, we might add, but also theories about how FLs are learned.

We shall spend a large part of this chapter clarifying what empiricism and rationalism (or 'mentalism' as we shall call it) are, and exploring how these opposing philosophies have exerted their influence in two particular areas – linguistics and learning theory (including the study of L1 acquisition). But first, Box 3.1 invites you to reflect on some issues relevant to what we shall be discussing.

B3.1 Contrary opinions

For every point of view that exists, there is always an opposite one. Below are some opposite points of view about FL (foreign language) learning and teaching. Match the opposites together (the suggested pairings are given in Note 1). How would you describe the issues raised in these pairs? Then ponder the opinions, particularly in the light of your own FL learning experience. Which opinions do you have most/least sympathy with?

All the issues raised here will make an appearance later in the book, particularly in Chapter 9, which deals with the recent history of language teaching.

(a) Learning a language is like learning any other habit. You don't have to think about it; it just develops automatically.

(b) Of course, to learn a language you have to hear others speaking it. But learners really develop a language 'inside themselves', forming their own views about how it works, and following their own sweet way.

(c) Amount of practice is not important. Sometimes you can learn a word after just hearing it once – particularly if you hear it in a context where its use is especially vivid.

(d) Practice makes perfect, so the more you practise, the more thoroughly you learn. The teacher should make you repeat sentences lots of times.

(e) We don't need to worry when a learner makes an error. After all, children make lots of errors when learning their L1, and these nearly always disappear over time. Indeed, errors can be a good thing. As the saying goes: 'we learn through our mistakes.'

(f) Thinking about how the language works is a very important part of learning. Understanding can be a very useful tool.

(g) We learn languages by copying what others say. That's why exercises which ask you to 'listen and repeat' are so useful.

(h) When you are learning a language the teacher must ensure you make as few mistakes as possible. This is because practice makes not just perfect, but permanent as well. A mistake repeated will often become ingrained.

3.2.1 Structural linguistics

At the end of the nineteenth and beginning of the twentieth centuries, a stimulus for the development of contemporary linguistics came from what at first sight might appear an unlikely source. This was the rapid disappearance of scores of American Indian languages. Take a look at CW3.1 (*Languages dying out*), which records the pessimistic thoughts of one linguist and anthropologist, J. W. Powell, on this matter.

Realization of the near extinction of so many languages led some linguists – particularly Franz Boas, whose huge *Handbook of American Indian Languages* (1911) is a monument to the movement – to develop what is sometimes called field linguistics. As the name suggests, this sort of linguistics involved going 'out into the field' to collect data, very often from a language that was in the process of dying out.

These data would then be used as the basis for the linguist to work out the language's structure. This idea, of working from data to an understanding of underlying structure, is an important one. Two terms coined by another early-twentieth-century linguist of the period, the Swiss scholar Ferdinand de Saussure, help to clarify the idea. He uses the French word *parole* (literally 'word') to describe actual concrete instances of language use – the utterances recorded by the field linguist, for example. To describe the more theoretical, underlying structure of the language (what we called the 'system' in 2.3), Saussure uses another French word *langue* ('tongue', 'language'). We can use these terms to express our important idea: it was believed that you could collect specimens of *parole*, and then use this recorded information to work out *langue*.

Linguists like Saussure developed a set of analytic procedures which they believed would enable them to achieve this aim of working from instances of a language's use to an understanding of how that language was structured. These procedures for analysing languages are still used by some linguists today. They involve techniques for breaking speech up into segments (words, phonemes, morphemes, etc.), and for classifying items into categories (like nouns, adjectives and adverbs). A central technique associated with these procedures entails looking at the <u>distribution</u> of items – exactly where they could and could not occur in relation to other items. If you would like to see an example of a distributional point, look at CW3.2 (*Looking at distribution*).

It was the American linguist Leonard Bloomfield who put together and systematized these analytic procedures in a highly influential book called *Language*, which appeared in 1933. The linguistics of Bloomfield and his colleagues has come to be called structuralism, and one of its central aims was to be *scientific* in its approach to linguistic analysis. But what did 'being scientific' mean? For Bloomfield, the answer lay in the philosophical tradition known as empiricism. It is a tradition that goes back to the seventeenth-century English philosopher John Locke (and beyond), and in Bloomfield's own time was associated with logical positivist philosophers like Rudolf Carnap, working in Vienna. Empiricism placed central importance on 'sense data' – concrete, material things that can be seen, touched, heard, recorded, measured – as the starting point and basis for scientific enquiry. In the study of language, this leads precisely to the procedure of using actual instances of speech (*parole*) as the starting point for analysis. Here are two quotations (cited in Stern 1983: 137) which illustrate Bloomfield's desire to be scientific, and which show what that entails:

- 'science shall deal with only such events that are accessible in their time and place to any and all observers';
- 'science shall deal with only such terms as are derivable by rigid definition from a set of … terms concerning physical happenings.'

For Bloomfield, then, science (and linguistics as science) was concerned with the observable and the physical.

In its concern with these attributes, structural linguistics became linked with a school of psychology also aggressively interested in the observable and the physical. This school was known as behaviourism.

3.2.2 Behaviourism

Four of the principal protagonists in behaviourism were: a nineteenth-century Russian, Ivan Pavlov; an early-twentieth-century American, John Watson (sometimes called 'the father of behaviourism'); another early-twentieth-century American, Edward Thorndike; and a mid-twentieth-century American, Burrhus Skinner. Behaviourism was concerned with how learning took place. The three basic behaviourist ideas about learning are:

(a) Conditioning (Pavlov and the dribbling dogs)

Learning is seen as a question of developing connections (known as <u>stimulus–response bonds</u>) between events. The process of developing connections is called <u>conditioning</u>. Pavlov's dogs are the best-known example of the conditioning process. In one famous experiment (described in Box 3.2), Pavlov taught dogs to salivate when they heard a bell ringing. Salivation is of course an entirely natural thing for a dog to do in the presence of food – no learning at all is required – and for this reason the response is known as an <u>unconditioned reflex</u>. But it is not normal for a dog to salivate when a bell rings, so we are here indeed talking about learning. The dogs were conditioned to respond in the way they did; their response is a <u>conditioned reflex</u>.

B3.2 How to teach dogs to salivate when a bell rings, in two easy lessons

Lesson 1. Ring a bell, and soon after give the dog food.
Lesson 2. Repeat many times. Soon the dog will associate the bell with food, and will salivate when the bell rings.

(b) Habit formation (Skinner and the sporty pigeons)

The behaviourists shared with the structural linguists a view of science which was grounded on the importance of physical events (what we earlier called 'sense data'). Hence they did not take easily to the idea of some unobservable, abstract entity called the 'mind' being involved in learning. For them, learning was a question of habit formation. When the behaviour to be learned was complex, it was developed by a process called <u>shaping</u>. To shape a behaviour, you break it down into small parts, and teach each one at a time, until eventually the whole complex behaviour is built up. By shaping, Skinner was able to teach pigeons unlikely behaviours, like playing table tennis (see Box 3.3 below), and in this way Skinner had remarkable success in teaching animals behaviours which are both complex and unnatural for them. As we shall see in CW9.1, the concept of shaping plays a role in some language teaching methods.

B3.3 How to teach a pigeon to play table tennis, in five easy lessons

Lesson 1.   First stand your pigeon behind a ping-pong ball. Whenever it approaches the ball (by chance at first), give it some food. Soon your pigeon will have been conditioned to approach the ball.

Lesson 2.   Now only give the pigeon food when it actually touches the ball.

Lesson 3.   When the pigeon has learned to touch the ball, start to reward it only when it pushes the ball forward.

Lesson 4.   Continue training in the same way until the pigeon can knock the ball over a net.

Lesson 5.   Your pigeon is now ready to confront an opponent (another pigeon). You now only reward them when they push the ball past their opponent. The championship can commence.

(c) The importance of the 'environment' (writing on a 'clean slate')

We can draw a distinction, sometimes useful in discussions about learning, between the *organism* and the *environment*. The organism is the person or animal that does the learning. The word *environment* is here being used in a very wide sense to refer to anything external to the organism. An event or a situation, or even another person (a teacher or parent for example), may be seen as part of the environment in this sense. Different learning theories give different degrees of importance to the organism and the environment. In behaviourism, the environment is all, and the role of the organism is considered insignificant. Two vivid metaphors are often used to describe this view of the organism. The child is said to be born as a 'clean slate' (the Latin phrase is *tabula rasa*) onto which experience 'writes' or 'draws' its 'messages.' A second, similar, metaphor is of the child as a piece of unused photographic paper, which, when 'exposed' to the world and to experiences, begins to reflect images of these. The simple diagram below shows a way of representing the roles of organism and environment in behaviourism; the size of the boxes indicates relative importance to the learning process.

Environment   Organism

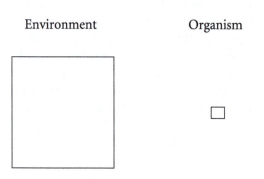

If you are interested in the development of ideas in language teaching you will want to know more about behaviourism than is given here. Many introductory texts dealing with learning theory will give the appropriate background (see 'Further reading' at the end of the chapter for suggestions).

3.2.3 Mentalism (rationalism)

Skinner applied his behaviourist views to language in a book, published in 1957, called *Verbal Behaviour*. Chomsky's 1959 review of this is a major and devastating attack on behaviourism in linguistics. Chomsky writes from within a philosophical and linguistic tradition known as 'mentalism' or 'rationalism', which stands in opposition to behaviourism in nearly all respects. Mentalism is the belief that the mind (and all things associated with it, like consciousness, thoughts, etc.) are important for determining not just human behaviour but also the way we 'do' science. Chomsky revolutionized linguistics and introduced a theory known as generative grammar (GG for short). His book *Syntactic Structures* (1957) introduced the theory, and his 1965 *Aspects of the Theory of Syntax* modified the model. Chomsky's views of both language and language learning have been highly influential in the study of FL learning (and language teaching as well). Lyons (1970) provides a brief and accessible account of Chomsky's early beliefs (his thinking has developed considerably since the GG days which we shall concentrate on here). We shall here look initially at his views on language and linguistics, and then at his thoughts on first language acquisition.

3.2.4 Generative linguistics

As we have seen, a main idea of the structuralists was the belief that the starting point for language analysis should be 'the observable.' A central plank of Chomsky's argument is that if we insist on restricting ourselves to the study of the observable, we shall fail to understand the most important aspects of language. We can illustrate this by looking at two of Chomsky's most famous sentences:

(1) John is easy to please.
(2) John is eager to please.

Structural linguistic techniques would recognize the clear structural similarity between these sentences. They both start with the noun (*John*), followed by part of the verb *be*, followed by an adjective (*easy/eager*), finishing with *to* and a verb (*please*). But despite these similarities, there are fundamental differences between the sentences. These are brought out by the fact that we can say (3), but not (4):

(3) It is easy to please John.
(4) *It is eager to please John.

Without entering into the technicalities of Chomsky's analysis, we can understand the gist of his argument by thinking about the relationships between the verb *please*, and the adjectives *easy* and *eager*. In sentence (2), the person wanting to do the pleasing is John. But sentence (1) means something like 'it is easy for someone (else) to please John'; the sentence has a 'passive sense': *John is easy to be pleased*. The relationship of the elements in the sentences are, then, quite different, and this accounts for the fact that we can say (3) but not (4). The important point is that these different relationships do not manifest themselves in the 'observable' sentences (1) and (2) themselves, which are superficially similar. It is only at a deeper level of analysis – when you start to think about the impossibility of saying (4) – that the true relationships between the elements become apparent. It is this more revealing, but also more abstract (and unobservable), level of analysis that Chomsky introduced into his linguistics. He called it <u>deep structure</u>. In terms of his analysis, he would say that sentences (1) and (3) are similar at deep structure level, while sentences (1) and (2), though superficially highly similar, are dissimilar at the deep level.

It is important to understand how Chomsky's willingness to talk in terms of a deep structure, which goes beyond the observable, leads him to abandon the structuralist belief that considering *parole* leads to an understanding of *langue*. In our example, the instances of *parole* (that a field linguist recording English might testify) are sentences (1), (2) and (3). Sentence (4) would never be heard, because it cannot exist – further evidence of the main point, that unobserved truths are important in understanding how *langue* works.

We may call this type of analysis 'mentalist' because it believes that in order to say important things about language it is necessary to go beyond the observable. This is where the essential methodological differences between Bloomfield and Chomsky become evident. Chomsky is always asking whether one can or cannot say certain sentences (like (4), for example). The person he asks is often himself, as a native speaker of the language in question. He is prepared to 'create his own data', to rely on native-speaker intuition, and above all to ask about what you *cannot* say as much as what you *can* say. It is considerations like this that led Chomsky (1966) to claim, referring to the structuralists' techniques mentioned earlier: 'I think there are by now very few linguists who believe that it is possible to arrive at the phonological or syntactic structure of a language by systematic application of "analytic procedures" of segmentation and classification.' Pause to reflect on this sentence for a moment. It will play an important part in the argument below.

3.2.5 Mentalist learning theory

The 'analytic procedures' just mentioned were those outlined earlier (in 3.2.1). They were developed for the linguist, particularly the field linguist anxious to describe a language before it disappears. As we have seen, Chomsky's views amount to a claim that however much linguists use these techniques, they will never arrive at a proper understanding of how a language system works.

Let us now turn our attention to another individual, in another situation. This is the young child born into a language community and attempting to learn their first language (e.g. English). This child has something in common with the field linguist. Both are faced with a new language which at first they know nothing of. Both have to use whatever resources are at their disposal to come to grips with the language. The young child is indeed a type of field linguist. How does the child manage to crack the secrets of their first language? Ask a behaviourist this question, and the answer would speak in terms of applying (in an unconscious way, of course) the same kinds of analytic procedures that the field linguist uses, one of which you explored in CW3.2.

But for Chomsky this way of 'working out' a language's structure is as unlikely for the child as it is for the field linguist. However long the child listened to *parole* and unconsciously applied the linguist's 'analytic procedures', they would never reach *langue*. Chomsky's statement given at the end of the last section, then, embodies a belief in how languages are *not* learned. The child does *not* listen, apply some rather general techniques and eventually end up speaking the language. Environmental help plus the use of some general procedures are just not enough.

How, then, does the child manage to learn their first language? Chomsky sees this problem as part of a more general one that he calls 'Plato's problem.' This problem is: how is it that human beings, whose contacts with the world are so brief and limited, know as much as they do? The association with Plato comes about because in *The Meno* Plato describes the philosopher Socrates demonstrating that an ignorant slave boy knows the principles of geometry. Socrates leads the boy through a series of questions to discover geometric theorems. Plato's answer to Plato's problem was reincarnation – we know so much from such an early age because we bring knowledge with us from previous existences. Chomsky's formulation of Plato's problem in relation to language is this: how does a child learn such a complicated system as language in such a relatively short time? The acquisition is quick, what is acquired is complicated; therefore the achievement needs explanation. As we have seen, one sort of explanation is that the child receives excellent teaching, from the 'environment' in general and the mother in particular. Chomsky has always denied the feasibility of this explanation. He points out that the data the child gets from the environment (parents and other adults) are 'degenerate' in the sense that they are full of false starts, poor examples, and do not contain anything like the full information the child would need to be able to work out how the language operates. Certainly they are not at all the kind of carefully planned and well-articulated language data that most trained FL teachers strive to give their learners. This argument against the 'child receives excellent teaching' explanation is sometimes called the <u>poverty of stimulus</u> argument.

How on earth, then, *does* the child learn? Chomsky's answer is that the child is born with a powerful piece of machinery – what he calls the language acquisition device (LAD) – which enables them to do the complex task. This piece of machinery works only for language (and not for other kinds of acquisition), and it contains a kind of blueprint of how language works. It is the existence of this blueprint that makes it unnecessary for the child to undertake the kind of analytic procedures the field linguists developed. These procedures are not necessary because children already know a lot about language when they are born. Though at first sight it may seem surprising, Chomsky (1987) notes that his answer to the problem is not so dissimilar to Plato's. Today (in the tradition of Western thought at least) we no longer believe in reincarnation. But the effect of a 'piece of machinery' like the LAD, developed by evolution and genetically passed on from age to age, is not really so different!

Chomsky's views about the LAD amount to a claim about 'what does the work' in L1 acquisition. The child's environment does of course have some role to play – after all, if the child hears no language then they will certainly not learn an L1. But this role is minimal, and the real work is done by children themselves. The diagram below shows this view of the relative roles of environment and organism in L1 acquisition. It stands in dramatic contrast to the diagram in 3.2.2:

Environment   Organism

Chomsky's views on language acquisition stimulated a huge number of studies on the subject, and most reach conclusions that negate behaviourist views. Box 3.4 illustrates the kind of data the generative grammarians were fond of.

B3.4 A child that nobody don't likes

In the following exchange, reported in McNeill (1970: 106), the linguist parent is attempting to correct the child (learning English as an L1):

Child: Nobody don't like me.
Parent: No, say nobody likes me.
Child: Nobody don't like me.

The child and parent repeat this exchange *eight* times. Then, exasperated at the parent who seems more interested in grammar than in what is being expressed, the child says, with some passion:

Child: Oh, nobody don't likes me.

Two questions:

1. What does this example suggest to you about the role of *habit formation* in learning the L1?
2. Where does the child's incorrect sentence *Nobody don't like me* 'come from'? Where does the child get it from?

If 'practice makes permanent' and learning proceeds through habit formation (as behaviourists claim), then we might expect the badly formed sentence *Nobody don't like me* to become well and truly permanent, since it is repeated eight times. But doubtless it does not become permanent. What is likely to happen is that when the child is good and ready to produce the right form, they will do so irrespective of how many hundreds of times they may, up until that point, have produced the wrong form. One might take the exchange as an example of how little the child is affected by their 'environment' – the child carries on in their own sweet way despite all parental attempts to change linguistic behaviour. And where do the child's utterances 'come from'? They have almost certainly never been *heard* by the child in the 'environment.' The child has 'invented' them. They come – like most of L1 acquisition for Chomsky – from somewhere inside the organism itself.

Before leaving Chomsky, it is worth noting where his view of an innate LAD takes him. It must of course be the case that all children possess the same piece of machinery. The notion that there is one LAD for those born in Japan, another for Italian children, another for the Dutch, is absurd. The idea only makes sense if we say that all children, wherever and whenever they are born, possess the same 'blueprint for language.' If this is the case, then it follows that all the world's languages must share important characteristics – those aspects of all human languages that our innate blueprint maps out. During recent decades, Chomsky and like-minded linguists have taken up a quest which has in fact fascinated linguists for centuries – to explore the possible nature of what is called Universal Grammar (UG). Finding deep underlying similarities between the world's languages, which are superficially so diverse, has become a major preoccupation of Chomskyan linguistics.

3.2.6   The swinging pendulum

We have here been looking at two opposing views of language and language learning, views which can be linked up to more general philosophical positions about the world and knowledge of it. As we look at the development of thought in both the language learning and language teaching spheres, we shall see the conflict between these two views enacted time and time again. Thus a familiar pattern in much language literature from 1940 to 1970 is for fairly strong empiricist assumptions to be replaced by fairly radical mentalist ones. Time and time again the movement is from Bloomfield/Skinner-inspired to Chomsky-inspired. This is why it has been worth devoting a good portion of one chapter to this particular swing of the pendulum.

B3.5 An earlier exercise revisited

In Box 3.1 you considered some contrary views about language learning and teaching. Look again at these views. For each pair of contrary views, decide which is associated with an empiricist position and which with a mentalist one.

Do these views (plus what you have just been reading about) enable you to make any general statements about the implications of empiricism and mentalism for FL learning and teaching? What does each approach say about how we learn? And about how we should teach? Your thoughts at this stage may be vague, but they should become clearer as the book proceeds.

The laws of gravity dictate that once pendulums have swung one way, they will swing back again. So it is that in recent decades there have been various reactions to Chomskyan linguistics. One of these sees the pendulum swing away from mentalism back towards empiricism. The development of powerful computers has been partly responsible. It is now possible to collect together a huge number of texts (spoken or written, or both), selected to be as representative as possible, in electronic form. Such a collection is called a <u>corpus</u> (plural <u>corpora</u>), and the branch of linguistics that is based on these collections is <u>corpus linguistics</u>. Corpora can be truly massive; three of the best known are the Birmingham/Collins Cobuild corpus (now known as the *Bank of English*) which stretches to 650 million words, the *British National Corpus* (around 100 million words), and the 450 million-word *Corpus of Contemporary American English* (affectionately known as COCA for short). To get a small taster of the power of corpora, you might like to take a look at the website of the British National Corpus – www.natcorp.ox.ac.uk. Click on the 'BYU-BNC' link under the heading of 'Search the British National Corpus online'; you will be invited to type in a word of your choice. It will tell you how many instances of your word appear in the corpus as a whole, and you will be able to look at these instances. My attempt just now with the word *empiricism* gave 121 examples in their textual contexts. Choose a word of your own and try for yourself.

Corpora provide a huge amount of information about how linguistic items are actually used. Notice how dramatically different a way of 'doing linguistics' this is from Chomsky's. As we saw in 3.2.4, he trusts to native-speaker intuition for his data; the phrase we used was that he 'create[s] his own data.' In contrast, the corpus linguist's data come from actual attested instances of use. Something else we saw in that same earlier section was Chomsky's belief that important aspects of language can only be revealed by looking at non-existent sentences as well as occurring ones – things that you *can't* say as well as things that you *can* say. Corpus linguistics is firmly based on what people have said or written (not on what *hasn't* occurred). Though there are many differences between corpus linguistics and structuralism, the two share in common the basic belief that studying how language is actually being used is the way to 'do linguistics.' To borrow some phrases from 3.2.1: both approaches are 'parole-based.' They take 'actual instances of speech as the starting point for analysis.'

Very often, looking at actual usage throws up surprises that a native speaker, sitting in their armchair thinking about language, might not predict. Here is an example. Sinclair and Renouf (1988) look at what corpora reveal about the word *see*. It would be natural for you to imagine (from the comfort of your armchair) that the most common use of this word is to do with visual perception, as in the sentence *I can see him in the distance*. In fact, computer evidence suggests that the most common usage is in the sense of 'understand' (as in *Yes, I see*, or *Do you see what I mean?*). In 11.2.2 we shall briefly consider the relevance of information like this for language teaching.

Another movement which challenges Chomsky's views is known as <u>cognitive linguistics</u>. Two aspects of this approach are relevant here. First, in 3.2.5 we mentioned in passing the Chomskyan belief that language acquisition is separate from other areas of mental (cognitive) development; as its name suggests, the LAD works for language alone. In contrast, cognitive linguistics argues that language and mental development are closely allied. A firm and un-Chomskyan link is established between language and cognition. Second, cognitive linguistics, like corpus linguistics, believes that to study language (and language acquisition) you need to look at actual instances of language in use. Here is how one introduction to the field (Evans and Green 2006: 108) puts it: 'knowledge of language is derived from patterns of language use, and ... knowledge of language is knowledge of how language is used.'

Thus it is that from around the beginning of the 1970s Chomsky's views were being challenged on a number of fronts. Another challenge relates not so much to the empiricism/mentalism issue as to the perception that Chomskyan linguistics failed really to consider the way language was used in society. One might refer to the movement which developed this perception as the 'sociolinguistic revolution',[2] and it had a great effect on attitudes towards language learning and teaching. It deserves its own separate section.

3.3 The 'sociolinguistic revolution'

3.3.1 Communicative competence

If you have ever seen a transcript of your voice recorded onto tape as you were taking part in some form of 'natural' conversation or discussion, you will probably have been shocked at the number of 'ums' and 'ahs' you make, the number of times you start a sentence one way and finish it in another, the number of times you make grammatical and lexical slips. If you have not seen such a transcript, it will not take you long to make one: record yourself in a short stretch of natural conversation with someone, and then transcribe exactly what you say – word for word, 'ums' and 'ahs' included.

Shock is a common reaction. Many of us think of ourselves as incisive, fluent, coherent speakers, and our self-esteem takes a cruel blow when we see what we have said written down. The speaker in Box 3.6 was not drunk, tired, drugged or mentally deranged. The slips and hesitations made are normal to nearly all speakers in informal situations. If you were given a copy of a similar transcription of your own speech, you would probably have little difficulty in editing out all the slips and hesitations, to convert it into a far more elegant piece of discourse. It may be said that the slips you made were 'performance-related', and that your actual 'competence' in the language is more truly reflected in the corrected version. This latter version, you might want to say, more accurately represents your true ability at English.

B3.6 Up the Amazon

Below is a part of a passage of normal speech, transcribed. It is taken from Hughes and Trudgill (1996: 52):

> Um ... in the days before husbands and children, um I did quite a lot of travelling and um ... one of the th ... places I went to was to the Amazon and um I hadn't really as why I ... I knew my husband and um ... then but ... just as a friend really and so we um decided that we, or he decided that we would go to Brazil and er I'd been travelling anyway ... came back for Christmas, two days to wash my rucksack and off we went to Rio ... and um I hadn't given it any thought at all and the next thing I knew we went up to Manaus ....

Chomsky draws this distinction between competence and performance, and it is similar to Saussure's between *langue* and *parole*. Saussure's *langue* – the underlying language system – is akin to Chomsky's 'competence', and Saussure's *parole* is related to Chomsky's 'performance.'[3] Chomsky states quite clearly that his concern as a linguist is not with performance but competence, and a highly abstract version of competence at that. In his influential 1965 book, which set out one version of GG, he speaks in terms of the competence of the 'ideal speaker-listener, in a completely homogeneous speech-community.' He is not interested in the way that John or Mary actually speak. One of them might have a speech defect, the other a particular way of pronouncing their 'r' sounds; one may have a London accent, the other an Australian one. But these are performance features, and Chomsky is interested in the abstraction, in what underlies performance.

At the beginning of the 1970s, the views of linguists coming from different traditions and countries, but sharing a more social approach to language study, came to have their voices heard. Sociolinguists (those interested in how language is used within society) began to show discontent with the Chomskyan way of doing things. One of the notions that came under attack was this idea of the 'ideal speaker-listener.' The American sociolinguist Dell Hymes, for example, was interested in the language of disadvantaged children, people who could hardly be described as ideal speaker-listeners. He wanted to be able (directly or indirectly) to help such children, and he found little of relevance to him in the rather rarefied atmosphere of Chomskyan linguistics.

We have already seen in 1.3 that Chomsky's other notion – of the 'homogeneous speech-community' – is not one that has much currency in today's world. Stern's (1983: 231) quotation summarizes arguments that we have already seen:

> since World War Two the profound social and political changes in the world have left a recognition that the reality of the language situation can no longer be forced into the simple mould of the single-language nation state with its single-medium school.

Little surprise that with perceptions like these in the air, Hymes should describe Chomskyan linguistics as a 'Garden of Eden' view.

In an important article entitled 'On Communicative Competence', Hymes (1970) argues that linguists, particularly of the generative school, have been concerned exclusively with what he calls 'the possible.' They have focused their attention on what the rules of the language system permit as possible structures, what we called 'systemic competence' in 2.3. If, Hymes argues, we restrict linguistics in this way, we shall learn nothing about how language is used as a means of communication among humans. Hymes suggests various other factors, apart from 'the possible', that we need to study. Hymes calls one of these factors 'the feasible.' There are sentences which, though perfectly grammatical, would never be said by anyone because they are so difficult to process. Box 3.7 exemplifies one of these.

B3.7 The woman who married a mouse?

An example of a sentence that is perfectly grammatical yet too difficult to process is: *The mouse the cat the dog the man the woman married beat chased ate had a white tail.*

> Split this up into smaller sentences to reveal what it means. Start with the mouse. Your first sentence might be *The mouse had a white tail*. Then move on to the cat, then the dog, and so on.
>
> Invent another similarly complex sentence, also containing five verbs, but having nothing to do with mice.

A further factor might be called 'the performed.' There are many phrases and sentences which, though they might well express what a speaker wants to say, do not happen to be used. We saw examples in 2.3.4, where we suggested that there is no real reason why a sentence like *It's a big shame* (as opposed to *It's a great shame*) should not be used. But it never is (in standard British English at least). Note that *It's a big shame* is perfectly grammatical – it just does not happen to be the way we express the idea.

The final factor is the one that has had the greatest effect on the study of language learning and teaching. It is what Hymes calls 'the appropriate', and it deals with the 'rules of use' discussed in 2.4.1 under the heading of 'sociolinguistic competence.' A number of examples were given there, one being Canale and Swain's inappropriate way the waiter spoke to the restaurant guests: *OK chump, what are you and this broad going to eat?*

If you want a summary of the factors which Hymes discusses, take a look at CW3.3 (*Hymes's communicative competence*).

3.3.2   An example of a 'sociolinguistic' approach

The work of Hymes and other sociolinguists on rules of use is a central part of what we have been calling the 'sociolinguistic revolution.' Here is an example of the kind of study that the approach led to. Sinclair and Coulthard (1975) set themselves the task of analysing interactions between teachers and pupils in the school classroom. Not surprisingly, at various points in their investigation they come across situations in which teacher and pupils misunderstand each other. In one lesson, for example, the teacher plays a recording of a television programme 'in which there is a psychologist talking with a "posh" accent. The teacher wants to explore the children's attitude to accent and the value judgements based on it' (1975: 29). When the recording is finished the teacher questions the students about the psychologist:

Teacher: What kind of person do you think he is? Do you – (pupil bursts
           out laughing) – what are you laughing at?
Pupil: Nothing.

The pupil says *Nothing* because they think the teacher is angry with them for laughing. They interpret the teacher's *What are you laughing at?* as an implied command to stop laughing. In fact the teacher does not mean it in this way. They intend it as a serious question; if they can make the pupil explain their mirth, this will provide them with an excellent opening for the topic they wish to discuss. As the conversation proceeds, the pupil realizes what the teacher really meant and the misunderstanding is cleared up.

It is easy to see why this misunderstanding should have taken place. Some question forms in English – such as *What are you laughing at? Why are you shouting? What are you standing up for?* – may be interpreted either as straight requests for information or as commands to do something (expressed in a rather indirect way). A parent may, for example, ask a child *Why are you shouting?* out of genuine curiosity at what the child is doing. But it might also be a veiled way of saying *For goodness' sake talk more softly.* Because sentences like these have two possible interpretations, the question arises of how a pupil (or indeed any native speaker – as well as the foreign language learner who is a central figure in this book) knows in any given situation which interpretation is the correct one. In the case we have considered, there was misunderstanding; but more often than not the listener will know immediately and unequivocally whether the speaker was asking for information or giving a command. Sometimes the speaker will give a 'linguistic signal' to make the meaning clear; for example, intonation or tone may indicate that a command is being given. But often there will be no overt signal, and only the context will help the listener towards the correct interpretation.

B3.8 Help or information?

In one of the boxes in Chapter 2, an example was given of a misunderstanding where a request for help was wrongly interpreted as a request for information. Try to find this example.

Also in Chapter 2 there is an example of an utterance intended as an order being wrongly interpreted. The utterance involves the structure *Would you like …?* Find this example also. The answers are in Note 4.

Sinclair and Coulthard try to draw up rules which specify what situational factors have to be present for a sentence to be interpretable as a command. One rule says that 'any declarative or interrogative [uttered by a teacher in a classroom] is to be interpreted as a command to stop if it refers to an action or activity which is proscribed at the time of the utterance' (1975: 32). According to this rule, utterances like *I can hear someone laughing, Is someone laughing?* and *What are you laughing at?* are to be taken as commands to stop laughing in situations where laughing is felt to be a 'forbidden activity.' Where laughing is *not* a forbidden activity, these three utterances would receive quite different interpretations. The first might simply be an observation, the second and third requests for information. The pupil's misunderstanding in the episode outlined earlier happens because (contrary to the teacher's intentions) they perceive of laughing as forbidden activity at that particular moment.

In fact, Sinclair and Coulthard give three rules for the interpretation of sentences as commands. But the details of the analysis are not relevant here. What is important is the nature of the questions the linguists are asking. They are not questions about the structure of the sentences, but about their use.

The work of Sinclair and Coulthard has been introduced to illustrate the shift in emphasis that occurred in linguistics in the early 1970s. If further exemplification is necessary, the titles of two books influential at that time may be cited. The first is a book by the linguist Michael Halliday concerned with the way children acquire their L1. Books in the generative school about this (of which there were very many) are predominantly concerned with the stages children go through when they acquire structures – how children 'learn to form', one might say. Halliday's 1975 book is entitled *Learning How to Mean*, and this clearly shows that the interest is not in syntax ('form') for its own sake, but in how language is acquired to perform actions.

The title of another influential book in the field is even more revealing. It was published in 1962, two years after the author's death. He was John Austin, a British philosopher with a particular interest in matters linguistic. The book is called *How to Do Things with Words*. The title says it all, and this idea of 'doing things with words' well captures a notion which played an important role in the 'movement' we have been describing. It is the notion of the speech act. We might say that Sinclair and Coulthard are looking at the teacher's utterance *What are you laughing at?* in speech-act terms. The study of speech acts forms an important part of the branch of linguistics central to the movement we have been discussing. This is pragmatics, defined by Widdowson (1996: 130) as 'the study of what people mean by language when they use it in the normal context of social life.'

It is worth reminding yourself, at the end of this rather theoretical section, that speech acts, pragmatics and the 'sociolinguistic revolution' are very important to language teaching. Look back to 2.4.1 where we talked a little about 'rules of use.' Because many of them are not universal, they will often need to be taught to the foreign learner. Chapter 9, section 9.6, explores the very practical issue of how this can be done.

3.4 Conclusion

In this chapter we have focused mainly on ideas that were developed some decades ago. We have spent time on them because of the influence they have had, and continue to have, on theories of language learning and teaching. The next chapter begins our consideration of language learning. In it, we shall immediately see evidence of how the empiricism/mentalism conflict has made itself felt – in this instance in the analysis and interpretation of learner errors.

Notes

1. The pairs are: (a) and (f); (b) and (g); (c) and (d); (e) and (h).
2. This term is a useful label, but we are here using it to refer to developments that go beyond what are usually considered as sociolinguistics. As is mentioned in 3.3.2, the concept of the speech act, and the study of pragmatics in particular, play an important part in the 'movement.'
3. Though similar, Saussure's and Chomsky's terms are not equivalent. Chomsky's 'competence' is a psychological concept, while Saussure's *langue* has a social dimension – it is the language of the entire speech community.
4. In example 3 of Box 2.11, the question *Excuse me, do you have a watch?* is wrongly interpreted as a request for information. In 2.4.1, the teacher's utterance *Would you like to read?* is not recognized as a command.

Issues to think or write about

1. In 3.2.6, language corpora are mentioned, and a number of available ones are named. Find out more about corpora. Discover what others are available; what aims they have; how they differ from each other. Find out more about what uses linguists have put corpora to, and in general about the field of corpus linguistics. You can concentrate on the corpora of a single language, or of more if you wish.
2. Section 3.3 talks about speech acts and gives some examples (such as 'requesting information' and 'giving orders'). Here are some more speech acts: Focusing on English or some other language, choose one or more of these

   greeting   *inviting*   *asking for permission*   *cursing (swearing)*

   speech acts. For each, outline some situations in which you would use them. Then consider some of the expressions that could be used to express the act. Finally, think about the 'rules of use' related to your expressions. When would you use each expression, and how do they differ from each other?

Further reading

Lightbown, P. M., and Spada, N. 2006 *How Languages Are Learned* 3rd edn Oxford: Oxford University Press
Includes an approachable section on behaviourism (and indeed on many other learning theories mentioned in this book).

Hergenhahn, B. R., and Olson, M. H. 2005 *An Introduction to Theories of Learning* 7th edn London: Pearson Education
Covers a number of theories, not just behaviourism, with sections on Pavlov, Thorndike and Skinner.

Chomsky, N. 1988 *Language and Problems of Knowledge* Cambridge, MA: MIT Press

One of Chomsky's more accessible descriptions of his ideas (including Plato's problem).

Brown, H. D. 2006 *Principles of Language Learning and Teaching* 5th edn Englewood Cliffs, NJ: Prentice-Hall

Brumfit, C. J., and Johnson, K. (eds) 1979 *The Communicative Approach to Language Teaching* Oxford: Oxford University Press

Section 1 contains substantial extracts from seminal papers associated with the 'sociolinguistic revolution', including Hymes' 'On communicative competence.'

Part II
Learning

4 Learners and their errors

4.1 Introduction

An FL learner's language is perhaps never more interesting than when they get things wrong. When they produce correct, error-free utterances, these may tell us little about what is going on in the learner's mind. But as soon as an error is made, we can look at its nature and try to work out why it was made. Errors can hold vital clues about the processes of FL learning. It is rather like the pain that tells the doctor more about what is wrong with you than all the parts that do not hurt. Box 4.1 gives a simple illustration.

B4.1 Being hungry or having hunger?

If you are hungry in German, you say *Ich habe Hunger*, literally *I have hunger*. You would not say *Ich bin hungrig*, literally *I am hungry*, which is of course the normal English way of expressing the idea.

If a German learner of English says *I have hunger*, you can be almost certain that they are translating literally from German; they are 'working through' German. But there is a second type of mistake which many learners make, irrespective of their native language. It is to say *I hungry*. If our German learner says this, we cannot conclude that they are 'working through' German, because this is not the German way of expressing the idea. They are in fact doing something which young children learning English as an L1 do, leaving out the verb *be*. Why do you think they are doing this?

In this chapter we shall discuss these two different sorts of error.

The unacceptable sentence *I have hunger* illustrates a type of error that formed the basis of a theory about foreign language learning which was developed by applied linguists in the 1950s and 1960s. We shall begin by discussing this theory.

4.2 Contrastive analysis: a theory about FL learning

The rationale for this language learning theory lies within behaviourism and the belief that learning is a question of habit formation. The behaviourists believed that when a new habit was learned, old (already existing) habits would have some effect on the learning process. Looking at the effects of one habit on learning another is known in psychology as the study of transfer. Two sorts of transfer are important to us. Positive transfer is where the two habits share common aspects, such that knowing one will help with learning the other. So if you are learning to ride a motorbike, it may be that being able to ride a normal bicycle will help the process. In this case we would say that there is positive transfer from bicycle to motorbike riding. Negative transfer is also called interference. When I bought my new car, the direction indicator (to signal a left or right turn) was on the side of the steering wheel where my old car had its windscreen wiper. The result was that for the first few weeks in my new car, every time I wanted to turn left, the windscreen would get cleaned.

B4.2 Further examples of transfer

Think of some more examples of learning to do (non-linguistic) activities. They might be learning a particular sport or a particular musical instrument. Think of some behaviours which might help or hinder your learning of these activities. Think of at least one example of *positive* transfer and one of *negative* transfer.

It is easy to think of language learning parallels to the motorbike riding and direction indicator examples. Chapter 2 contains many. We noted (in 2.1), for example, that a German learner of English will not have great difficulty with the concept of the article system, because both languages have systems that are conceptually similar. We can therefore say that learners are likely to experience some positive transfer from native to target language. We also saw there that Japanese does not have a comparable article system, so Japanese learners will experience negative transfer from the L1 when learning German or English. Our German learner who said *I have hunger* for *I am hungry* would also be displaying negative transfer.

One of the major figures interested in such matters was Robert Lado, whose influential book *Linguistics across Cultures: Applied Linguistics for Language Teachers* appeared in 1957, the same year that a book mentioned in 3.2.3 appeared – Skinner's account of language in behaviourist terms, entitled *Verbal Behaviour*. Lado was interested in what made some things easy for learners, and other things difficult. He believed that by comparing the native language (its structure, its sounds, its lexis) and the target language, we would be able to find out about ease and difficulty of learning. This belief was a kind of manifesto for what came to be called the 'contrastive analysis (CA) hypothesis.' Here is a clear statement of it, from Lado (1957: 2): 'those elements that are similar to the [learner's] native language will be simple for him, and those areas that are different will be difficult.' This hypothesis led to a very large number of research projects throughout the world, which aimed to compare various languages in order to identify potential learning difficulties. The Center for Applied Linguistics, founded in Washington in 1959, was particularly active in this area, with large-scale projects comparing aspects of English with German, Spanish, Italian, Russian and French. If you want a taste of what CA involves, take a look at CW4.1 (*CA in action: personal pronouns in English and Polish*).

Because it makes sense to suppose that as a general rule learners will learn simple things before more difficult ones, it was imagined that CA projects like those undertaken by the Center for Applied Linguistics would tell us something about the *order* in which learners would acquire items in the target language. We might expect that a learner will acquire parts of the target language which are similar to their native language before those that are different. It follows from this that learners with different native languages will acquire items of a target language in different orders. So, to take up an earlier example: we might expect Germans learning English to master the article system before Japanese students learning English.

B4.3 Transfer in language learning

Think about your own FL language learning experience. Make a list of three examples of mistakes you are aware of making in an FL which are due to negative transfer from your L1. If you have any FL teaching experience, you may also think of L1 transfer mistakes that your learners make in the FL.

Positive transfer is sometimes more difficult to detect than negative, but try to think of three examples where your L1 and an FL you have learned are similar, and where positive transfer might occur.

The early days of CA were heady ones, and it was believed that comparing native and target languages would tell you almost everything you needed to know in order to devise a language teaching programme. This extreme view came to be known as the strong CA hypothesis. Here is an expression of it, from Lee (1968: 180): 'the prime cause, or even the sole cause, of difficulty and error in foreign language learning is interference.'

The problem with the strong CA hypothesis is that it is clearly not true. We have touched on one example already, in Box 4.1, where we noted that some learners, even of languages like German, do produce sentences like *I hungry, even though contrastive analysis would predict *I have hunger. Where does the error *I hungry come from? If it is not caused by negative transfer, then this would be a case where the strong CA hypothesis breaks down.

Problems like these led to the development of what Wardhaugh (1970) calls the weak CA hypothesis. This is more reasonable in its claims. It says that CA may help us identify and explain some learner errors *once they have occurred*. But the hypothesis is 'weak' because it does not claim any predictive power for CA – to foresee errors with any certainty in advance. So, if the German learner does say *I have hunger then the contrastive analyst can draw on their knowledge of German to provide an explanation for the mistake. But the weak theory allows that the learner may also produce errors like *I hungry, which cannot be explained in terms of interference. The problem with the weak hypothesis is that it does not seem worth the immense effort of large-scale comparison of languages (such as those the Washington Center for Applied Linguistics undertook), just to be able to explain a proportion of error occurrences.

It was behaviourist learning theory that gave birth to CA, and the Chomskyan attacks on behaviourism which we considered in the last chapter contributed significantly to its temporary demise. But notice the word 'temporary.' CA became unfashionable for a time; but it was never truly killed off and still attracts interest today, though not within the original behaviourist framework. This continued interest is not really surprising. All language teachers know that L1 to FL interference not only happens but is an important aspect of language learning. The behaviourist framework may be discredited, but it would be a grave mistake to lose the idea of transfer with it.

What aspects of transfer have continued to interest applied linguists beyond the behaviourist era? One issue is *when* transfer occurs. Does it happen in some situations more than others? A possible factor is *learner level*. It has been suggested that lower level learners are particularly prone to negative transfer, and CW4.2 (*Transfer: when and where?*) describes one study that shows this. Perhaps because beginners have fewer resources at their disposal in the target language, they tend to rely heavily on their native language to help them in times of trouble. When they do not know a word or a structure, for example, they may simply fall back on their L1 equivalents and use these. If you have any experience as a language teacher, consider whether you have found that learner level makes any difference to amount of transfer. Another factor which many think has an effect is *language area*. It is generally recognized that pronunciation is an area where much transfer occurs; another is lexis.

4.3 Non-contrastive errors

B4.4 A strange way to ask a question

Imagine that a learner produces the utterance *Did she wanted?* (for example in the sentence *Did she wanted to go to the cinema yesterday?*). Specify first how this sentence deviates from the correct form (something you did with other sentences in CW2.4). Then try to imagine how this error came about. A linguist assures you that the sentence is not based on the learner's L1. Where, then, does it come from? How might you account for it?

In English questions, we often place the tense marker (the element which indicates the time of the 'action') on the auxiliary verb. In Box 4.4's question, the auxiliary is *do*, and the form *did* is what indicates that the action took place in the past. The learner gets this part right. But they in fact mark tense twice – as well as having *did* they also put an *-ed* on the end of the verb *want*. The morpheme *-ed* is indeed the way that the past tense is marked in many non-question forms – *She wanted to go to the cinema yesterday* is right, for example. But in questions the tense marker moves from main verb to auxiliary verb.

Where does the error 'come from'? Although it is not impossible that for some learners of some L1s there may be elements of transfer at work here, it is unlikely to be the main cause, since languages do not usually mark tense like this, on both an auxiliary and the main verb. The fact that the learner remembers to put *do* in the past tense, but forgets that they should not put the main verb, *want*, in the past tense, strongly suggests that their error comes about because they are a little mixed up about how questions are formed in English. Maybe they have developed a mistaken view of how English works. Or perhaps in the heat of a conversational moment they forget what they have learned and put every verb in sight into its past form!

By the end of the 1960s, interest in CA had waned, and the field was ready for a less restricted view of learner errors – one which would deal not just with interference but also with errors of the *Did she wanted?* sort. One paper which clearly shows this shift towards a more wide-ranging consideration of error types is by Richards (1971). The paper's title – 'A non-contrastive approach to error analysis' – announces the new perspective.

Richards is interested in errors whose 'origins are found within the structure of English itself', or the way it is taught; that is, in non-contrastive causes. He calls non-contrastive errors of this sort intralingual, meaning 'coming from within the language itself', as opposed to interlingual, meaning 'coming from differences between L1 and FL.' Another term which Richards uses to describe

67

some non-interlingual errors is <u>developmental</u>. This term is revealing, and points up an important characteristic of these errors – that they are often similar to the errors made by children learning their L1. This similarity is mentioned in Box 4.1, in relation to the German learner's use of the *I hungry* form which, we noted, cannot be explained in contrastive terms. If you want to look at another example of an intralingual error, go to CW4.3 (*No mices? Then the cats are useless*). It involves the 'Cats' essay from Box 2.2.

Richards' paper was one of a number with a similar perspective written around the beginning of the 1970s. Other important ones are Selinker (1972), Corder (1967) and Nemser (1971). The term <u>error analysis</u> (EA) is often used to describe this perspective, which provides a wider coverage of errors than the more restricted contrastive analysis.

4.4 Creative construction: another theory about FL learning

Things are taken a step further by two American applied linguists, Heidi Dulay and Marina Burt. In the first of two exciting and important papers (Dulay and Burt 1973), they begin to develop an alternative to CA which they call <u>creative construction theory</u>. They are particularly interested in errors that learners bring upon themselves – like Richards, they use the word 'developmental' to describe these. To understand why the word 'creative' appears in the theory's name, ask yourself again where a form like *Did she wanted?* 'comes from.' We have noted that it is unlikely to be modelled on the learner's L1. It is even more unlikely that the learner has ever heard it uttered by a native speaker – or even another learner (though the latter cannot be entirely discounted, of course). The place it is most likely to 'come from' is the learner's own head; it represents their own attempt to put into practice rules about question formation that they have learned. There is, in other words, a sense in which they have 'created' the form.

Dulay and Burt's 1973 paper reports on two studies. In the first, they are interested in what proportion of errors is caused by interference, and what proportion may be said to be developmental. They took 145 Spanish-speaking children living in the United States and analysed 388 of their English errors produced in natural speech, attempting to classify these as contrastive or developmental. If, to pursue our earlier example, a child produced *I have hunger*, then this was taken to be an error of transfer (this is the Spanish as well as the German way of expressing the idea). But if the learner produced *I hungry* (not the direct equivalent of a Spanish expression), then this was taken to be a developmental error. Burt and Dulay make the important point (which we noted earlier) that this error, of omitting a part of the verb *be*, is one that L1 children also commonly make. It seems to represent a 'developmental' stage learners go through when acquiring a language naturally.

It is easy to imagine how the results of Dulay and Burt's research rocked the hitherto CA-dominated world. They are:

Interference	3% of the errors considered
Developmental	85% of the errors considered
Others (i.e. where no decision could be made)	12% of the errors considered

The second part of their research was based on work being done in the study of L1 acquisition, particularly by the linguist Roger Brown. In 1973 he looked at three children – Adam, Eve and Sarah – over the period they were acquiring some basic morphemes in their L1, English (2.3.2 mentioned some of the basic ones). He plotted their progress monthly and then compared the order in which they learned these morphemes – their morpheme acquisition order. He found a remarkable degree of consistency from one child to the next. This led him and others to the idea that maybe L1 learners have a kind of 'internal syllabus' (a 'programme inside their heads') that leads them to acquire their native language in the same way. Dulay and Burt wanted to know whether FL learners acquired some important morphemes of English in a specific order. Their subjects were children with the same L1, and they focused on eight morphemes. They did indeed find an acquisition order common to their learners.

But what would happen if children with different L1s were considered? Would the same morpheme acquisition order be found? As we noted earlier, CA would predict otherwise, since the belief was that a learner's acquisition order would be based on the differences and similarities between target language and L1. Imagine, for example, two learners – Learner A and Learner B. Learner A's native language has a form similar to the English possessive *-s* (as in *John's book*, *Mary's car*), while Learner B's does not. CA would expect Learner A to acquire this morpheme in English before Learner B. If this does not happen, and both learners acquire this and other morphemes in the same order, this would indeed be a final nail in the coffin of the strong CA hypothesis.

In a second paper, Dulay and Burt (1974) looked at two groups of children – Spanish and Chinese speakers – and tackled the question: do learners with different L1s acquire morphemes of a foreign language in the same order? The answer, according to their study, was yes. The acquisition order of the two groups was virtually the same. This led them to an exciting and rather far-reaching speculation – that there is perhaps a universal morpheme acquisition order which all learners follow, irrespective of their mother tongue.

Some details of their findings: the English auxiliary verb *be* was acquired at about the same time by both groups, even though there is no comparable verb in Chinese but there is in Spanish (suggesting to adherents of CA that the Spanish speakers would acquire it before the Chinese). Then there was the noun plural morpheme *-s*, used to turn a singular noun like *hat* into the plural *hats*. This was acquired by both groups at roughly the same point in the sequence, even though there is one in Spanish but not Chinese. If this study and ones like it are taken at face value, then the lid of CA's coffin is firmly in place.

69

Both the Dulay and Burt studies were with children, and the question arises whether the same results would be found for adults. This was studied by Bailey *et al.* (1974), who found roughly the same acquisition order with adult FL learners.

Let us pause and take stock. We seem here to have findings which suggest:

- most learner errors are developmental, not the result of interference;
- both children and adults follow a sequence in the acquisition of grammar items in the FL. There is what might be called an 'internal syllabus';
- this sequence is 'universal', occurring whatever the learner's L1.

This research has been much criticized for its methodology, and in a moment we shall consider some of these criticisms. But before this, here are two observations.

First, you need to be clear on the intellectual roots of these ideas, which need to be linked to what was discussed in Chapter 3. The shift from CA to EA is a clear instance of the movement from behaviourism to mentalism that we plotted in that chapter. CA has its basis in behaviourist learning theory, while the work of Dulay and Burt is pervaded by Chomskyan ideas. You can see this in the very notion of 'creative construction.' We have seen that Chomsky's view of L1 acquisition places a great deal of importance on the role of the acquiring organism – language comes from inside the individual; it 'grows' rather like a plant grows. The form we discussed earlier – *Did she wanted?* – is similarly one that comes from within. The very word 'creative' carries echoes of Chomsky and his language acquisition views. The phrase 'internal syllabus' which we used earlier in this section similarly suggests the notion of 'everything being within the organism.' Indeed, it would not be far-fetched to suggest that Chomsky's LAD contains or implies some kind of 'internal syllabus', for L1 acquisition at least.

The second observation also relates to this notion of an 'internal syllabus', which we earlier described as a 'programme in the learners' heads.' Consider for a moment the possible implications for *language teaching* of this notion. Most learners in most classrooms have a syllabus imposed on them from outside. The textbook or the teacher (and often, ultimately, the Ministry of Education) tells them what morphemes and grammatical structures they will learn, in what order. There is, in other words, an 'external syllabus' imposed on the learners. But if learners really do have their own learning order, is there any point in imposing another order on them? What is the point in having an *external* syllabus if learners have their own *internal* one?

This exciting idea has hovered round the edges of much discussion about language teaching in recent decades, and it tends to evoke strong passions. Some rightly point out that Dulay and Burt's subjects were living in the target-language environment, potentially hearing English all the time in their surroundings. This is crucially different, it may be argued, from people learning the target language in their own native country, perhaps in classes which meet for just a few hours each week, with no word of the FL ever heard between classes. So, findings that are true in one situation may not hold in the other. But there are counter-arguments: perhaps the differences between the situations are not that significant; perhaps a good teacher should make the FL classroom as much like the L1 environment as possible. These are important ideas and arguments which we will return to more than once in later chapters. If you would like to give some initial thought to the teaching consequences of the internal syllabus idea, take a look at CW4.4 (*Yes, but what does it mean in practice?*).

Since the heady days of Dulay and Burt's work, many criticisms have arisen which cast doubt on their findings.[1] An obvious restriction of this work is its small scope – in terms of the number of languages considered, the number of learners covered, the number of language items studied. Given such small samples, the use of the phrase 'universal morpheme acquisition order' seems rather cavalier. There are also problems with the research methodology used. All this explains why Dulay and Burt's percentages for interference and developmental errors have been bitterly disputed. Ellis (1994: 302) gathers together some figures for percentages of interference errors from six other studies, and they are all well above Dulay and Burt's 3 per cent (23 per cent, 31 per cent, 33 per cent, 36 per cent, 50 per cent, 51 per cent, in fact). Certainly Dulay and Burt's low figure would go against the instincts of many experienced teachers. Experienced or otherwise, what do *your* instincts tell you?

4.5 Conclusion

This chapter has been about learner errors. We have seen how important a part they may play in understanding the processes of foreign language learning. Indeed, we have considered two theories that are centrally based on two differing views of learner errors.

Both these theories have had their moment at the centre of the applied linguistic stage, and although neither continues to hold that position, neither has yet made its final exit. We have seen that the 'CA hypothesis' received major setbacks as Chomskyan mentalism (here in the form of Dulay and Burt's work) replaced behaviourism. But we have also seen that CA still remains today a subject of interest to applied linguists.

The second of these theories, 'creative construction', has also been attacked, and the various problems and doubts we have just discussed certainly led to a diminution of interest in morpheme acquisition studies in the 1980s. But even more than with CA, 'creative construction' is still very much alive and kicking. Its underlying ideas continue to excite, and they persist in finding a place in discussion about language learning and teaching, even today. The idea of the internal acquisition order is an attractive one which for many has a ring of truth to it. As we shall see in the next chapter, it is certainly another idea that refuses to go away.

We shall also see in the next chapter, and indeed in later ones, that errors continue to play an important part in the study of foreign language acquisition. We have begun to look at errors, but we are by no means finished with them.

Note

1. McLaughlin's 1987 book has a succinct discussion of some of these criticisms (pp. 33–4).

Issues to think or write about

1. If you have access to a language learner (perhaps someone learning your L1), collect some information about their errors. You could listen to their speech for a while (if possible recording some of it) and/or look at their writing. If you know about their native language, you could try to work out which of their errors were interlingual and which intralingual. If you do not know their native language, you could ask the learner why they think each error was made. Either way, try to arrive at explanations (as detailed as possible) for the errors, both interlingual and intralingual.
2. How important is it that a language teacher should be able to speak the L1 of their learners? Some would say it is essential, and that a native speaker of English should only be allowed to teach English in Japan if they know Japanese. Others say it is less crucial.

   Consider both sides of this issue. Think, particularly in the light of what has been discussed in this chapter, of how knowing Japanese will help the native-English-speaking teacher. But think also of ways in which it will be of restricted value, and of how many factors other than knowing the learners' L1 will be important for the teacher. Try to reach some conclusions.

Further reading

Ellis, R. 1994 *The Study of Second Language Acquisition* Oxford: Oxford University Press
Chapter 8 provides a useful introduction to language transfer. Creative construction is referred to at various points in the book.

Odlin, T. 1990 *Language Transfer* Cambridge: Cambridge University Press
A thorough consideration of transfer, not just in syntax, but for other linguistic areas too. The book also considers issues like the relationship between transfer and age.

James, C. 1980 *Contrastive Analysis* London: Longman
A less recent book about CA, which provides detailed coverage.

Richards, J. C. (ed.) 1974 *Error Analysis* Longman
This describes the genesis of the EA movement. It contains the paper discussed in this chapter, Richards (1971).

5 Input, interaction, and output

5.1 Acquisition and learning

5.1.1 Language acquisition: a powerful and exciting concept

If ideas can symbolize the spirit of an age, then the symbol of the recent applied linguistic age is undoubtedly 'language acquisition.' But what does this term mean? What exactly is 'language acquisition'? In the next section we shall see how some have answered these questions; for the moment we may characterize it as the process by which individuals 'pick up' a language through exposure to it. There are two immediately obvious sorts of language acquisition. The first is L1 acquisition, which every normal child manages at an early age. The second is FL acquisition, where someone, child or adult, picks up a language, for example while they are living in a target language country. The subjects of Dulay and Burt's work, which we considered in 4.4, were of this sort. The study of foreign or second language acquisition (SLA) is today a major field of enquiry.

Chomsky's ideas stimulated the interest that there has been over the past few decades in L1 (and, indirectly, FL) acquisition. For him, L1 acquisition is a conundrum, even a miracle. The big question (which, as we saw in 3.2.5, he refers to as 'Plato's problem') is: how is it that the very young child, so poorly developed in many areas, is able to learn the rudiments of their native language so quickly and so successfully? Chomsky's answer was, as we have seen, that the individual has a machine in the head, an LAD, that does the job for them.

The words 'quickly and successfully' hold the key to one of the main reasons why applied linguists are interested in the acquisition idea. In an important article that appeared in 1968, Newmark and Reibel make the point that L1 acquisition is the quickest and most successful instance of language mastery that we know of. Since this is so, they argue, we might do well to study in some detail what is known about the L1 acquisition situation. What does the child do that makes acquisition so quick and successful? How do the adults who talk to the child behave? What assistance do they give to the acquisition process? What are the important aspects of the acquisition environment? Notice, though, that only one of these questions is about the 'organism'; the others are about the 'environment' (using these words as discussed in 3.2.2). This indicates that we are prepared to consider a role for the latter beyond that suggested by Chomsky.

If we have answers to these questions, perhaps they will be of inspiration to foreign language teachers. Of course, you will immediately say, there are huge differences between L1 acquisition and what goes on in foreign language classrooms around the world. There are also big differences between FL acquisition in the *target language country* and language teaching for a few hours a week in the *learner's native country*, and we made mention of these differences in 4.4. But even bearing these considerable differences in mind, perhaps we really should ask the questions above, and, for both L1 and FL, find out what we can about the mysterious phenomenon of language acquisition. It is certainly the case that applied linguists from the end of the 1960s have been inspired by such questions. The notion of language acquisition really is a powerful and exciting one.

In this chapter we shall be dealing with two sorts of people and their behaviour. We look first at the people who give acquirers their language, and we shall call these people 'language providers.' In the case of L1 children, they are those (often the parents) looking after the children, sometimes referred to as caretakers. The language they use to the children is often called caretaker talk (a more general term than the word motherese, once much used but which suggests only mother-to-child communication). In the case of FL learners, the language providers will be people who communicate with the acquirer, including in the classroom. When these people are native speakers of the target language, the term foreigner talk is used to describe their language. Then we shall look at acquirers themselves, and the language they produce. Some of what we say in the following discussion will apply more clearly to L1 than FL acquisition. At other times it may be the other way round. We can justify moving freely from one to the other on the assumption that, in many respects at least, the two are indeed comparable.

As the chapter unfolds, it will become clear that three concepts are central to it. The first is the concept of input. This is the language that the learner receives from those who communicate with them. Second, there is the language that they themselves produce, which we call output. The third concept involves both input and output; it is interaction – the exchanges which occur between the language providers and the acquirers – which many feel to be important to the acquisition process.

Input, interaction and output in language acquisition – what are they like? What relevance do they have to FL teaching? You will be encouraged to think about this latter question at various points during the chapter. We will also see, later in the book, how others in the field have tried to answer it by incorporating characteristics of acquisition into FL classroom teaching. This is particularly apparent in a recent approach to language teaching called task-based teaching. There is a lengthy discussion of task-based teaching in 9.9.

B5.1 Thinking about L1 acquisition

Paragraph 3 of the section above poses the following questions:

1. What does the child do that makes L1 acquisition so quick and successful?
2. How do the adults who talk to the child behave? What assistance do they give to the acquisition process?
3. What are the important aspects of the acquisition environment?

In the course of this chapter we shall provide some answers to these questions. Now, before you read on, would be a good time for you to ponder how *you* would answer them.

5.1.2 The learning/acquisition distinction

The applied linguist Stephen Krashen is one of those interested in foreign language acquisition. In fact he argues (in Krashen 1982 for example) that there are two quite distinct ways of mastering an FL, and he calls these <u>acquisition</u> and <u>learning</u>. Acquisition first: he describes this process as a 'natural', subconscious one, where there is no 'conscious focusing on linguistic forms' (of the sort that you find in most language classrooms). It is what we have already informally called the process of 'picking up' a language, just as you do if you go and live in the target language environment. Indeed Krashen says that the minimal condition for acquisition to occur is 'participation in natural communication situations.' As we saw earlier, FL acquirers sometimes make the same kinds of mistakes as L1 acquirers (our earlier example – in Box 4.1 – was omitting the verb *be*, as in **I hungry*), and indeed Krashen claims that what is known about L1 acquisition is in general applicable to FL acquisition. He also uses the term 'creative construction' to describe the process, clearly indicating that he comes from the same stable as Dulay and Burt.

Learning, on the other hand, is a conscious process, and it usually takes place in the language classroom. For Krashen it is particularly marked by two characteristics. First, there is 'error correction' (EC). When learners make mistakes, it is normal for the classroom teacher to draw explicit attention to them, and to correct the errors. As we shall later see, with some exceptions parents do not usually do this. The second characteristic is what Krashen calls 'rule isolation.' In the language teaching classroom it is normal for a lesson (or part thereof) to focus on one language point. It may be a grammatical item like a particular tense, or a pronunciation point, or some 'rule of use.' The word *isolation* indicates that in this procedure language points are dealt with one by one. Again, as we shall see, L1 parents do not usually focus on individual items in this way.

But is the acquisition/learning distinction a useful one? Many have pointed out that it is not at all clear-cut. Certainly I can think of examples in my own experience where I have been living in an FL environment and generally acquiring the language, but at the same time augmenting that acquisition by using grammar books to help me 'learn.' Equally (though less easy to demonstrate) I feel that sometimes as a learner in an FL classroom there have been points that I have 'picked up' (perhaps just by listening to and 'soaking up' the language the teacher produced) rather than 'learned.' These experiences suggest that when we attempt to master a language (in whatever environment) we are doing a bit of learning *and* a bit of acquisition.

Because of these difficulties, we will not be making major use of the distinction. It is the case that the research described in this chapter has acquirers as its subjects, while the next is much more concerned with learning. But Chapter 5 is not *about* acquisition and Chapter 6 is not *about* learning. In both chapters our overriding concern is to look at what happens when people try to come to grips with a language; and a major secondary concern is how we can learn from that about what we can best do in classrooms to help them.

B5.2 Acquiring and learning: a consumers' comparison

Acquiring a foreign language can be very successful, but it can have its drawbacks. The same is true of learning.

Reflect a little on the pros and cons of each process. If you have experience in your own life of acquiring and learning different FLs, be sure to base your reflections on this.

5.2 Language providers and their input

At the beginning of this chapter we mentioned Newmark and Reibel's (1968) article and the idea that L1 acquisition is the quickest and most successful instance of language mastery that we have. This might lead us to wonder whether the best language teachers in the world are in fact those parents or caretakers who provide children with the input that leads them to acquire their L1. After all, *every* child, bar those with some severe impairment, successfully acquires their L1 to an astonishing degree (as regards speaking at least – writing is another story). This is why it makes sense to look closely, as we will do in the following sections, at what those language providers both *do* and *do not* do when they give children language input. Perhaps these 'L1 language teachers' have some secrets to convey to FL language teachers … about what to do, and also what not to do.

5.2.1 Some things that caretakers do *not* do

Whether or not caretakers can justifiably be called 'L1 language teachers', one thing that they do not do is give 'language learning lessons' – or at least not of the sort that FL teachers traditionally provide. To appreciate this, consider one FL teacher in action. Her name is Winnie, and she teaches at a school in Hong Kong. The evening before her class, she consults the school's English syllabus, which has been endorsed by the country's Ministry of Education, to decide what language items to teach the next day. The syllabus tells her that the students are ready for the simple past tense (*yesterday I worked* …, *last year I visited* …). So Winnie prepares her lesson round this. When she enters the class, she begins by talking in Cantonese. 'Good morning', she says, 'today we're going to look at the simple past tense in English – how it is formed and how it is used.' She then explains how the tense is constructed for regular verbs, by adding *-ed* to the verb stem. She also describes how questions and negative forms are made, and gives some examples of the tense's use. She has prepared some simple drill-like exercises to follow. In one, she says sentences in the simple present (like *he works*), and expects the learners to change the sentences into the simple past (*he worked*). Learner errors are immediately corrected. Winnie provides an excellent introduction to the tense, and she plans to elaborate on this in the next lesson.

There are at least four things here that L1 caretakers *do not* do:

1. They do not follow a syllabus. Our FL teacher might say 'my learners are now half way through their intermediate course, and the syllabus says that the time has come to introduce the simple past tense.' As we shall see later, caretakers have a very good sense of the rough linguistic level of their children. But mums chatting to their friends do not say 'Sarah's three and a half now, so next week I'm going to introduce the simple past tense to her.' As a result, we may say that caretakers do not <u>fine tune</u> their language, keeping careful tabs on what language is known to the child, and using just that language. There is no syllabus document lurking in the nursery cupboard.
2. Caretakers do not normally provide explanations for their offspring. They may find themselves *using* the simple past tense, but there would be no talk about *-ed* or verb stems.
3. Caretakers do not drill. They might, very indirectly, encourage the child to produce some piece of language, but the 'change the simple present into the simple past' formula would not normally be used. Nor anything like it.
4. As an introduction to the fourth point, look at Box 5.3.

B5.3 What parents do and do not correct

Brown and Hanlon (1970: 47) study the L1 development of three pre-school children (Adam, Eve and Sarah). As part of that study, they look at adult responses to child utterances. Here are four of their examples:

Child utterance	Adult response
(a) *Draw a boot paper*	*That's right. Draw a boot on paper*
(b) *There's the animal farmhouse*	*No, that's a lighthouse*
(c) *Mama isn't boy, he a girl*	*That's right*
(d) *And Walt Disney comes on Tuesday*	*No, he does not*

Look first at the child's utterances. Some of them contain 'grammatical' mistakes, some do not. Identify each. Then look at the adult's responses. Some signal approval, some disapproval; again, identify each.

Based on these four sentences, what can you say about what adults *do* and *do not* correct?

Point 4 is that caretakers do not often correct errors of grammar. What they *do* frequently correct is the 'truth value' of what a child says; whether, that is, a statement is true or false. But grammatical errors are often not consciously drawn attention to. The examples in Box 5.3 show this. So even though child utterance (a) is poorly formed, the child receives parental approval, because it is true. Child utterance (b) on the other hand is 'corrected' because it is false, even though its grammar is perfect.[1]

One way of encapsulating these four ideas is to say that caretaker communication is largely message-focused, and not normally form-focused. In other words, much of the caretaker's effort is put into getting the message across, into being understood, and not in dwelling on the nuts and bolts of the language. The concentration tends to be on content and not means, the 'what' and not the 'how.' This distinction, between message- and form-focus, will come up again, not only in the next chapter (6.6.3) which is about learning processes, but also in our discussion on language teaching. You may like to sneak a look forward to 9.5, which is entitled 'The shift from "how" to "what".' This will show you what an impact the distinction has had on language teaching.

Any reader who is a parent will understand why words like *normally* have frequently been used in the above discussion. We are here discussing what generally, but not always, happens. So, many caretakers will *occasionally* focus on form, correct and give explanations, particularly if the child asks a language-related question. Caretakers who are professionally engaged in language studies or language teaching are probably particularly abnormal in this respect. I personally found myself on occasions even *drilling* our son when he was young – the price a child pays for having a parent interested in language education. For the antics of another language-studies-related person, turn back to Box 3.4, where the linguist caretaker tries very hard to correct the child's error.

A final point on the *do nots*. We have here been discussing L1 acquisition specifically. But some (if not all) of the points made apply equally to FL acquisition, where a learner acquires the language in the FL environment. In 2.5 we met a Japanese adult called Wes, studied by Schmidt (1983). Wes was living in Hawaii and picking up English from the environment. Schmidt has the following comment to make about Wes's language providers: 'I have observed Wes', he says, 'in interaction with many native speakers, including at least a dozen language-teaching professionals, and have not noted a single instance of feedback explicitly focused on grammatical form' (1983: 166).

5.2.2 Some things that caretakers *do* do

B5.4 Thinking about caretaker talk

You probably decided when thinking about L1 acquisition in Box 5.1 that parents 'modify' their language when talking to a young child. But how exactly? How is their language different from when they are talking to another adult? Make a list of as many characteristics of caretaker talk as you can think of.

Clark and Clark (1977 – Chapter 8), and Snow and Ferguson (1977 – an entire book devoted to the matter) provide excellent accounts of the important characteristics of caretaker talk (now often referred to as CDS, for child-directed speech). Here is a 'Rough Guide to What Caretakers Do', taken from the above-mentioned sources and elsewhere.

Rough Guide to What Caretakers Do

- Caretaker talk is intelligible and grammatically well formed (indeed, it is perhaps not quite as 'degenerate' as Chomsky claimed – see 3.2.5).
- Caretakers often talk to children about objects that can be seen and events that are happening in front of their eyes. They talk about the <u>here-and-now</u> (a term in common use in the field). As Cross (1977: 169) puts it: 'the vast majority of expressions the child hears encode events that are perceptually,

---

cognitively and semantically available and salient to the child.' Another term used by applied linguists (various contributors in Gallaway and Richards 1994, for example) to describe this is <u>semantically contingent</u>.

- Caretakers simplify. Snow (1972) found that adults use fewer grammatical morphemes in speech with two-year-olds than with ten-year-olds, and fewer with ten-year-olds than with adults. In addition, caretaker sentences tend to be shorter. Phillips (1973) found that utterances to two-year-olds averaged less than four words each. Adult–adult speech averages over double this figure.
- CDS includes a lot of redundancy; caretakers often repeat things several times to make sure that the child understands. Newport *et al.* (1977) give the following example: *Go get the duck – the duck – yes, get it – that's right – get the duck.* You can easily imagine the movements, particularly pointing (possibly even quacking), that accompany this utterance.
- Caretakers may not fine tune their input, but this does not mean that they are oblivious of child language level. They <u>rough tune</u> their language. This means that they have a very good general sense of what the child will understand, and they apply that general sense as they talk – avoiding ways of expression that are clearly over-complex. For example, no one would dream of saying to a three-year-old 'I can scarcely believe my eyes. You certainly have increased in size since the time that I last saw you, some weeks ago now.' Common sense tells the speaker that, in all sorts of ways, this sentence would be inappropriate.

This section has largely been about input to L1 acquisition, and at several points it has been suggested that the input FL acquirers receive shares common elements. In fact, both these types of language are examples of what are called <u>simplified codes</u>. These are special ways of communicating which have developed for use with groups of people who, for one reason or another, are likely to have problems with the 'normal' language. These groups include children, non-native speakers, those with cognitive disabilities and the deaf. As the term 'simplified codes' suggests, these languages are simplifications or 'reductions' of the language on which they are based.

But even though CDS and the input FL acquirers receive may share elements in common, is the language caretakers use to children really relevant to FL learning? Surely, you may cry, the two situations – L1 and FL learning – are so different that we cannot draw useful parallels. Let us for the moment put the differences between these two situations on the shelf and consider Box 5.5. It is an important box. It stands at the focal point of this chapter, explicitly asking the type of question you are encouraged to ask throughout – about implications for language teaching in what we know about L1 and FL language acquisition.

B5.5 What can language teachers learn from L1 caretakers?

Forget for a moment the differences between the L1 and FL learning situations. With disbelief suspended, consider what FL teachers would have to do in class to make their input similar to L1 caretakers.

If language teachers modified their input in these ways, what do you predict the effect would be? Would learners learn? Would modification of input in this way be enough to ensure acquisition of the FL? Would there be any negative results?

5.2.3   The Input Hypothesis

The role of input in FL teaching virtually took centre stage in language teaching discussion during the 1980s, with the development by Krashen of the Input Hypothesis. This is the idea that input is the most crucial factor in determining whether an FL will be learned or not. 'The hypothesis states simply', say Krashen and Terrell (1983: 32), 'that we acquire … language by understanding input that is a little beyond our current level of (acquired) competence.' To make this idea concrete, consider the imaginary situation given in Box 5.6.

B5.6 Can you speak Flipspraek?

Imagine that three friends of yours, native speakers of English, are learning an (imaginary) language called Flipspraek. They are at different levels: Friend 1 is almost a beginner, Friend 2 is more advanced, and Friend 3 is the best of all. The three friends go to stay with a family in Flipspraekland. Early on in their stay, someone in their host family says to all three of them:

(a) Glop ti indo ap tugen, molim maegt ti blippo un grinop int mag?

Since Friend 1 does not understand a single word of this utterance, they can only smile sweetly and nod their head energetically.

Friend 2 understands some words. These are written in English in (b):

(b) If you're indo ap tugen, molim could you blippo a grinop for me?

Do you think that Friend 2 knows enough to understand the meaning of the whole utterance? Or to decipher any of the individual unknown words? Consider what they are likely to *understand* and *not understand* of the utterance.

Friend 3 understands much more, and this is what they 'hear':

(c) If you're indo into town, please could you post a grinop for me?

Is Friend 3 able to work out roughly what 'indo' and 'grinop' mean? What are you able to say about their meanings?

Friend 3 will probably guess that *indo* is some verb of movement, though they will not know whether it signifies 'going', 'driving', 'walking' or something else similar. In the same way, they cannot know whether a *grinop* is a 'parcel' or a 'letter' or a 'postcard', but they are probably fairly sure that it is some item that can be posted.

This example shows how language 'a little beyond our current level of (acquired) competence' can often be worked out by a learner. Friends 1 and 2 have little hope of understanding *indo* and *grinop*, because they understand so little of the context in which the words occur. For Friend 3, on the other hand, the Flipspraek sentence is likely to lead to a degree of learning. They may not be able to work out the exact meanings of the two unknown words. But the general meanings will be clear, and with time and a few more examples of their use, the words will be learned.

Krashen's claim is that acquisition will occur when unknown items are *only just* beyond the learner's present level. As with Friend 3, context will help this to happen, but so will other devices found in simplified codes and employed by caretakers – such as using gestures (e.g. pointing at things), focusing on the here and now, repeating items. Above all, the learner needs the help of a friendly language provider who will rough tune, modifying their language so that it does not wander too far away from the learner's level of competence.

Krashen has a formula that neatly expresses his idea of <u>comprehensible input</u>. He describes the acquirer's present level of competence as i, and the level immediately following i as $i+1$. The Input Hypothesis claims that learners progress by understanding language containing $i+1$ – language just above their present competence. In this formulation, we may say that rough tuning consists of knowing, roughly, what a learner's i is, and hence being able to gauge $i+1$.

5.2.4   The silent period

Krashen's position is that input is *the* important determiner of acquisition, the main factor which dictates how successfully it will occur. What then of output? The story of 'Hitomi and the Ball' in Box 5.7 reveals his views on this.

B5.7 Hitomi and the ball

Here are two accounts of the early stages of FL learning:

1. Krashen (in Palfreman 1983) tells the story of a four-year-old Japanese girl called Hitomi, who lived with her parents for a while in an apartment neighbouring on Krashen's. Hitomi spoke no English on arrival in the US, and Krashen tells of his attempts to get Hitomi to speak in the early months of her stay. He would say things like *Hitomi, say 'hi'*, but here would be no reaction. He tried *Hitomi, say 'ball'*, and even *I won't give you the ball till you say ball*. All these attempts met with silence. Hitomi was more or less silent for five months ('more or less' because children in these circumstances do produce set phrases, like *Leave me alone*. They have picked such phrases up as entire units, without really understanding how they are made up).

   Eventually, after five months, language came tumbling out. One characteristic Krashen notes about Hitomi's speech is that it resembled the speech of his own young children, particularly in the way it developed from shorter to longer utterances. By the time Hitomi returned to Japan, her English was, Krashen says, approaching that of his own children. There are indeed similarities between L1 and FL acquisition!

2. Ervin-Tripp (1974) describes a group of 31 English-speaking children attending school in Geneva, where French was the language of instruction. Ervin-Tripp's observations go back to the time the children arrived and first began to be exposed to French. 'Some of the children', she notes, 'said nothing for many months … My own children began speaking six and eight weeks after immersion in the school setting' (p. 115).

Do you have any thoughts about what these two examples reveal regarding learner output?

These two examples show that acquirers often go through a 'silent period.' This means that quite a considerable period of time may pass between the acquirer first being exposed to a new language item and their beginning to produce it. To Krashen, this silent period says something about the role of output in acquisition. He asks what was going on during the five months that Hitomi was silent. His answer: 'She was listening … When she started to talk, it was not the beginning of her language acquisition. It was testimony to the language acquisition she had already done.' Output is evidence that input has done its job and that acquisition has occurred.

Krashen's ideas received much criticism during the 1980s and after, and indeed some speak of 'Krashen bashing' – hitting out, that is, at the man's ideas, a procedure which became a fashionable applied-linguistic blood sport for a while. But several of his ideas have remained with us. One is the notion of the silent period. Another is that making input comprehensible is an important aspect of language acquisition. As Long (1983: 138) puts it: 'only comprehensible input will do. The question is, how does that input become comprehensible to the learner.' Though none would deny that the nature of input plays a role, Long developed another hypothesis which changed the emphasis away from input as we have so far been considering it. This was the Interaction Hypothesis, which we will now look at.

5.3 Language providers and their interaction

Long notes that many characteristics of CDS are also present in foreigner talk (or what he and others call <u>NS–NNS speech</u> – for 'native speaker to non-native speaker'). We have seen some of these characteristics in our earlier 'Rough Guide to What Caretakers Do.' But Long does not want to focus just on input. He is interested in how interactions – whole exchanges between NS and NNS speakers – are different from NS–NS interactions. To illustrate the difference between *input* and *interaction*, Long (1983) considers the following two exchanges:

(a) NS: What time you finish?
    NNS: Ten o'clock.
(b) NS: When did you finish?
    NNS: Um?
    NS: When did you finish?
    NNS: Ten clock.
    NS: Ten o'clock?
    NNS: Yeah.

In (a) the speaker is modifying their speech in the hope of making it more comprehensible to the non-native listener. In fact they make it ungrammatical, omitting the use of the verb *do* to form the question (go back to 2.3.3 to refresh your memory on how this piece of syntax works). This is the kind of feature that the input studies we have so far been considering would concentrate on. It is an example of modified input. But what happens in (b) is different, and is to do with the interaction as a whole. Here is what Long (1983: 128) says about it:

> After the native speaker's initial question fails, s/he uses an exact self-repetition, which succeeds in eliciting an appropriate response from the non-native speaker. The response is sufficiently ambiguous, however, to make the native speaker employ a confirmation check (*Ten o'clock?*),

which serves to establish that the non-native speaker's reply had in fact been correctly heard.

The native speaker's interaction involves self-repetition and a confirmation check.

What kind of interaction modifications do NSs make? Before we look at some, you might like to ponder this yourself:

B5.8 You to NNSs

How do NSs modify their interactions when speaking to NNSs? A way to tackle this question is to think how you yourself might 'manage' a conversation when speaking to someone whose knowledge of your language is not very good, and who would not understand if you interacted normally. How might your interactions be different from when you are speaking to a native speaker? Try to focus on interaction management – as in Long's example (b), rather than input modifications like the one in his example (a).

Pica (1987) mentions three of the most commonly discussed interaction modifications. One is the <u>confirmation check</u>. This is where a speaker seeks confirmation of what has been said to them, by repeating the utterance, or part of it, usually with rising intonation – just what happens in Long's example (b). Then there is the <u>clarification request</u>. This is where the speaker seeks help in understanding something not understood. Phrases like 'I don't understand' or 'please repeat' are useful here. Pica's third modification type is the <u>comprehension check</u>, where a speaker tries to find out whether something said has been understood. Another interesting form of modification is mentioned in CW5.1 (*The topic-focused question*).

Pica *et al.* (1987: 740) express the claims of the Interaction Hypothesis like this. 'In the course of interaction', they say:

> learners and their interlocutors negotiate the meaning of messages by modifying and restructuring their interaction in order to reach mutual understanding. As a result of this negotiation, learners come to comprehend words and grammatical structures beyond their current level of competence and ultimately incorporate them in their own production.

Two things are noteworthy about this definition. One is that the hypothesis clearly stays with Krashen's idea of comprehensible input. The other is that the quotation contains the phrase 'negotiate the meaning of messages', and <u>negotiation for meaning</u> is a central idea in the hypothesis; so central, indeed, that it has earned itself an abbreviation – NfM. When speakers interacting with each other fail to understand something, they negotiate meaning.

B5.9 Recognizing NfM

Would you recognize an instance of NfM if you met one? Here is an example from Gass and Varonis (1994), cited in Ellis (1997). It illustrates a common form of interaction which we have not so far mentioned – non-native speaker to non-native speaker: not NS–NNS, but NNS–NNS.

> Hiroko: A man is uh, drinking c-coffee or tea with uh the saucer of the uh uh coffee set is uh in his uh knee.
> Izumi: in him knee.
> Hiroko: uh on his knee.
> Izumi: yeah.
> Hiroko: on his knee.
> Izumi: so sorry. on his knee.

Try to express in your own words what happens in this example.

Find an example of a *confirmation check* in it.

This example is often given to illustrate how NfM can lead to improvements in learner language. Can you see how? The 'answers' are discussed in Note 2.

Time perhaps to pause and take stock. We have been looking at two forms of acquisition – for L1 and FL. Because we always have half an eye looking in the direction of language teaching, we have been wondering whether the teacher has something to learn from what happens in the acquisition situation. What would happen – you are encouraged to ask yourself throughout this chapter – if the language teacher tried to 'copy' aspects of the acquisition situation in the classroom. We have so far focused on two aspects of this situation – input and interaction, and have considered the modifications that language providers offer in order to make what they say comprehensible. But which are more useful – input or interaction modifications? There is a growing body of research suggesting the answer is the latter, and one such piece of research is exemplified in CW5.2 (*Interaction versus input*). After you have had a look at that, it is time to turn our attention to a third concept to complete the trio with input and interaction: output, the language that learners themselves produce.

5.4 Language acquirers and their output

5.4.1 The Output Hypothesis

What is the role of output in acquisition? According to Krashen's Input Hypothesis, it is almost none. For him, acquisition takes place when the learner hears (or sees) language. When language is produced by the acquirer, that is evidence of acquisition having taken place, not acquisition itself. You may readily accept that input has an important role to play in acquisition. But many will think that there is a role for output too. Surely our learners need to use the language – to practise – as well as understand. Not surprising then that along with the Input and Interaction Hypotheses, we should find the emergence, in the 1990s, of an Output Hypothesis, principally associated with the name of the Canadian applied linguist Merrill Swain.

Swain points out that output is generally accepted as having value as a way of providing practice, and hence contributes to the development of fluency. But, claims Swain (1995), there are other reasons why it is important. One is that producing output is often more challenging for the learner than understanding input. Often it is possible to understand what a person is saying by intelligent guesswork, perhaps without very much comprehension of the individual linguistic elements used in the message. Perhaps you yourself have even sometimes 'cheated' a little (as I certainly have on occasions) when it comes to comprehension, 'faking' understanding by vigorous nods of the head and smiles, when in fact you have not really understood very much. But you cannot fake output. In Swain's words: 'the importance to learning of output could be that output pushes learners to process language more deeply (with more mental effort) than does input' (1995: 126). She discusses various other ways in which output is valuable for learners, and these are to do with making learners aware of how the language works, noticing differences between what they themselves say and how native speakers express themselves, leading to conscious reflection on how the language works. After all the (valuable) discussion about how input and interaction are important for language learning, Swain's ideas remind us that producing language – and not just understanding it – is important. Teachers brought up to believe that we 'learn by doing' will doubtless be in sympathy with her message. You are invited to think about what the implications of this are for language teaching and for what should go on in classes.

5.4.2 Fish and chips

What happens if you allow learners to produce language output without the kinds of 'control' (like the error correction) associated with classrooms? This is often what occurs when a learner comes to live in the target language country and picks the language up without the help of a teacher. Will plenty of input plus opportunities for output produce acceptable language use? One study that has looked at this situation is Cancino *et al.* (1978). Their subjects were six Spanish-speakers, aged between 5 and 33, acquiring English while living in a target-language country. The researchers plotted the progress of these learners over a period of ten months, particularly focusing on the acquisition of one structure – making sentences negative in English (<u>sentence negation</u>). At the beginning of the study all six of the learners made sentences negative by the highly effective but inaccurate means of putting the word *no* in an utterance. Examples are **I no can see*, **They no have water*. Two things are noteworthy about the learners' progress over time. The first is that by the end of the ten months, all except one had gone well beyond the 'putting-*no*-in-the-sentence' solution, and had acquired the rudiments of the English negation system. This fact is important because it suggests that if left to their own resources (that is, acquiring the language in the natural environment without tuition), some learners will indeed progress. Just like L1 acquirers, they are able to 'grow out of' their mistakes and move towards mastery of the language. It is a fact that has highly thought-provoking implications for the attitude of language teachers towards learner errors. One legacy of behaviourist thinking is the still widespread view that errors should be avoided at all costs, because 'practice makes permanent', suggesting that if errors are left uncorrected they will never be grown out of. But it is clear that in the case of L1 learning, and for nearly all of Cancino *et al.*'s subjects, repeating the inaccurate *no* negative ('practising' it) certainly does *not* make permanent. Error correction is a topic taken up in 15.3.

The second noteworthy point relates to the one learner who did not progress. His name was Alberto, and he was a 33-year-old Costa Rican. Over the ten-month period, poor Alberto made no progress at all. He finished as he started, with the 'putting-*no*-in-the-sentence' solution. Box 5.10 chronicles a similar sorry tale.

B5.10 A sorry tale

The subject of Shapira's (1978) study is Zoila, a 25-year-old Guatemalan woman. She was a native speaker of Spanish who had lived in the United States for three years, working as a housekeeper in English-speaking families. Shapira plotted Zoila's progress with ten selected morphemes. The sad conclusion: 'during the 18 month observation period, there appears to have been little, or quite insignificant, development in the acquisition of any of the 10 grammatical categories studied.' The title of Shapira's paper is 'The non-learning of English: a case study of an adult.'

Any of you who have had contact with immigrants coming to live in your own country and trying to pick up your own L1 will know that cases like Alberto's and Zoila's are unfortunately not that rare. Some learners seem to reach a stage beyond which they fail to progress. This process, in which 'stabilization of erroneous forms' occurs, is known as <u>fossilization</u>. Many learners <u>fossilize</u>.

Fossilization is a phenomenon of great interest both to FL acquisition researchers and to language teachers. Why? Because if we can find out why fossilization occurs not only will we understand the processes of FL acquisition better, but we may even be able to do something (in the classroom perhaps) to prevent its occurrence. One member of the Cancino *et al.* team, John Schumann, makes a special study of fossilization. Why does it occur, and what can stop it from occurring? His book, Schumann (1978), is all about this.

B5.11 Thinking about fossilization

In the paragraphs you are about to read, suggestions are given as to what might cause fossilization. Before you read these paragraphs, consider this issue. What are your thoughts on the causes of fossilization?

If possible, base your considerations on some 'fossilized individuals' that you have yourself come across.

A common view of fossilization, and possibly one that occurred to you when looking at Box 5.11, is that it happens when the language a learner has acquired is sufficient to meet their needs. In these circumstances there is, quite simply, no reason for the learner's language to continue to progress towards the 'norm.' This is illustrated by what I like to call the *Fish-and-Chips Syndrome*. Imagine a learner visiting Britain as a tourist. Perhaps they are in a restaurant and want to partake of that celebrated piece of local haute cuisine, fish and chips. Maybe if their English is not so good, they will say something like: *Give to me fish and chips*. This structure is 'unacceptable' in various ways, and certainly no English language teacher would condone its use. But it is also likely to succeed. That is, its use is likely to result in the appearance of a plate of fish and chips. And if it works, the argument goes, what incentive is there for the learner to abandon it and develop some more acceptable phrase, such as *I'd like fish and chips, please*?

The *Fish-and-Chips Syndrome* is discussed in more abstract (and much more academic!) terms in CW5.3 (*Fish, chips and feedback*), where objections to it (particularly in relation to L1 acquisition) are also put forward.

Schumann (1978) bases his approach to fossilization on the work of Smith (1972), who argues that language serves three general functions. Two of these are particularly relevant to us.[3] The first is what Smith calls the *communicative*, and it relates to the simple transmission of information. So when someone asks what the time is, or indeed requests a plate of fish and chips, it is this function that is being fulfilled. Smith's second function is the *integrative*. Here the user wants their language to mark them as a member of some social group. Some aspects of L1 use are easy to associate with this function. For example, people may deliberately either maintain or avoid a local dialect to make a statement about the social group to which they belong. Using or not using a particular dialect is sending signals to the world about how you see yourself in relation to some group.

The *Fish-and-Chips Syndrome* well illustrates the communicative/integrative distinction. Providing the utterance results in fish and chips, then it succeeds on a communicative level. But for a learner who has some integrative ambitions, who wants perhaps to be seen as urbane, a well-travelled person-of the-world who is as at home ordering food in English as in their native language, the utterance would send all the wrong signals. It might succeed communicatively (and digestively) but it would fail integratively.

Schumann uses the communicative/integrative distinction to develop what he calls his <u>acculturation model</u>, which explains why FL learners fossilize. This is described in CW5.4 (*The acculturation model*), which also briefly discusses pidgin languages. You might like to take a look at this now. Schumann's approach is sometimes described as a 'sociolinguistic' one, and his solution to the problem of fossilization revolves round the relationship between language learners and target language cultures. His views may account well for the occurrence of fossilization in immigrants, but the solutions to fossilization which his approach implies are not obviously applicable to many FL learners. For more practicable solutions applicable to more normal learning situations, we can turn again to Swain's Output Hypothesis. Does the fact that some learners fossilize compromise her Output Hypothesis in some way? We need first to remember that five out of Cancino *et al.*'s subjects did not fossilize; their output moved towards standard English as time passed. But where fossilization does occur, are there any practical suggestions for moving learners' language along? For Swain, the answer lies partly in creating language teaching tasks which not only provide opportunities for output, but also push the learner to notice aspects of how the target language 'works', and focus attention on elements of 'form', rather than just message. This is a topic which will be revisited again in the next chapter (particularly in 6.6.3).

This chapter has concentrated on just one of the many approaches to SLA – the one which focuses on the 'discourse aspects' (the term is from Ellis 1997) of input, interaction and output. Schumann's acculturation model provides a small taste of another ('sociolinguistic') perspective. But the field of SLA is vast and growing, and the picture provided here is not a full one. For that fuller picture, you will need to turn to the further readings suggested. But before this chapter ends:

B5.12 More implications?

In the all-important Box 5.5 you were asked to think about what would happen if language teachers modified their input in the ways that caretakers do. Now, at the end of this lengthy chapter, it is worth asking more questions about implications for language teaching.

Imagine then that the Interaction Hypothesis were shown to be 'true.' What would be the implications for classroom language teaching? And what about fossilization? Can you think of any ways that classroom language teaching can either stop fossilization from happening, or attempt to 'defossilize' the fossilized learner?

Notes

1. Although adults may be tolerant of poor grammar, there are some linguistic areas they do care about. Two of these are rude words and forms that they consider socially unacceptable (so a dialect form like *I ain't* might well get remarked upon).
2. Izumi's utterance *in him knee* is a confirmation check, to clarify she has understood Hiroko's *in his knee*. Both these utterances contain errors. Hiroko corrects Izumi, and also himself, producing the correct version *on his knee*, which Izumi then repeats.
3. Smith's third function, not discussed, is called the 'expressive.' This goes beyond the integrative, and through it the user seeks respect in the particular realm of language use, perhaps as a storyteller or a poet.

Issues to think or write about

1. This chapter has made mention of 'simplified codes', particularly 'adult to child' and 'native speaker to non-native speaker' speech. Perhaps you have access to people who speak one of these codes – a parent talking to their child, or a teacher talking to language learners. If so, try to collect some examples of their language, preferably recording a lengthy stretch of speech. Do an analysis (as detailed as you can) of the way your subject (the parent or teacher) modifies their language when talking to the child or language learner. Consider how their speech modifications might help to make their language more comprehensible.
2. Pidgin languages are mentioned briefly in CW5.3. Find out something about these languages, and also about 'creoles' – a related type of language. Define what these languages are, and give a number of examples from various countries around the world. Finally, give some thought to a matter just hinted at in this chapter – the possible relevance of pidgins to SLA and FL learning.

Further reading

Mitchell, R., and Miles, F. 1998 *Second Language Learning Theories* London: Edward Arnold
A detailed introduction to the world of SLA.

Gallaway, C., and Richards, B. (eds) 1994 *Input and Interaction in Language Acquisition* Cambridge: Cambridge University Press
A useful look at caretaker language, and more.

Krashen, S. 1985 *The Input Hypothesis: Issues and Implications* London: Longman
Krashen has outlined his theories in a number of publications. This one provides a good overall description of his views.

Doughty, C. J., and Long, M. (eds) 2003 *The Handbook of Second Language Acquisition* Oxford: Blackwell
The book as a whole is an excellent reference work for anyone really interested in the area. Susan Gass has a chapter in it entitled 'Input and interaction.'

Swain, M. 1995 'Three functions of output in second language learning.' In Cook, G., and Seidlhofer, B. (eds) *Principle and Practice in Applied Linguistics* Oxford: Oxford University Press, 125–44
A good, easy-to-follow description of the Output Hypothesis.

6 Some learning processes

6.1 Introduction

In the 1990s I was invited to be a member of a small team sent to visit a university in a country which shall remain nameless. Because English was an important language for study there, the university ran English language courses for all its undergraduates. The powerful views about acquisition which we discussed in the last chapter had made their mark on the university, and several years before our visit the courses had become 'acquisition-based.' Formal methods of conscious teaching had been dropped, and they had been replaced by an emphasis on providing comprehensible input. Instead of following classes studying grammar, pronunciation and essay writing, the students (who could not believe their luck) spent their time watching videos in English, reading books and listening to English-speaking radio. Though the students were indeed overjoyed, the experiment had turned out to be something of a failure. Standards of English dropped, and this had its effect on the overall performance of students in their degree courses. Our team was asked to propose ways of replacing the 'acquisitional approach', to come up with a theoretically sound 'learning-based' alternative to acquisition.

But are there any recent theories of learning? Is there just behaviourism (the learning theory of earlier decades), or does some more up-to-date theory exist that perhaps does for learning what applied linguists like Krashen, Long and Swain do for acquisition? The answer is yes. Mention has already been made (in 3.2.6) of cognitive linguistics, which regards language (and its learning) in relation to mental or cognitive processes. There are also recent theories of learning which spring from current approaches to psychology and which offer real alternatives to the acquisition view. McLaughlin (1987) calls them 'cognitive theories.' McLaughlin *et al.* (1983) outline one such theory, while Johnson (1996) and Skehan (1998) develop others. Theories like these attempt to explain how learners sitting in classrooms, receiving tuition from a teacher, can come to master a language as proficiently as by the acquisition route. We shall begin this chapter by looking at some of the concepts underlying these cognitive theories and considering how they relate to FL learning. They are concepts that can be used to describe many types of skill, not just FL learning. This is why, as the chapter unfolds, we will find ourselves discussing skills that have nothing to do with language. At one point we even discuss learning how to drive a car. This comes about because what we are in fact discussing is 'skill learning' in general, of which FL learning is just one type.

B6.1 Language learning and learning other skills

Is learning a language like learning other skills? Think of a skill you have learned. It may be related to sport, or music, or driving a vehicle. Think about similarities and differences between learning that skill and learning a foreign language. Are the two comparable? In what ways are they the same? In what ways different?

6.2 Consciousness and noticing

In the last chapter, we talked a lot about *i* and *i+1*. The former is the learner's state of knowledge at a given moment (which may be inadequate in some way), and the latter is a slightly more 'advanced' or 'more adequate' state of knowledge which they may come across in the input they receive. But how does *i* turn into *i+1*? According to Krashen (1982), one of the ways in which this can happen is through a 'noticing the gap' principle. The learner becomes aware of a difference between their inadequate *i* and the superior *i+1* which they encounter in input. This awareness leads to development in the direction of *i+1*. In Krashen's view, this awareness is on a subconscious level. Indeed, Krashen sees second language acquisition as a whole (like Chomsky sees first language acquisition) as a subconscious process in which there is no role for consciousness. Look back to the 'learning/acquisition distinction' in 5.1.2 and you will see the word 'subconscious' right there in our working definition of acquisition.

But can't 'noticing the gap' be a conscious process? Schmidt and Frota (1986) suggest that it can. Their paper describes Schmidt's efforts – inside and outside the classroom – to learn Portuguese during a five-month visit to Brazil. He kept a journal of his learning experience, which was also plotted by other means, including tape recordings. The paper contains a long discussion of what this experience has to say about various current issues in language teaching. One of the issues is: *the 'noticing the gap principle' – conscious or subconscious process?* While in Krashen, acquisition (converting *i* to *i+1*) is subconscious, Schmidt and Frota's position is that something will only be mastered 'if it is present in comprehended input and "noticed" in the normal sense of the word, that is, consciously' (p. 311). So comprehensible input remains an important idea, and for it to play a real role in learning, the learner needs to 'notice a gap.' But this process will normally be a *conscious* one.

The data that Schmidt and Frota collect on Schmidt's learning of Portuguese provide evidence for this view. Schmidt says that he and his co-researcher found 'a remarkable correspondence between my reports of what I had noticed when Brazilians talked to me and the linguistic forms I used myself' (1990: 140). Some details: they looked at Schmidt's performance on 21 verbal constructions, 14 of which had been explicitly taught in the class Schmidt attended. The fact that a construction was taught in class did not (lamentably) guarantee that it would appear in Schmidt's output. The number of times that he heard a construction did relate to whether he would use it himself, but this was not, in his words, 'the whole story.' What emerged was a strong connection between the things that he says in his diary that he has noticed and the things that start to appear in his output. Schmidt is cautious in the claims he makes. He does not say that noticing is *enough* for a form to be learned, nor that in the study it was *always* shown to be necessary. But the strong connection exists. CW6.1 (*Schmidt notices*) gives an example of noticing during Schmidt's learning of Portuguese.

Schmidt's 1990 paper develops the noticing idea, discussing what factors can make it happen. *Frequency in input* is clearly one. As we saw above, if a construction occurs a lot in the learner's hearing, that may make it more likely to be noticed. Another factor is *perceptual salience in input*. Schmidt and Frota observed for example that when a form is 'reduced' in some way it becomes less noticeable. An example of a reduced form is the contraction *We'd* instead of *We had* (you may also recall, from CW2.2 that some vowels have 'reduced' forms, a common reduction being to /ə/). Another factor which is particularly interesting from the teaching point of view is *task demands*. If you set up a teaching activity which relies heavily on some sorts of language items being understood or used, then the chances are that these items will be noticed (whether or not the teacher intends this).

So Schmidt helps to put consciousness back into language learning. When we turn in Part 3 of this book to teaching, we will find how this is reflected in ideas about what may happen in classrooms. In 12.2, for example, we discuss the concept of consciousness-raising – helping to make learners consciously aware of how the language works. And when, in 9.2, we outline seven important questions to ask about different teaching methods, the role of consciousness is right there: the third question is *How much 'engagement of the mind' does the method expect?*

B6.2 Yes, but how?

You may be ready to admit that noticing and consciousness-raising are important in language learning. But how can they be introduced into the classroom? Try to think of some ways this might be done. Be as specific and as concrete as possible.

6.3 Declarative and procedural knowledge[1]

Another concept which makes its way into cognitive approaches to language learning is the old distinction made in philosophy between 'knowing about' and 'knowing how to.' It is a distinction that makes perfect sense to those involved in skill training of any kind. Driving instructors, for example, understand that 'knowing about' driving (what a steering wheel is, what function it performs, and so on) is quite different from 'knowing how to' drive. Indeed, a driving test which concentrated on declarative and not procedural knowledge would be a recipe for disaster. Language teachers also understand the distinction well. They realize that having declarative knowledge of a language is quite different from being able to speak it. The world is full of people who know a great deal *about* English, but who find it difficult to create a sentence in the language. Box 6.3 describes one.

B6.3 Putting dad to shame

I once had a neighbour who was an eminent professor from overseas. He was an expert on the English language, and had written many a learned paper describing aspects of English grammar. But his use of English was almost non-existent. He could not understand what was said to him, and his attempts to speak were filled with errors and such poor pronunciation that it was almost impossible to understand a word. He had high declarative knowledge, but low procedural knowledge. This situation did not change over the year that he was in England.

The professor was accompanied by his family. This included his eight-year-old daughter, who was attending a local school. Though her English was almost non-existent when the family arrived, within a year it was of a very high standard indeed. It was certainly very much better than her professorial father's. Her procedural knowledge was very good, but her declarative knowledge was probably very small.

Perhaps you have also come across individuals who 'know about' a foreign language but cannot speak it well? And others who can speak it well but know nothing about it?

There is a burning issue that my neighbour and his daughter raise. You probably have no problem with the idea that 'knowing about' a language is very different from 'knowing how to' speak it. But here's the issue: can 'knowing about' help you in the process of learning 'how to'? If your aim is to speak a language fluently, is there any value in understanding how it works? How you answer these questions will have massive implications for language teaching. What would those implications be if we decided that declarative knowledge did *not* help in the development of procedural knowledge? And the implications if it *did* help?

6.4 Automization

Automization means 'making automatic', and Box 6.4 gives an example of the process at work. It is a very important process, and indeed two cognitive psychologists, Shiffrin and Dumais (1981), describe it as 'a fundamental component of skill development', playing a vital role in the development of any skill (including, presumably, the skill of using a foreign language).

B6.4 A seven-year course in cigar rolling

Crossman (1959) studied several girls whose job was to roll cigars in a factory, using a purpose-built machine. These girls were studied over a period of about seven years, during which time they each made over ten million cigars. They continued to improve over this time, becoming more and more automatic at the job. Indeed, by the time the study finished it was only the slowness of the machinery that was preventing the girls from getting faster. When it comes to rolling cigars, practice does indeed make for speedy performance!

Crossman's study (and indeed this whole section on automization) reintroduces the issue of the role of practice in learning. Take a look back at Chapter 3's Box 3.1, where points (c) and (d) are about this. Remind yourself of any thoughts you had on the issue at that time.

Exactly why is automization important? Precisely what role does it fulfil? When a skill is newly learned, its performance takes up a great deal of conscious attention – what is sometimes called <u>channel capacity</u> ('room in the mind'). Take an aspect of learning to drive a car as an example. Learners who have just been taught how to change gear will at first only be able to do it if they concentrate on the gear change and nothing else. They need to take their eyes off the road, to look down at the gear stick, to think about which direction to move it in, to remember which pedal is the clutch and which foot should be on it. Then they have to coordinate all these actions together; there is a lot to do at once. Until the learner has progressed from this stage, they are a danger to themselves and anyone near them. Taking eyes off the road is clearly dangerous, and a driver simply cannot stop doing everything else whenever a gear change is called for. One might say that there are 'higher-level skills' which require available channel capacity. In driving, these skills include paying attention to what is happening around you, anticipating the movement of other traffic and of pedestrians. Will that lorry pull out? Is that man about to cross the street in front of you? Are the traffic lights about to change? Channel capacity can only be made available to handle such matters if 'lower-level' skills like changing gear have been made so automatic that they occupy no 'room in the mind.' When novice drivers have automated gear changing, they will be able to perform the action without even being aware that they are doing it. The role of automization in skill learning is therefore to free valuable channel capacity for those more important tasks which require it. Before reading on, take a look at CW6.2 (*Higher-level and lower-level skills*). It invites you to think about high-level and low-level skills in areas other than car driving, including language learning.

It is easy to apply the automization concept to language learning. When the learner first comes across a new tense, for example, they may need all their available effort to produce it. What auxiliary is used? What ending goes on the auxiliary? What part of the main verb is needed? As with changing gear in a car, there is at first precious little time for anything else. The higher-level skills in language use relate generally to understanding messages being conveyed to us, and ensuring that our own messages are properly conveyed. You may yourself be able to think of language learners who are struggling so hard with the mechanics of the language that holding a conversation with them is very hard work indeed. You are in the conversation to find out something from them and to tell them something in turn. But all their attention seems to be on trying to produce the correct tense. You want to scream out to them: *Don't worry about the correct tense. Just tell me what you want to say*. Indeed, you have probably passed through this learning stage yourself. It is the pre-automization stage. Over time the learner will come to use that tense so automatically that it occupies no thought-space for them to do so, at which point they are free to think about *what* they are saying, not *how* they are saying it.

Therein lies the importance of automization. But how does the process come about? How does the learner move from the first stage of full conscious attention to the stage of effortless production? One theory, associated with the American cognitive psychologist John Anderson and his colleagues, was developed in relation to the learning of skills in general, not specifically language learning. In fact in the first instance it was applied to the learning of geometry.[2] The following paragraph briefly describes the model.

In much traditional teaching, the teacher starts by giving the learner declarative knowledge on the chosen topic, telling them *about* what they have to do. The driving instructor, for example, may well begin to teach gear changing by describing the required movements and how they are done. Similarly the language teacher may begin their treatment of a particular tense by giving an explanation of how it is formed. Anderson's model conceptualizes automization as the process of converting that declarative knowledge into procedural knowledge. The model has two main stages.[3] Stage 1 is called the <u>declarative stage</u>. Here, the learner is given knowledge which is memorized. When they want to perform an action, the stored knowledge has to be dragged from memory. Whether the action is gear changing or using a new tense, the learner more or less suspends performance of other actions, and consciously brings back to mind what to do next. We shall call Stage 2 the <u>proceduralization stage</u>.[4] At this stage, the learner converts 'knowledge about' into 'knowledge how to.' The knowledge, in other words, becomes <u>proceduralized</u> or <u>automized</u>. The model and its movement from declarative to procedural can be represented in a simple diagram:

Declarative knowledge → procedural knowledge

Because the movement here is from DEClarative to PROcedural knowledge, the model has been described as DECPRO. It is discussed in more detail in 6.6.1.

B6.5 Facilitating proceduralization

1. Anderson's model deals with the process of proceduralization. But how, in actual practice, is proceduralization achieved? The cigar maker in Box 6.4 illustrated the process at work. What causes the skill to become auto-mated in that case? What about FL learning? Is there anything a learner might do to help the process on its way? What about the teacher – how can they help?
2. Think now about the DECPRO model. What would it 'look like' in the classroom? 12.2 deals with this in detail, but you might like to think about it yourself at this stage. Presumably you would start off by giving your learners 'declarative knowledge.' How? Then you would 'procedur-alize' that knowledge (which you have just thought about in paragraph 1 above).

When you have done this, you might like to sneak a quick look forwards: 12.2 (entitled *Conveying language*) deals with ways of developing declarative knowledge, while 12.3 (*Practising language*) is to do with proceduralizing that knowledge.

6.5 Restructuring

Although automization is very important in skill development, McLaughlin (1987) says that there is 'more to learning a complex cognitive skill than devel-oping automaticity through practice' (p. 138). The additional element is to do with the idea of <u>restructuring</u>. As people learn, the way they conceptualize what they are learning changes. McLaughlin uses an example from Cheng (1985) to illustrate the principle at work. The example involves the simple mathemati-cal problem of adding up ten twos. The first way is to view the problem as one of addition. This way entails nine operations, each adding two to the running total (2 + 2 = 4 + 2 = 6 and so on). The second way is to see the problem as a multiplication one. This involves just one operation (2 × 10 = 20). A young child will use the first solution until they have been taught their multiplication tables.

When this has happened, they will be able to 'restructure' the problem, seeing it as multiplication rather than addition.

One of McLaughlin's examples for language learning involves the learning, by L1 children or FL acquirers, of irregular simple past tense forms in English – forms like *came, went, saw*. An L1 child will hear these forms and may well produce them correctly for a while. But with time they will realize that there is a general rule for the formation of simple past forms – you add *-ed* (so *help* becomes *helped*, *want* becomes *wanted* and so on). This 'restructuring' of their knowledge will lead them to replace the correct *came, went* and *saw* with the incorrect *comed, goed* and *seed*. Only later, after more restructuring, does the child return to the original correct forms, realizing that these verbs are exceptions to the general rule.

One important characteristic of restructuring, McLaughlin (1987 and 1990) points out, is that it often occurs suddenly; the 'new way of seeing things' comes about in a flash. In this respect, restructuring is quite different from automization, which usually occurs over time as more and more practice is given. A learning theory needs to have some way of accounting for 'sudden flash' learning, because it does indeed happen. Perhaps you can think of an example in your own experience of where you have had a 'sudden flash' of understanding, or where you have suddenly been able to do something which up to that point you were unable to do.

6.6 Towards a model

6.6.1 DECPRO and PRODEC

In this chapter so far we have discussed various concepts which are associated with a cognitive language learning theory. We have talked about conscious engagement in the learning process (associated with noticing), movement from declarative to procedural knowledge, and restructuring. Whether or not these concepts taken together add up to an actual model of language learning, they are certainly its building blocks, and when we come to consider teaching in Part 3 of this book, we will see how they have had an effect on what goes on in classrooms.

B6.6 Learning and acquisition together?

In Johnson (1996) I suggest that the concepts of declarative and procedural knowledge can be used to describe both learning and acquisition. The argument goes like this:

Learning, as we have seen, can be called DECPRO, and characterized as the movement from declarative to procedural knowledge through a process of proceduralization or automization. The process is important to free up channel capacity.

It is possible, I argue, to say that acquisition is the development of procedural knowledge without an initial declarative stage. The acquirer picks up ways of saying things which come into use immediately. It is procedural knowledge without declarative knowledge. Just PRO.

But PRO without DEC – procedural without declarative knowledge – is inadequate. The learner who does not have the latter will not understand how the language 'works' and will therefore be restricted in how they can use it. So someone who has acquired the language (just picking it up in the target language country for example) must, if they are not to fossilize, somehow develop declarative knowledge. I call this model PRODEC, moving from procedural to declarative knowledge. The process involved is declarativization (converting procedural to declarative knowledge), and it is important as a way of helping the learner develop an understanding of how the language works.

So the argument is that the two possible pathways to language mastery, learning and acquisition, can be described in terms of the declarative/ procedural distinction. In one the starting point is declarative knowledge which converts into procedural knowledge (through proceduralization). This is learning. In the other the starting point is procedural knowledge which needs to be converted into declarative knowledge (through declarativization).[5] This is acquisition.

I say that it is possible to look at language teaching techniques in terms of whether and how they assist in one of the two fundamental processes of proceduralization and declarativization.

A model of language learning. And also perhaps for the learning of skills in general?

6.6.2 Combining formal and informal instruction

In Chapter 9, which looks over the recent history of language teaching, we shall see that it is possible to identify approaches which place emphasis on the development of either declarative or procedural knowledge. At the declarative end of the spectrum, we find 'formal' approaches where lots of attention is given to grammar explanation, accompanied by a severely restricted amount of very controlled practice. Other more informal methods place the emphasis on 'learning how to' rather than 'learning about.' Little attention is given to learning rules, and students are encouraged to undertake communication activities where actual use of the language is required.

B6.7 Declarative and procedural classrooms

In 1.5 we looked into five very different language classrooms. Go back to these descriptions. Identify one classroom where the focus of attention is most obviously on declarative knowledge. Then find one where the main focus is on procedural knowledge.[6]

But if both declarative and procedural knowledge really are important for students (as argued in Box 6.6), then perhaps it is important for teachers to pay attention to both. There are some pieces of research which may suggest this, and these are of two types. Some suggest that there is benefit to adding procedurally oriented practice to teaching that is basically focused on the declarative. CW6.3 (*Adding some acquisition to learning*) looks at a paper by Montgomery and Eisenstein (1985) where the conclusion is that 'a combination of form-oriented and meaning-oriented language teaching was more beneficial than form-oriented teaching alone.'

The second type of research evidence suggests that language teaching programmes that concentrate on the development of procedural knowledge can benefit if a declarative element is added. Ellis (1994), mentions Harley (1989) and White (1991) in this respect. Both report experiments involving the introduction of formal instruction into an informal approach to language teaching. In both cases the effect was beneficial, though this is only part of the picture. Take a look at CW6.4 (*Adding some learning to acquisition*) which shows just this.

Both these sorts of evidence are far from conclusive. But, taken together, they may suggest that where teaching concentrates on the DEC side of things, some PRO may need to be added. And where the focus has been on PRO, some additional DEC can be useful.

6.6.3 Two different formulations of one major issue

To conclude the chapter, we shall revisit a question which was discussed in 5.4.2 in relation to output and fossilization. We argued there that if learners are left to produce output without any of the 'controls' associated with classrooms, there is a danger that fossilization will occur. In that section we discussed Swain's view that this might be avoided by creating language teaching tasks which not only provide opportunities for output but also push the learner to notice aspects of how the target language 'works.' To develop this idea, let's restate it in terms of a distinction made in 5.2.1, and very much used in discussions on language learning and teaching today. The distinction is between message-focus and form-focus. Message-focused activities in the classroom are ones where we concentrate on leading the learner to get their message across, even though they may make language mistakes in their attempt to do so. Such activities are useful – indeed necessary – in the classroom. But they run the risk that the learner will be satisfied with whatever (imperfect) language gets the message across. This is precisely the *Fish-and-Chips Syndrome* and, as we saw in 5.4.2, this leads to fossilization. To avoid this syndrome, our classroom strategy needs to find ways of introducing form-focus into the learners' work, putting the emphasis on the mechanics of the language, concentrating on correct language use. So message-focused work, the argument runs, needs to be supplemented by form-focused work to ensure the learner's language develops.

Notice how similar this conclusion is to the one reached in CW6.3, which said that procedural knowledge needs to be supplemented by declarative knowledge if fossilization is to be avoided. And notice in turn how close this is to the formulation discussed in 6.6.2, that what is required is a 'combination of form-oriented and meaning-oriented language teaching.' So the notions of declarative/procedural and form-focus/message-focus are very similar. They are slightly different ways of expressing the same major issue.

It is very important to concentrate, finally, on the major issue itself – not just on the different ways of formulating it. You will probably readily accept that language teaching approaches that place the emphasis on declarative knowledge and form-focus run the danger of producing learners who know *about* the language but find it difficult to use their knowledge to communicate effectively. Many language teachers spot this danger early in their career. But the opposite danger often goes unnoticed. It lurks inside approaches that place the emphasis on learning to communicate, on getting messages across. It is the danger that learners' language will not develop, but will fossilize into an unacceptable pidgin-like form. The fish and chips will arrive, but the learners will fail their English exam. As we will see in Chapter 9 (in Box 9.14 for example), this is a major issue in recent approaches to teaching, particularly communicative language teaching and task-based teaching.

Now for a dramatic change of focus. So far in Part 2 we have been looking at theories of FL learning. In Chapters 7 and 8 we turn our attention to the characteristics that make learners different from each other. You might say that we are about to move from a consideration of *learning* to a focus on *learners*.

Notes

1. Approaches to language learning which utilize the declarative/procedural distinction are sometimes called 'information-processing approaches', because procedural knowledge is involved in the skill of being able to formulate and encode (i.e. process) language quickly.
2. This description of Anderson's learning model is based on two sources: Anderson (1982) and Neves and Anderson (1981).

3. There is a third, less important stage, which is not discussed here. Anderson (1982) calls it the 'Procedural Stage.'

4. The use of the term *proceduralization* in this sense departs somewhat from the terminology of Anderson and his colleagues.

5. Though I argue that neither pathway (DECPRO or PRODEC) is inherently superior to the other, there may be many reasons why, in a particular situation, one is to be preferred to the other (or is, quite simply, more likely to happen). For example, if a learner is living in a country where the target language is spoken, in a situation where there is some pressure to communicate in that language, then it may be that PRODEC becomes the predominant pathway.

6. In Classroom 2 (the grammar-translation class) the emphasis is almost entirely on declarative knowledge. The students are learning *about* Italian. Classroom 1 (immersion) is perhaps the one where there is most focus on procedural knowledge.

Issues to think or write about

1. Here is an opportunity to delve into the applied linguistic/SLA literature. Choose one of these topics and find out all you can about it:

consciousness-raising	noticing
declarative and procedural knowledge	restructuring
automization	

2. Here is a research-based question, related to what you have seen in CW6.3 and CW6.4. Imagine that you are asked to do research comparing (particularly in terms of success) a language teaching Method A and a Method B. How would you set up the research? What stages would you need to go through? What challenges are you likely to face in ensuring your research results are valid? How would you tackle them?

Further reading

McLaughlin, B. 1987 *Theories of Second-Language Learning* London: Edward Arnold
A useful book about FL learning theories in general. Chapter 6 focuses on 'cognitive theories.'

Skehan, P. 1998 *A Cognitive Approach to Language Learning* Oxford: Oxford University Press
The title says it all.

Johnson, K. 1996 *Language Teaching and Skill Learning* Oxford: Blackwell
Focuses particularly on declarative/procedural knowledge and automization.

Schmidt, R. W., and Frota, S. 1986 'Developing basic conversational ability in a second language: a case study of an adult learner of Portuguese.' In Day, R. (ed.) *Talking to Learn: Conversation in Second Language Acquisition* Rowley, MA: Newbury House
This paper describes the initial 'noticing' research, and it is written in an accessible way.

Batstone, R. 1996 'Key concepts in ELT: noticing' *ELT Journal* 50/3: 273
A clear and succinct (one-page) outline of the noticing idea.

7 Individual language learners
Some differences

7.1 Introduction

B7.1 A good language learner: the ingredients?

A major theme of this chapter and the next is what makes people good or bad language learners.

What do *you* think makes a good language learner? Make a list of the qualities you think a good language learner possesses. Think about bad language learners also. What makes them bad?

Try to think of specific individuals you know. You might start by thinking about yourself. Are *you* a good or a bad language learner? What makes you one?

A few years ago I joined a class to learn Russian. There were about twelve people in the class. Our learning experience had much in common. We all had the same teacher, of course, and followed the same textbook. It is true that some worked outside the class more than others … and yes, remembering back, there was one student who had a friend of a friend who was Russian, and she managed a bit of conversational practice outside class. But even in this respect the differences were small – we all had full-time jobs and were usually unable even to finish the modest pieces of homework that we were given. Yet despite these similarities of learning experience, what was really dramatic was the very different levels of success reached by individuals in the class. At one extreme was the poor fellow who by the end could barely manage a heavily accented *good morning*, and whose progress with the alphabet never really got beyond a heartfelt expression of sheer amazement at how clever Russian children must be to master it. At the other was the lady with a clear flair for languages who seemed to pick up words and structures on hearing them once only, and who seemed to be moving rapidly towards being able to read *War and Peace* in the original. Between those two fell the rest of us, displaying a truly diverse spread of achievement.

Why these differences? Apart from the odd 'environmental' advantage (like the student who had the chance to converse with a Russian), most of the differences must have lain within ourselves – with what we ourselves brought to the learning task. But what exactly are the factors (or <u>variables</u> as they are called) that make the difference? In past decades applied linguists have given a great deal of attention to trying to identify them and to developing some kind of a profile of what the 'good language learner' is like.

The variables that contribute to individual differences are usually divided into three broad categories. Some are called <u>cognitive</u>, meaning that they relate to the mental make-up of the person. Intelligence is one such factor; another is language aptitude, the phrase used to refer to an ability specific to language learning and different from general intelligence. Other variables are called <u>affective</u>. Psychologists and applied linguists use this adjective and the associated noun *affect* to mean 'to do with the feelings' and 'feelings' respectively. The word root is the same as in the more everyday English words *affectionate* and *affection*. The most commonly studied affective variables are motivation and attitudes. The third set of factors we shall look at are the <u>personality</u> variables. The one that springs most readily to mind is 'extroversion/introversion', but there are other less obvious (and possibly more important) ones.

In this chapter we shall look at variables related to two of these three categories – cognitive and affective. Personality variables will be saved for Chapter 8, where we also look more closely at the concept of the 'good language learner.'

7.2   The cognitive variables

7.2.1   Intelligence

B7.2 Intelligence and FL learning

Do *you* think there is any relationship between intelligence and language learning? Do more intelligent people learn languages better, or faster?

As always, if possible make your starting point specific individuals that you know personally.

Early in the twentieth century, intelligence was considered an important factor for FL learning. It was believed that a certain degree of intelligence was useful, if not essential, for success. This was a reason why learning foreign languages was often left until university level, so that only the most intelligent would take it on. It was also a common belief that FL learning actually helped to develop the intelligence, and even today one occasionally hears (in Britain at least) the learning of Latin supported in this way. It may not be a useful language to know, some people argue, but learning Latin helps build intellectual powers. Occasionally this argument is expressed in its 'Pain Is Good For You' form – Latin is so hard, and hurts so much, that it must be doing you good. Take a look at CW7.1 (*Learning to say 'a cup of tea' by the 'Pain Is Good For You' Method*) which gives you an example of painful learning.

As we saw in 3.2.5, Chomsky's views about language stimulated a large number of studies of how children acquire their first language. In these it was a common belief that L1 learning, at least as far as speaking and listening were concerned, is relatively unrelated to cognitive development. One of the major figures in this field was Eric Lenneberg. In his 1967 book he argues that at the time language acquisition takes place, the child is at a rather low level of mental development. A rather sobering and dramatic fact he cites is that in normal children L1 acquisition is related in terms of developmental stage to the ability to control bowels. So almost everyone learns to speak their L1 irrespective of intelligence.

Although the work of Lenneberg and others was concerned with L1 and not FL acquisition, it was very much in the spirit of Chomsky's views not to consider intelligence and FL language learning to be related. In the FL area, two Canadian researchers are particularly associated with looking at the relationship between intelligence and FL proficiency. Robert Gardner and Wallace Lambert's influential book (1972) is called *Attitudes and Motivation in Second-Language Learning*. It has an appendix which includes a paper entitled 'Language aptitude, intelligence and foreign language achievement.' In it, they report on a 1961 study of 96 children learning French in Louisiana. The basic finding is that there is little relationship (<u>correlation</u>) between intelligence and achievement in FL learning.

Canadian scholars like Lambert and Gardner have for a long time been major contributors to the field of applied linguistics, one important reason being that Canada is a bilingual country, with French- and English-speaking provinces. Issues of foreign language learning are hence of particular interest to Canadians. One of their major contributions was to pioneer immersion programmes (you met immersion in 1.5's Classroom 1; take a look also at CW6.4). The first experiment with immersion took place in St Lambert, a suburb of Montreal, in 1965, and is described in Lambert and Tucker (1972); it is also discussed in Chapter 9, Box 9.5.

In the following years immersion programmes mushroomed in Canada. In the early days the children on these programmes were in selected schools; they had passed certain tests and hence were considered 'intelligent.' One Canadian researcher, Genesee (1976), was interested to know whether these programmes were worth running with less intelligent pupils. To find this out, he used a basic research method which you will find in different permutations (related to different variables, not just intelligence) throughout this chapter. He first tried to find out how good all the pupils in his study were at French, by giving them various tests. He then tried to measure their intelligence, by other tests. Finally he attempted to correlate French achievement with intelligence, using statistics to find out whether being 'good at French' was related to 'being intelligent' (and whether 'bad at French' correlates with 'not-so-intelligent'). Genesee was interested to look not just at overall ability in French, but at performance in different skill areas like listening, reading, speaking and writing. So in fact he gave his subjects five sub-tests in French, dealing with the different skills. In order to measure intelligence, he gave the subjects an IQ (for 'intelligence quotient') test. Doubtless many of you will have come across IQ tests in some context or other. You may have suffered them at school, since in some countries (including Britain) they have been used to measure intelligence as a means of helping to make decisions about a child's future. You can also find something that passes for them in books and magazines purchased at railway stations, where you are invited to 'measure your own intelligence' or 'find out how clever you are.' Genesee's attempts to correlate French achievement and intelligence find no relationship between intelligence and what he calls 'communication skills' (basically, speaking and listening). But he *does* find a correlation between intelligence and what he calls 'academic language skills' – that is, reading and writing. This suggests that being intelligent will help you to learn reading and writing, but not speaking and listening. So the answer to the question 'does intelligence relate to FL learning?' may be: 'it depends on which language skills you are talking about.'

The distinction between 'communication skills' and 'academic writing skills' reappears in the work of Cummins (1980). He distinguishes between 'basic interpersonal communicative skills' (BICS for short) and 'cognitive/academic language proficiency' (CALP). The latter, Cummins finds, is 'strongly related to general cognitive skills … and to academic achievement' (Cummins 1980: 176).

B7.3 Intelligence and different language skills

As we have seen, more than one applied linguist has suggested: (i) a relationship between 'academic skills' and intelligence, but (ii) no relationship between 'communication skills' and intelligence.

Think about both (i) and (ii). Do these suggestions sound sensible to you? If so, can you explain these relationships? Why should 'academic' but not 'communication' skills involve intelligence?

Genesee's findings lead towards another interesting perspective. Perhaps IQ correlates not with FL learning ability but with *ability to profit from certain types of instruction*. Perhaps, that is, you have to be intelligent to succeed in learning languages when using particular methods. This idea was investigated by Chastain (1969). He compared IQ scores with the achievement results of students learning a foreign language by two different methods. One of these was the popular method known as audiolingualism. We came across a version of audiolingualism in 1.5's Classroom 4, and you will read much more about it in Chapter 9 (9.3), which deals with the recent history of language teaching. At its basis is the behaviourist view that language learning is a question of habit formation, in which the 'mind' has no role. The other method was called 'cognitive code' (also to be touched on in 9.3). In 'cognitive code' teaching, learners are expected to understand grammatical explanations and to learn rules; so it might be said that the method involves exercise of the intelligence. Sure enough, Chastain found that the more intelligent learners did well in cognitive code classes, but that there was no such correlation for the audiolingual classes (where intelligence did not seem to relate to success). So a further answer to the question 'does intelligence relate to FL learning?' may be: 'you have to be intelligent to learn from those methods which utilise the intelligence.'

We shall leave intelligence for the moment. But this is not the end of the story. We shall find ourselves having cause to mention it again very soon …

7.2.2   Aptitude

B7.4 Christopher (from Box 1.5) again

Savants are people who may be backward in most areas yet who have extraordinary skills in just one area. Christopher is a savant who is described by Smith and Tsimpli (1995). He was born in 1962, and was diagnosed as brain-damaged at the age of six weeks. Smith and Tsimpli (1995: 1) describe him like this:

> Christopher is unique. He is institutionalised because he is unable to look after himself; he has difficulty in finding his way around; he has poor hand-eye co-ordination, turning many everyday tasks such as shaving or doing up buttons into a burdensome chore; but he can read, write and communicate in any of fifteen to twenty languages.

Christopher's languages include Danish, Dutch, Finnish, French, German, Modern Greek, Hindi, Italian, Norwegian, Polish, Portuguese, Russian, Spanish, Swedish, Turkish and Welsh. Notice what a variety of language families are represented here.

Smith and Tsimpli note that one of the astonishing things about Christopher is the speed with which he learns. An example with yet another language, not listed above:

> when he began learning Berber … he took to the language enthusiastically, seeming 'thoroughly to enjoy teasing out the details of the subject agreement system; and after a few minutes he was able to suggest the correct verb form to accompany a masculine as opposed to a feminine subject … despite there having been only two relevant examples.'
>
> (Smith *et al.* 1993: 286)

In addition, 'on the occasion of his second lesson (three weeks after the first) he was able to translate simple sentences on demand, despite having spent only an hour or so on revision in the intervening period' (Smith and Tsimpli 1995: 18).

How can this be? How can individuals like Christopher, with such gross cognitive deficits, be so good at just one thing – FL learning? His case seems to provide strong evidence for the idea that there is such a thing as an aptitude for FL learning that is separate from general cognitive ability. We have already noted, earlier in this chapter, that this idea was appealing to the Chomskyan way of thinking, because – at least as far as the L1 is concerned – acquisition is not seen as intimately connected with general cognitive growth. It may be that this idea, related though it is to the L1, stimulated interest in the FL aptitude area in the 1960s. Certainly we do find at that time an upsurge of interest in the subject.

B7.5 FL learning and other subjects

In the popular imagination, language learning ability is associated with being good at certain other skill areas. People say 'if you're good at languages you're probably good at Subject X as well.' One 'Subject X' is music. People sometimes express the view that being good at foreign languages goes with being good at music.

Can you think of any other subjects? Do you have any ideas about what these subjects (including music) may have in common with language learning?[1]

A second reason for this upsurge in interest is the purely practical desire to predict – to be able to recognize who will succeed at language learning before they do any. To understand this idea, you need to distinguish aptitude from achievement and proficiency. Achievement and proficiency tests measure 'how well you have done.' An aptitude test looks at 'how well you would do.' It has a strong predictive element to it. The hope of the 1960s was that rather than spending a great deal of money teaching individuals who might not have any natural talent, aptitude tests would be able to identify in advance those worth focusing the training effort on.

B7.6 A Big Question

There is one question which will dominate this section: how on earth can aptitude be measured?

Give some initial thought to the question, and to what kinds of quick test might be given to individuals to predict their future success in FL learning.

Do not expect at this stage to reach any firm conclusions. A few thoughts will do.

What *is* language aptitude? According to Carroll (1973: 5) it is the 'rate at which persons at the secondary school, university and adult level [will] successfully master a foreign language.' Notice that this definition accepts that everyone can acquire; it is just that some people do it *faster* than others. But this definition takes us only so far, and Box 7.6's Big Question can only really be answered usefully if we can somehow develop a more detailed notion of what language aptitude entails. One of the big aptitude tests, developed by Carroll and Sapon (1959), was called the *Modern Language Aptitude Test* (MLAT for short). It has five sub-tests. The way the authors developed their test was interesting. They drew up a long list of factors which they thought might be related to language aptitude. Then, over time, they undertook research to see which of these factors correlated with actual language learning performance. As a result, their list was reduced to manageable size. Four major areas were in fact identified (in Carroll 1965). We shall look at the two most important of these – phonetic coding ability and grammatical sensitivity – in some detail, just making mention of the other two (inductive learning ability and rote learning ability).

7.2.3 Phonetic coding ability

B7.7 Spelling clues

One of the sub-tests in MLAT is called 'Spelling Clues.' An approximate phonetic spelling of an English word is given. These are the underlined words on the left below; the first, luv, represents the word *love*. You have to find the word on the right which has approximately the same meaning. The answer to (a) is *affection*. Example (a) is taken from MLAT itself; the other examples are invented, following the MLAT principle.

In order to get an idea of what it feels like to do part of an aptitude test, work through the examples below. The test is written specifically for native speakers of English. If you are not one, do the examples anyway; you might also like to invent some examples of your own, for your own native language.[2]

(a) <u>luv</u>	carry	exist	affection	wash	spy
(b) <u>cawz</u>	men	jobs	cattle	helmets	ravens
(c) <u>wor</u>	hat	battle	train	waterfall	window
(d) <u>layk</u>	river	handbag	pond	similar to	dam
(e) <u>hansum</u>	good-looking	money	football	writer	journey
(f) <u>cntri</u>	open	plant	habit	walk	nation

What on earth has this sub-test of MLAT got to do with ability to learn a foreign language? The answer is suggested by a phrase often used to describe someone with linguistic flair. We say they have 'a good ear' for languages, and this expression carries the idea that language aptitude has a component which deals with sound. Carroll, along with others in the field, accept that this is the case, and accordingly the first of his four areas is called <u>phonetic (or phonemic) coding ability</u>. He defines this (1965: 128) as 'the ability to code auditory phonetic material in such a way that this material can be recognized, identified, and remembered over something longer than a few seconds.' This ability is important because 'individuals lower in this ability will have trouble not only in remembering phonetic material, words, forms etc., but also in mimicking speech sounds' (p. 129).

It is important to understand that this skill is something more than the simple ability to *hear* differences between sounds. There is more than the ear involved. One extra element is memory, and the quotation above talks about phonetic material being *remembered*. There is also the element of being able to associate sounds with symbols, what might be called 'sound-symbol association ability.' This element is particularly strongly present in the MLAT sub-test you looked at in Box 7.7, where you are asked to make associations in the L1 between sounds (the 'approximate phonetic spellings' on the left) and meanings (the appropriate words on the right). In addition, Carroll talks about 'coding' material, and this suggests how not just the ear but also the brain is involved. Carroll is speaking of the ability to see some kind of order in the stream of foreign sounds bombarding the FL learner. Gardner and Lambert (1972: 289) describe this same ability in similar terms, as 'a higher cognitive skill in which the individual actively seeks to impose a meaningful code on ... material.' Their own research shows how important this ability is for FL learning. So does the work of Pimsleur *et al.* (1964). CW7.2 (*How to do badly at French*) describes what they discovered about students who were underachieving in French.

▍ 7.2.4   Grammatical sensitivity

Box 7.8 may perplex you. How can it be, you may wonder, that asking questions about the function of words in a person's L1 will help to know how good they will be at FL learning? Carroll's claim is that there is a connection.

B7.8 Words in sentences

Another of MLAT's sub-tests is called 'Words in sentences.' In this, you are given a 'key sentence' which has one item underlined and in capital letters. In (a) below this is the word <u>LONDON</u>. After the key sentence come one or more other sentences with five items underlined and given a letter: A, B, C, D or E. You have to decide which item 'does the same thing' in its sentence as the word in capitals in the key sentence. In (a) below the intended answer is A, because (to use MLAT's own words): 'the key sentence is about "London" and the second sentence is about "he".' Examples (a)–(d) are the practice items in MLAT itself; the other examples are invented, following the MLAT principle.

Work through the examples below. The test is written specifically for native speakers of English. If you are not one, do the examples anyway; as with Box 7.7, you might also like to invent some examples of your own, for your own native language.[3]

(a) <u>LONDON</u> is the capital of England.
    <u>He</u> <u>liked</u> to <u>go</u> <u>fishing</u> in <u>Maine</u>.
    A   B   C   D   E

(b) Mary is cutting the <u>APPLE</u>.
    <u>My brother John</u> is beating <u>his</u> <u>dog</u> <u>with a big stick</u>.
     A   B   C D   E

(c) <u>MONEY</u> is his only object.
    Not so many <u>years</u> <u>ago</u>, <u>most</u> <u>farming</u> was done by <u>hand</u>.
             A B   C   D   E

(d) There was much <u>TALK</u> about a rebellion.
    Where is <u>John?</u> There is no <u>doubt</u> about <u>it</u>.
         A   B   C
    There lay the dead <u>horse</u>. There I found my <u>answer</u>.
               D   E

(e) I gave <u>HIM</u> the book.
    When <u>Peter's</u> <u>mother</u> died, <u>Mary</u> wrote <u>a letter</u> <u>to him</u>.
        A   B   C   D E

(f) Peter likes swimming <u>AND</u> Mary likes dancing.
    Yesterday <u>we</u> <u>all</u> went to the theatre, <u>but</u> Mike stayed <u>at</u> home.
           A B   **C**   **D**   **E**

<u>Grammatical sensitivity</u> is to do with how aware you are of the workings of your first language. In Carroll's words (1973: 7), it is 'the individual's ability to demonstrate his awareness of the syntactical patterning of sentences in a language.' There is a longer quotation below from Carroll (1973). In it, he suggests that individuals possess this grammatical sensitivity to varying degrees, and he claims that it is related to success in a foreign language:

> although it is often said that linguistic 'competence' in the sense defined by Chomsky (1965) involves some kind of 'knowledge' of the grammatical rules of the language, this 'knowledge' is ordinarily out of conscious awareness ... nevertheless, some adolescents and adults (and even some children) can be made to demonstrate an awareness of the syntactical structure of the sentences they speak ... Even among adults there are large individual differences in this ability, and these individual differences are related to success in learning foreign languages, apparently because this ability is called upon when the student tries to learn grammatical rules and apply them in constructing and comprehending new sentences in that language.
>
> (Carroll 1973: 7)

It is important to understand that this awareness is not the same thing as knowing grammatical *terminology*. So, for example, someone may never have heard the word *adjective* or have the remotest idea what it means, but may at the same time have some kind of subconscious awareness of what an adjective is. It is rather like Socrates' slave boy whom we met in 3.2.5. The philosopher was able to show that the boy had an understanding of the principles of geometry without the boy being able to articulate a single mathematical rule.

Research in the area suggests that grammatical sensitivity is indeed an important skill for the FL learner to possess. According to Skehan (1989: 27) the sub-test of MLAT that measures it (described in Box 7.8) 'has proved to be the most robust of all the sub-tests used in the language aptitude field, and withstands study-to-study variation.' Gardner and Lambert (1972) record a particularly interesting finding. They observe that grammatical sensitivity correlates with grades in *all* areas of academic achievement, not just FL learning. And this brings us back to the notion of 'general' intelligence; for although grammatical sensitivity is clearly a language-related concept, Gardner and Lambert are suggesting that it has relevance to non-language areas. The implication is that FL learning and other sorts of learning are somehow linked together. We have already discussed this link in an earlier chapter, and mention was made in this context of cognitive linguistics. You may wish to look back and find that discussion.[4]

7.2.5 Inductive learning ability and rote learning ability

We shall pass briefly over Carroll's other two areas. One is <u>inductive learning ability</u>. This is the ability to 'examine language material ... and from this to notice and identify patterns of correspondences and relationships involving either meaning or grammatical form' (Carroll 1973: 8). Though Carroll is talking about language learning here, you might think that the ability to identify 'patterns of correspondences' and 'relationships' will be useful in learning almost any subject. So perhaps once again we are dealing with an ability related to general intelligence. Finally, there is <u>rote learning ability</u>. This is to do with the ability to learn things by heart. In the language field, it relates particularly to the area of vocabulary learning.

Boxes 7.7 and 7.8 illustrate how two of Carroll's areas can be tested. Box 7.9 describes MLAT as a whole. Think about which of the four areas we have described are being tested in each sub-test:[5]

B7.9 The sub-tests of MLAT

1. *Number learning*. Subjects are given numbers in an artificial (made-up) language. They are asked to reproduce these numbers in combined sequences. For example, they might be taught 1 and 5, and be asked to produce 15.
2. *Phonetic script*. Subjects are given a rudimentary phonetic 'alphabet', and are then asked to underline words they hear on tape.
3. *Spelling clues*. This is the sub-test illustrated in Box 7.7.
4. *Words in sentences*. This is the sub-test illustrated in Box 7.8.
5. *Paired associates*. Subjects learn some Kurdish vocabulary items for two minutes, and are then tested on them.

Another important test, developed at around the same time as MLAT, is Pimsleur's (1968) Language Aptitude Battery (LAB for short). Although LAB differs from MLAT, there are striking similarities. For example, two of LAB's underlying components deal with 'verbal intelligence' and 'auditory ability.' Both have clear counterparts in MLAT.

7.2.6 Aptitude since 1970

Aptitude tests like MLAT and LAB were reasonably successful as predictive tools. But perhaps you have noticed that the work we have been describing in this section all took place before 1970. What has happened since then? There was something of a fallow period during the 1970s and 1980s. Doubtless one reason is that the idea of testing people in order to decide whether they are 'good enough' to undertake an activity became an unpopular one. It could be seen as a 'closing of doors' on people who might be able to overcome poor aptitude and do well at language learning anyway. They might, in other words, be able to walk on (however slowly) up the road were doors not slammed in front of them. But a revival of interest in language aptitude took place in the 1990s. This happened partly because developments in cognitive psychology brought new ideas and frameworks into play. Dörnyei (2005) gives an overview of the developments, and according to him a starting point was the book edited by Parry and Stansfield (1990). Its title – *Language Aptitude Reconsidered* – carries the message very well.

One aspect of the 'reconsideration' was to look at language aptitude in a more contextualized way, considering how different facets of it come into play in different learning situations. Skehan's work shows this well. In his 1989 book – a book all about individual differences – he discusses the idea that tests like MLAT are entirely concerned with what in 2.3 we called systemic competence. But, as we saw in Chapter 2, there are other areas of competence relevant to communicative ability. It is possible that there are different 'aptitudes' related to these different areas. Recall Wes, the Japanese artist we met in 2.5 (and again in 5.2.1). His strategic competence was particularly far advanced. Perhaps we can say that he has good 'strategic aptitude', but not-so-good 'grammatical aptitude.' Skehan identifies the search for possible different sorts of aptitude as a worthwhile research agenda. More recently (Skehan 2002), he turns his attention to how different elements of aptitude come into play at different stages in the learning process. Other recent developments in language aptitude testing are briefly described in CW7.3 (*Some more recent approaches to aptitude*).

7.3 The affective variables

7.3.1 Motivation

B7.10 Why, why ... oh why?

In 1.2 we considered the motives for language learning of five individuals. Look back to that section and remind yourself of those five types of motivation. Also in that chapter (Box 1.2) you were asked to think of other reasons for language learning. Remind yourself of your thoughts there also. Have any further motives occurred to you since then?

Can you identify, from among all these motives that you have been thinking about, some that you predict will be the most likely to lead to language learning success? Do these particularly strong motives have anything in common?

In other words, is it possible to make any kind of general statement about what particularly motivates language learning?

These issues will be considered in the present section.

In all areas of human activity, there are many reasons why people do things, and learning foreign languages is no exception. Among the wealth of motives for FL learning, one of the more grotesque is what is known as 'machiavellianism' – where one seems to learn the foreign language not for love of the target country and its culture, but to contribute to its destruction. Spies sometimes have to be word-perfect in the target language in order to carry on their sinister trade. In this context the notion of 'target' has rather unpleasant military overtones!

Consider particularly two of the individuals mentioned in 1.2. Wai Mun Ching is learning Mandarin 'so that she will feel more integrated with the country she is now a part of.' People with Wai Mun's kind of motivation often do well in FL learning. The other learner is Lilian from Chile. She is learning English so that she can study abroad. The key to her ambition is a good score on an English test.

These two learners exemplify a distinction that is commonly made in motivational studies, between <u>integrative</u> and <u>instrumental</u> motivation. We say that someone is 'integratively motivated' if they are learning the foreign language through a desire to learn more about a culture, its language and people – to 'integrate' more within the target language society. Wai Mun is integratively motivated. Instrumental motivation involves learning in order to achieve some other goal. So if you learn French because you will get a better job if you speak that language, then your motivation is, like Lilian's, instrumental.

If asked, you would probably predict that Wai Mun will do well at Mandarin, and integratively motivated people often do succeed at language learning. Indeed, one way of viewing Schumann's acculturation model (described in CW5.4) is to say that it is based on the notion of integrative motivation and its importance. Gardner and Lambert (1972) carried out another major study of this area. They looked at learner groups in Montreal, Louisiana, Maine, Connecticut and the Philippines. They find a high correlation between integrative motivation and proficiency. The correlation is particularly striking in Montreal.

B7.11 Striking in Montreal

Why 'particularly striking in Montreal'? Can you think of any reason why integrative motivation should relate to FL proficiency particularly in that context? To ponder this question you need to bring to mind anything you know about the language situation in Canada in general and Montreal in particular.

In Gardner and Lambert's study, by the way, the foreign language in question was French.

We will be considering this issue of motivation and context later in this section.

Though some studies find that integrative motivation is more effective than instrumental, there is also no shortage of research showing the importance of instrumental motivation as well. An oft-cited study is Lukmani (1972) who looked at sixty girls from a high school in Mumbai (formerly Bombay). Their motivations for learning English were instrumental, the commonest reasons being to get a good job, to cope with university classes, to travel abroad. What is more, the subjects' instrumental motivation scores correlated significantly with their English proficiency. Gardner and Lambert (1972: 130) find the same in the Philippines: 'that students who approach the study of English with an instrumental outlook and who receive parental support in their views are clearly more successful in developing proficiency in the language than are those who fail to adopt this orientation.'

B7.12 Instrumental or integrative?

Look back to Box 7.10 and the list of motives for language learning you drew up there. Try to identify which of these motives might be called integrative, and which instrumental. How well does the distinction work when applied to all these motives?

Earlier we spoke of a 'wealth of motives' for foreign language learning. Precisely because of that wealth, many have found the integrative/instrumental distinction a little simplistic, unable to capture all that needs to be said about motivation. One major study which reaches this conclusion is Burstall *et al.* (1974). Burstall and her colleagues undertook a large-scale research project concerned with the teaching of French at primary schools in England. The resulting 'Burstall report' was extremely influential. Its main finding cast doubt on whether there was any real advantage to an early start in FL learning, and this finding influenced policy (in England and outside) for a long time. Part of the study looked at how a number of psychological variables relate to the learning of French in English schools. Regarding motivation, the report finds that the motivational characteristics of individual pupils appeared to be neither exclusively integrative nor wholly instrumental. The motives of the pupils were often complex and difficult to categorize completely in terms of the integrative/instrumental distinction.

B7.13 Gender differences

Another finding of the Burstall report relates to gender differences in motivation. Before reading the next paragraph, think whether you would predict any differences between boys and girls as regards motivation for learning a foreign language at school.

Two other findings in the Burstall report are relevant to us. The first relates to gender differences. Burstall found consistently more integrative motivation in girls. One reason perhaps is that girls appear more confident of parental support for language learning. Whatever the rights and wrongs of the matter, some parents seem to regard learning languages as suitable for girls, while the boys are encouraged in the direction of subjects (like electronics and mechanics perhaps) which some might regard as more 'macho.' Second, the report finds a difference between 'word' and 'deed' in integrative motivation studies. When asked, nearly all the pupils talked about their strong desires for intercultural contacts. But did they really mean it? This points to a very common problem in the study of many affective areas, and in fact one which Cancino *et al.* (1978) encountered when studying Alberto, whom we met in 5.4.2. The fact is that if you ask someone about their feelings for a foreign culture, for example, many are unlikely to admit negative feelings to a stranger (the researcher). But their true feelings might be quite different.

In general, writers have tended to find the integrative/instrumental distinction unsatisfactory. Gardner (1985), for example, accepts that the picture is complicated by such factors as the 'machiavellianism' we mentioned earlier. Spies may be rare individuals, but even when dealing with 'normal' people, attitudes towards languages and cultures are often far from straightforward.

The study of motivation also raises the interesting 'chicken-and-egg' issue of cause and effect. Motivation may lead to success; but success can also lead to motivation – and it may be very difficult to work out which of these two is in fact happening. Burstall *et al.* (1974) came to the conclusion that high motivation in the pupils they were studying was the *result* of success, not vice versa. There are some other studies that suggest the same. The idea that success leads to motivation is called the <u>Resultative Hypothesis</u> by Hermann (1980).

When we were discussing aptitude, we noted that there was something of a fallow period during the 1970s and 1980s, with a revival of interest in the 1990s in line with developments in psychology. A characteristic of the new approach was that it looked at language aptitude in a more contextualized way. The same happened with motivation. There was a fallow period at the same time, followed by a revival for similar reasons. And the new emphasis on contextualization was there too. In his overview of this field, Dörnyei (2005) describes the period which we have so far been looking at as the *social psychological period*. The period beginning in the 1990s he calls the *cognitive-situated period*, and as the word 'situated' suggests, a main characteristic is to look at specific situations and variables rather than to seek sweeping general statements.[6] Looking at specific contextual factors – like the teacher, the curriculum, the class – can (Dörnyei argues) explain a 'significant portion of the variance in the students' motivation.' A variable that has attracted recent attention is task. The activities or tasks that a learner undertakes in class can have an important effect on how motivated they are. Perhaps as well as finding out whether our learner is instrumentally or integratively motivated, we should also be asking whether they enjoy the learning tasks they are given in the language classroom.

But what happens if the learner doesn't enjoy a task? All is not necessarily lost, as CW7.4 (*Problem solving in pairs*) shows. It describes a study which well illustrates the kind of specific detail the 'situated' approach goes into.

You may have noticed that hovering around the edges of our discussion of motivation is the concept of attitude. In integrative motivation, it is attitude towards a foreign culture and people, and in CW7.4 it is attitude towards language courses, learning tasks, materials, methods and teachers. Attitudes really are extremely relevant to motivation; looking at how people feel about things can say a lot about why they do things. So we will now turn the focus fully on attitudes and consider in a more systematic way the kinds of attitudes relevant to language learning.

7.3.2 Attitude

B7.14 Relevant types of attitude?

So far we have mentioned just a few types of attitude relevant to language learning. One of these is 'attitude towards the target language culture.' What others, not yet mentioned, can you think of? One way of doing this would be to write a list, with each item beginning 'Attitude towards …'

The attitude most studied in relation to language learning is one that we have already touched on. It is attitude towards the target language speakers, sometimes called the <u>reference</u> or <u>aspirational</u> group. If you are learning French, how important is it that you should like French speakers? Some of the Canadian work looking at the learning of French in Montreal came to the conclusion that attitude towards reference group is extremely important, such that students with negative attitudes are likely to do poorly in school French, whatever their aptitudes or motivation. Jakobovits (1970) is particularly firm. His view is that if you dislike French speakers you are wasting your time even attempting to learn French.

B7.15 Poor attitudes – what effect?

How important do *you* think attitude towards the speakers and culture of the target language is? Can a learner with poor attitudes in these areas succeed? If possible, think of someone you know who has poor attitudes in these areas. How successful have they been as FL learners?

Think about how such attitudes might affect learning. Are there any specific aspects of the language that are particularly likely to suffer through poor attitudes?

But is attitude towards reference group *always* so important? Surely there are many situations where learners know very little indeed about the reference group. Indeed, I fear that it is not unheard of to meet learners who are not terribly sure where in the world the countries speaking the target language are located.

Learner level is likely to be one factor governing how important this type of attitude might be. It is possible that at the advanced level attitude towards reference group will be more important than lower down. At the advanced stage, 'getting inside the culture' is important. It is then that you study the literature and culture of the target language, and for these activities a degree of sympathy towards that language and culture will be necessary. One might also say that having a good accent becomes more important at the higher level. Developing a good foreign accent may certainly be said to depend on a sympathy for the culture and people.

B7.16 Accent and attitude

Do *you* think a good target language accent depends on attitudes towards reference group? Did you identify it as an important language area in Box 7.15?

Why should accent depend on such attitudes?[7]

But what about at the elementary level? At that stage learners do not have to put much of themselves into the lessons. Indeed, learning may be seen as just an 'academic exercise.' Green (1975) studied the learning of German in British schools. One finding was that liking German seemed to have no relationship with favourable views towards German people. This is a conclusion that can perhaps be explained in terms of learner level.

Geographical setting is almost certainly another important factor. You will by now have realized that many studies of individual differences emanate from bilingual Canada. In bilingual countries, cultural stereotyping is often very strong. Hence in a city like Montreal, English speakers will often have strong views about French speakers, and vice versa. These views are likely to be highly influential in language learning. French speakers who strongly dislike English speakers are likely actively to resist learning English (and may often refuse to speak it even if they are able to). But in other parts of the world, and in relation to certain languages, serious cultural stereotypes may not even exist. To pluck an example at random: it may well be that most Romanian children have no discernible attitudes towards Spain and the Spanish language. There will doubtless be a degree of non-serious stereotyping (with the Spanish it may be to do with bullfighting and flamenco), but nothing more than this. In that type of situation, one would not expect attitude towards reference group to be important. Perhaps this accounts for Gardner and Lambert's aforementioned findings, that integrative motivation was most important in Montreal and less so in places like the Philippines.

What about other attitude types? Here are some that have been discussed in relation to language learning:

> *Attitude towards success* (sometimes called <u>need achievement</u>): This is 'the degree to which a student strives for accomplishing goals in life.' It may be that people tend to divide themselves into 'high achievers' and 'low achievers' in general. The 'high achievers' will strive to do well at everything, including learning languages. It is interesting to note that Pimsleur's aptitude test, the LAB, looks at the overall grades of learners in all subjects, in order to help predict success in language learning. The testers are trying to identify 'individuals that do well overall.'

> *Attitudes towards teacher*: It is a common belief that you will not learn French if you dislike the French teacher. This is doubtless sometimes true, and as we saw in CW7.4, the teacher can be an important motivator (or demotivator!). This is also suggested in the good language learner study we shall look at in the next chapter (Naiman *et al.* 1978). There, one of the weakest students they looked at is one of the few (of those studied in depth) to report not getting on very well with the teacher. But it is often *not* true, and indeed the same good language learner study reports that bad learners as well as good learners liked their teacher (a finding you will see reported in CW8.3). It seems that in many cases, learners are quite capable of 'distinguishing the messenger from the message.'

B7.17 Messenger and message

How important is the teacher as a motivator? Can you think of examples in your own experience where attitude towards the teacher seems to have had an effect on learning? A case perhaps where someone you know disliked learning a language (and did badly at it) because they disliked the teacher? Or where liking a teacher seems to have affected language learning positively?

There is one other type of attitude that has been studied in relation to FL learning. CW7.5 (*Attitude towards your own country*) looks at how your feelings towards your own culture may influence success in learning the language of another culture.

7.4   Finding out about affect

Earlier in this chapter, in relation to both Cancino *et al.*'s Alberto and the Burstall report, we mentioned the difficulties in finding out what people really think where feelings are concerned. How can it be done? The obvious method is to ask them, and indeed attitude questionnaires (or <u>scales</u>) have commonly been used for this purpose. Jakobovits (1970) offers many examples. The <u>Likert scale</u> is a common technique, named after Rensis Likert, the American educator who developed it. It involves specifying your level of agreement with a statement. A scale of 1–6 is common, ranging from *strongly disagree* to *strongly agree*. Below are two example statements from an 'Anomie Scale', written for Canadians and taken from Jakobovits (1970: 266–7):

1.   Having lived this long in this culture, I'd be happier living in some other country now.
2.   The big trouble with our country is that it relies, for the most part, on the law of the jungle: 'get him before he gets you.'

Have a look at CW7.6 (*Finding out what they really think?*), which illustrates another common technique for finding out about attitudes.

Questionnaires have become extremely popular in applied linguistic research, but they have disadvantages as well as advantages. Though questionnaire-based research can carry an aura of 'being scientific', there is more to 'good science' than a questionnaire and some accompanying statistics. Take a look at CW7.7 (*Questionnaires and interviews*) which looks at the pros and cons of questionnaires, in comparison with the other major way of sounding people's views: by interview.

To what extent can (and should!) teachers attempt to control attitudes? As we noted in our discussion of learner level, in many situations learners do not arrive in class with fixed attitudes, and the teacher's role then is more like 'attitude former' than 'attitude changer.' But where negative attitudes do exist, it needs to be realized that though attitudes can be changed, they tend to be somewhat deep-seated and enduring. Psychologists have done fascinating work in attitude changing, in non-linguistic areas. A problem of attitude change was, for example, posed in the Second World War when the war with Germany, but not with Japan, was finished. The natural reaction of allied troops was to want to go home, and they had to be persuaded to continue fighting. But it would be unrealistic to expect teachers to engage in elaborate attitude changing programmes.

A little gentle persuasion perhaps, but not much more. Dörnyei and Csizér (1998) suggest 'ten commandments for motivating language learners' that the teacher can follow. Their commandments include exhortations like: 'familiarise learners with the target language culture', 'personalise the learning process' and 'create a pleasant, relaxed atmosphere in the classroom.'

7.5   A sad conclusion

But, when all has been said, how important are attitude and motivation? Though there can be no doubt that highly motivated learners with the right attitudes will have a head start, these are not necessarily enough. We conclude this chapter with part of a sad story. It shows that attitudes and motivation will not take you all the way. A second instalment of the sad story comes in 8.2.3.

B7.18   The Sad Story of Student A: Part 1

The sad story comes from Naiman *et al.* (1978), and is about one of the students they studied in depth. They call her Student A. She has much going for her. She is full of the right attitudes and has plenty of integrative motivation. Here are some of the things said about her:

- 'she appeared to be attentive, very jovial and relaxed, obviously enjoying some of the activities';
- 'she indicated that French was her favourite subject and expressed a general love of languages';
- 'outside the classroom she occasionally listened to the French radio station and talked to her friends in French – "for fun"';
- 'according to her teacher, Student A was a "beautifully adapted person", not afraid of making mistakes, very motivated, and a hard worker.'

But life can be very cruel. Despite these very positive traits, Student A is, sadly, second-lowest in class. What kinds of reasons may have caused this to happen?
   A possible explanation will be given in 8.2.3.

Notes

1. A subject often mentioned in this respect is mathematics. Perhaps FL learning shares with mathematics, and music, the ability to see patterns and relationships. This ability is discussed in 7.2.5.

2. The intended answers are: (b) cattle; (c) battle; (d) pond; (e) good looking; (f) nation.
3. The intended answers are:

(b) D. Like *apple*, *dog* is the direct object of the sentence;

(c) D. Like *money*, *farming* is the subject of the sentence;

(d) B. In the third and fourth sentences, the word *there* has a different meaning from the one in the key sentence. In the second sentence the meaning is the same, and the words *talk* and *doubt* both come after the verb *be*;

(e) E. *Him* in the key sentence means *to him*, and like *him* in the following sentence is the indirect object;

(f) D. The words *and* and *but* are used in the same way, to join together what otherwise might be separate sentences.

4. The language/cognition link is discussed in 3.2.6 and again in 6.1; in both cases cognitive linguistics is mentioned.
5. *Number learning* clearly involves inductive learning ability. The main component of *Phonetic script* is phonetic coding ability, as with the *Spelling clues* test. As Box 7.8 illustrates, *Words in sentences* is said to involve grammatical sensitivity. Ability at rote learning is a main part of the *Paired associates* sub-test.
6. Dörnyei in fact identifies a third period, starting around 2000, which he calls the process-oriented period. This is characterized by studies that break down the motivational process into stages.
7. Accents are a very strong marker of identity, and of association with a social group. Many people cherish local or class accents in their L1 for that reason. Some such attitudes make their way into FL learning, where a learner may only put effort into improving their accent if they can feel a part of the target language society. Sometimes you even hear of learners who have a very good 'ear', and who are capable of a near-native accent in the FL. But they may intentionally keep some foreignness in their accent, just to indicate to the world that however well they speak the FL, their true identity is not as a member of the target language group.

Issues to think or write about

1. Here is a chance to find out something about the background to a topic discussed in the chapter, outside of its applications in FL learning. Choose one of these topics:

   • intelligence and intelligence testing
   • savants
   • aptitude tests
   • gender differences in different school subjects.

   Find out all you can on the topic, paying particular attention to non-language-related areas.

2. Think of a particular group of people – they may be school pupils you teach, or friends of yours – young or old. Devise a questionnaire to discover what you can *either* about their motivations for FL learning *or* about their attitudes to something relevant to FL learning (for example, to native speakers of the FL). Your questionnaire can use whatever sorts of questions you like

(Likert scales, for example). If you have the opportunity, use your questionnaire on some 'guinea pigs.'

Further reading

Skehan, P. 1989 *Individual Differences in Second-Language Learning* London: Edward Arnold
A major publication in the area of individual differences.

Dörnyei, Z. 2005 *The Psychology of the Language Learner* London: Lawrence Erlbaum Associates
Dörnyei's book provides thorough treatment of the area.

Gardner, R. C. 1985 *Social Psychology and Second Language Learning: The Role of Attitudes and Motivation* London: Edward Arnold
As the title suggests, this is particularly useful for the affective variables.

Dörnyei, Z., and Skehan, P. 2003 'Individual differences in second language learning.' In Doughty, C. J., and Long, M. H. (eds) *The Handbook of Second Language Acquisition* Oxford: Blackwell, 589–630
Quite a short, succinct account.

Skehan, P. 1998 *A Cognitive Approach to Language Learning* Oxford: Oxford University Press
Chapter 8 focuses on research into language aptitude.

8 Good language learners and what they do

8.1 Introduction

The Sad Story of Student A which closed Chapter 7 suggests perhaps that there are factors other than those we have so far considered that can contribute to individual success or failure in language learning. Perhaps the key to her lack of success has something to do with the personality variables we shall now consider. When we have discussed these, we shall look in detail at the study Student A's story comes from, Naiman *et al.* (1978). This was the largest of a number of studies undertaken in the 1970s to look at what makes a good language learner. As we shall see, these studies partly attempt to identify the characteristics that go to make up good language learners. But they also consider an issue we shall finish the chapter with. This is the question not of what good language learners are *like*, but of what they *do*. What processes, or strategies, do they use in the course of learning that make them so good at it?

8.2 Personality variables

8.2.1 Extroversion and introversion

B8.1 Extroverts and introverts

Before you read below about research that has been done in this area, here are three issues for you to consider:

1. You probably have a general idea of what makes an introvert and an extrovert. Try to make this general idea as specific as possible. What exactly is an introvert? And an extrovert?
2. Do you regard yourself as an introvert or an extrovert?
3. A question about research: how can you find out whether a person is an extrovert or an introvert? Can you think what kind of research techniques might tell you?

4. Which do *you* think are likely to learn languages better – extroverts or introverts? What advantages and disadvantages are there to being an extroverted FL learner? What about an introverted one?

Skehan (1989: 100) identifies two characteristics of the extrovert. One is sociability – they are the gregarious, people-oriented individuals. The other is impulsivity; extroverts often act on the spur of the moment, and are prepared to take risks. Introverts on the other hand tend to be introspective, reserved and even distant, distrusting impulse and often planning ahead. A test which aims to measure such characteristics is Eysenck's Introversion–Extroversion scale. It operates in much the same way as the scales described in the last chapter, consisting of statements to which the subject agrees or disagrees to a greater or lesser degree. Two questions from Eysenck's scale will give you the flavour:

• Do you sometimes say the first thing that comes into your head?
• Can you usually solve a problem better by studying it alone than by discussing it with others?

Can you think of some more questions that might go into an Introversion–Extroversion scale?

Do extroverts or introverts make better language learners? Some feel that extroverts should have the advantage. After all, they engage in conversation a lot, exposing themselves to input and producing output – both characteristics which, as we saw in Chapter 5, are thought important for language learning. Among the attempts to relate these factors to language learning is a paper by Pritchard (1952) which finds a correlation between the 'sociability' side of the extrovert's personality (measured by observing how much pupils talked in the school playground) and fluency in spoken French.

In Naiman *et al.*'s (1978) good language learner study (which we will look at in detail in 8.3), Eysenck's scale is used with a large number of pupils. No correlation is found with language learning success. But the researchers express surprise at this result, because their informal observations of the pupils did suggest an advantage to the extroverts. They speculate whether the Eysenck scale was in fact doing its job.

Common sense might suggest that there could be a connection between extroversion and *oral performance*. But you may also feel that introverts are really just as competent in all areas, the only difference being that the introverts do not speak so much. You might then ask yourself whether you really have to speak a lot to learn a language. Can you not take everything in without opening the mouth much at all? It is a pertinent question to ask.

8.2.2 Tolerance of ambiguity

Perhaps there are people you know who become very agitated if the future is unclear to them. People like this simply must know, in any given situation, what is going to happen to them next. Others, on the other hand, seem quite happy living in a state of uncertainty. The term tolerance/intolerance of ambiguity is used to characterize these personality traits. Budner (1962) describes intolerance of ambiguity as 'the tendency to perceive … ambiguous situations as sources of threat.' As with several other variables we have been considering, this factor is measured by a scale. Budner's Intolerance of Ambiguity Scale invites subjects to agree or disagree with statements such as 'what we are used to is always preferable to what is unfamiliar.'

Naiman *et al.* (1978) administer Budner's test and attempt to correlate results with French proficiency. Interestingly, this is one of the few personality traits where a correlation *is* found, particularly with results on a listening comprehension test.

The suggestion is that those who are tolerant of ambiguity are better language learners than those who are not.

This piece of research finds another interesting, and related, connection. This is between intolerance of ambiguity and the degree to which learners want their L1 to be used in class. The researchers find differences between learners regarding attitude towards the teacher's use of the FL in class. Some learners are quite happy to be 'immersed' in the FL, even though they may not understand everything that is being said. But other learners are disoriented by not understanding, and are upset that the teacher does not use the L1 to help communication where necessary. 'She keeps talking away in French', they might say. 'How am I supposed to know what she's saying? She ought to say it in English.' Naiman *et al.*'s study shows that the individuals who do not mind use of the FL in class are the ones shown by Budner's test to be tolerant of ambiguity. Those who object to overuse of the FL are intolerant of ambiguity. There is also a suggestion in the research that those tolerating more use of the FL fare better as learners. Putting all these connections together, we find that not minding extensive use of the FL is connected to being tolerant of ambiguity, and both these factors are related to success in FL learning.

This connection between proficiency and tolerance of ambiguity is particularly strong at the early learning stages, and this leads Naiman *et al.* to wonder whether individuals who are intolerant of ambiguity might decide to give up learning the language at an early stage.

Two other factors that have been studied in relation to FL learning are discussed in CW8.1 (*Empathy/ego permeability and sensitivity to rejection*). Though no convincing connections with learning success have been established for either factor, it is worth taking a look at this CW for an interesting research method problem that it raises.

8.2.3 Cognitive style and field dependence/independence

When we are given a problem to solve, we all have our own preferred ways of tackling it. These 'ways of thinking' are sometime referred to as 'cognitive styles.' Messick (1970) calls them 'habitual modes of information processing.' Interesting research has been done into the different cognitive styles of individuals. In the language learning field, some of the most fascinating is related to what is called field independence. Witkin (cited in McDonough 1981: 131) describes this as 'an analytical, in contrast to a global, way of perceiving [which] entails a tendency to experience items as discrete from their backgrounds and reflects ability to overcome the influence of an embedding context.' In simpler words: some individuals seem more able than others to extract things from the context in which they are met, and to see them as separate entities. People who can do this easily are said to be field independent, while those who cannot are field dependent. One area in which this has been studied is visual perception, and there exists an 'Embedded Figures' test. This asks subjects to find a given shape and isolate it from a complex figure which contains it. Box 8.4 gives an example.

B8.4 What Embedded Figures tests look like

Below is an example of an item of the sort that might be found in an Embedded Figures test. It is an invented example, but is very similar to some in Witkin *et al.* (1962). The task is to find the figure (a) 'embedded' in each of the figures (b), (c) and (d). Try it. This example is not difficult, though some of the items in Embedded Figures tests can be very hard.

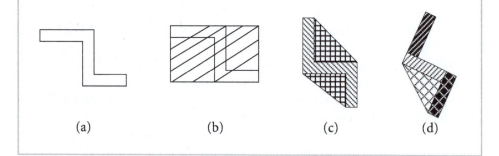

(a)   (b)   (c)   (d)

But there is more to field independence than visual memory. Indeed you may have come across an Embedded Figures test as part of those tests which (as we mentioned in the last chapter) you can buy on railway stations to 'measure your own intelligence.' Their presence in IQ tests suggests that the ability to isolate shapes in this way has a cognitive side to it, and is felt to relate to general intelligence.

Naiman *et al.* (1978) gave their subjects a field independence test. The results were interesting. They found positive correlations between field independence and language learning success, particularly at later learning stages. The field-independent subjects seemed to be better learners. The researchers also make fascinating and explicit claims about the sorts of errors field-dependent people make. It is worth taking a moment to look at some of these errors because they show the kinds of problems field-dependent learners meet. They are described at CW8.2 (*Field dependent errors*).

Naiman *et al.* (1978) gave a number of personality and cognitive style tests to their subjects, only some of which have been described here. Of these, only two gave positive correlations with language learning success – tolerance of ambiguity and field independence. The researchers themselves were disappointed not to have more results in this area. As we have mentioned on more than one occasion, they speculated that perhaps it is the difficulty in measuring some variables that made for such disappointing findings.

We have considered just some of the personality variables studied in relation to language learning, and there are others we have not covered. Principal among these are anxiety, and one of a rather different sort to those we have looked at: age. Box 8.5 invites you to think about these two variables.

B8.5 Thinking about anxiety and age

(a) Being an anxious person is likely to affect many aspects of an individual's life. What about using a foreign language? What effects would you expect anxiety to have on that? Would all the effects be bad? Is there anything good about being anxious?

(b) Think about the relationship between age and language learning, particularly about starting a language early in life (at the age of eight, for example). What advantages and disadvantages do you see to that? What about making a late start (say over the age of 45). Is the picture gloomier the older you get, or does the older person have any advantages?[1]

In this chapter and the last we have treated variables in isolation. But remember that within any real learner many more than one variable is present. These variables exist in different strengths; sometimes one will be so strong as to dominate all the others; sometimes they will be of equal strength and will 'cancel each other out.' Certainly it is possible for a learner to compensate for some important characteristic that is missing, and it is equally possible for some strongly present negative element to destroy what might otherwise be a promising learner profile. 'Profile' is the important word here. If we want to make predictions about performance, we need to bear in mind *all* the characteristics a learner possesses, taken together. Spolsky (1989) developed a model of FL acquisition which considers many variables together to provide a learner profile. He lists a full 74 factors (or 'conditions', as he calls them) that contribute to language learning success. He notes that 'the effect of any one condition can be masked by the strong influence of other conditions; thus aptitude might be masked by attitude' (p. 204). He uses the term 'preference model' to describe a framework which, like his, takes different variable weightings into consideration.

This is the point to revisit the Sad Story of Student A. As you will recall from Box 7.18, she had very good attitudes and strong motivation. It was a mystery why she did so badly at learning French. Perhaps the answer lies in the Embedded Figures test she was given by Naiman *et al.* (1978). This revealed that she was highly field dependent, apparently not a good characteristic for language learners. For her, this might be what Shakespeare's Hamlet calls the 'vicious mole of nature' – the one small feature that grows until it destroys all the good that surrounds it.

8.3 Good language learner studies

B8.6 Doing the right things

At the beginning of the previous chapter (Box 7.1) you were asked to consider what characteristics a good learner might possess. You thought about bad learners as well. Here are some related questions: What do you think good language learners *do* as they learn? What kinds of strategies do they use? Try to be as specific as possible. Do they, for example, learn lists of vocabulary items by heart? Do they pay a lot of attention to grammar? What else? And what about bad learners?

As always, try to think of specific individuals you know – including yourself perhaps.

You will by now have gathered that at this point in the book our main interest is in an abstract, fictitious and perhaps even mythological person – the good language learner. How can we find out what good language learners are like? Carroll's (1967) suggested way of doing this was inspirational. Why not, he suggested, gather together a group of people who were self-evidently good language learners and try to find out what they have in common? Like many brilliant ideas, it seems entirely obvious once someone has thought of it.

Around the mid-1970s, a number of studies did just this. The largest so-called good language learner study is one that we have mentioned a number of times already – Naiman *et al.* (1978) – and in this section we shall spend time describing in some detail what was done and found. Another study, Pickett (1978), has much in common with parts of Naiman *et al.*, but is much more modest in scope. A further two studies, by Stern (1975) and Rubin (1975), are also well known. They are theoretical and do not involve any direct research. You might regard them as statements of belief as to what good learners will (or should) be like, and part of their interest is that they give a clear idea of the view of language learning predominant at that time. Rubin's study is particularly interesting as a view from the 1970s of what strategies were felt to be important for success, and Naiman *et al.* use her speculations as the basis for part of their study. Box 8.7 lists Rubin's good learning strategies, as adapted by Naiman *et al.* Compare the list with the one you developed in Box 8.6. Take time, also, to reflect on Rubin's list itself. Which strategies on the list do *you* feel are particularly important?

B8.7 Seven hypotheses about good language learners

1. The good language learner is a willing and accurate guesser.
2. The good language learner has a strong drive to communicate, or to learn from communication. He is willing to do many things to get his message across.
3. The good language learner is often not inhibited. He is willing to appear foolish if reasonable communication results. He is willing to make mistakes in order to learn and to communicate. He is willing to live with a certain amount of vagueness.
4. In addition to focusing on communication the good language learner is prepared to attend to form. The good language learner is constantly looking for patterns in the language.
5. The good language learner practises.
6. The good language learner monitors his own and the speech of others. That is, he is constantly attending to how well his speech is being received and whether his performance meets the standards he has learned.
7. The good language learner attends to meaning. He knows that in order to understand the message it is not sufficient to pay attention to the language or to the surface form of speech.

(Rubin 1975, adapted by Naiman et al. 1978)

Naiman *et al.*'s study really was large-scale. It had three main aims. One was to identify the strategies that good learners used. In particular: were Rubin's strategies (in Box 8.7) used by good learners? Second, were there any correlations between successful learning and the variables we have been looking at, particularly the personality and cognitive style ones? A third and less central aim was to learn something about what teachers do in classrooms.

The study was done in Canada using subjects whose L1 was English. It had two main parts. For the *adult interview study* they identified 34 individuals who were self-evidently good language learners. They also chose, for comparison, two people who were bad at languages. All the chosen subjects were given a questionnaire asking about their experiences and background, and trying to find out about their learning strategies. Three of the good learner subjects were then chosen for special in-depth case studies.

The *main classroom study* dealt with pupils learning French at school. A group of 72 pupils was selected from learners studying at different institutions chosen to represent the variety of schools in the area. As well as proficiency tests, they were given a series of personality and cognitive style scales, including those which we have been describing. Each pupil was also observed in class for a total of 250 minutes, with many aspects of their behaviour noted down. Both students and teachers were interviewed. Six pupils were selected for in-depth case studies, one of these being the Student A we have already met. Large-scale research indeed!

The Naiman *et al.* study provides a veritable treasure trove of interesting pieces of information. Some of the small but nevertheless instructive findings are given in CW8.3 (*Small-but-fascinating*). Treasure troves apart, what about more major findings, related to the study's three main aims? As regards *learning strategies*, five of Rubin's strategies found some support, particularly in the adult interview study. Here they are:

1. Active learner participation is important. The better learners did appear to be making positive efforts to create opportunities to use the language. As one of the good adult learners put it: 'I would try to get involved as much as possible ... Language is a skill you've got to use all the time ... Participation seems really essential' (p. 10).
2. The better learners realized that they did have to come to grips with language as a system. They showed willingness to learn grammar. In the questionnaire, learners were asked whether they learned systematically or unconsciously. Of the good learners, 94 per cent answered that their approach was highly conscious and systematic. They wrote statements like 'just absorbing the language doesn't get you very far.' Naiman *et al.* add an interesting comment. 'It may be significant', they say, 'that the two subjects [in the adult interview study] who regarded language learning as a totally unconscious process were the unsuccessful learners' (p. 11). It would be difficult, perhaps, to square this finding with Krashen's views about the subconscious nature of language learning. You may like to go back to Chapter 5 and find where this view was described.
3. But at the same time the good learners saw it necessary to view language as communication, realizing the need to go and seek opportunities to talk to real people. The learner who was about the best of the adults studied claimed to have a girlfriend in every language. He says the language comes alive when you get to know individuals who speak it.
4. Good learners do appear to monitor their own interlanguage (the word commonly used to describe a learner's language which falls somewhere between the learner's L1 and the target language). They are constantly correcting themselves. In one class, the best pupil answered (silently, to himself) all the teacher's questions, whoever the teacher had addressed them to. He compared his own answers with those given by others in class.
5. Good learners realize that learning a language involves affective problems, which they have to come to terms with. They know that you have to be prepared to appear foolish while you are learning. One learner picked up Icelandic from a five-year-old, and only realized later that some of the expressions he was learning were childish (*Mr Copper-wopper* for

policeman, for example). Another learner notes that 'one good characteristic is to be outgoing, to be willing to take risks.' For her, this involved being prepared to go up to native speakers and practise on them, even though it was sometimes obvious that the native speakers would rather be speaking among themselves, without the presence of a non-native who would need 'special attention.'

Another major finding regarding learning strategies was to do with how you find out about them. The researchers found that information on strategies is more usefully collected through interviews, not observation. They had hoped that watching pupils in class would give them plenty of information on strategies. But this did not happen. This is not so surprising when you think how much of language behaviour in general is 'covert', or hidden. There is not much to see or hear – most of what happens goes on in the head. Reading and listening are the obvious examples of covert language behaviour. This introduces an interesting problem relating to research methods:

B8.8 Seeing into the unseen

How can you find out what is going on when a learner reads or listens? Just watching the learner will not tell you much. What other research techniques are available for seeing into the unseen?

What about when a learner writes? The *results* of writing are visible but, as with reading and listening, a lot of what is going on is in the head and cannot be 'seen' on the page.

These issues will be looked at later in this chapter (8.4.2).

We have already come across two of Naiman *et al.*'s three main findings to do with *cognitive styles and personality traits*. Here are the three:

- Tolerance of ambiguity correlated at lower levels, and may perhaps be important in decisions concerning whether or not to continue with the language.
- Field independence correlated at higher levels.
- A general measure of attitude (not just one of integrative or instrumental motivation) does correlate with success, particularly at early stages. It is perhaps *necessary*, but it is not *sufficient*.

Our Sad Story of Student A illustrates this last point. As we saw, she is full of the right attitudes and has plenty of integrative motivation. But this is not sufficient to guarantee her success.

Naiman *et al.* also have some findings about teacher behaviour. CW8.4 (*What teachers do*) describes the three main ones.

Since Naiman *et al.* there have been a number of other good language learner studies, including ones by Gillette (1987), on the learning of Spanish and French, and Lennon (1989), on Germans learning English. These studies, like the others we have mentioned, raise an issue which has perhaps been in your own mind as you read: to what extent can we really expect all good learners to be similar and to follow the same strategies? After all, as we noted in 1.5, there are 'very many ways of skinning the language-learning cat.' It is true that we have to expect differences as well as commonalities, and Naiman *et al.* find just this. For example, they note that there is a lot of variation among the good learners over such matters as preference for formal versus informal learning conditions, and in their preferred way of being taught. There were also substantial differences in learning styles. Some learners would learn vocabulary by memorizing lists of words, for example, while others found different ways of doing this. In yet another good language learner study, Stevick (1989: 128) witnesses the same thing. His seven successful learners 'differ markedly with regard to what ... they prefer to do and not to do.' Observations like this lead Ellis (1994: 546) to the conclusion that 'it is easy to overstate the commonalities in strategy use among good language learners.' But some commonalities there undoubtedly are, and the good language learner studies have contributed immensely in our efforts to identify them.

These studies are essentially concerned with <u>expertise</u>, trying to identify the characteristics that expert language learners possess. There have been many expertise studies, looking at a large number of areas of human skill – such as mathematics, playing chess, medical diagnosis and many others. In Johnson (2005), I look at these general expertise studies and consider what they have to tell us about language-related skills, including language teaching.

8.4 Learning strategies

8.4.1 Types of learning strategies

When I started to learn French as a schoolboy in my early teens, I developed a rather bizarre strategy for remembering what I learned in class. I started to write my own 'textbook' for teaching French to others. My unfortunate sister, some years younger than me, was the one who suffered the consequences of my strange language learning experiment. I would sit her in a corner, I recall (as she still does, painfully), and give her French lessons using the 'teaching materials' I had produced. I found this learning strategy, peculiar though it was, very effective. My sister may have learned little French through it, but I learned a lot!

As we have seen, learning strategies (usually a little less weird than this) were a topic of major interest to the good language learner studies. In fact research like Naiman *et al.*'s led to a spate of enquiries into learning strategies during the

1980s and 1990s. But what exactly is a learning strategy? Box 8.9 contains some examples.

B8.9 Six learning strategies

Here are six examples of learning strategies, taken from a category system developed by Oxford (1990). Use these examples to try to develop your own definition of what a learning strategy is. In a moment you will be able to compare your definition with Oxford's.

A *Taking risks wisely*: 'Pushing oneself to take risks in a language learning situation, even though there is a chance of making a mistake or looking foolish. Risks must be tempered with good judgement' (p. 144).

B *Remembering new language information according to its sound*: One of Oxford's examples is a way of learning FL vocabulary. You think of a word in your L1 (or any other language) which sounds like the word you are trying to learn. You try to associate the two words. For example, if you are trying to learn the Russian word *brat* (meaning 'brother'), you could associate it with the English word *brat* (an 'annoying young person'). Bringing to mind this association may help you remember the Russian word. Under this heading, Oxford (p. 42) also mentions the use of rhymes to remember a word.

C *Finding out about language learning*: 'Making efforts to find out how language learning works by reading books and talking with other people, and then using this information to help improve one's own language learning' (p. 139).

D *Cooperating with peers*: 'Working with other language learners to improve language skills. This strategy can involve a regular learning partner or a temporary pair or small group. This strategy frequently involves controlling impulses toward competitiveness and rivalry' (p. 147).

E *Switching to the mother tongue*: 'Using the mother tongue for an expression without translating it, as in *Ich bin eine girl* [used when a native speaker of English learning German cannot remember the German word for *girl*]. This strategy may also include adding word endings from the new language onto words from the mother tongue' (p. 50).

F *Repeating*: 'Saying or doing something over and over: listening to something several times; rehearsing; imitating a native speaker' (p. 45).

Here is Oxford's own definition of learning strategies (1990: 8): they are 'specific actions taken by the learner to make learning easier, faster, more enjoyable, more self-directed, more effective, and more transferable to new situations.'

That is simple and clear-cut, you may think. But, as Dörnyei (2005: 162) puts it: 'learning strategies are immensely ambiguous phenomena and nothing is clear-cut about them.' If you were to attempt a characterization more elaborate than Oxford's, you would face problems. One would be to distinguish learning strategies from another sort of strategy discussed by applied linguists – commu-nication strategies. These are the 'techniques for coping' that learners develop in relation to strategic competence. Recall the Japanese artist Wes (whom we have met several times) and the sorts of ruses he developed for getting his mes-sage across using his rather restricted knowledge of English. These 'ruses' are communication strategies. The problem of definition comes about because com-munication strategies can also be learning strategies. Here is an example from Hawkins (1998). A learner may develop the habit of asking people they are talking with to explain the meaning of a word. This is a communication strat-egy because it helps the learner over a linguistic deficit. But it can also be a learning strategy – it may be a very good way of getting to learn the meanings of new words.

A second point relevant to the definition of learning strategies is whether or not the word *strategy* should be confined to conscious actions. Learners do lots of things in the process of learning that come naturally and are out of conscious control. Are these strategies, or should they be called by some other name, such as 'processes'? Although applied linguists disagree over this, most say that learning strategies involve some degree of 'consciousness.' But does it really matter, you may ask? From one point of view it matters very much. As we shall see in a minute, attempts have been made to 'teach' strategies. You might argue that it is only really possible to teach things that are at least poten-tially conscious.

Rubin developed her list of learning strategies in 1975. Since then, much more elaborate classifications have been devised. One of the best known appears in Oxford's (1990) book *Language Learning Strategies*. Her classificatory system makes a distinction between what she calls 'direct' and 'indirect' strategies. She explains these (pp. 14–15) by an analogy from the theatre. When using direct strategies, the language learner is like the performer in a play. An actor's task is to come to grips with the play itself. Similarly the language learner's direct strat-egies help them to come to grips with the language. They deal with things like memorizing vocabulary and getting to understand new grammar rules. The lan-guage learner's indirect strategies are more akin to the role of the play's director. They deal with regulation and control. In the case of the language learner, this would include planning issues (like how many hours you spend on learning, and what you do in preparation for each lesson), as well as issues to do with affective demands – coping with the 'strain on the nerves' that speaking and learning a foreign language can involve.

Oxford's classification has six main categories of strategy, three under the heading of 'direct', and three under 'indirect.' You can see the full list at CW8.5 (*Oxford's strategy system*). You are also asked there to think about your own learning strategies. Another book dedicated to the study of learning strategies is by O'Malley and Chamot (1990). Their classificatory system is different from Oxford's, but one common element is the category of metacognitive strategies. These important strategies 'involve thinking about the learning process, planning for learning, monitoring the learning task, and evaluating how well one has learned' (O'Malley and Chamot 1990: 137). Here are three examples of metacognitive strategies (described in O'Malley and Chamot's own words, p. 137):

- *Directed attention*: Deciding in advance to attend in general to a learning task and to ignore irrelevant distractors; maintaining attention during task execution.
- *Self-management*: Understanding the conditions that help one successfully accomplish language tasks and arranging for the presence of those conditions; controlling one's language performance to maximize use of what is already known.
- *Problem identification*: Explicitly identifying the central point needing resolution in a task or identifying an aspect of the task that hinders its successful completion.

How useful to the learner are metacognitive strategies? There is a lot of research to suggest that metacognition is very important for academic success in general, not just in language learning. Here is an example of their importance in an area not related to language use. Schoenfeld (1985) is interested in how people solve mathematical problems. Look at his observations on one expert problem-solver:

> the critical point to observe … is that a monitor-assessor-manager was always close at hand during the solution attempt. Rarely did more than a minute pass without there being some clear indication that the entire solution process was being watched and controlled … there was an extraordinary degree of executive control at all times … Plans and their implementations were continually assessed, and then acted upon in accordance with the assessments.
>
> (pp. 310–13)

Goh (1998) reaches similar conclusions in her study, which is directly concerned with language learning. She notes that learners who have a high degree of metacognitive awareness seem better able to control and manage their learning in terms of understanding and storing new information as well as finding the best ways to practise and reinforce what they have learned.

From what Schoenfeld and Goh suggest above, it seems clear that learning strategies are important for good language learning. But remember Dörnyei's words quoted earlier: 'nothing is clear-cut' about learning strategies, and in fact when one asks what we know about the usefulness of learning strategies for language learning, the answer is not at all clear-cut. In one of O'Malley and Chamot's (1990) studies, they give tasks to learners at different levels. These include filling in blanks with vocabulary items, writing about a picture, and listening to a dialogue. The researchers try to find out what strategies learners are using as they do the tasks. The conclusion:

> in general, more effective students used a greater variety of strategies and used them in ways that helped the students complete the language task successfully. Less effective students not only had fewer strategy types in their repertoires but also frequently used strategies that were inappropriate to the task.

> (p. 140)

Others, like Goh (1998) reach similar conclusions. Good learners, it seems, have a rich repertoire of strategies from which they can draw. But not all the research reaches the same conclusion. Chen (1990) looked at six good and six bad learners at Guangzhou Foreign Language Institute in China. The better students used fewer strategies. The suggestion is that better learners went straight for the right strategies, while the bad learners used trial and error (and hence in effect used more strategies).

When we were considering learner errors in 4.2, we saw that they would often vary from language group to language group according to the relationship between the learner's L1 and the target language. A similar reason helps to explain why 'nothing is clear-cut' in the learner strategy field. The strategies people use will naturally fit in with what they believe about the learning process, and this will differ from one culture to the next, from one educational system to the next. CW8.6 (*Not clear-cut at all*) gives examples of this. It is a theme which we will pursue in 10.4.

8.4.2   Researching learning strategies

The study by O'Malley and Chamot mentioned earlier reintroduces an issue brought up in Box 8.8. This is the question of how we can hope to 'see into the unseen', to find out what is going on in a learner's head as they learn to use language. One technique, employed by Naiman *et al.* and many others, is simply to ask the learner. Interviews and questionnaires can be used to persuade learners to state what their learning strategies are. You may like to remind yourself what was said about these methods in CW7.7.

But there is another set of techniques, also involving introspection, which has the potential to tell us a great deal about strategy use. They are called <u>think-aloud techniques</u>. In these, the learner is given some language learning task to do, and is asked to say aloud whatever thoughts go through their head as they do it. They may be asked to do this after the task has been done, but a common version of these techniques is known as <u>concurrent verbalization</u>. This involves the learner in actually talking as the task is being done. O'Malley and Chamot use this type of verbalization in the study we have just discussed. Think-aloud techniques give the researchers some 'way in' to the otherwise silent world of learning strategies. But they are not everyone's cup of tea. At the very least, learners will usually need some training to be able to verbalize as they work. Even then, by no means everyone is able to think aloud successfully. Some subjects protest strongly against the technique, saying that they can either do the task or talk about how to do it … but not both at the same time. CW8.7 (*Talking drivel*) vividly records the protest of one person who was subjected to concurrent verbalization.

8.4.3 Teaching learning strategies

If we accept that a good repertoire of learning strategies will benefit the learner, the next question we need to ask is: can strategies be taught? What do you think? You are invited to look back over some of the specific strategies that we have mentioned (for example in Box 8.9). How would you go about teaching these? What kinds of exercises or activities could be given to learners to help develop strategies like these? If you ask applied linguists such questions, at present you are likely to receive answers that are statements of faith rather than views based on hard evidence. But the interest in learning strategies has understandably led to attempts to try to teach them. CW8.8 (*Attempts to teach strategies*) describes two – one from the general field of educational psychology, and another focused on language learning.

Oxford's (1990) book might be described as a training manual, and it includes many interesting exercises geared to develop learning strategies in students. Box 8.10 describes one which many others have thought to be useful – getting one's learners to keep diaries of what happens as they learn.

B8.10 Dear Diary …

Below is part of Oxford's (1990: 190–1) description to teachers on how to get learners to keep diaries:

Instructions

Tell your students the following in your own words: Use a diary or journal to express your feelings about learning the new language. Feel free to write whatever you want, but write something every day. The diary describes how you are learning the language and how you feel about it. Diary entries do not have to be long and involved. In fact, a few lines or a few paragraphs a day might be enough. When you want to explore a particular problem or a happy event in more detail, you can write more than usual. The diary is for you, and you can use it any way you want: to describe emotions, desires, issues, difficulties, achievements, other people, learning strategies, conversations, how

---

you spent your time. You will probably want to use the diary to evaluate the general progress (or lack of it) that you feel you are making.

Oxford's instructions do mention learning strategies, but many students will have difficulty understanding what learning strategies are. Imagine that you particularly want your learner diaries to give you information about learning strategies. What would you add to the instructions above to help your learners understand what you want?

How would you evaluate an approach like this? If you have language teaching experience, would you expect Oxford's diary idea to work with your students?

As well as books like Oxford's which deal with learner training in depth, it is now quite common for teaching materials and coursebooks to incorporate exercises geared to develop learning strategies. J. McDonough (1998) gives the example of a coursebook called *Signature* (Phillips and Sheerin 1990). This is a standard three-level course for adults learning English as a foreign language. One element which suggests it was written in the 1990s is that it includes exercises aimed at training the learner in efficient dictionary use, as well as sensitizing them to the need to develop good learning strategies.

But even supposing learning strategies can be taught, there is the question of whether it is worth the time to do so. Arguments in favour might be based on the old saying: 'Give a man a fish; you have fed him for today. Teach a man to fish; and you have fed him for a lifetime.' Teaching learning strategies, you could say, feeds the learner for a lifetime. It will teach him, as it were, to catch his own fish. The argument against might be that if the time taken to teach learning strategies were spent on direct language teaching, much more good would be done. Give a man a freezer full of fish, perhaps, and he will not need to learn how to catch them.

As far as language learning (if not fishing) is concerned, the jury is still out. As J. McDonough (1998: 195) puts it, there is not yet 'much hard evidence that strategy training leads to improvement in language learning outcomes.' We do not yet know whether strategies can be taught. Take a look at CW8.9 (*The jury is out*) for the description of one attempt at strategy training.

What's new in learning strategies? Nisbet and Shucksmith's work in the general educational field was mentioned in CW8.8, and the point was made that many of the interesting ideas about learning strategies have come from that area. According to Dörnyei (2005) educationalists have in recent times begun to replace the notion of learning strategies with the concept of self-regulation. The learning strategies approach involves, as we have seen, trying to identify techniques or strategies which can be associated with successful learning. But our discussion of Naiman *et al.* showed that there are as many differences as there are commonalities in the strategies good learners use. Perhaps a more fruitful approach will be to look at why successful learners 'self-regulate', relating the search to their motivations and attitudes, among other things. Dörnyei feels that this change of approach – from learning strategy identification to the study of self-regulation – is where the future lies.

This chapter concludes Part 2 of the book, and our look at language learning. In Part 3 the focus switches to language teaching. In a perfect and logical world, you would expect what we say about language teaching to be firmly based on what we know about language learning. Certainly in Part 3 we shall make efforts to refer back to Part 2 as often as possible, and we will indeed frequently find ourselves seeking justifications for teaching procedures in terms of what is known about learning. But alas, as many have lamented since time immemorial, the world is neither perfect nor logical. It is a sad and shameful truth that in applied linguistics, as elsewhere, division and compartmentalization exist where there should be unity and oneness. There are, in fact, two worlds rather than one. The world of language teaching, which we are about to enter, exists alongside the world of learning. But they really *are* different places. They often seem like two separate countries, in which people drive on different sides of the road.

Note

1. You might expect anxiety to have some bad effects on language performance, particularly in speaking, when you are likely to feel particularly exposed. But in all areas of learning, some – but not too much – anxiety may be useful if it makes you more aware and alert.

   We have seen various examples in the book (in Box 6.3 for example) of how young children have the advantage of being able to pick up languages in a natural way. But they also tend to be poor at learning rules and generalizations. Elderly people are perhaps slower to learn, but can be more organized, and often have the very great advantage of being well-motivated.

Issues to think or write about

1. A main concern in the chapter has been what good language learners are like, and what they do. We are now about to move from language learning to – in Part 3 of this book – language teaching. As preparation for this, think about good language teachers, rather than learners. What are good language teachers like, and what do they do? Express your own thoughts. But also, if you can, seek the views of others, collecting together as many opinions as you can.

2. If you want to know what concurrent verbalization feels like, here is your chance to try doing one. Below are three tasks to choose from, but you can think of some other puzzle if you prefer:

    (a) An anagram (a very short task). Here is the name of a Shakespeare play, with the letters mixed up; the title has three words: AJIMRDOONUELTE. Work out what the title is.

    (b) A jigsaw (a longer task). If you have a jigsaw puzzle available, spend about fifteen minutes doing as much of it as you can.

    (c) A game of chess (also long). If you can play chess, and have a computer with a chess programme available, spend fifteen minutes playing a game against the computer.

Speak aloud (in your L1) as you do your task. Say everything that is going through your mind. If possible, record what you say. Listening back to what you said will give you an idea of what concurrent verbalizations sound like. Note some of the strategies that you use when doing the task.

Further reading

Since this chapter, like Chapter 7, is about individual differences, the further reading mentioned at the end of the last chapter is also relevant here, particularly Skehan (1989) and Dörnyei (2005).

Oxford, R. 1990 *Language Learning Strategies: What Every Teacher Should Know* Rowley, MA: Newbury House
One of a number of books dealing with learning strategies. This one is particularly accessible, and is relevant to practising teachers.

Oxford, R. 1996 (ed.) *Language Learning Strategies around the World: Cross-cultural Perspectives* Honolulu: University of Hawaii Press
A collection of papers looking at learning strategy differences between cultures.

Hawkins, R. 1998 'Learning strategies.' In Johnson, K., and Johnson, H. *Encyclopedic Dictionary of Applied Linguistics* Oxford: Blackwell, 195–7
Useful if you want just a short discussion of the learning strategy area.

Part III
Teaching

9 Language teaching
A brisk walk through recent times

9.1 Introduction

There are, as we saw in 1.5, many ways of skinning the language learning cat. The same is true of the language teaching cat. The history of language teaching does indeed display a bewildering variety of different methods and approaches, all jostling for our attention, often by means of extravagant claims of the 'learn a language in three months without any effort at all (even while you're asleep)' variety. This chapter's 'brisk walk' will take us along a path through the forest of methods, paying some attention to the background ideas and intellectual traditions which lie behind the actual classroom procedures. But reflect first on your own experience.

B9.1 Methods: a consumer's view

Think about your own classroom language learning experiences. Identify some of the main characteristics of each 'method' (or 'approach') that you have experienced. Has a specific name been used in relation to each method?

For each method, try to list some of the advantages and disadvantages you noticed, viewed from your position as a learner – the 'consumer.'

In the late 1960s, Kelly (1969) produced an overview of language teaching history which began in the period around 500 BC. His long historical perspective carries a message for anyone looking at the development of language teaching. It is that there is nothing new under the sun. As he himself puts it (1969: 394): 'ideas accessible to language teachers have not changed basically in 2000 years.' It is indeed a sobering thought to find that issues which we consider today to be at the cutting edge of debate, and methods we like to think of as 'state of the art', are likely to have been around in Aristotle's time. Each generation, in ignorance and through vainglory, pats itself on the back for reinventing the language teaching wheel.

A second introductory point: in this chapter we describe methods as if they existed in some pure, uncontaminated form. But in fact you rarely come across pure, uncontaminated examples of any method. This is because methods are put into practice by human textbook writers and human teachers. These groups of humans have the wisdom to inject their own beliefs, preferences and experience into what they produce. So you almost never find a pure example of communicative language teaching (to select one of the methods we shall describe). What you find instead is 'Textbook writer A's version of communicative language teaching', or 'communicative language teaching as taught by Teacher B.' Richards (1985) has a delightful phrase to describe this phenomenon. He speaks about the 'secret life of methods', capturing the idea that behind all the public statements about what a given method is like, there lurks a back-street existence – the secret life that the method really follows.

9.2   Seven questions to ask about a method

Before beginning our 'brisk walk', it will be useful to try to identify some ways in which methods are different from each other. Here are our 'seven questions to ask' about any method you come across. Answers to them will help you to view methods in relation to each other.

1. What are the method's 'Big Ideas'? Many are based on a small number of central insights, which act as guiding inspiration. If you can identify these Big Ideas, you are well on the way to 'understanding' the method.
2. What are the theoretical underpinnings behind the method? In an ideal world, it would be supported by a view both of language and of language learning. This rarely happens. Sometimes just one of these – a view either of language or of language learning will be behind the method. Sometimes, shamefully, neither is there. As you read about the various methods in this chapter, try to relate them to the theories of language and language learning discussed earlier in this book.
3. How much 'engagement of the mind' does the method expect? As you will have gathered from Chapter 3, different learning theories have very different views about the role of the mind in learning. At one extreme is behaviourism, where the mind plays no part at all, and learning is viewed as habit formation. In mentalist views this is not true at all. A useful way of characterizing language teaching methods is to identify how they stand in relation to this factor.
4. Is the method <u>deductive</u> or <u>inductive</u> in approach? Deductive learning is where the learner is first given a rule. These rules are then demonstrated working in practice. The sequence is from 'rule' to 'example', and the term RULEG is a useful way of remembering it. In the contrasting sequence, EGRUL, examples are first given, and the learner works out the rules for themselves. Often the rules are given at a last stage, and indeed are sometimes never explicitly stated at all. EGRUL is inductive learning.

5. Does the method allow use of the L1 in the classroom? Some methods shun this at all costs; 'the L1 must never be used, however desperate the struggle to communicate becomes' is a common dogma. In some other methods, you may find a major part of each lesson is given in the learners' L1, with the target language only making an occasional guest appearance. Sometimes the 'deductive versus inductive' question may determine this issue. A deductive method involves giving rules, and in practice this will often have to be done in the learners' L1. It is often not practicable to explain grammatical rules to a learner (particularly at the early learning stages) in the target language.

6. Which of the four skills are given emphasis in the method? The four skills are listening and speaking (the 'spoken' skills), reading and writing (the 'written' skills). Methods can differ dramatically as to where they place the emphasis. In some, learners do nothing but read and write; in others they do little other than listen and speak.

7. How much importance does the method give to 'authenticity of language'? In our survey, we shall see that there are methods which take great pains to make the language the learner is exposed to as 'realistic' as possible. In other methods, no effort at all is made in this direction.

Some of these points have already been covered in earlier portions of this book, and by its end all seven will have been given an airing. At this stage we want them just to give us a starting point on that path through the forest. But where should we join the path? The earlier we join it, the more sense of direction it will give us. But the earlier the starting point, the longer the journey will be. As a compromise, we shall pick the path up in mid-twentieth-century America …

9.3 Audiolingualism

We saw audiolingualism (AL) in action in 1.5's Classroom 4. Practical need was its starting point. Towards the end of the Second World War, the Americans were deploying soldiers in different parts of the globe, especially in South-East Asia. The soldiers needed to learn languages, and this simple fact involved the Army Specialized Training Program (ASTP, started in 1943) in an exciting and unique language teaching experiment. There were two new and important ingredients in the situation. The first was the sheer number of learners involved. According to Howatt with Widdowson (2004: 304) as many as 15,000 soldiers were enrolled, and this posed applied linguistics with a new set of logistical problems. The second element concerns the languages being taught; they were not the usual few 'run-of-the-mill' languages like French and German. There were 27 in all, and these included South-East Asian languages like Japanese and Korean – languages which for North Americans and Europeans might be described as 'exotic' (a term which native speakers of Japanese and Korean might equally legitimately use to describe what European tongues are for them).

From the teaching point of view these languages posed problems which more well-trodden languages – with their many published grammars and well-studied syntactic systems – did not pose. For learners also the task was daunting, because exotic languages confront English-speaking learners with difficulties not encountered in languages more closely related to their own. Out of the ASTP emerged what is sometimes called the 'GI Method'; and out of that developed audiolingualism.

In its heady early days, two claims were made for AL – that it was 'scientific' and 'new.' We have already seen, in 3.2, that there is some justification for the first claim, because AL based itself on a combination of the new 'science of language' (structuralism) and the 'science of behaviour' (behaviourism). These two areas of scientific enquiry did indeed provide AL with theoretical underpinnings. The claim to newness is less justified, and it is possible to find characteristics of AL in methods which preceded it.

What does AL teaching look like? In Box 9.2 is an example of part of a lesson.[1] It deals with two sentence types (or sentence patterns as they are often called): *HAVE* + *just* + *-ed*, and *HAVE* + *not* + *-ed* + *yet*. Notice this way of describing sentence patterns. Writing HAVE in capitals is one way of showing that we are talking about the verb 'to have' as a whole, including all its various forms (like *has*, *have* and *had*); *-ed* is here a shorthand way of referring to the past participle of verbs, which usually ends in *-ed* (e.g. *worked*, *wanted*). These two sentence patterns are associated with the present perfect tense in English. Look through the box and identify exactly what is being taught at each of the three stages. Notice at what points the teacher is 'demonstrating', and at what points there are drills. Then think about what the sentences there show you about when the present perfect tense is used in English.

B9.2 Picking up pens, opening doors, reading books…

Objectives: to teach the present perfect tense, with 'just' and 'yet.' Some example sentences:

I have just picked up the pen.	I haven't picked up the pen yet.
She has just opened the door.	She hasn't opened the door yet.
They have just read the book.	They haven't read the book yet.

Step 1   Demonstrating the sentence pattern HAVE + just + -ed
Actions are done in front of the class, sometimes by the teacher and sometimes by a pupil. For example, the teacher picks up a pen and says 'I have just picked up the pen.' Then a pupil opens the door and the teacher says 'She has just opened the door.'

Step 2   Practising HAVE + just + -ed
(a) Drill   Pupils form sentences from a table like this:

I			(to close) the window
We			(to switch on) the light
They	(to have)	just	(to play) football
He/she			(to walk) home
You			

(b) Drill   The teacher says sentences like the ones on the left below. Chosen pupils make **HAVE + just + -ed** sentences (as in the example on the right):

She's closing the window.   She's just closed the window.
She's going to switch on the light.
They will play football.

Step 3   Demonstrating and practising HAVE + not + -ed + yet
(a) Demonstration   Show a diary for the day:

7.30 get up   10.00 phone Bill
8.00 wash   12.00 visit Jane (for lunch)
9.00 eat breakfast   2.00 take dog for walk

Teacher says: It's 8.30. I'm late. I haven't washed yet.
                It's 9.30. Mary's late. She hasn't eaten breakfast yet.

(b) Drill   Pupils form sentences from the table:

I		(to eat)	John	
We		(to phone)	the dog for a walk	
They	(to have) not	(to visit)	dinner	yet
He/she		(to take)	Mary	
You				

This is only part of a lesson. Think of what is needed to finish it (you can set 'homework' if you wish). Also, think about this lesson in relation to our 'seven questions to ask' (in 9.2). The lesson will not enable you to answer all of them, but the answers to some are suggested.

What are AL's 'Big Ideas'? Rivers (1964), an important book on AL, lists six. They are:

- Primacy of speech
- A 'stimulus-response-reinforcement' (S-R-R) model
- Habit formation through repetition
- Incrementalism
- Contrastive linguistics
- Inductive learning

You will probably be able to say what each of these means (with some help from Chapter 3 perhaps). For details about all these ideas, take a look at CW9.1 (*AL's Big Ideas*). You may be particularly intrigued to read there about the language-teaching equivalents to the food pellets that Skinner gave to pigeons.

AL was extremely widespread throughout the world up to the 1960s. It was often supported with great enthusiasm. As Cioffari (1962: 65, cited in Rivers 1964: 10) complains: 'small groups enthused with missionary zeal … have come to feel that they alone have the secret formula for bringing about improvement in the profession.'

What happened to AL after the beginning of the 1960s? It certainly did not die anything like a complete death, and teaching of the sort we saw in 1.5's Classroom 4 still continues in many places today. But two developments damp-ened the 'missionary zeal' mentioned above.

The first of these developments was research looking at the effectiveness of AL teaching. One of the hallmarks of the 1960s in applied linguistics was the num-ber of large-scale research projects which involved comparing methods. These projects usually entailed teaching two competing methods in a number of classes over a long time, and then comparing the results through tests on learner achieve-ment. The hope was that research like this would answer the question it is per-haps natural for us all to ask: 'what is the "best" method for teaching languages?'

B9.3 Answering the question it is natural to ask

As you are about to discover, there are big problems associated with doing 'method comparison' research using the procedures just described. Can you imagine what these problems might be? Why is it so difficult to find answers to the question it is natural to ask: 'what is the "best" method for teaching languages?'?

Probably the best-known of the method comparison experiments involved AL and a method known as <u>cognitive code</u>, already briefly mentioned in 7.2.1. This was really a version of Classroom 2's grammar-translation (in 1.5), and in fact

Carroll (1966: 102) calls it 'up-to-date grammar-translation theory.' The experiment is described in CW9.2 (*Dampening the missionary's zeal*).

The second reason for dampened missionary zeal was that, as we saw in 3.2, Chomsky's views on language and language learning dealt a devastating blow to AL's theoretical underpinnings – behaviourism and structural linguistics. Without these supports, AL found it difficult to stand up.

But what did Chomsky suggest replacing the discredited method with? On one level the answer is an anti-climactic 'nothing.' This is because Chomsky is the first to recognize that care is needed when applying the findings of linguistics to language teaching matters. Here is what he says (in Chomsky 1966: 52): 'I am, frankly, rather sceptical about the significance, for the teaching of languages, of such insights and understanding as have been attained in linguistics …' So perhaps there are no direct applications of Chomsky's views to language teaching. But if we look for rather more indirect influences – implications rather than applications – there is no doubt that Chomsky's ideas have had a very profound effect on language teaching. Arguably the time of greatest influence of these ideas was in the 1980s. But an influence was first felt in the 1960s when his ideas were new. We shall consider this influence now.

9.4   Oiling a rusty LAD

Chomsky, as we saw in 3.2.5, credits the 'organism' (as opposed to the 'environment') with the major part of the work of L1 acquisition, achieved by means of the LAD. The concept of an innate LAD was a powerful one in L1 acquisition studies. But there is an apparent restriction on the use of the idea for foreign language learning; namely that the life of LAD seems rather short. Like various biologically endowed mechanisms, LAD seems to have a 'critical period' – a time when it is called on to do its job, does it, then disappears from the scene. An enlightening metaphor might be to compare it to the stage of a rocket going into space. When a certain stage has done its job, it falls away and burns up. In the heady days of Chomsky and GG, there was much research and argument to show that the stage at which LAD falls away is around puberty, though research since then has suggested a much earlier age.

So we all have an innate, and very powerful, language-learning machine – the LAD. The obvious question is: why don't we use it for foreign language acquisition? Perhaps in fact we can: as long as the acquisition takes place *before* puberty – before the LAD rocket stage has fallen off and burned up. But the clear and devastating argument against the use of LAD for foreign language learning is that it cannot help in the very situation which most of us are interested in: language learning *after* puberty. Or is the argument so devastating? What happens if we change our metaphor and view LAD not as a rocket stage falling away but as a piece of machinery that, having done its job, has fallen into disuse and simply 'gone rusty'? If this is the case, then perhaps there is some way in which we can 'oil' LAD back into operation for the purpose of foreign language learning.

But how do you lubricate a rusty LAD? What does this metaphor actually imply? An answer that language teaching since the 1960s has explored is to try, as far as possible, to recreate in the FL classroom the conditions which are present when the learner's L1 is acquired. Perhaps if these conditions are recreated, the LAD will be able to do its job yet again. Notice the words 'as far as possible.' They are important because a classroom can never, of course, simulate all the conditions which are present in natural acquisition (the point was made in CW4.4). Everyone accepts that. But supposing we decided that the best way to use classroom time was to simulate *to the restricted extent possible* what happens in acquisition, what would we do in class? What, in other words, would we need to do in the classroom to make it a place where acquisition can happen? You have already been asked to think about this (in Box 5.12). But perhaps before we look at how language teaching has answered this question over the past few decades, we need to remind ourselves of what we know about language acquisition, and of the conditions that are present when it takes place.

B9.4 Revisiting acquisition

Remind yourself of important aspects of language acquisition (for both L1 and FL) by going back to Chapter 5. Look first at the section entitled 'Language providers and their input' (5.2), and revisit the things caretakers do and do not do. What is the Input Hypothesis (5.2.3)? And the 'silent period' (5.2.4)?

Then consider interaction (5.3). What are the important characteristics of the way in which language providers interact with language acquirers? What is NfM? Now take a look at the section dealing with language acquirer output. What is fossilization? Why does it happen? How might it be avoided?

Finally, remind yourself of the distinction we came across first in 5.2.1, and then again in 6.6.3 – between form- and message-focus. Look back and check what was said about the distinction in those chapters.

Several interesting suggestions for oiling LAD were put forward in the 1960s, and to illustrate the lines along which applied linguists were thinking, we shall take a brief look at a 1968 paper by Newmark and Reibel. Their starting point is the idea that L1 and FL learning are not substantially different. They observe that we already have a highly successful way of 'teaching' children their L1, evidenced by the fact that all normal children succeed in learning it. Why then do we not use this 'way of teaching' for an FL, rather than replacing it with 'unnatural' methods that have a very poor success rate? It is a mistake, in short, to give up a way of teaching which we *know* works for children, for one which *might* work for adults. We should instead try somehow to recreate in the FL classroom what happens for L1 learning. The LAD will then do its work.

For Newmark and Reibel an important feature of the L1 situation is that the language the child receives is 'structurally random.' In conventional FL teaching there is usually finely tuned structural control. This means that in the lesson the teacher restricts their language to those grammar items they know the learners are familiar with. But as we saw in 5.2.1, caretaker talk is not finely tuned in the same way; 'there is no syllabus document', we said, 'lurking in the nursery cupboard.' In this sense the child's exposure to the language is 'structurally random.'

Newmark and Reibel's arguments lead them away from the rigidly controlled grammatical teaching of AL, towards a loosening of the grammatical reins in the FL classroom – in other words, not controlling the grammatical content of lessons in the way that many teachers have been taught to do. As Newmark says elsewhere (1963: 217): 'the whole question of the utility of grammatical analysis for language teaching needs to be reopened.' The very idea must have come as a shock in a language teaching world still dominated by AL. Their suggestion is that structurally organized teaching should be replaced by teaching which is organized around 'situations' rather than structures. As we shall see in the following pages, the idea of organizing language teaching around something other than structures was a highly influential one which took many forms. Box 9.5 describes one.

B9.5 Parent power at work in St Lambert, Montreal

The 'St Lambert experiment' is an example of parent power. It started in 1963 when a group of twelve parents met 'to discuss what they considered a lamentable situation in the local school system' (Lambert and Tucker 1972: 220). Children from an English-speaking background were going through the system 'with little more knowledge of French than their parents had had.' In a country committed to bilingualism, this was considered unacceptable by the parents.

Their idea to begin an 'immersion programme' was met with a good deal of scepticism. Here is what the Association of Catholic Principals of Montreal said: 'we are of the opinion that the average child cannot cope with two languages of instruction and to try to do so leads to insecurity, language interference, and academic retardation' (Lambert and Tucker 1972: 5). But thanks to the parents' persistence and the support of experts at McGill University in Montreal, the project got under way. The first class of English-speaking children to be taught in French was set up in 1965.

Lambert and Tucker's description of the experiment includes the comments of one Mme Benoite Noble, an experienced teacher from France, who attended classes. Here is how she describes what was happening by grade 5:

the children read very well, with practically no accent. When they speak, an English accent is apparent and they make grammatical mistakes that

> a French-speaking child would not. They answer orally questions asked about the reading, and then answer other questions in writing.
>
> (Lambert and Tucker 1972: 241)
>
> Overall, 'the teachers speak French all the time; they like, are even enthusiastic about their work; they are competent, experienced elementary school teachers, not second-language specialists' (p. 242).
>
> Before you read the following paragraphs, think about what the values of immersion programmes might be. And possible disadvantages?

The St Lambert experiment was counted a great success, and it was the first of a large number of immersion programmes in Canada. In fact, Brinton *et al.* (2003) report that by 1987 no fewer than 240,000 Canadian children were participating in bilingual immersion programmes. These spread to the United States in the early 1970s (the first being a Spanish Immersion Programme in Culver City, California), and in the 1980s there were more than 25 such programmes in the US, teaching a variety of languages.

What is the 'Big Idea' behind bilingual immersion programmes? It is that the main focus of attention in the teaching is not on language but on the other subjects in the curricula that are being taught *through* the FL. Language is acquired in an almost 'incidental' way. So what appears to be 'subject teaching' can in fact be language teaching. This has interesting implications for language teaching progammes or syllabuses. Imagine that you were one of the concerned parents described in Box 9.5. You ask to see the programme being followed by your child in the immersion programme. The piece of paper you receive does not list sentence patterns nor any other language-related items. It is not really a language-teaching syllabus at all. Instead, what it lists are the topics to be covered under the subject headings – history, geography and so on. We might say that the programme or syllabus is expressed in 'other-than-linguistic' terms. The phrase well captures the incidental nature of language learning in bilingual education.

9.5   The shift from 'how' to 'what'

This is the moment to make explicit some connections between what we have just been discussing and some concepts introduced in earlier sections of this book. A further dimension to the 'other-than-linguistic' idea relates to the distinction – by now familiar to you – between form- and message-focus. How is that distinction relevant here? Well, teaching English through other subjects is one way of creating message-focus. The learner's attention is focused on history or geography, and not on how the language operates. Message-focus is, we saw in 5.2, a characteristic of L1 acquisition. Its presence seems to be important for making LAD work. So any attempt to 'oil' LAD back into service is likely to involve trying to create message-focus in the classroom. This is why the pursuit of message-focus is something that has been sought one way or another in most approaches to language teaching in the past few decades. We could indeed say that one of the great changes that has occurred in language teaching over the past 50 years is a move from form-focused methods like AL (where the emphasis is on *how* to say things in the FL) to the kind of message-focus found in immersion programmes (where the emphasis is on *what* is being said in the FL). The shift is from *how* to *what*.

What has just been said explains why the idea of message-focus is going to make its presence felt regularly in the following pages. But what about form-focus? Is that idea going to disappear? The answer is no, and the reason is to do with fossilization and the *Fish-and-Chips Syndrome* we discussed in 5.4.2, and again in 6.6.3. It was suggested there that if the FL learner's full attention is on conveying messages, they will develop the habit of doing this without giving a thought to correctness. The result will be the emergence of a kind of pidgin language, which will become fossilized because it is doing its job (of conveying messages) and therefore need not develop. This thought has led applied linguists to realize that although we do indeed need to make language teaching message-focused, we need also to find ways of introducing elements of form-focus into it. This is another of the Big Themes of language teaching in the past few decades – how to combine elements of form- and message-focus. You have in fact already seen two attempts to do just that, in CW6.3 and CW6.4. Take a look now at CW9.3 (*CBI*). It describes a way in which immersion programmes have developed in recent times. It is called <u>content-based instruction</u>, or CBI for short. You will notice once again that although message-focus is centre stage, form-focus is not ignored.

These ideas, and the terminology associated with them, will resurface later in the chapter. But first we need to return to the 'sociolinguistic revolution', as we described it in 3.3. You may like to go back to that chapter and remind yourself of how in the early 1970s the emphasis given in linguistics to grammar was replaced by an interest in 'language in use.' Hymes's (1970) paper 'On communicative competence' was mentioned (3.3.1), with its exploration of the notion of 'the appropriate' as an important dimension in language studies. The effect of this 'revolution' on language teaching was indeed dramatic.

9.6 Notional/functional

In a paper published in 1966, Newmark expresses the discontent which language teachers were feeling towards the structure-oriented AL teaching of that time. The result of this teaching, Newmark says, is a learner who may be entirely 'structurally competent', yet who is unable to perform even the simplest communicative task. This type of learner will know their grammar well, and will be able to produce structurally correct sentences without problems. But deposit them at an airport in the target language country, and they may not know how to ask for a taxi, or request simple services. Newmark's amusing example of the 'structurally competent' but 'communicatively incompetent' learner is the one who wants to ask for a light from a stranger in the street – not something that happens much in many countries nowadays, but common enough in the smoky 1960s. There are various sentences that they might use, and Newmark suggests three. Notice that although these sentences are entirely inappropriate, and would never be used by a native speaker, they are nevertheless perfectly grammatically correct. They are: *Have you fire?*, *Do you have illumination?* and *Are you a match's owner?* No grammatical mistakes here; but no one would ever use these sentences.

What is the solution to the problem of the structurally competent but communicatively incompetent learner? One answer (though not in fact the one explored by Newmark) is related to the field of syllabus design, and is associated with the work of an organization known as the Council of Europe. This organization has as part of its brief the unenviable task of fostering cooperation among member states in Western Europe; a little like trying to herd cats, perhaps. In the early 1970s their Council for Cultural Co-operation brought together a team of language teaching experts to look at the possibility of developing language teaching systems for the teaching of all member-state languages. The team confronted the sociolinguistic insights of writers like Hymes, and was responsible for the development of a type of syllabus which aimed to cater for the teaching of language in use – of communicative competence. In his 1973 paper, one member of the team, Wilkins, developed categories which might be used for a new type of syllabus oriented towards communicative competence. The two most important of these categories are illustrated in Box 9.6.

B9.6 New categories for new syllabuses

Here are some examples of Wilkins' two main category types. Can you see how these category types differ? Attempt to describe each and say what sort of 'item' each contains.

Category Type 1	Category Type 2
past time	greeting
frequency	inviting
dimension	making plans
location	expressing gratitude
quantity	complaining

Decide whether each of the following is a Type 1 or Type 2 category:

* *introducing yourself*
* *possibility*
* *futurity*
* *asking for information*

Wilkins called Category Type 1 above 'semantico-grammatical', and Type 2 'categories of communicative function.' Semantico-grammatical categories, or <u>notions</u> as they came to be almost universally called, are what we might in everyday English describe as 'concepts.' The functional categories, or <u>functions</u>, are what in everyday English we might call 'uses' of the language. They have something in common with the concept of 'speech acts' introduced in 3.3.2. *Possibility* and *futurity* in Box 9.6 are notions; *introducing yourself* and *asking for information* are functions.

The thinking behind the Council of Europe's work was that notions and functions would form the basis for syllabuses that listed concepts and uses, rather than (initially at least) grammatical structures. This in turn would lead to a type of teaching in which each lesson would deal not with a structure but with a 'concept' or 'use.' Box 9.7 shows how a functional textbook might be organized:

B9.7 What a functionally organized textbook looks like

Here is part of the contents page from a functionally organized textbook, by Johnson and Morrow (1979). This shows what functional areas will be covered in the first nine teaching units:

1. Talking about yourself
2. Meeting people
3. Asking about things
4. Asking for things
5. Inviting
6. Making arrangements
7. Asking the way
8. Asking for help
9. Asking for permission

Think about what language items might appear in each of these units. In which unit might Newmark's *asking for a light* be covered?

Have you ever come across a textbook organized in a similar way?

It may well be that Unit 4 in Box 9.7's textbook, *asking for things* (or *requesting services* as it might be called more formally), would cover the function of *asking for a light*. This is where you would teach your students how to – and how not to! – ask for a light. The syllabus as a whole shows how Newmark's problem might be solved. It provides, in effect, a vehicle for teaching learners how to 'be appropriate' – how to be communicatively competent.

The development of the notional/functional (n/f) syllabus had quite a dramatic effect on language teaching syllabuses in the 1970s, and a large number of textbooks in the 1970s and 1980s were based on notional/functional syllabuses. We shall look in much more detail at this syllabus type in 11.3.

9.7   Communicative methodology

The sociolinguistic revolution also left its mark on classroom techniques or 'methodology', and contributed significantly to what is commonly called communicative methodology (often abbreviated to CM). Part of that methodology came about as a consequence of the new syllabus types. It may sound odd to suggest that syllabuses should affect techniques – after all, you might say, syllabuses deal with the *what* of language teaching, and techniques with the *how*. But actually 'how we teach' and 'what we teach' can be intimately connected. Consider the portion of a functional syllabus in Box 9.7 for example. Unit 5 covers *inviting*. How can you practise *inviting* in the classroom? Drills of the sort associated with AL can play a part. But quite soon you are going to have to say something like this to your learners: 'Pretend that you are not in a classroom at all, but are walking down a street. You meet a friend you haven't seen for a long time. You want to invite him out for a meal. What do you say?' The exercise type you are involved in here is known as role play. In role play exercises, learners act out parts in a small-scale scenario specifically set up to practise chosen functions. Role play became an important technique in CM, almost as a direct result of n/f syllabuses and the aspects of language they focus on. We will look at role play (and an associated technique – simulation) in more detail in 12.5.3, which contains examples of these techniques.

But it is possible to relate aspects of CM back to the sociolinguistic revolution in more general terms than this. Hymes attacked Chomsky for having an over-restricted view of linguistics. As we saw in 3.3, Hymes attempted to elaborate and enrich linguistics by adding extra dimensions to the notion of language competence. These extra dimensions made their way into language teaching partly through the notional and functional categories we have just been discussing. But language teaching methodology in the 1960s was also over-restricted in terms of the small range of skills it covered. The most pervasive of these was the 'skill of being grammatical', which (as we saw in Box 9.2) methods like AL prized above all others. As in linguistics, the extra dimensions added to previous practice by CM relate to communicative skill – the ability to understand messages and to get messages across. Use of the word 'message' twice in the last sentence suggests a way in which these ideas about communication connect with the form/message-focus distinction discussed earlier in this chapter. The distinction is relevant here because an important characteristic of CM is that it tries to create classroom activities where the learners are encouraged to 'understand and express messages.' The development from AL to CM clearly shows the shift from *how* to *what* which we discussed earlier. We shall pursue this theme more fully in Chapters 12 and 13, and we will see specific examples there (e.g. in 12.4.3 and 13.3.5) of how the new emphasis on message-focus revealed itself. But just to give a flavour of the kinds of activities CM uses, one example is given in Box 9.8.

B9.8 A short tour round Oxford

The exercise below (from White 1979) practises reading comprehension. The instructions to the learner have been left out. What do you think the exercise involves doing? What is the learner expected to do?

Since the text given in White (1979) is quite long, about half of it has been omitted here; only half the tour, in other words, is described.

Short tour: 1 hour

Begin at Queen's College (39) *on the* **HIGH STREET**. The entrance to Queen's College opens onto the High Street. In style, the buildings of the college are neo-classical and contrast with those of nearby St Edmund Hall, founded in the 13th century. From Queen's, walk up Queen's Lane and turn right into the quadrangle of St Edmund Hall (48), the only remaining medieval hall at Oxford. The domestic scale of the buildings is of interest, giving us some idea of what the original colleges were like.

From St Edmund Hall, *continue along* **QUEEN'S LANE**, noting the ancient church, recently restored and now used as a library, to the right. Follow Queen's Lane where it turns left, passing between Queen's and New Colleges. At the junction of Queen's and New College Lanes, continue straight ahead and turn right into the entrance of New College (31). This college was new in the 14th century when it was founded by William of Wykeham, Bishop of Winchester. The college quadrangle is particularly handsome, while the chapel is one of the finest in Oxford.

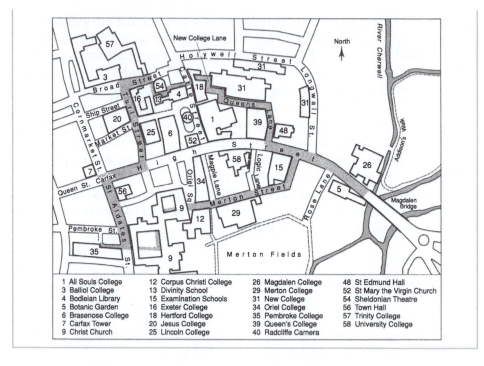

1 All Souls College	12 Corpus Christi College	26 Magdalen College	48 St Edmund Hall
3 Balliol College	13 Divinity School	29 Merton College	52 St Mary the Virgin Church
4 Bodleian Library	15 Examination Schools	31 New College	54 Sheldonian Theatre
5 Botanic Garden	16 Exeter College	34 Oriel College	56 Town Hall
6 Brasenose College	18 Hertford College	35 Pembroke College	57 Trinity College
7 Carfax Tower	20 Jesus College	39 Queen's College	58 University College
9 Christ Church	25 Lincoln College	40 Radcliffe Camera	

The text of White's exercise is from a guide book, and it describes a short tour round Oxford. The numbers in the text refer to numbered places on the map. Learners read the text and follow the route of the tour on the map. They can be asked to mark the route in pencil.

Not so long ago, reading exercises involved going line by line through a text, dwelling on the meaning of every word and structure until 100 per cent comprehension was achieved. White's exercise above is not like this at all. To do it successfully, the learner will not have to understand every word of the text. They need just enough comprehension to fulfil the task of plotting the route on the map. Indeed, there will be very many difficult words that the learner can simply ignore. This is acceptable to modern eyes because we realize that in real life 100 per cent comprehension is rarely required. In fact, what the learner *does* need to be able to do in real life is to concentrate on extracting important pieces of information, ignoring other less important parts of the message, and not worrying too much about unknown, difficult words that are not relevant to the task in hand. The '100 per cent comprehension' school is actually a hindrance here, and in fact it prevents the learner from developing these skills. Exercises like the one in Box 9.8 represent a significant development and enrichment of our idea of what skills are involved in language use.

B9.9 The '100 per cent comprehension' school

I vividly remember an occasion when I used an activity like the one in Box 9.8 with a group of learners who had been taught by the '100 per cent comprehension' method. As soon as they came across an unknown word, they were frozen into inaction and could not continue to read. Unfortunately, in this case, the unknown word came in the title of the passage, so the freezing process occurred early on. The passage was not even embarked upon and remained unread.

Since the activity the learners were doing did not involve 100 per cent understanding of the title, I did what might first appear as a very 'un-teacher-like' thing – I refused to tell them what the difficult word in the title meant. My motive was to encourage them to focus on the passage's overall message rather than on the meaning of individual words. But the result was near revolt. *How can you, a teacher, refuse to tell us what something means? It's a teacher's job to tell us things*, they mumbled in a rebellious and surly fashion.

Perhaps they were right. What do you think? Ponder the arguments for and against what I did (or refused to do!) in this lesson.

Now think more generally about the idea that 'in real life 100 per cent comprehension is rarely required.' Have there been examples when you were abroad where you have been conscious of not having understood very much of the language around you, yet have still been able to 'get by'?

Now to move on. N/f and CM might arguably be described as the European view of 'communicative language teaching' (CLT).[2] Its impetus was the changing perception of language associated with the sociolinguistic revolution – a new answer, in effect, to the question 'what is language?' But there is another question that can be used as the starting point for language teaching innovation. It is: 'How do people learn language?' We have already seen some answers to this question, in sections 9.4 and 9.5. These largely draw inspiration from parallels with L1 acquisition. In the following section, we'll look at how others (particularly in North America) have sought elsewhere for answers to the 'learning question.'

B9.10 'Learner-inspired' and 'language-inspired' methods

Think back over the teaching methods that have so far been mentioned in this book. Make a list. Identify some that have been motivated mainly by the 'how do people learn?' question, and others motivated by the 'what is language?' question.

A warning: do not expect absolutely clear-cut results to your survey. It is natural that some methods should be motivated by both questions, or by some mixture of the two.

9.8 Humanistic approaches

The next group of methods we consider ask the 'learning question.' But unlike others we have looked at, they answer it by appealing (in most cases at least) not to L1 learning but to a set of principles associated with the concept of 'humanism.' The roots of humanism in language teaching are various. A central one is the 'discovery learning' movement, particularly associated with the work of the educational psychologist Jerome Bruner in the 1960s. Discovery learning emphasizes the learner's own activity and enquiry, rather than the transmission of information by the teacher. An applied linguist who relates the principles of humanism to language teaching is Gertrude Moskowitz. The title of her book – *Caring and Sharing in the Foreign Language Class* (1978) – well summarizes the preoccupations of humanistic teaching. At the beginning of this book she expresses the discovery-learning view that the focus of conventional teaching is on 'information transmission', and that humanistic teaching helps learners discover the personal meaning of the information that we provide them with. She goes on to list the principles of humanism, including the following: learner achievement of their full potential; striving for personal as well as cognitive growth; recognition of the important role of feelings; and understanding the significance of self-discovery for learning.

B9.11 But what does it mean?

Another influential book in this area is Stevick's *Memory, Meaning and Method* (1976). It is worth pondering the book's last sentence, which says a lot about humanism in language teaching: 'Of the three subjects of this book, Memory is a by-product of Meaning, and Method should be the servant of Meaning, and Meaning depends on what happens inside and between people' (p. 160).

But what does this mean? Try to explain what Stevick is saying here about how his three main concepts – memory, meaning and method – relate to each other. A version is given in Note 3.

What are humanistic approaches like? The Silent Way, Total Physical Response and Dogme are three of the best known. CW9.4 (*A Rough Guide to some Humanistic Approaches*) describes these.

9.9   Task-based teaching

We have already discussed the idea of LAD lubrication at some length, especially in 9.4. We return to it now to see how it led towards an approach to language teaching which is very popular, even dominant, today – task-based teaching, or TBT for short. We begin by looking at some work which represents a particularly coherent attempt to simulate key aspects of acquisition in the classroom.

9.9.1   The procedural syllabus

Prabhu is an applied linguist who worked in Southern India. In the late 1970s his concern to improve English language teaching in the region led him to find out about CLT and the n/f syllabus. He came to the conclusion that while this movement was adding a valuable new (sociolinguistic) dimension to language teaching, it was not doing much to tackle the problem India faced – that structure-based language teaching was failing to teach structures! His thinking led him to undertake an experiment in language teaching often referred to as the 'Bangalore experiment.'

Prabhu's starting point is an answer to the 'learning question.' It is the idea – at first sight paradoxical – that the best way to teach grammatical structures is to focus not on the structures themselves but on 'meaning' or 'message.' If, the argument goes, classroom activities succeed in concentrating learners' minds on *what* is being said (message) rather than on *how* it is being said (form), then ultimately the structures will become absorbed.

You are by now well familiar with the distinction between form- and message-focus, and may already be asking how Prabhu's approach differs from others which show the *how* to *what* shift we referred to earlier in this chapter (9.5). The novelty lies in where the distinction leads Prabhu. The next stage in his argument is to claim that you cannot really focus on meaning if you are at the same time following a language syllabus. How can you expect your learners to concentrate on *what* is being said if your syllabus dictates that you should on that day be practising a certain tense? To give an example: you might decide to practise the simple past tense with your learners by asking them on a Monday morning to tell you what they *did* at the weekend. The chances are that the learners will recognize that you are not really interested in their message (what they actually did at the weekend) but on their grammar (using the simple past tense). 'Pretending to ask about message when you're really interested in form' is, Prabhu claims, a fruitless as well as a deceiving practice. Box 9.12 gives another example:

B9.12 Ten o'clock? Is that so good?

Woodward (2001: 5) gives this example of a teacher/student dialogue:

T: What's the time now?
S: It's ten o'clock.
T: Good!

'Why', Woodward asks, 'is it a good thing that it's ten o'clock?'
What's the answer to Woodward's question? Why on earth does the teacher say 'Good'?

The teacher's answer in Box 9.12 relates of course to the form, not the content, of the student's message. They are saying to the student 'you gave a good answer', rather than 'it's good that it's ten o'clock.' Form-focus masquerading as message-focus is a practice much followed even in approaches which claim to recognize the importance of message-focus. CM, for example, sees the value of message-focus. But often, as we will see later in 12.4.3, it tries to create message-focus while practising structures.

Prabhu's thinking leads him to devise a language teaching programme which does not list the language items that his course will cover. He has instead a programme, or syllabus, of tasks. This task-based syllabus tells the teacher what kinds of activities they will be doing in class each day, but not what language items will come up. The idea is that whatever language necessary to do the task will be used, and over time this language will be unconsciously absorbed. In addition to this, Prabhu's teachers model themselves on the L1 caretakers we met in 5.2, largely avoiding the kinds of activities (like drilling and error correction) that caretakers do not use.

B9.13 What would you expect?

The following paragraph briefly describes what happened in the Bangalore experiment. Before reading this, think about what *you* would expect to happen if you taught in such a way. What would be the consequences of avoiding drilling and error correction? What about the idea of not having a language syllabus, but allowing whatever language is necessary for an activity to be used? What kind of benefits would you expect? What kind of problems would you predict? What kind of learners would you produce?

Prabhu experimented with what is sometimes called the <u>procedural</u>, or task-based, syllabus over a number of years in India, first with intermediate learners and then with beginners. What happened? Well, at first the children had severe problems with the lessons, largely due to unfamiliarity. They had never come across classes like that before. But gradually the pupils began to come to terms with the new approach, and when it was formally evaluated, in Beretta and Davies (1985), the results showed some advantages to this way of teaching. There are of course problems. As you might expect from our earlier discussions on the *Fish-and-Chips Syndrome*, 'naturalistic' approaches like this tend to result in pidgin-like language which, in the absence of any stimulus to improve, soon fossilizes. You can read about another approach, quite similar to Prabhu's, in CW9.5 (*The 'Natural Approach'*).

Perhaps you have by now seen connections between Prabhu's procedural syllabus and the bilingual immersion programmes we spoke about earlier. It is worth making the connection explicit. In relation to bilingual education, the phrase 'syllabus in other-than-linguistic terms' was used (in 9.4) to describe the incidental nature of language learning in the approach. The programme or syllabus being followed in bilingual teaching would be stated in terms of subjects (history, geography and so on), not language items. Prabhu's syllabus is also stated in 'other-than-linguistic' terms. The only difference is that Prabhu's lessons do not revolve round subject areas, but round tasks or activities. His is a task-based syllabus.

There is another piece of terminology which also describes Prabhu's syllabus. The phrase, used by Breen (1983), is 'syllabus of means.' Most conventional syllabuses, Breen says, are syllabuses of 'ends.' That is, they are lists of the items that are to be taught. Although structural and notional/functional syllabuses differ from each other in important respects, they are both syllabuses of 'ends' – the structures, notions, functions listed are what is being taught. Prabhu's syllabus does not list ends. It is important to understand that it is not the aim of the teaching to increase the learners' proficiency in doing tasks. These tasks are not an end in themselves. They are means – vehicles for teaching something that is given no mention at all on the syllabus: language. They are pegs on which to hang language.

9.9.2 TBT: some developments and some questions

How has TBT developed since Prabhu's procedural syllabus? Task-based teaching has become a subject of keen contemporary interest, and different task-based approaches exist today. Some differ substantially from Prabhu's, often not being based so centrally on the parallel with L1 acquisition. But one underlying principle holds for all the approaches – to place the emphasis firmly on activities or tasks that learners do in class. It is possible that the late 1990s and following will be known in applied linguistics as 'The Age of the Task.'

But what exactly is a task? We saw an example of one in Chapter 1's Classroom 5 (section 1.5). In the lesson, which took place in Beijing, the learners were put together in pairs and asked to select a holiday for themselves, based on information they were given. You may recall that the learners became very engaged in the task, which involved plenty of NfM, and it took much longer to do than the teacher expected. This 'choosing a holiday' activity has the five characteristics of a task discussed by Wesche and Skehan (2002). The first is that in a task, *meaning is primary*. This does not imply that form is necessarily ignored, and it may be that the teacher in Beijing decides to inject some form-based work into his lesson – he might decide to introduce and practise some vocabulary items, for example. But the prime focus is on holiday selection. Second, there should be *a communication problem to solve*. The learners need to communicate in the FL to solve the task's problem. In the case of Classroom 5 this happens because the learners work in pairs; they need to 'negotiate' their choice through communication with each other. Wesche and Skehan's third characteristic is that there should be some sort of *relationship with real-world activities*. This is regarded as particularly important by Long (1985) who characterizes tasks as 'the things people will tell you they do if you ask them and they are not applied linguists.' So Long identifies activities like making an airline reservation or buying a pair of shoes as tasks, since they are things which people really do. Our activity fits well into this, because people often spend time discussing holiday choice, with either friends or family. The fourth characteristic is that *task completion has some priority*. This means that the way the task is presented to the learners should emphasize that the aim is to reach a conclusion, rather than simply practise the language for the sake of it. Finally, Wesche and Skehan say that *assessment of the task is in terms of outcomes*. The learners will be judged (even perhaps assessed) not primarily in terms of how many grammar mistakes have been made, or even how well the learners have expressed themselves, but on whether the holiday choice is actually made. The word 'primarily' is important here. The Beijing teacher may well take note of grammar mistakes and draw attention to them at some point, but not in a way that detracts from the essential message-focus of the activity.[4]

Given the recent amount of interest in tasks, it is not surprising that a number of ways of classifying tasks should have emerged. Jane Willis's book, *A Framework for Task-Based Learning* (1996), identifies six task types. You can find these in CW9.6 (*Six task types*), which contains an activity matching example activities with task types.

As we saw earlier, an important characteristic of Prabhu's version of TBT is the recreation of the message-focused nature of acquisition. He is also guided by what we know that language providers do and don't do when they give input. But other versions of TBT find their rationale in different aspects of acquisition or learning. Indeed, the question 'Why TBT?' is likely to receive as many answers as there are practitioners. CW9.7 (*TBT: reasons and realizations*) mentions three of the most common answers. It also looks at some of the various ways that TBT has been realized in language classrooms.

We may say that TBT is today a 'work in progress' – still developing, still finding questions it needs to answer. What are the 'burning issues' in TBT today? Here are three:

B9.14 Burning issues in TBT

1. We have already seen that although in tasks 'meaning is primary', a degree of form-focus is often involved. Indeed, many see this as a necessity if fossilization is to be avoided (think of fish and chips yet again). But how can form-focus be introduced in a way that ensures meaning remains 'primary'? Take a look at the framework Willis (1996) proposes, in CW9.6. How does form-focus make its way into that model? Can you think of other ways a focus on form can be introduced into a task (you might find it useful to concentrate on one task here – the 'choosing a holiday' task perhaps)?

2. Now, here is a deceptively simple question: what makes some tasks harder than others? Try to draw up a list of characteristics which will contribute to task complexity. And (again, deceptively simple?): why might it be useful for teachers to know which tasks the learners will find easy, and which difficult? How might that information be used?

3. One of the characteristics of tasks that has been researched is pre-task planning. Stay with the 'choosing a holiday' task. Imagine that you give your class some time to prepare for the activity. What effect would you expect this preparation time to have on their performance of it? Would it lead to improved performance? If so, try to say as specifically as possible what kinds of improvements you might expect.

What do applied linguists have to say about these burning issues? Several ways of introducing form-focus have been discussed. One mentioned by Wesche and Skehan (2002) is Samuda's. She suggests that it should be possible to 'seed' tasks with language features – ensuring that specific structures are salient, and hence likely to be noticed. This could be done, Samuda argues, while still maintaining the naturalness of the task (Samuda 2001). Another mentioned in the same source is Long's idea that if a task involves NfM that will in itself lead learners to focus on form, asking themselves, and perhaps the teacher, questions about how things are done in the FL. H. Johnson's solution (1992) tries to develop tasks which will 'stretch' the learners' language, and she allows time spent on form-focused activity (such as looking for vocabulary items, for example) as part of the task itself.

There has also been quite a lot of discussion on what makes tasks difficult or easy to do. Take a characteristic like 'familiarity of information', for example. Presumably if a task involves topics and information which are well known to the learners and within their sphere of interest, they will find the task easier. If on the other hand the task introduces unfamiliar material, the learners will find the task difficult and even, perhaps, stressful. Other features whose influence have been researched in this way are how the task is structured and exactly what kind of outcome is required. One reason why these questions are important is that their answers help us to develop a notion of task grading – a first step, one might suppose, towards developing a graded 'syllabus of tasks.' Syllabuses and grading are a main topic of 11.2.

The effects of pre-task planning have attracted a lot of research interest (and there is indeed an entire book on the matter – Ellis's *Planning and Task Performance in a Second Language*, 2005). Much of the research shows that planning time leads learners to be more adventurous in their task performance, using more complex language. They also become more fluent. Other research has looked at the effect of giving a post-task. A study by Skehan and Foster (1997), for example, suggests that if learners are told in advance that they will have to repeat a task in front of the class, this has some effect on accuracy in doing the initial task itself. Bygate (1996 and 2001, for example) has done a number of studies looking at what happens when learners are asked to repeat a task. Usually there is some improved performance second time round.

And where does the future lie? The 'Age of the Task' is certainly not yet over, and TBT is likely to continue opening up exciting new dimensions for language teaching. *New* dimensions? Remember Kelly at the beginning of this chapter? Who knows? It might turn out that among the obscurer works of Aristotle is a treatise entitled *In Defence of TBT and NfM*. Written in Classical Greek, of course.

9.10   Post-method pedagogy

Methods, methods, methods. This chapter is full of them. You might like to make a mental list of the ones that have been mentioned. But do we need methods? They can certainly provide coherence and theoretical justification to what teachers do in class. But there are disadvantages too. What are these? Before reading on, you might like to think of reasons why adoption of one method – for example in an entire country, for all teachers and learners – might not be a good idea.

In recent decades, a number of applied linguists have moved towards what has been called <u>post-method pedagogy</u>. The titles of two papers appearing in the 1990s say what this is all about. One is by Prabhu (1990), entitled 'There is no best method – why?' The other, Allwright (1991), really does say it all. The title is 'The death of the method.' Post-method pedagogy has been developed and elaborated by Kumaravadivelu, particularly in his 2006 book.

You may remember that in Chapter 3 (3.3.1), when we introduced the notion of communicative competence, we came across Hymes' criticism of Chomskyan linguistics. He called it a 'Garden of Eden view.' Methods too have a touch of the Garden of Eden about them. They are abstract and idealized concepts, developed by applied linguists largely in relation to theories, and heavily based on a world of 'should be' rather than the world as it is. But, important as abstract and idealized concepts may be, language teaching is an activity that involves people – particularly teachers and learners – living in real contexts. To be successful, one might argue, teaching must be sensitive to what teachers, learners, and contexts are like.

Thinking about teachers first: at the beginning of this chapter we talked about the 'secret life of methods', and how teachers frequently modify the methods they are supposed to follow. There is a tendency for Ministries of Education, and their teacher trainers, to regard such modifications as unacceptable. 'You should follow the communicative approach' (or direct method, or natural approach, or whatever the favoured method is), teachers might be told. Indeed a teacher may face dire consequences if they fail to adhere to the favoured method. But there is another way of looking at the teacher deviations. Teachers, you might argue, develop great expertise through long experience. When they deviate from the favoured method, they are often improving on rather than detracting from what goes on in class. To put this argument the other way round, we may say that methods can sometimes be like straitjackets, preventing teachers from utilizing their expertise where this does accord with what the recommended method dictates.

Methods can be straitjackets for learners too. As we saw in Chapter 7, learners are very different from one another, and the good language learner studies highlight these differences. 'There are many ways of skinning the language learning cat' was how we put it in the first sentence of the present chapter. How can one method, you might ask, deal with all these individual differences and different learning styles? Not just teachers, but learners too, will benefit from deviating from fixed methods.

Then there are contexts. A method that works well in Britain – and was perhaps developed by British applied linguists – may not work so well in Pakistan, or Chile, or Russia, where the cultural and educational contexts will be quite different. One might even see the imposition of an approach to learning developed in one country as a form of cultural imperialism when applied in other parts of the world.

These, in sketchy outline, are the arguments against language teaching that is too firmly method-based. But, you might wonder, won't 'methodless language teaching' end up in chaotic eclecticism, allowing teachers to do whatever comes into their head, without any principle? Whatever your view, perhaps we should look in some detail at the contexts in which language teaching take place. This is the subject of the next chapter.

Notes

1. In order to provide a short, 'self-contained' example, this one has been invented.
2. 'Arguably' because the term communicative language teaching has been used in very many different ways by applied linguists, and there is no agreement over its proper use. Indeed, Howatt (1984: 279) distinguishes two separate (and quite different) versions of CLT, which

he calls 'weak' and 'strong.' The weak version is what is being described here, where learners are being trained in communicative skills through exercises of the sort illustrated in 9.6. The strong version is much closer to Prabhu's procedural teaching, described in 9.9.1, where the claim is that communication is learned through the actual process of communicating.

Certainly some applied linguists will feel that notional/functional syllabuses are a development that should be kept separate from CLT.

3. Stevick is saying that meaningfulness is what makes things memorable, and hence learned. So the aim of methods should be to 'make meaningful.' Meaningfulness comes by thinking about people and how they relate to each other.

4. You have probably asked yourself how much the 'choosing a holiday' task is different from the kinds of communicative activities found in CM. You may also have noticed that the characteristics of the tasks listed here are very similar indeed to the characteristics of the communicative activities applied linguists were describing in the early 1980s. The similarities cannot, and should not, be denied because they clearly signal that TBT comes out of CLT. Note 2 above makes the point that there are very many different versions of CLT, some being called 'strong' and others 'weak.' Some would regard TBT as a 'strong' version of CLT. But the rationales for the two approaches are not always similar. CW9.7 asks 'why TBT?' The first answer would apply to CLT, but the second and third not so clearly.

Issues to think or write about

1. In 9.2, you were given seven questions to ask to help identify important characteristics of a method. Ask these questions about a method, or perhaps just a textbook, that you are familiar with. Discuss what the answers to your questions reveal about the method or textbook. If you are familiar with more than one method, or textbook, compare how they relate in terms of the answers to the seven questions.

2. In Box 9.2, you we given a framework for a lesson teaching the present perfect tense using 'just' and 'yet.' Prepare a similar framework for another structural point involving two words which learners often find difficult – 'since' and 'for' – and how they differ in phrases like 'since last week' and 'for two days.' If you are not sure about the use of these two words, consult a grammar book. Prepare your framework in as much detail as you can, including thinking of example sentences and the actual procedures you would use in class.

Or as an alternative: in Box 9.8, you saw an activity in which learners read the description of a tour and mark the route on a map. Think of another activity which involves reading something and transferring information from it into some other medium – which might be another map, or a diagram, or a table or something similar. Plan your activity in detail, thinking about exactly how you would use it in class.

Further reading

Howatt, A. P. R., with Widdowson, H. G. 2004 *A History of English Language Teaching* Oxford: Oxford University Press
This is, with good reason, the standard history of ELT.

Richards, J. C., and Rodgers, T. S. 2001 *Approaches and Methods in Language Teaching*, 2nd edn Cambridge: Cambridge University Press
As well as providing coverage of most of the methods mentioned in this chapter, this book also explains the distinction between *approach* and *method*.

Brumfit, C. J., and Johnson, K. (eds) 1979 *The Communicative Approach to Language Teaching* Oxford: Oxford University Press
A collection of papers dealing with the background to CLT. The introductory section includes excerpts from Hymes' paper, 'On communicative competence.'

Prabhu, N. S. 1987 *Second Language Pedagogy: A Perspective* Oxford: Oxford University Press
Provides a detailed account of the Bangalore experiment and its theoretical background.

Carter, R., and Nunan, D. (eds) 2001 *The Cambridge Guide to Teaching English to Speakers of Other Languages* Cambridge: Cambridge University Press
This contains 32 chapters (written by different authors), dealing with a wide range of topics related to the practice of language teaching. It is relevant to all chapters in Part 3 of this book.

10 Contexts

10.1 Introduction

B10.1 Language teaching and politics

One of the points that will be made in this chapter is that language teaching has a political side to it. Before reading the chapter, think what this might mean. What aspects of the language teaching operation might be regarded as political?

Those who are new to the language teaching profession may (for a short while!) believe that becoming a good language teacher is only a question of equipping yourself with a good knowledge of the target language, learning how to conduct the sorts of activity which go on in classrooms, as well as acquiring more general teaching skills to do with managing classrooms and the people in them.

These aspects of language teaching are of course very important. But something that may not be immediately apparent to novice teachers is that language teaching has a social and even a political side to it. These aspects will be particularly important to the teacher who is a native speaker of the target language and who plans to go abroad to teach that language, perhaps to a culture that is entirely different from their own. They will find that there is an immense amount to learn about becoming a 'good' teacher that has nothing to do with nouns and verbs, or drills, or keeping discipline in class. But even teachers who are working within their own country, generally teaching a language that is not their own L1, will benefit from a realization that teaching a language is a social, and even a political, act. As Stern (1983: 284) puts it: 'language teaching can be looked upon as a deliberate intervention into ethnolinguistic relations which can be planned more or less efficiently and which, in this way, can contribute to the bilingualism of a society.'

In this chapter we shall look at language teaching as it operates within a society. We shall begin by thinking about aspects of what is called 'foreign language planning' – the decisions made by a society about language teaching. These decisions can be made at a governmental, local or institutional level. They are perhaps unlikely to be made (yet, at least) by those reading this introductory book. Nevertheless, teachers operating within the society will be better at their job if they understand why and how these decisions are made.

We shall then focus on one issue related to language planning which is currently attracting much attention – the role of <u>English as an International Language</u> (abbreviated to EIL) or, as it has become in its most recent incarnation, <u>English as a Lingua Franca</u> (ELF). Then finally in this chapter we shall concentrate on questions of more direct relevance to individual teachers. These are largely to do with 'appropriate methodologies' – ensuring that the way we teach is in line with what is accepted within the society in which we work. A major aim of this chapter is to raise your awareness of how teaching practices have a social dimension.

10.2 Language planning

10.2.1 Some questions language planners ask

Language planning is a large area which deals, on an 'official' level, with the language problems of a society. Have a look at CW10.1 (*Some language planning questions*) which lists some general language planning issues.

One of the questions in CW10.1 is about foreign language planning, asking which foreign languages should be taught in the society. It is not difficult to find examples in the history of language teaching where there has been bad foreign language planning, or even none at all. It might be said (though not everyone would agree) that continuing to give such importance to Latin and Greek in Europe during the earlier part of the twentieth century, long after they served any obvious communicative purpose, is an example of bad planning. But as time passes and the world gets smaller, nations are becoming more and more aware that deliberate language teaching policies are required.

What sorts of questions do foreign language planners ask? We shall here look at a few. They will show you that nouns, verbs, drills and discipline are indeed a small part of the overall language learning and teaching picture.

Which languages should be taught? A major consideration will of course be the learners' communication needs. These will in turn depend on whether the main use of the FL is likely to be for international communication, or for communication within the borders of the country. Sometimes there is a political dimension to the issue. In the days of the Soviet Union, for example, many Eastern European countries taught Russian; perhaps not so much for reasons to do with communicative needs, but as a recognition of the existence of a sphere of influence. With the demise of the Soviet Union came widespread replacement of Russian by English as the first FL in that area. But the story is not over yet, because (as Jaworski 1998 notes) Russian is beginning to gain importance again in the area as a *lingua franca* for trading purposes.

Another dimension to the question can be how closely related the L1 and target language are. For example, there are good reasons why languages like Japanese and Chinese should be taught in Western countries at the present time. Both provide a doorway into cultures whose economic influence is now high and is likely to increase in the future. Although there are some signs that these languages are being taught more, they are not as widespread in schools as perhaps their importance warrants. Why not? One reason may well be that the European learners' L1s are so different from Japanese and Chinese. They would be very difficult languages to learn, and an impracticably large amount of time would have to be allocated for teaching them in schools. So they are not taught.

Which 'version' of which language? This is also a question that can generate heated debate. English is a good example. Countries where English is taught as the main FL may have agonized long and hard with one small corner of this problem – whether British or American English should be the norm. The Arabic-speaking Middle East, for example, divides itself into British and American 'camps.' The standard, well-rehearsed arguments are: *for British English* – it is the 'real thing', the proper language, as spoken in the country where the language originated; and *for American English* – English is an international language not because the British use it, but because it is the language of superpower America. Other English-speaking countries are also of course in contention, for good reasons. If you live close to Australia, for example, then it probably makes good sense to use Australian English as your norm.

But does the norm have to be associated with a native-speaking country? What about using a local variety of English as the model? These are questions we will consider in detail in 10.3.

In which order of importance should foreign languages be placed? Many countries find it useful to specify this. So an 'important' Language A might be taught from an earlier age and for more hours weekly, and a 'less important' Language B started later and taught for fewer hours. Again, as well as actual communicative needs, other considerations may be relevant. Stern (1983: 278) gives the example of France, which has Spain, Germany, Italy and Britain among its neighbours. The importance given to Spanish, German, Italian and English in different parts of France reflects this geographical reality. The influence of geography is also illustrated (as Stern again notes) in the Burstall report, which we mentioned in 7.3.1. The report shows that children in the south of England have more positive attitudes towards learning French than those in the north. There are many parts of Scotland that are closer to Norway than they are to France. Indeed, a few are closer to Oslo than to London, but that is another story!

Who learns? is another important question. One provocative argument suggesting the folly of attempting to teach entire populations a language is illustrated in CW10.2 (*Too much English for too many people?*). It is difficult to escape the conclusion that sometimes reasons for language teaching stated in terms of utility actually mask political motivations to do with cultural imperialism. Colonial powers want their language to be taught in colonies, whether there is a need for it or not.

How well? and *How much?* also need to be asked. Until recently, many societies had a simple view of level. Learners strove to attain near-native-speaker standards. But in many situations this is impracticable; there is not enough time for it to be anything like achieved. Indeed, such lofty aims will often be unnecessary, particularly in ESP situations. It is vitally important that airline pilots, for example, should have enough English for the crucial job of communicating properly with air-traffic controllers and others. But what the airline pilot does not have to do with English also needs to be recognized. For example, they do not need to read literature (for professional reasons anyway) or be able to articulate a political argument. Different levels, in different language areas, need to be accepted as aims for different types of learner.

10.2.2 Things foreign language planners need to bear in mind

In order to answer the questions we have been considering, foreign language planners – and the teachers who put their plans into action – need to know a lot about the *context* in which the teaching takes place. Context is all important, and applied linguists who try to make lists of the factors that are relevant to language teaching always include a set called 'contextual.' We need a framework for describing these factors. Stern's framework is shown below. It is in fact an amalgam of two other models, from Spolsky *et al.* (1974) and Mackey (1970).

Contextual factors in language teaching

Stern mentions a number of language teaching situations that can illustrate the relevance of the factors in his model. They are: an English class for adult immigrants; French in a comprehensive school in Great Britain; English in a German primary school; and Spanish in a US high school. Each of these situations occurs within a school environment, and teachers as well as administrators therefore need to know something about the school's policy on language teaching – how much importance is given to it, how it fits into the curriculum, and so on. The school is located within a 'home environment and neighbourhood', and once again the teacher needs to know something about this. An interesting example of how home and neighbourhood background can affect language teaching comes from Burstall's report. Here is one finding from her study of French teaching in Britain: 'for pupils of both sexes in each group of primary schools, high mean scores on the Listening, Reading and Writing tests coincide with high-status parental occupation and low mean scores with low-status parental occupation' (Burstall *et al.* 1974: 24). And again (p. 31): 'children with parents in higher-status occupations receive greater parental support when they approach new learning experiences than do those with parents in lower-status occupations' (both these quotations are cited in Stern 1983).

We have already seen how region affects language teaching in our earlier example of language teaching patterns in the areas of France, according to the neighbouring countries. Burstall again provides some interesting information. In her study, it was consistently found that a high level of achievement in French occurred in small rural schools, not large city ones. We have also seen earlier in this chapter how national and international factors are relevant to language learning.

The outer perimeter of Stern's model shows the six general factors that will influence the teaching. CW10.3 (*Matching variables and examples*) puts some flesh onto these six categories and contains an activity that uses them.

10.2.3 How do you plan foreign language teaching? An initial look

We have looked at various considerations which need to be taken into account when answering the question: how do you plan foreign language teaching? Important as these variables are, when we come to look at the details of foreign language planning, one consideration becomes paramount – the communication needs of learners. To arrive at specific answers to the sort of questions raised in this chapter, we need to find a way of analysing learners' needs. It is the process of needs analysis that will tell us just how much, and for what purposes, our learners will need which foreign languages. We shall look in detail at needs analysis in the next chapter, which focuses on syllabus design. But to illustrate how the process can help with general language planning issues, Box 10.2

contains an example of how one study provided a profile of learner needs that led in the direction of very concrete suggestions for language teaching practice in Holland.

B10.2 Needs in Nijmegen (based on van Els *et al.*'s (1984) description of the work of Claessen and his colleagues in Nijmegen, the Netherlands)

The late 1970s was a time of some upheaval in the Netherlands' language teaching scene, as a result of some changes in educational policy. Some educationalists felt that these changes did not reflect the language needs of the country, and Claessen and his colleagues therefore undertook research to establish what these needs were. Needs were looked at in three ways, in relation to: (a) secondary schools; (b) trade, industry, public administration and tertiary education; and (c) other relevant areas. The researchers produced a list of 24 language use situations, dealing with the areas of leisure, work and education. Here are three items from the list (taken from van Els *et al.* 1984: 168):

- light reading (illustrated periodicals, detective stories);
- writing a short business letter, asking for a report, registering at a congress;
- having a conversation with a colleague or fellow-student on one's own special subject.

The list of situations was given to relevant people – school pupils, staff of companies, government services and many others. They were asked how often these situations would be met for each of the major languages taught. Van Els *et al.* list a number of findings of the research. Here are three:

1. there are different patterns of need for French, German and English. This includes different levels of required proficiency (something that the examination system did not take account of);
2. learners found French more difficult than English or German, and hence many gave it up early at school. This problem might be answered by allocating more time to French than to the other languages;
3. minor needs for other languages – particularly Russian, Spanish and Italian – were revealed. Perhaps these minor needs could be catered for by making available provision outside the school system.

Think about your own country, or a country where you have worked. What do you know about the educational policy as regards FL teaching there? As far as you can tell, does it meet the true language needs of the people?

10.3 English as a global language: from Gandhi to Rushdie

Here, to start, are some statistical questions. The answers might surprise you.

B10.3 What percentages?

What would be your guesses for the answers to these questions:

(1) What percentage of English spoken around the world is between native speakers?
(2) What percentage is between native speakers and non-native speakers?
(3) What percentage is between non-native speakers?

Graddol (2007) provides the answers: for (1) it is 4%; for (2), 22%; and for (3), 74%. It will be useful to keep these figures in mind as you read this section.

Earlier in this book (1.3), we noted that the world is getting smaller. By the day. We now live, as Crystal (2003) puts it, in a global village. This is largely because systems of transport and communication have developed so dramatically. We can now travel to any part of the globe in not much more than a day (assuming easily accessible airports). And we can exchange messages across the world by email faster than we can type them. This means that people with different first languages find themselves increasingly wanting to communicate with each other. A global *lingua franca* is needed.

There are, it is true, some unfortunate consequences to this idea. One danger is that the birth of a global language may lead to the death of little-used, regional ones. People are often shocked to realize that languages, like the world's rain forests, are disappearing at an alarming rate. Crystal (2003: 20) reports that 'at least 50% of the world's 6000 or so living languages will die out within the next century.' This is sad; a language disappearing is like a species becoming extinct.

Another issue is that while a global language has the advantage of allowing international communication, people feel at home with their own 'local' languages, which provide them with a sense of identity. People want to have a language which they can call their own. It will be different from other languages. It will mark their own character, say who they are. This leads many to resist the pull of a global language. Crystal's example of resistance comes from Gandhi: 'to give millions a knowledge of English is to enslave them', he laments. 'Is it not a painful thing that, if I want to go to a court of justice, I must employ the English language as a medium' (2003: 124).

Gandhi is talking about English because when he was writing this (in 1908), English was already well on the path to becoming the global language. It is very much farther along that path today. We can all think of examples in our daily lives of how widespread the use of English has become. One that springs to my mind today as I write is that my teenage son spends time (too much, I say!) playing computer games online. His fellow players come from all round Europe. They have to communicate with each other, and they do so in English.

B10.4 English around you

Think of some examples you have come across of English being used for international communication.

Have you ever sensed any resentment from those whose native language is not English, forced to use it in this way? If your native language is not English, do you yourself feel any resentment?

So globalization increases the necessity for a world *lingua franca*, and English seems to be occupying this role. Why English? One might be tempted to argue, especially if one comes from an English-speaking country, that it is to do with special virtues that the language possesses. Typical virtues often associated with English (by the English!) are that the language avoids complicated grammatical constructions (remember the complex Russian noun and adjectival endings you saw in CW2.3?). It is also often claimed that English has a large and rich vocabulary. But, as Crystal (2003) says, arguments like this are 'misconceived.' He points out that Latin – a major international language in former times – is like Russian in terms of its inflectional complexity. So easy grammar does not seem to be crucial. Much, much more important is power, and with English this springs from two sources. The first is the development of the British Empire, which coloured much of the globe red and let English seep into the red bits. Then, today, there is the status of America as a superpower.

If a global *lingua franca* is required for international communication, it is important, you may argue, that we should all adopt some generally accepted model – a version of English that everyone agrees to take as a standard. It is British and American English that have traditionally played that role, and this naturally gave Native Speakers of English (very much with the capital N and S), great prestige. They were the people who 'knew what the language should sound like.' The world had to copy them. The individual who particularly benefited from this view was the person Medgyes (1994) calls the NEST – the native English-speaker teacher. For many decades, and in many parts of the world, Being A Native Speaker (worthy of capitals again) was the highest qualification a teacher could aspire to – more important than how much training or how much experience they had had. This state of affairs is part of what Holliday (2005) calls 'native-speakerism.'

It would be nice to be able to say that the days of native-speakerism have now gone. This is alas not true, though the arguments against it are being marshalled. Let's look at the case of the NEST first.

B10.5 NESTs and non-NESTs: the dark and bright sides

The title of Medgyes' (1994) book is *The Non-Native Teacher*. In two chapters – entitled 'The bright side of being a non-native' and 'The dark side of being a non-native' – he looks at the advantages and disadvantages of being a non-NEST.

Think about NESTs and non-NESTs, teaching English in a country that you know, where English is not the L1. What advantages and disadvantages will each have – both for the learners and for the teachers?

Medgyes sees many advantages to being a non-NEST. His list includes being more likely to be able to anticipate the difficulties their learners will meet. Also, being from the same culture as the learners, the non-NEST will be more sympathetic to the learners' problems, and will understand their attitudes. Along with this awareness that being a non-NEST has a bright side has come a realization that teaching qualifications and amount of experience are likely to be more reliable indicators of a good teacher than just being a native speaker.

But an awareness of the pros of being a non-NEST is just one reason for the (albeit gradual) wane in native-speakerism. Behind it is also a revised attitude towards what should be the model or standard for English as an International Language (EIL). The Native Speaker has lost their privileged position here too. Here's what Kachru (1983) says: 'the native speakers [of English] seem to have lost the exclusive prerogative to control its standardization.' English is no longer 'owned' by the native speaker. Indeed, the statistics you saw at the beginning of this section (following Box 10.3) show that they are not the majority speakers of it. The ownership is now more general, encompassing all those countries worldwide where English is used. So a change really is taking place. Remember the indignation Gandhi felt that he had to use a foreign language if he wanted to conduct a legal case? Compare this with the attitude of a more recent Indian, the author Salman Rushdie. Kachru shows how Rushdie has 'made English his own.' He 'stands up to English language as an equal', Kachru says, 'and relentlessly plays with its grammar, syntax and spellings until it become pliable enough faithfully to express the way an Indian thinks, feels, talks, laughs, jokes and relates to language' (p. 49). Kachru's book is entitled *The Indianization of English*, and the title says it all. The language Rushdie uses is not the English of an ex-colonial power. It is his own language, the means of expression of an Indian. Here is yet another Indian expressing the same attitude: 'we shall have the English language with us and amongst us, and not as a guest or friend, but as one of our own, of our caste, our creed, our sect and of our tradition' (Rao 1978). This process has occurred not just in India, of course, but in countries over the globe. Along with *Indianization*, one might equally well speak of the *Nigerianization*, or the *Singaporeanization* of English, for example. These <u>world Englishes</u> have almost become dialects of the same original language.[1]

Earlier we spoke of the threat to identity which many see in the development of a global language. People want their own language to express who they are. The shift in attitude – from Gandhi to Rushdie – has partly removed this threat. The world Englishes that are developing may be versions of the same original language, but they are sufficiently different to be able to express the various cultures of those who speak them. But surely, you might think, the more the identity issue is solved, the more acute the intelligibility issue becomes. This is the problem with all dialects. As they develop they become different, and the danger is that they will end up being mutually incomprehensible. When the people of Singapore, Nigeria and India (for example) all accepted the 'native-speaker model' of English, they had no problems understanding each other. But today they no longer accept the model, and we speak not of 'world English' but of 'world Englishes.' As their respective 'dialects' move apart, unintelligibility will surely result.

Or not? Perhaps the danger is exaggerated. McKay (2002) looks in detail at the types of differences that develop between various Englishes, and suggests that though problems of intelligibility do exist, they are not perhaps as serious as one might imagine. As regards vocabulary, for example, context will sometimes, but not always, clarify meaning. McKay's examples are taken from Butler (1999). They include the Thai English expression *minor wife*, whose meaning (mistress) is fairly transparent. But the Singapore and Malaysian English word *outstation* (a place or station at distance from HQ, or from the centre of population) cannot perhaps be so easily guessed. You will find some grammatical illustrations at CW10.4 (*What do they mean?*).

McKay's findings relate to specific world Englishes. But what about English being used as a *lingua franca* across the world? How different are they from each other, and do whatever differences there are detract from international communication? The statistics following Box 10.3 show that the most common use of English is as a *lingua franca*. To what extent can ELF stand as a viable standard for learners to follow? If we want to find out, we need to collect instances of ELF and study its nature. Seidlhofer (2001) argued the case for a corpus of English as a Lingua Franca, and this led to one: the Vienna-Oxford International Corpus of English (or VOICE). There is also now an Asian ELF corpus (ACE), developed by Kirkpatrick, and discussed in Kirkpatrick (2011).

In his paper, Kirkpatrick lists some of the common features of 'European ELF' and 'Asian ELF.' You can find some examples of grammatical features at CW10.5

(*ELF features*). One of these is dropping the -*s* of the third-person simple present verb – saying *She like* rather than *She likes*. ELF speakers tend to do this. They also have characteristic pronunciation features, and these have been particularly studied by Jenkins, another pioneering figure in the ELF kingdom. Jenkins (2000) notes that the native speaker's weak forms like [ə], and the distinction between [ð] and [θ] (as in 'this' and 'thin') are among those that tend to disappear in ELF. You can see Jenkins talking about her work online at www.youtube.com/watch?v=YD4xDVMUh5E.

Can, and should, ELF stand as a model for learners? There are some features of ELF which may impair communication, but many – like the absence of that simple present -*s* and the [ð]/[θ] distinction – are not likely to do this in most situations. This suggests that the learner who masters ELF will have a powerful language for international communication. Some will argue that the English language is being destroyed by the kinds of simplifications ELF makes. But the statistics that follow Box 10.3 have a compelling logic of their own. They show you who the main users of the English language are, and the ELF studies show you just what that language is like.

In this section, we have been discussing the international context within which much language teaching today takes place. We have mainly been concerned with models for language learning. In the next section we will look at the importance of context to teaching methods.

10.4 Appropriate methodology

Context is not just important for the language planner. Teachers need to know about context as well. Knowledge of context is most likely to be an issue in the case of the expatriate teacher going abroad – for example, an Australian going to work in Africa. If they are to operate successfully in their new context they will have to understand it, and realize that it is different from their own. But sensitivity to context is also an issue for the FL teacher working in their own country. This is particularly true if they have been trained to use ideas and techniques that originate abroad. The fact is that many FL teaching situations involve the coming together of people and ideas from different cultures. When cultures meet, the result may be happy union. Unfortunately there is often also an element of clash. Language teachers must be ready to handle clash.

Someone who explores clash in detail is Holliday. His 1994 book is entitled *Appropriate Methodology and Social Context*. The book results partly from his experience working in Cairo as part of a joint British–American–Egyptian language teaching project. During his stay, he took copious 'observation notes' on various classes he attended, as well as on other events relevant to his topic. Here is an extract from his observation notes on a class in a faculty of education in Egypt, conducted by a local lecturer. The extract well conveys his bewilderment on meeting a way of teaching alien to his own:

anyone walking in would have thought there was chaos because a lot of students were talking at once and the lecturer did not always seem to be in control... The lecturer asked some students to be quiet, but not some others who appeared to be talking out of turn... One particular student in a group which always seemed to be talking out of turn was clearly in contact with the lesson because they often initiated very cogent comments... The end of the lesson was left apparently without a concrete conclusion.

(Holliday 1994, p. 38)

After the lesson, Holliday discussed it with the local lecturer. She said that

she knew exactly what was going on and that, yes, it was culturally normal to be talking and listening at the same time ... and that although some students were talking a lot, perhaps only 60% about the lesson, they were very much in touch. The ones she told to be quiet were [the ones who were] really off the point.

This example shows the 'foreignness' an expatriate teacher experiences when going to work in a different cultural context. It is important to realize that this foreignness works in two directions. Individuals in the host culture are likely to find aspects of the expatriate's views as bizarre as the expatriate finds theirs. Many expatriate teachers are surprised by this. Here is a common scenario: our novice teacher, trained, let us say, in Canada, sets off for their first job abroad. In their suitcase, among their other private effects, they carry a set of views about language teaching and a collection of techniques provided by their training course. The shock they receive during their first few weeks of teaching abroad is not a trivial one. The 'locals', the teacher discovers, are not as enthusiastic about the contents of their suitcase as they were expecting. In fact, the locals seem downright hostile to some of the teacher's favourite ideas and techniques. Their reaction is as human as it is illogical. They blame the locals. Muttering under their breath, they call the locals 'backward', not yet ready for their advanced notions. They protest: 'Certainly it is they, not I, who must change.'

Just to give an example, let us explore this issue in relation to one particular item in their baggage – the idea of groupwork. This technique has become very popular in recent years. In the past, classes were traditionally 'fully frontal.' That means that the teacher would stand at the front of the class, with the pupils in serried ranks facing them (sometimes the benches would actually be bolted down, as if deliberately to crush any attempt at communication in any direction except frontwards). Interaction was traditionally teacher to pupil, one pupil at a time, perhaps occasionally (as in a Handel oratorio) alleviated by some choral work, with all the pupils repeating in a chant something that the teacher had said. In groupwork on the other hand, pupils work together in small groups (from two to five or more members). Most of the interaction in this configuration is pupil to pupil.

One of the obvious advantages of groupwork for the language teacher is that it increases the amount of learner talk possible in the classroom – lots of people in the class can be speaking for lots of the time. This is particularly important if one holds the view that interaction is crucial for language learning (the 'Interaction Hypothesis' we mentioned in 5.3). Another major advantage is that students who are perhaps too nervous to speak directly to the teacher may be less inhibited when talking to their peers in a group. Long and Porter (1985) provide a list of the assumed advantages of groupwork for language teaching. The list is a long one, which is precisely why groupwork finds its way into our novice teacher's suitcase.

As you have probably guessed, we are going to find that groupwork is not well accepted in the context where our novice teacher works. Given all the advantages to groupwork, how can it possibly be unpopular or unacceptable? Before reading on, consider what the possible reasons might be.

Our novice teacher's attempts to introduce groupwork may meet with some resistance. Why? They need to know that the idea of groupwork has its origin not in language teaching, but in the field of educational studies, where it is associated with a particular educational philosophy. The philosophy is one which attempts to shift the centre of 'power' away from the teacher, and to involve learners more in their own learning. It is part of a movement away from teacher-led classes towards more interactive, learner-oriented ones. Reynolds (1994) provides a good background to the concept of groupwork as used in education.

A number of writers have noted that some cultures are hostile to groupwork because it involves learner–teacher relations that are at odds with those held in the culture. Shamim (1996: 124), for example, notes that in Pakistan most classes are teacher-fronted. She gives three reasons for this. They are: (a) 'the teachers' lack of awareness and/or feelings of insecurity in using other types of classroom organization'; (b) 'the effect of culture, whereby the teacher is traditionally seen as an authority figure and is given respect for his or her age and superior knowledge'; and (c) 'the view of teaching/learning that is prevalent in the community where teaching is viewed as transmission of knowledge'.

Other objections to groupwork are discussed in Kramsch and Sullivan (1996). They note that groupwork (along with the communicative approach and the idea of learner-centredness) 'have long become for many non-native teachers and learners synonymous with progress, modernization, and access to wealth' (p. 200). But then they take a close look at ELT classes in Vietnam. As well as points discussed in Shamim (1996), there is another aspect of local culture which is likely to make groupwork unpopular in class there. This is the idea of the 'classroom-as-family.' In Vietnam, students are placed in classes which stay together over years. The class becomes like a family, and class members are likely to stay in contact with each other long after they have left school. In this context, breaking classes up for groupwork does not go down well. One student reports that: 'all the students were connected by a thread, and that if they were divided up, that thread was broken.' And again: 'if the other students are separated from me, I feel like my right arm is cut off' (Kramsch and Sullivan 1996: 203).

So our novice teacher may, to their astonishment, find that they are being accused of a kind of cultural imperialism (if not indeed of cutting off students' arms!). In their innocence they thought that groupwork was just a way of getting learners to talk more. They discover that in fact it is a whole philosophy of education, even perhaps of life.

In an interview reported in Phillipson (1992: 260), Widdowson discusses the general problem of which our groupwork example is a particular instance. He says that although in recent years our expertise and awareness of various aspects of language teaching has increased impressively,

> where I think things have not been really effective has been in the mediation, the way in which these ideas have been integrated into local social, political and educational conditions of the countries where they are applied … We've tended always to make the same basic error, which is to assume that somehow it is the local conditions that have to be adjusted to the packaged set of concepts we bring with us rather than attempt to look into the real issues, practical as well as ideological, of implementation and innovation within these local contexts … I don't think we have brought into the operation [of language teaching] an awareness of local conditions nor an effective involvement of local people, so that one can see these as in some sense, even though enlightened and benevolent, well-meaning, but nevertheless to some degree impositional.

Recent writers, particularly Phillipson (1992) and Pennycook (1994), remind us that all too often language teaching can indeed be highly 'impositional', perhaps even constituting a form of cultural imperialism. CW10.6 (*Some issues about going global*) tells you about two more writers who feel the same way.

What is the answer? Should our novice teacher abandon their efforts to use groupwork, on the grounds that it does not fit in with the local cultural context? The issue is not a simple one, and in recent years there has been a growing literature on the subject of 'innovation', looking at how to introduce new ideas into a context in such a way that they will become accepted and 'sustainable.' Some books on this subject, like Fullan and Stiegelbauer (1991), deal with educational change in general; others (like Markee 1997) focus on language teaching.

Part of the answer lies in compromise and gradual movement. If the novice teacher is genuinely convinced about the value of groupwork but does nothing to fit into local educational practice, they will get nowhere. They may have a degree of success if they manage to integrate small portions of groupwork into the local diet in a clever and subtle way. But even then, they need to have the backing of others locally involved in the profession. You can argue that this backing is needed not just to ensure success, but also for ethical reasons. You should not try to change a context, you might say, unless that context wants to be changed.

What we have been discussing here may be called the relativism of methodologies. It leads us back to the idea of post-method pedagogy that we discussed in 9.10. It expresses the view that there is no single 'best' way of doing anything. Instead, there are ways that may be more or less appropriate according to situation. Holliday uses the phrase 'appropriate methodology' to describe this idea. Take a look at CW10.7 (*Methods as plausible fictions*), which looks at the issue from a slightly different viewpoint.

We may all be tempted to believe that this message – that there are no 'best' ways of doing things – applies to other people, not ourselves. But what our own conviction persuades us is the 'best' may be just as culturally determined and as relative as the views we find so strange in other cultures. CW10.7 talks about theories and methods as 'fictions.' Really wise teachers, I believe, are blessed with the sense to be aware of what their own 'fictions' are. And to recognize them as fictions, not facts.

Earlier in this chapter, we took an initial look at the question: how do you plan foreign language teaching? Our answer pointed up the importance of needs analysis. In the chapter about to begin we look more closely at this question, as it relates to the business of drawing up detailed language programmes specifying the content of courses, perhaps on a day-to-day basis. Detailed programme specification is the area of syllabus design. It is an area in which needs analysis continues to play an important role.

Note

1. There are three quotations in this paragraph, and I have taken them from secondary sources. Kachru (1983) is cited in McKay (2002) and in Widdowson (2003). Rao's quotation is taken from Kachru (1985).

Issues to think or write about

1. Section 10.2 and CW10.1 are about language planning. What are the language planning issues in your own country, or in another country that you know well? Describe and discuss these issues. If you wish, you can restrict yourself to foreign language planning, using the list on CW10.1 as the starting point for your deliberations.

2. Section 10.4 looks at how groupwork can prove to be unacceptable or unpopular in particular contexts. Think of some other techniques that you imagine might be similarly unpopular in certain contexts, even though they are often recommended for use by teacher trainers living elsewhere. Consider why the techniques might be recommended by trainers, and why they might be unacceptable in a different context.

Further reading

Phillipson, R. 1992 *Linguistic Imperialism* Oxford: Oxford University Press
A book that well illustrates how some see the political dimension to language teaching.

Wright, S. 2004 *Language Policy and Language Planning: From Nationalism to Globalisation* Basingstoke: Palgrave Macmillan
A lengthy consideration of language planning issues.

Crystal, D. 2003 *English as a Global Language* Cambridge: Cambridge University Press
A highly accessible introductory book on EIL.

Jenkins, J. 2000 *The Phonology of English as an International Language* Oxford: Oxford University Press
This book also has a lot to say to the teacher. It focuses on phonology.

Holliday, A. 1994 *Appropriate Methodology and Social Context* Cambridge: Cambridge University Press
Key reading on the topic of appropriate methodology.

11 Plans and programmes

11.1 Introduction

A good number of people who are professionally involved in language teaching will at one time or another in their lives have the responsibility of producing a syllabus, or part of one. But what exactly is a syllabus? Essentially it is a statement of *content*, a plan of what your programme will cover. In Chapter 9 we saw that the *what* and *how* of language teaching can be closely connected, so that a statement of content is likely to carry with it methodological implications (perhaps you can find where this was said, in 9.7). Syllabuses therefore rarely confine themselves to content alone. Often they talk about methodology as well, and are likely also to contain statements about aims and objectives, and even about the form of evaluation to be used for the teaching programme. But content remains the main element of most syllabuses.

In 3.1 the point was made that 'in the field of applied linguistics nothing ever happens in a vacuum.' This applies to syllabus design as much as to any other area. The way you organise teaching reflects what you consider important, and what you want to draw attention to. If you believe the main task of foreign language learning is mastering the grammar of the language (a view held in the 1960s), you will organize your teaching around grammar points, using a structural syllabus. If on the other hand you want to focus on language use, you will probably go for a notional/functional syllabus. You can learn a lot about someone's beliefs regarding language teaching by looking at the syllabus they use.

The present chapter takes a detailed look at the major syllabus types, particularly the structural and the notional/functional. It deals with the nuts and bolts of syllabus design, aiming to give you a feeling of how syllabuses are actually constructed. We will also look at different sorts of language teaching programmes, particularly language for specific purposes (LSP) programmes, and general courses where the purposes are far less specific.

A good place to begin is by looking at the contents page of a textbook, a location where many teachers come closest to seeing a syllabus at work.

B11.1 Nuts and bolts: an initial look

In some language teaching textbooks, the contents page of the Teacher's Book reveals details of the syllabus. Below is part of this page (for the first 12 units) from Teacher's Book 1 of a course called *Now for English* (Johnson 1983). I wrote these materials for primary-level children who were starting to learn English as a foreign language at the age of eight. Here are some questions to draw your attention to aspects of the contents page. You will find the answers in Note 1.

1. There are three columns. The titles of each column appear in the shaded boxes at the top. They have been omitted. What do you think they are for the first two columns? What about the third column? This is more difficult because we have not yet fully discussed the items that occur in this column. But go on: make a guess at what the title may be.
2. Though you cannot tell for sure without seeing more of the book, which of the three columns do you think tells you most about how the book is organized?
3. The book contains revision units at regular intervals. Identify these units and the intervals at which they occur.
4. In the second column, some items are given in italics. What do these items have in common? Other items are in capitals. What do they have in common? Say what the difference is between these two types of item.
5. Concentrate now on *verb forms*. The units focus on one verb in particular. Which one?

Introductory lesson	*What's your name?* *My name's John.*	names (asking for names and saying who you are) colours countries of the world
1 Good morning everyone	*I'm Anne.* *I'm not Peter.* *Who's this?* *It's Sam.*	the characters of the book introducing yourself
2 Who's this?	*This is Mr Porter.* *This is my father.* *he's/she's* numbers 1–10	family relations (talking about the family) children's ages
3 Oh Sally!	*What's this?* *It's a …* (positive, negative, interrogative, short answer)	objects commonly found in the street or house

4	What a mess!	*Whose is this book?*	common classroom
		Whose book is this?	objects talking about
		It's Sam's.	who owns things
		It's his/her book.	
		Is that/it your book?	
5	Kate's farm	*What colour is it?*	farm animals
		It's red.	
		It's a red horse.	
		this/that	
6	Games to play	revision, and Progress Test 1	
7	Gee up, Sam	*I'm a …*	exciting jobs
		You're a …	(talking about jobs)
		(positive, negative,	
		interrogative, short answer)	
8	Circus time	*He's a …*	the circus
		She's a …	
		(positive, negative,	
		interrogative, short answer)	
9	Stop, Bella, stop	IMPERATIVE	simple actions
		(positive, negative)	giving orders
10	Shirts and	*What are these?*	articles of clothing
	skirts	*They're …*	
		These are …	
		PLURAL NOUNS	
		NO ARTICLE + PLURAL	
		NOUN / a + SINGULAR	
		NOUN	
11	Cowboys and	*We're …*	cowboys and Indians
	Indians	*You're …*	
		They're …	
		(positive, negative,	
		interrogative, short answer)	
		numbers 11–20	
12	Games to play	revision, and Progress Test 2	

(Part of contents page from Teacher's Book 1 of *Now for English* (Johnson 1983))

11.2 The structural syllabus

11.2.1 Constructing a structural syllabus

Question 2 in Box 11.1 asks about how *Now for English* is organized. If you had the opportunity to look more carefully at the book itself, it would become apparent to you that its main organization is in terms of the structures. Each unit focuses on a number of grammatical structures. You can see (even from the contents pages, though more clearly by looking at the book itself) that these have been ordered and graded through the course. This is a way of saying that the book follows a <u>structural syllabus</u>.

How are structural syllabuses actually constructed? One way to find out would be to interview someone who has designed syllabuses. At several points in my career I have done just that. So in CW11.1 (*MAAL interviews MAMD*), I interview myself. MAAL (Me as Applied Linguist) talks to MAMD (Me as Materials Designer). The interview revolves around the *Now for English* syllabus that you have just seen. Take a look at it now.

As you can see from the *Now for English* contents page, the verb *be* has been divided into a series of sentence patterns (the phrase was introduced in 9.3). For example, there are positive statements (called <u>affirmatives</u> in grammar), some negatives and some question forms (<u>interrogatives</u>). Find examples of these.

Syllabus designers frequently have to divide structures into sentence patterns – 'bite-sized chunks' – that can be taught one by one. From Unit 13 onwards in *Now for English*, the main structure introduced is the simple present tense. Box 11.2 asks you to think about the sentence patterns this can be divided into.

B11.2 Liking chocolates

Here are some of the main sentence patterns associated with the simple present tense in English:

'Basic' form (the affirmative)	She likes chocolates.
Negative	She doesn't like chocolates.
Question (interrogative)	Does she like chocolates?

Note that all these examples use the third-person singular (*she*). Think of the equivalent sentences using a different person (e.g. *I* or *they*).

If you feel in the mood for a linguistic challenge, use the examples above to work out the rules for forming simple present negatives and interrogatives. Be as explicit as you can, and if possible use grammatical terminology in your explanation. (If you have difficulty with the interrogative forms, look back at how you tackled the task in Box 2.7.)

Note 2 gives a short explanation.

11.2.2 Criteria for structural syllabus ordering

How do syllabus designers decide on the ordering of items on their syllabus? One criterion was mentioned by MAMD in CW11.1. What does he call that criterion? Before reading on, you might like to consider other criteria that structural syllabus designers might use.

Here is a short 'Rough Guide' to the most common criteria structural syllabus designers employ to decide on the order they will introduce items.

Rough Guide to Syllabus Design Criteria

Simplicity criterion

What it is: moving from simple to more complex structures.
   Comments:

- We need to distinguish *formal* and *conceptual* simplicity. Formal simplicity relates to how the item is 'constructed.' For example, in Box 11.2 you were asked to think about the structure of simple present negatives and questions, which are quite complex (using *do*, *does*, *doesn't*, etc). But a structure may be formally simple and conceptually difficult. The indefinite article, for example. The form is easy: you just put *a* or *an* at the beginning of the noun phrase. But it is very difficult to explain as a concept if the learner does not have it in their L1.
- Linguists have sometimes tried to develop 'scientific' definitions of simplicity. But their attempts have never really worked. One reason is that what makes a sentence simple or difficult for you to process is not just a question of its structure. Many 'psychological' factors are also involved.
- Simplicity and complexity are complicated by contrastive linguistics. Look back at 4.2 and the idea that a structure may be more difficult for the speakers of one language than another, according to the relationship between the target language and the learner's L1.

Sequencing or grouping

What it is: putting things together that 'go' together.
   Example: *some* and *any*. Though the rule is a simplification, learners are often taught that *any* is used for negative and interrogative sentences: *Did she eat any chocolates?* and *She didn't eat any chocolates*, as opposed to *She ate some chocolates*. It makes sense to teach these words in the same or adjacent units.

Frequency

What it is: teaching the most frequently used forms first.

Comments:

- A 'frequency count' is a study which counts the frequency of items in a language. Many deal with vocabulary, but sometimes they look at grammatical structures. George (1963), for example, finds that the 'simple' tenses (e.g. in *She eats chocolate* and *She ate chocolate*) far outstrip the 'continuous' ones (*She is eating chocolate* and *She was eating chocolate*). Perhaps this suggests the simple tense should be taught before the continuous ones? Many syllabuses teach them the other way round.
- Recently, information about frequency has been taken from corpora. Look back to 3.2.6 to remind yourself about corpus linguistics and what corpora are. One reason why they are useful to language teachers is because they show us how words are really used. They can also give firm information about word frequency. An example which shows both these advantages was given in 3.2.6. It was Sinclair and Renouf's (1988) findings regarding the word *see*. It would be natural, we noted, for you to imagine that the most common use of this word is to do with visual perception (as in the sentence *I saw him in the distance*). In fact, computer evidence suggests that the most common usage is in the sense of 'understand' (as in *Yes, I see*, or *Do you see?*). Since this is the most frequent usage, perhaps it should be the first taught. Corpora can also provide frequency information about grammatical structures (more efficiently than a single 'computerless' person, like George, possibly can).

Utility

What it is: teaching the most useful things first.

Comment: 'Most useful' often means 'most frequent.' Sometimes a sentence pattern may be so useful for the actual process of teaching that it is worth covering early. Sentence patterns like *Open the door* (the imperative) and *What's this?* often occur early in courses, because they are so useful in the classroom. Once the imperative is learned, many classroom actions can be practised. Look back to the contents page of *Now for English* and note how early it is taught. Why is *What's this?* such a useful form to teach early?

Teachability

What it is: teaching structures that are easy to convey before ones that are difficult to teach. So it is simplicity from the *teaching* point of view.

Comment: All teachers know that some structures are easier to teach than others. Two examples from earlier: The *some/any* distinction is a favourite for some teachers because it is easy to explain and practise. The indefinite article, on the other hand, can be fiendishly difficult to teach.

A controversial statement to think about: perhaps with very difficult structures all you can do is expose learners to them, and offer explanations if asked, rather than trying to teach them in a formal way. What do you think?

Designing a syllabus can be a very messy business, and one reason is that the criteria we have been discussing can conflict. We noted, for example, that it can be very useful to teach *What's this?* early on in a course. But the simplicity criterion might suggest this pattern should come a little later – after all, it is a question form, showing <u>inversion</u>, where the subject *this* comes after the verb *is* or *'s*. A small example, but if you ever come to design a syllabus yourself, you will find it is a process full of uncertainties and compromises. Messy, and certainly an art rather than a science.

11.2.3   A recent perspective on the structural syllabus

In section 4.4 we looked at morpheme acquisition studies which suggest that learners have their own order for learning structures – what amounts to an *internal syllabus*. The morpheme acquisition studies, and the Chomskyan tradition which inspired them, ask a challenging question that structural syllabus designers cannot avoid confronting. In CW4.4 we posed the question like this: 'What is the point in having an *external* syllabus if learners have their own *internal* one?' Applied linguists have reacted in different ways to the existence of the internal syllabus. Here are three reactions:

> *Reaction 1*: 'Since the learner has their own internal syllabus, there is no point in imposing an external one. We should let the learner follow their own internal learning order.' This is really what Prabhu does. Find the section in Chapter 9 where his procedural syllabus is described, and make sure you are clear that this is what he is advocating.
>
> *Reaction 2*: 'Yes, well, doubtless the learner has an internal syllabus, but for the purposes of classroom teaching we can just ignore that, and carry on using our external syllabus. Don't forget that the morpheme studies were done in a naturalistic context. Where we are dealing with classroom learning, an external order for learning should be imposed.'
>
> *Reaction 3*: 'Let's keep an external syllabus, but as far as possible make this reflect what we know about the internal syllabus. In other words, we would use the information given by the morpheme acquisition studies to help us decide on the order of structures introduced in textbooks.'

One applied linguist who follows this third argument is Pienemann, who developed what is called the Teachability (or sometimes the Learnability) Hypothesis. His hypothesis 'predicts that instruction can only promote language acquisition if the [learner's] interlanguage is close to the point when the structure to be taught is acquired in the natural setting' (Pienemann 1985: 36). In his research he shows that learners will not fully master a language item if it is too far in advance of the point that the 'internal syllabus' has reached. The implication is that teaching programmes should take information about acquisition orders into account when they decide how to order teaching items. Rogers (1994) shows that this does not normally happen. She looks at seven textbooks teaching German as a foreign language, and finds that the order in which items are taught does not follow what is known about German natural acquisition orders.

It could be argued that we do not yet know enough about natural acquisition orders for Pienemann's Teachability Hypothesis to have much impact on language teaching. But the hypothesis does carry a very important message that syllabus designers ignore at their peril. It is that syllabus construction is not just the application of simplicity criteria, frequency counts and the rest. The notion of 'learner stage' is an important consideration. Whether this is measured in a formal way by acquisition order studies, or is just based on teacher experience of the way learners progress, it should be in your thoughts as you design a syllabus. Which you might not yet have done, but may well have to do some day.

11.3 Notional/functional syllabuses

11.3.1 Needs analysis

In 9.6 we described the development of the notional/functional (n/f) syllabus by the Council of Europe team. We related it to the 'sociolinguistic revolution', to discontent with structural teaching in general, and with the structural syllabus in particular. In this section we shall look more carefully into the machinery of the n/f syllabus.

Selection is a big issue for this syllabus type. In structural syllabus design, selecting what to teach is very much a question of deciding on ordering. Remember what MAMD says in CW11.1 about *Now for English*: he feels he can teach all the major structures of English over the three years of the course. This concept of total coverage – starting with beginners and proceeding over a period of time until all the structures of the language have been taught – is a common one in much language teaching. But it is not a concept that can be applied easily to n/f syllabuses. Take functions, for example. It is clear that the uses to which a language can be put are very many. We simply cannot teach *all* the functions of English. We therefore have to find some means of identifying which functions to teach, and which to exclude, from our course.

The member of the Council of Europe team who considered this problem was the Swiss applied linguist René Richterich. His answer was related to a procedure which we met briefly in 10.2.3. Needs analysis has its roots in educational studies going back at least as far as the work of the American educational psychologist Benjamin Bloom, who developed a way of classifying educational aims (Bloom 1956). The procedure is widely used today in relation to many study areas, including engineering and management. In the field of language teaching, Richterich defines language needs as 'the requirements which arise from the use of a language in the multitude of situations which may arise in the social lives of individuals and groups' (1972: 32). But the key word in Richterich's definition – *situation* – poses problems. One dictionary (the *Concise Oxford*) defines it as a 'set of circumstances', and another member of the team, van Ek (1973), thinking specifically about language use, talks of 'the complex of extra linguistic conditions which determines the nature of the language act' (p. 13). The words *set* and *complex* convey the idea that the factors which go to make up a situation are complex and numerous. This suggests that if the concept of situation is to be really useful for syllabus design, it will have to be broken down into component parts. This is just what the Council of Europe does. The 'components of situations' as described by van Ek (1975) include these three: setting (where the user is); topic (what the user talks about); and role (the relationships between the users in an interaction). You can find more details about these elements in CW11.2 (*The components of 'situation'*).

So Step 1 of needs analysis *à la* Council of Europe involves listing the *situations* – broken down into settings, topics and roles – relevant to the learner in their use of the target language. But a further three steps are needed. Step 2 is to identify the language *activities* likely to occur in the situations. Van Ek says that these 'may be as comparatively "simple" as understanding the weather forecast on the radio or as complex as summarizing orally in a foreign language a report written in one's native language' (1975: 104). Step 3 is to list the *notions and functions* associated with the situations and activities. Then there is an important Step 4. This is to identify the actual language forms most useful to express the notions and functions. The word exponent is used in this context: we say that such and such a phrase expounds such and such a function. For example, in English two ways to expound the function of *greeting* are *Hi* and *Good morning*. These differ very much in formality, and it may be that for particular students one is more appropriate than the other. You would let your needs analysis identify which exponents it will be appropriate to teach.

These four steps – *situations* → *activities* → *notions and functions* → *exponents* – take us from needs to language content. They provide a way of selecting the most relevant material for our language syllabus. To put a little more flesh onto these bones, imagine that you are developing a syllabus for a group of secretaries learning English. Box 11.3 invites you to undertake a mini needs analysis for these learners.

B11.3 Doing a mini needs analysis

Here is a short example of part of a needs analysis for a secretary; just part – it is very incomplete.

Step 1	**Components of situations**
Setting	learner's L1 country; in the office
Topics	hotel bookings, transportation arrangements, appointments
Roles	stranger to stranger; secretary to boss

Step 2	**Language activity** making phone calls to the FL country in relation to a business trip their boss is to undertake
Step 3 *Notions* *Functions*	**Identifying notions and functions** dates, times, futurity, giving information, requesting information, making arrangements
Step 4	**Identifying exponents** She'll be staying for … days I'd like to … Could you please tell me … on + date; at + time; will be + -ing; by + form of transport

(a) Think of three more language activities in which this secretary may want to use their target language. For one of these activities, work through Steps 3 and 4 as above.

The Council of Europe's needs analysis model was one of a number that were developed in the 1970s. But by the beginning of the 1980s, there was a growing realization that a proper needs analysis should look at more than the target situation. A broader approach was provided by Hutchinson and Waters (1987), and this is described in CW11.3 (*Necessities, lacks and wants*). As you will see, their model involves finding out about learner perceptions. But are learner perceptions reliable? Can learners really be trusted, you might ask, to identify what they require? Brindley (1989) points out that many teachers feel learners are incapable of discussing their requirements in a sensible manner. Certainly, many cultures do not encourage learners to develop views regarding their needs. So (some say) many learners are simply incapable of expressing their needs. And when they do express views, Brindley suggests that these are often not well articulated or enlightened. True as this may be, it is indeed a foolhardy course designer who plans teaching without giving some consideration as to what the learners feel they need, however poorly they express themselves. The 'cautionary tale' in CW10.7 shows just how foolhardy it is to ignore learners' views. After all, they are the principal 'stakeholders' in the language learning business (you need learners if you want to teach languages!). You ignore learners' feelings at your peril.

How can you make sure that the wants of learners are properly heeded? One suggestion (discussed in Clarke 1991) is to involve them directly in the process of syllabus design, by developing a <u>negotiated syllabus</u>. This means that you make a point of asking your learners what they want out of your course, and you bear what they say in mind as you design the programme. This negotiation will naturally occur at the initial course planning stage. But it should happen later on too, and this reveals an important insight about how programmes should be developed. There is a rather widespread belief that syllabus design is something which takes place once only, at the beginning of course preparation. You first decide what you will teach, the myth goes, then how you will teach it. Finally you do the teaching. But recall that earlier in this chapter we described syllabus design as a 'messy business.' Part of the messiness is that syllabus designers will (and indeed should) find themselves returning to their syllabus and modifying it as the course develops, and even after it has finished. This is how it should be, because learner wants (as well as their lacks and necessities) will come to light as a course progresses. They will rarely oblige by entirely revealing themselves early on, at the needs analysis stage. Dudley-Evans and St John (1998: 121) have a pair of diagrams which nicely illustrate the idealized theory and the messy practice of how courses are constructed, taught and evaluated. The diagram on the left shows the sequence of events as it would be in an ideal world. The complexities of the procedure in reality are shown on the right. Notice how many more lines there are in the diagram on the right.

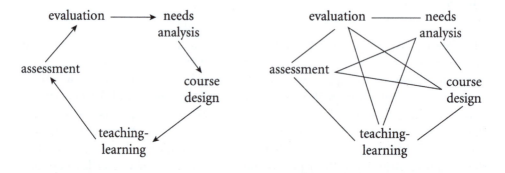

Earlier we used the word 'stakeholder' to describe the learner. There are of course various other stakeholders involved in the language teaching operation, and a full needs analysis will need to consider the views of a number of them. Jordan's (1997) example is of a Nepali man, Gopal, who wants to go to the UK to study for an MA in Economics. Jordan shows that besides considering Gopal himself, we need also to take into account the point of view of the Nepalese Ministry of Education, the British Council (who are sponsoring Gopal), the staff in the UK who teach the course he wants to attend, and the ESP teachers who will prepare him for that course. The various perceptions of all these stakeholders may differ in subtle but important ways. For example, ESP lecturers, as Hutchinson and Waters (1987) point out, sometimes exaggerate the importance of English for a person's study, giving it more priority than the student or the lecturers in their subject department would. More than one perspective on needs should be consulted to achieve a rounded picture.

The most obvious way to collect stakeholders' views is to ask them, through questionnaires or interviews. But other forms of data collection may also be useful; indeed, Jordan (1997) lists no fewer than 14 different methods for collecting information. You may for example want to see for yourself how English is used in target situations, and this may involve videotaping people as they use language in their workplace. Think again about the secretary you considered in Box 11.3. Spend some time considering how you could collect information on their needs. Think about the target situation's *necessities*, but don't forget *lacks* and *wants* as well. How would you find out about them?

This short section on needs analysis has perhaps succeeded in convincing you what a complex operation needs analysis can be. Jordan (1997: 40) has an amusing illustration of what he calls the 'needs analysis juggler.' His sketch shows a stick man (the needs analyst) juggling 17 balls in the air at the same time. Each ball represents one of the considerations that the needs analyst must bear in mind. Examples are language level, subject-to-be-studied, expectations, constraints of money and time, and educational background. Complicated! You may also have noticed how many acronyms there are associated with this field. The ones mentioned are barely the tip of the iceberg. I have mentioned TSA (in CW11.3), but not LSA (Learning Situation Analysis) or PSA (Present Situation Analysis). In fact, it is the areas of ESP and EAP (English for Academic Purposes) in general which are so soaked in acronyms. ESP and EAP are, one is tempted to say, truly ESAP – Entirely and Severely Acronym Plagued.

11.3.2   LSP programmes and n/f

This chapter, which started off considering different syllabus types, has now slipped imperceptibly into consideration of a particular type of programme: the LSP course (the general term, meaning language for specific purposes). This is nowadays an extremely widespread form of language teaching. It took me no more than five minutes on Google this morning to come up with the following list of LSP courses: Spanish for librarians, German for singers, Italian for banking, Portuguese for business professionals, French for food and wine lovers, Chinese for lawyers, Swedish for exchange students, Russian for lawyers, Japanese for doctors (as well as another in Japanese for anime lovers). CW11.4 (*LAP or LOP?*) shows a common way of classifying LSP. It also includes an activity. LAP and LOP: yet more acronyms!

LSP and n/f syllabuses developed hand in hand, because the latter provided such a useful way of describing and classifying language needs. They were to a large extent twins who grew up together. But as J. McDonough (1998) points out, the beginnings of LSP certainly predate n/f. An influential pre-n/f paper was written by Strevens, an applied linguist who himself went on to produce ESP materials in the form of a textbook for teaching seafaring English. Strevens (1971) argues that general English courses with a high literary content are not the only way of doing things. The paper's title is 'Alternatives to daffodils.' The reference is of course to Wordsworth's poem 'I wandered lonely as a cloud.' The language teaching world has indeed moved far away from hosts of golden daffodils.

If LSP and n/f are twins, they are also clearly related to CLT. So it is not surprising that LSP should have a concern with language as discourse. Genre analysis, which looks at the features of discourse associated with different genres, grew out of LSP. A genre is, in the words of Swales (1990, the major book in this field), a collection of 'communicative events' (texts for example) which 'share some set of communicative purposes.' You doubtless know the word genre used to describe a type of literature (tragedy, comedy or epic poetry, for example), and also in relation to types of film – horror, romantic comedy and so on – which share some 'family resemblances.' In the field of academic writing, we can identify genres like academic papers, dissertations, textbooks. To give you a sense of what genre analysis looks like, have a read of CW11.5 (*Analysing genres*), which shows how Swales (1990) analyses the characteristic patterns occurring in the introductory sections of academic articles. CW11.5 also includes an activity which allows you to think of genre analysis in relation to language teaching.

LSP teaching is often very demanding. J. McDonough (1998) mentions two ways in which your job as an LSP teacher may differ from the 'normal' language teacher's work. One is that you will often become more involved in course planning and development. The business of needs analysis, for example, may well fall on your shoulders. Second, you have to come to terms with your learners' specialist subject field. So if you are teaching a course entitled *English for Physicists*, you will need to have some rudimentary knowledge of the area. A Nobel Prize in physics is not necessary, of course (though it might help). But without a degree of interest in the field, and a rudimentary knowledge of it, you will find life difficult. LSP teaching involves a marriage of two disciplines – a language and a subject area. Like in real marriages, there are various ways of handling the relationship, with varying degrees of success. One particularly attractive possibility involves team teaching. The LSP teacher works together with the physics, chemistry or management studies teacher, attending lectures in those areas and making the language classes follow on from the subject area classes.

11.3.3   TENOR programmes and n/f

One of the attractive features of ESP is that it is relatively easy to identify language needs. But this is not true of another very common teaching situation, called TENOR. This, as we saw in 1.7, stands for 'teaching English for no obvious reason', and it includes all general courses, where the learners have divergent reasons for learning, or (as in many school situations) where we simply cannot know what their eventual uses (if any) of the FL will be.

Needs analysis does not work easily for TENOR students because their needs are either unknown or can only be specified in the most general terms. How then can you do the job of selection which the notional/functional syllabus seems to require? The Council of Europe's answer lies in the concept of the common core. All learners, whatever their eventual uses of the FL, will (the argument runs) need a certain common core of notions and functions. In the functional area, these are particularly uses associated with general socializing, like *greeting*, *requesting information* and *inviting*.

The Council of Europe needed to develop a language teaching system that would work in the many highly diverse situations met throughout the member countries. Flexibility was all-important, and the Council's needs were met by a <u>unit/credit system</u>. In this, teaching units deal with distinct areas of language use. Learners select which units to cover according to their particular language needs. Credits are given for units completed, and when a number of credits have been gained, a qualification is awarded.

The system identifies five levels of proficiency. The lowest was called the 'Threshold Level' (or 'T-Level'), though later a lower level called 'Waystage' was introduced. Next up is 'Basic', then 'General Competence', 'Advanced' and 'Full Professional.' The idea is that each level should have a common core unit, plus additional specialized units. Van Ek was given the task of developing a syllabus for the common core of the Threshold Level. His document, called *The Threshold Level*, is a landmark document in n/f syllabus design. It appeared in two forms: *The Threshold Level* (van Ek 1975) for the adult learner, and *The Threshold Level for Schools* (van Ek 1978) for the secondary-school student.

One of the advantages of n/f is that until you start to consider actual exponents, you are dealing with ideas (like 'situation', 'notion' and 'function') which are non-language-specific, and can therefore be applied to the teaching of many languages.[3] Consequently the notions and functions you identify as useful for a German person learning English are likely to be equally useful to the British person learning German, the American learning Spanish, or the Italian learning French. This means that a document like the *Threshold Level* can exist in a number of versions, for different languages. So it is that alongside the T-Level, there are comparable documents in other languages – the French *Niveau-Seuil*, German *Kontaktschwelle*, Spanish *Nivel Umbral* and Italian *Livello Soglia*, for example. If you want to get to know the T-Level a little, take a look at CW11.6 (*Getting to know the T-Level*), which contains a short activity.

11.3.4 N/f for general and specific programmes

Are there any teaching situations in which n/f is particularly useful? One clear, and very large, audience was immediately apparent when n/f syllabuses came into existence. In fact, it was the audience for which n/f came into existence. These were the learners suffering from the epidemic of 'syntax syndrome' that (as we saw in 9.6) Newmark diagnosed so well. These students knew their grammar but lacked communicative ability. They existed in droves around the world, a legacy of structural teaching. N/f teaching was able to add a communicative dimension to their knowledge, to 'activate' this knowledge so that it could be used for doing things with language. Because of the size of this audience, very many n/f courses are pitched at the intermediate level and above, the assumption being that the learners already know their grammar. Implicit in this approach is a view of language teaching that became very common. It is a two-stage model:

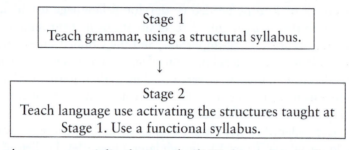

> **Stage 1**
> Teach grammar, using a structural syllabus.
>
> ↓
>
> **Stage 2**
> Teach language use activating the structures taught at Stage 1. Use a functional syllabus.

What about other, more specialized, uses of n/f? We have already discussed LSP. As we have seen, because of n/f and needs analysis, we are able to say to our students: 'We have analysed your needs, and are teaching you just those parts of English that are relevant to those needs.' Being able to claim this should give our courses great face validity.

There is another type of course which is becoming increasingly widespread throughout the world. We touched on a version of it earlier in this chapter, and met it first in 1.2 with the Chilean student Lilian Rivera. She has just six months in which to bring her English up to a particular standard. What she requires might be called an 'urgency course.' Its essence is to teach a large amount of language in a short space of time. The urgency course is popular, because the world is full of people in Lilian's circumstances.

The traditional approach to the urgency course is not very satisfactory. Often a structurally organized textbook intended for a long course would be used, and then abandoned when time ran out. So learners might cover the verb *be*, the simple present tense and not much else. N/f provides a much better way of selection, again by looking at needs – this time urgent ones. One common version of the urgency course is the <u>pre-sessional</u> course. This gives language training to students about to follow some study programme in which the FL is the language of instruction. Many pre-sessional courses are held in the target language country. It is possible to predict the learners' urgent needs as from the moment they arrive. They will, for example, soon want to open a bank account, to search for accommodation, to register at the Health Centre (in Britain they will probably have caught a cold in the first few days). These needs can form the basis of highly relevant teaching in which the notions and functions urgent for them are introduced.

11.3.5   A bursting bubble

In the 1970s and early 1980s, it is no exaggeration to say that n/f syllabuses dominated syllabus design in language teaching. Ministries of Education worldwide jostled to change their syllabuses from structural to n/f, and private language schools would boast of their up-to-date notional/functional-based teaching. It was a bubble that had to burst. When it did, this was not just the result of theoretical objections to the notional/functional syllabus, but also of concrete problems encountered by practitioners – the teachers who actually went into classrooms to teach with n/f textbooks.

Here are two anecdotes to illustrate these problems. The first took place in the early 1980s, when I was invited to sit in on a planning meeting at a major language teaching institution in Italy. The purpose of the meeting was to select the teaching books for the coming year. Because it was the early 1980s, I was confident that fashion would dictate that all the chosen books would be notional/functional. But I was wrong, and in the event almost all the books were structurally based. One teacher, who had been using n/f books for a number of years, explained: 'In n/f books the students learn lots of phrases, but they don't come out of the lesson with one major thing learned. In structural teaching they do.' This objection is grounded in the fact that it is difficult to make clear and strong generalizations about language use. So if you are not careful, your n/f lesson ends up providing not very much more than an elaborate phrase book (ten ways of *inviting*, five ways of *making plans*, and so on). The problem with phrase books is that you are not taught any general knowledge that enables you to go beyond the phrases given. The phrase book may tell you how to ask for a cup of tea, but what happens if you want a cup of hot chocolate?

The second anecdote makes the same point. In the late 1970s a colleague and I were writing n/f materials to be taught on a pre-sessional course.[4] One lesson dealt with one of those urgent activities – opening a bank account. The campus bank set aside a lunch hour for arriving overseas students to open accounts, and in the morning of that day we taught our group of recently arrived students some language appropriate to that activity. One sequence we introduced and drilled was *Good morning. I'd like to open a bank account please.* At lunch time I thought I would go to the bank and eavesdrop on the results of the morning's lesson. One short dialogue overheard was most depressing. The bank clerk knew of course that the students all wanted to open accounts, so they said to one student: *Hello. You want to open an account I expect.* The reply that came back was the drilled one: *Good morning, I'd like to open a bank account please.* Hardly a successful piece of dialogue! The learner had produced, parrot-like, exactly what they had been taught. They did not have the knowledge to handle the unexpected.

The bubble may have burst. But n/f never disappeared, and indeed it is almost inconceivable today to produce a syllabus without a notional/functional dimension. The heady days of 'notions and functions and nothing else' may have gone. But the movement has left an indelible mark.

11.4   The multidimensional syllabus

Syllabus designers and textbook writers today commonly follow similar procedures to van Ek's, producing their own syllabus inventories. But because of the burst bubble, the resulting syllabuses are rarely exclusively notional/

functional. They are more often hybrids, or mixtures. These are sometimes called <u>multidimensional syllabuses</u>. The basis of the multidimensional syllabus is that it has more than one 'unit of organization' (the phrase was used by MAMD in CW11.1). There are two main ways these syllabuses can be produced from an inventory like the T-Level. In the first, you can shift the focus at different points in the course. You might for example have some structural units followed by the occasional unit dealing with a situation; later you might change the focus yet again with some functional units. Morrow and Johnson (1979) use this method.

The second way is very common nowadays. It is to have more than one focus operating in each part of the course. A widely used textbook which follows this solution is Swan and Walter (1990). CW11.7 (*A multidimensional syllabus*) gives part of the book's plan. It shows that the content of each unit has been mapped out in four different ways. So there are in effect four syllabuses. To ensure that over the course as a whole each of these syllabuses is properly covered involves some very complex and clever planning.

B11.4 Spotting how a textbook is organized

You might think it easy to tell just by a quick glance how a textbook is really organized. But it can in fact be very difficult. As we have seen, the contents page can help, but often it will tell you very little, because unit names do not always reveal much about organization. Column 1 of *Now for English*'s contents page (in 11.1) is a good example. The units have names like *Oh Sally!* and *What a mess!*, which are not very revealing linguistically. Beware also of what a book says about itself. Many books say they are functional, and contain units bearing functional titles like 'Describing people' or 'Introducing yourself.' But the unit on 'Describing people' may in fact be a unit about the verb *be* followed by an adjective, as in *He's tall*, and *She's thin*. Similarly, 'Introducing yourself' may just consist of *be* plus a name – *I'm Keith*. The organization may, in other words, really be structural.

How to tell the true from the false? The secret lies in the concept of 'unit of organization.' You need to look closely at the lessons themselves, to see what they are really covering. If there is a clear structural thread running through a unit, while the functions within it seem to be disorganized, then that unit at least is a structurally based one. Looking at all the units in a book should enable you to say something certain about its underlying syllabus.

You are invited to look closely at a textbook that you know. Try to work out what kind of syllabus it is based on. This may take you some time!

11.5   Technology-assisted learning[5]

11.5.1   A virtual learning environment

This chapter concludes with consideration of a type of learning which is defined not by what kind of students follow it, or by how its content is organized, but by the resources it uses. It is technology-assisted learning.

It is certainly not surprising that modern technology – computers, emails, the Internet – evokes quite different reactions in people. At one end of the scale there are the Luddites (defined in the *BBC English Dictionary* as 'people who strongly oppose … the introduction of new machines and modern methods'). At the other are those who uncritically like anything modern simply because it is modern. It is a moot point whether there are more 'lovers' than 'haters' of technology, but even the most passionate haters know that the battle is already lost. Computers, email, the Internet and smartphones are all here to stay. They have devoured modern life with breathtaking speed. Take a look at CW11.8 (*Moodle: the real benefit of the virtual*). It illustrates one way in which technology has made its presence felt in language teaching.

11.5.2   The Internet and email

One reason why the Internet is powerful is because it can make a world of resources available to an individual sitting in one small room. Windeatt *et al* (2000) is full of examples of activities that use the Internet to practise vocabulary, grammar and the four skills. To illustrate: one of their vocabulary activities is called *Everywhere you go, always take the weather with you*. It is designed to introduce and practise weather-related vocabulary. The teacher prepares for the activity by finding websites describing international climate patterns and current weather. They go through weather vocabulary with the students in class before the activity begins. Then students imagine they will visit an English-speaking country of their choice. They are asked what they know about the country's climate, and what they think the weather there will be like now. They visit the identified websites to check whether their guesses were right, and this can lead to discussion about what clothes they should take with them, and what kinds of things it will be possible to do on their holiday. Windeatt *et al.*'s book is supported by an Internet resource at https://elt.oup.com/teachersclub. This is the Oxford Teachers' Club, which is free to join.

In 10.3, I mentioned that my son found himself chatting to children from other European countries while playing a computer game. Communication over the Internet by email is another resource with huge potential for language learning, because it enables people from around the world to communicate instantly. No three-week wait for a letter to emerge from the postal system. Robb (1996) discusses using electronic penfriends (keypals) worldwide for language teaching purposes. His paper gives a list of websites which will help teachers to develop contacts with educational institutions abroad. It suggests ways in which learners can be prepared linguistically for email correspondence – being given useful phrases about how to begin and end letters, for example. Robb also illustrates how learners' correspondence can be tracked by the teacher, who can for example be copied in to some of the communications. Teachers can also set up guidelines regarding how many lines of text they expect to be exchanged by learners. But be careful: Robb gives an amusing example of how the system was abused by one learner who sent the full text of Shakespeare's *Hamlet* to a keypal in order to maximise the number of words in their communication. Robb also discusses the types of activities that can be done with keypals. Perhaps it is enough for them just to correspond freely, describing their own countries, lifestyles, etc. But they can also make up stories together, or work together on written assignments. Sometimes practical difficulties make it problematic to match every learner in one class with every learner in another class overseas. For this reason, Robb (working in Japan) collaborated with colleagues in Prague and Melbourne to set up the Student List Project. In this scheme, students send their messages to an email list rather than to individuals. A variety of lists can be created, focusing on different areas of interests, like sports or films.

A good part of the value of email (and of Moodle, as described in CW11.8) is that it allows for rapid interaction, learner to learner or learner to teacher. Other means of achieving this have grown with the Internet. There are blogs ('web logs') which learners can use to express and collect views on given topics, or to write personal diaries online. Wikis are another similarly interactive resource. The word *wiki* means *fast* in Hawaiian, and the name has been adopted to describe a means of speedy communication over the Web. An important characteristic of the wiki is that material on a wiki website can be modified by anyone with access. Wikis are beginning to make their appearance in language teaching (I have just googled *wiki* and *language teaching* and got 169,000 hits). One use is as a tool for collaborative writing, where learners (even in different parts of the world) can work together on a text, suggesting modifications which can be immediately incorporated in the developing text. Dudeney (2007) has a section on the use of blogs and wikis in language teaching.

11.5.3 From CALL to MALU

Be prepared for yet more acronyms. CALL is computer-assisted language learning. It is defined by Levy (1997: 1) as 'the search for and study of applications of the computer in language teaching and learning.' It goes right back to the 1960s. Since then technology has moved on considerably, and there have been calls for a new acronym to reflect this development. One of the suggested alternatives is MALU, for mobile-assisted language use. Jarvis and Achilleos (2013) describe it as using 'a variety of mobile devices in order to access and/or communicate information on an anywhere/anytime basis for a range of social and/or academic purposes in an L2.' What is in a name? There are two differences between CALL and MALU. 'Computer' is replaced by 'mobile', and this reflects the growing popularity of mobile devices. But also 'learning' is replaced by 'use.' According to Jarvis and Achilleos (2013) this reflects a 'shift from viewing the computer as a tutor or tool to a medium.' Rather than as learning tools, mobile devices are being used as a means of communication, which is just how they are used in the real world.

Because computers, in the CALL model, are seen as a learning tool, they are often regarded by users as an aid for conscious learning. As you will recall from 5.1.2, this is opposed to acquisition in the theory put forward by Krashen. According to Jarvis and Krashen (2014), more recent mobile devices, such as smartphones and tablets, can be 'a major source of comprehensible input.' They help acquisition.

Jarvis (2015) gives examples of the sorts of activities in which mobile technologies can play a useful part. One describes a lesson on practising the simple past tense. Learners are asked to talk about what they did last weekend, and to decide who had the most exciting time. They use mobile devices to take pictures at home showing what they did. These devices are then used for discussion between learners. Jarvis also talks about setting up Facebook groups for class members. 'What's on your mind' posts can involve uploaded pictures and videos. Classmates can respond to these with a 'like' or by using the 'comments' tab to make points or ask questions.

11.6   And finally...

For many people, syllabus design is a dry, yawn-inducing subject. Whether or not this chapter has succeeded in stifling the yawns, it has hopefully indicated how much has happened in syllabus design in recent decades. Much of what has happened has been an enrichment and a 'complexification.' Syllabuses once could be short, simple documents, listing what structures would be taught, in what order. Nowadays, they are likely to be based on large-scale syllabus inventories containing many different sorts of lists.

But it is also true to say that along with developments in syllabus design has come an interest in the 'how' of language teaching – in methodology. At this point in the book, we imagine you have your syllabus ready and waiting. You now have to go into the classroom and teach it. But how? We have already dipped one toe into this river by considering, in the last section of this chapter, some techniques used when teaching with electronic resources. Now is the time to plunge fully into the river and immerse ourselves in methodology. The following chapters do just that.

Notes

1. Column 1 is entitled 'Unit', and the column just gives the unit names (like the chapter titles of a book). Column 2 is 'Main teaching points (structures).' This column lists the structures

to be covered in each unit. Column 3 is 'Topics (lexical areas) and functions.' The concept of 'topic' will be discussed later in the chapter.

Column 2 is the one which tells you most about how the book is organized.

The revision units are 6 and 12.

In column 2 the items in italics are sentence patterns. Those in capitals are structures. Sentence patterns and structures were discussed in 9.3, as was the use of capitals in this context.

The units focus particularly on the verb *be*.

2. To form negatives and interrogatives (from the basic affirmative form), you need to use part of the verb *do*. It is this verb that shows the tense (*do/does* in the simple present, *did* in the simple past) and carries the negation (*didn't*). The main verb *like* appears in the 'infinite' form, without an ending. In the interrogative, the subject (*she*) comes between part of the verb *do* and the main verb *like*.

3. This sentence illustrates that the term 'n/f' can be used alone, without the word 'syllabus' following. This usage is continued in the following pages.

4. The colleague was Keith Morrow, and the materials were a pilot version of what eventually became Morrow and Johnson (1979).

5. Thanks to Huw Jarvis for suggestions on how to update this section from the second edition.

Issues to think or write about

1. Box 11.3 gives an example of part of a needs analysis for secretaries. Think now about a different group of people with specialist needs – travel agents would be a possibility, but you may prefer to think of some other group. Do a 'mini needs analysis' like the one for secretaries. List, in as much detail as you can, situations, language activities, notions, functions and exponents.

2. Section 11.5 is about technology-assisted learning. Can technology really play a useful role in FL learning? Take a long, hard look at the advantages and disadvantages of using technology (in all forms, including the Internet, email, smartphones). Do they really help? Are they really an important step forward for language teaching?

Further reading

White, R. V. 1988 *The ELT Curriculum* Oxford: Basil Blackwell
An excellent book offering a broad overview of syllabus design within language teaching.

Trim, J. L. M., Richterich, R., van Ek, J. A., and Wilkins, D. A. 1980 *Systems Development in Adult Language Learning* Oxford: Pergamon Institute of English
A book containing the important early Council of Europe papers.

Hutchinson, T., and Waters, A. 1987 *English for Specific Purposes* Cambridge: Cambridge University Press

One of a number of excellent books on LSP, most of which contain a chapter on needs analysis.

Swales, J. 1990 *Genre Analysis* Cambridge: Cambridge University Press
If you want to read more on genre analysis, this book is recommended.

Dudeney, G. 2007 *The Internet and the Language Classroom* 2nd edn Cambridge: Cambridge University Press
As well as the Internet, this covers the use of email. Provides a wealth of practical ideas for various levels of teaching, and also deals with the use of blogs and wikis.

12 Ways and means

12.1 Introduction

In Chapter 6 (take a look back to Box 6.6) we identified two processes important in the mastering of a foreign language – declarativization and proceduralization. This chapter is about how we, as teachers, might help learners with these processes. With declarativization we are concerned with showing learners how some aspect of language 'works.' There are various ways this can be done. One is by actually 'presenting' the aspect to learners, by showing them examples, or giving them some kind of explanation. Another involves developing <u>language awareness</u> – trying to find ways of drawing learners' attention to language items. We shall use the term 'conveying language' to refer to all these different ways of showing how a language works. This may seem a curious term, and it is not one generally used in the literature. But it does capture the diversity of the activities that can achieve this aim in the classroom. The term we shall use in relation to procedural knowledge is less curious – it is 'practising language.' This also captures a range of procedures – many of which made a brief appearance in Chapter 9 – from very controlled drilling to activities like discussions, where learners are free to express themselves however they wish. In this chapter we shall look at techniques which are chiefly associated with teaching *spoken* English. In Chapter 13 we shall look at the teaching of other skills.

12.2 Conveying language

To start you thinking about how to convey new language to students, take a look at the activity in CW12.1 (*Teaching prepositions … with an army of helpers*). It asks you to consider how you might introduce some English prepositions to students.

Two characteristics can be associated with the good presentation of new language. One of them is *clarity*. The language point you are conveying to your learners needs to be clear. The second one is *memorability*. For the point to remain in the learners' heads, it needs to be presented in a memorable way. When I was at school, my history teacher wanted our class to understand the hardship suffered by workers during the British Industrial Revolution. He did so by dropping to the floor and crawling on all fours between the rows of desks, to show what it was like inside a coal mine. That was memorable. I still remember it.

Unfortunately, these two characteristics often lead in opposite directions. Clarity often suggests keeping the language content down to a minimum, so that the new item can be focused on without a cluttering context. 'Baldness' and 'focus' are key words. Memorability, on the other hand, often leads in the direction of a full context, trying to make the presentation as alive and meaningful as possible. 'Richness' and 'discursiveness' suggest themselves as key words. As we now consider some of the main modes of presentation available in language teaching, make a point of thinking of each in terms of the possibilities for clarity and memorability.[1]

One way of conveying information about language is by *explanation*. Here, a language rule is explained to the learners in explicit terms. It is associated with highly deductive teaching approaches like the grammar-translation approach. This was used in one of the five classrooms described in 1.5. Look back and find out which classroom.

A potential problem with explanations is that they can be highly intellectually challenging, thus making them inaccessible to many learners. This inaccessibility can be heightened by the use of linguistic words – like *noun, adverb, noun phrase* – which some learners will simply not have come across before. We use the word <u>metalanguage</u> to describe such 'language about language.' Explanation can be useful to introduce something for the first time, as the starting point for the proceduralization process. They can give the learner a kind of 'mental map' of what is to be learned. Fitts and Posner (1967) give a non-linguistic example. They report how the time taken to lead novice pilots up to their first solo flights can be reduced by more than half by giving an initial explanation in which the manoeuvres involved are discussed and explained.

But over-complex explanations can be particularly troublesome as a starting point, and it is very easy for them to become so long and contorted that they actually hinder performance. You can probably think of examples from your own experience, again related to non-language skills. Learning how to serve in tennis, for example, or how to drive a car perhaps. A tennis instructor may give such elaborate instructions on what to do – *Hold your arm at an angle of x degrees, with the wrist moving flexibly in an up and down position. The racket should be pointing directly ahead* – that the learner not only fails to serve, but also risks a nervous breakdown at the same time. As the skill psychologist Holding (1965) succinctly puts it: 'it is possible to disrupt the operator's performance in a quite lasting way by the over-elaboration of instructions.'

Simplicity is clearly an important characteristic for good grammar rules. What others are there? Swan (1994) is one of the few people who have tried to draw up a list of the characteristics a good language teaching rule should have. He lists six in all. One of them is indeed *simplicity*; another is that the rule should be *true*. Easier said than done, of course, and these two may conflict with each other. Often the language teacher has to simplify a rule to make it clear, but in so doing may arrive at a statement that is 'economical with the truth.' The *some/any* rules we saw in the 'Rough Guide to Syllabus Design Criteria' in 11.2.2 are a case in point. The rule that *any* is always used in questions (like *Did he eat any chocolates?*) is not strictly true. Think of examples where *some* is used in a question. Then look at CW12.2 (*Explaining* any *and* some) to see how one grammar book handles the difference.

All teachers, including language teachers, often need to do some explaining, so learning how to do it will certainly come in useful. You may like to try your hand at explaining some English grammar. Look back to Box 2.7, where you worked out the rules for forming English interrogatives. Restrict yourself to interrogatives of the type found in sentences (a), (b) and (c) there. Imagine you have to write a short explanation of these rules to a learner of English as a foreign language. What would you write? As in the *any/some* explanation above, keep the explanation short, and support it with examples.

A second way in which language is conveyed is by means of *key sentences*. Box 12.1 gives an illustration.

B12.1 Who dunnit?

Take a look at these key sentences (from Oxenden and Latham-Koenig 1999):

ACTIVE   PASSIVE

1a *Spielberg directed ET*   →   1b *ET was directed by Spielberg*

2a *They nominated the film for* →   2b *The film was nominated for*
    14 Oscars   *14 Oscars*

These sentences are used to show how to change the active into the passive. Focus first on sentences 1a and 1b. Use your own words to explain to a learner how 1a 'becomes' 1b. Then do the same for 2a and 2b. Think about clarity and memorability. Give the key sentences points out of ten for each.

Sentences 1b and 2b are different. How? (The title of the box gives a small clue.) Oxenden and Latham-Koenig use 2b to describe a common use of the passive (not found in 1a). What is this use? Try to explain it to a learner. The 'answer' is in Note 2.

Good marks for clarity, perhaps. But memorable? The words 'baldness' and 'focus' spring to mind, certainly more than 'richness' and 'discursiveness.' No one (including the textbook writers) would expect the learners to be excitedly telling their family about these key sentences when they return home after the lesson.

Dialogues/written texts are another extremely popular way of presenting new language in textbooks. Sometimes these are as bald and focused as the key sentences above, little more than a collection of sentences intended to 'carry' a grammatical point. We shall see an example of such a dialogue later, in Box 12.3.

In the following example of a written text (taken from Crace and Wileman, 2002), effort has been put into making the text interesting and hence memorable. The topic for this unit, and of the text itself, is *The Ice Maiden*. Before the learners read the passage, there are various warm-up activities, geared to arouse curiosity in the topic and prepare learners for what they will read. Then the text is read and some comprehension questions are asked. The passage is very much more than a carrier for the new structure that is being introduced, and it is likely to contain words and phrases unknown to the learner. At this stage the emphasis is on memorability rather than clarity. The focusing comes later, in an exercise which asks the learners to find instances of the structure being taught. This is followed by some practice in using the structure. As you read *The Ice Maiden* passage below, try to guess what the structure is. It is not too easy, testimony to the fact that the passage is indeed more than just a carrier of grammar. In fact you may have to go to Note 4 to identify the structure. So it might be argued that though the procedures here make the text memorable, it is, possibly, at the expense of clarity.

An amazing discovery

In 1993, an amazing discovery was made in the Siberian mountains. A team of archaeologists found a woman – she was 2500 years old. They called her the Ice Maiden because the ice had preserved her body, her clothes and her possessions. They discovered that she was from the Pazyryk people who had once lived there. And by looking at her things, they realized that she must have been someone very special. But who was she? And what was her position in society?

One metre seventy The team found that the ice maiden was one metre seventy in height – extremely tall for a woman at that time. It is not clear why she was so tall – she might have had extra food because of her status.

Dressed like a man The Ice Maiden was dressed exactly like a man, which means that she could have worked as a soldier. And only important people wore tall headdresses. It was covered in gold which clearly showed she was a rich and powerful woman.

Hole in the head The archaeologists found a large hole in the back of her head. This was probably part of a process for preserving important people when they died. This young woman clearly can't have been an ordinary member of society.

Fabulous tattoos Her body was covered with fabulous tattoos. The archaeologists now think that she must have been a storyteller. Storytellers were very important members of the Pazyryk society. They memorised the history of their people and used the tattoos of animals to illustrate the stories. In this way, they passed on the beliefs and traditions to future generations.

Teacher actions/descriptions can also be used to convey language to learners, and you can find an example of this in CW12.3 (*Teaching righteous indignation*). The technique is suited to some structures more than others. One of the structures it *is* commonly used for is teaching the present continuous tense.[3] One major use of this tense is to describe actions taking place at the present moment (<u>contiguous</u> actions). Since contiguous actions can be done in class, a common technique for conveying the tense's meaning is for the teacher to perform a series of actions, and to commentate on them as they are being done: *I am walking to the door*, *I am writing on the blackboard* and so on. Other members of the class then do the same actions, and the teacher produces sentences like *He is walking to the door*, *They are writing on the blackboard*. This procedure makes the contiguous action meaning of the tense very clear.

But the procedure has a danger, which Widdowson (1972) discusses. He makes the point that although this way of presenting the tense clarifies its *meaning*, it says nothing about how the tense is actually *used*. In fact, the use made of the tense in the examples just given is to 'commentate on your own actions and the actions of others.' Since everyone in the class can see what is happening, this use is unnatural and – if you look at it in terms of natural communication – even a little silly. It certainly leaves the learners without any feeling for when the tense is really used. Widdowson uses the terms <u>signification</u> and <u>value</u> for what we have called 'meaning' and 'use' above. He makes the point that learners need to be taught not just the signification but also the value of the grammar they are learning. This insight contributed significantly to the development of a communicative approach to language teaching.

How can we avoid the danger Widdowson discusses? Textbook writers nowadays take more care to ensure that the language of their texts is used in communicatively appropriate ways. Box 12.2 invites you to think about how this could be done for the present continuous tense:

B12.2 Contiguous but unseen?

Try to think of some situations where it would be natural to use the present continuous to commentate on actions taking place. This will probably need to involve actions which the listener can't for some reason see taking place. When you have thought of several situations, give a moment's thought to how one of them might form the basis of a language teaching exercise. Just a few vague ideas will suffice.

The way I tackled this problem in *Now for English* was to invent a situation where the children (the book's characters) have played a trick on their friend Sally, hiding something in her school desk. They are concealed behind desks in the classroom, waiting for Sally to come in. One of their number is peeping out from behind a desk and reporting to the others what is happening (*She's opening the door. She's coming in …*). The commentary is natural because the other children cannot see what is going on.

Widdowson's discussion raises the point that even in structural teaching we need to think about naturalness of language to situation. How much more so when we are teaching a function, like *asking for permission*, for example. In functional teaching, an essential part of the teaching point is to indicate the situations in which the exponent being taught would be used. 'Naturalness to situation' is not just important. It is what you are teaching.

B12.3 EFL or the Theatre of the Absurd?

It is easy, and unfair, to make fun of dialogues from less recent books because they do not have the same aims as books today. The dialogue below was clearly produced to contain examples of grammatical structures, and not to teach anything about communicative value. But though unfair, it can be very instructive sometimes to look at dialogues as a piece of communication. Do this with the dialogue below by thinking about what people would *really* say in the situation presented. Then compare it with what the dialogue has.

To start you off: as the dialogue unfolds it becomes clear that Y is a rail passenger (not a rail employee). One would not usually approach another passenger and say the first sentence without (at the very least) an introductory *Excuse me*. And is *It goes to Millville* a likely answer to that particular request? Go through the dialogue considering it in this way, to the point where the interactants say goodbye and apparently get on the same train together!

At the station

X: Does this train go to Newtown?
Y: No, it goes to Millville.
X: Where is the train to Newtown?
Y: It comes at a quarter to three.
X: When does it go to Newtown?
Y: Every half hour, and on Sundays it goes every two hours.
X: When does the bus go to Newtown?
Y: The bus goes from the bus station every fifteen minutes.
X: Are you going to Newtown?
Y: Yes, I go there every day. Where do you come from?
X: I come from Puerto Rico.

> Y: When did you come to this country?
> X: I came here in April last year.
> Y: This is our train. Goodbye.
> X: Goodbye.

In most of the examples we have so far considered, the teacher or textbook is directly 'presenting' a language item to learners. Allowing learners to find out for themselves, with guidance from the teacher, is a popular approach today, and has given rise to the procedure mentioned at the beginning of this chapter – developing language awareness. Another closely connected term is <u>consciousness-raising</u>, which Rutherford and Sharwood Smith (1985: 274) define as the 'deliberate attempt to draw the learner's attention specifically to the formal properties of the target language.' Perhaps this term will remind you of the concept of noticing that was discussed in 6.2. Go back to that section, entitled 'Consciousness and noticing', and remind yourself about the concept. There is also a discussion there on the factors that can help make noticing happen. The three factors mentioned are *frequency in input*, *perceptual salience in input* and *task demands*.

While you are in Chapter 6, look up Box 6.2, which asked you to think of ways in which noticing can be encouraged in the classroom. If you did this activity, take a moment to remember your thoughts on this. Thornbury (1997b: 333) gives a list of techniques to help develop noticing strategies in learners, and you may wish to compare your thoughts with his. One of Thornbury's techniques is to provide students with some input, and ask them 'to count the number of instances of a particular word or structure.' Other techniques include asking students to spot the difference between two similar texts, to report on the differences between a draft and a rewritten version of a passage. Teachers are also encouraged to provide opportunities in class for silent study and reflection, because noticing is more likely to happen under these conditions.

A distinction relevant to the process of conveying language is between induction and deduction. It was mentioned in 9.2, and CW12.4 (*Induction versus deduction*) tells you more about it.

12.3   Practising language

If you are fortunate (or perhaps unfortunate) enough to live next door to a pianist, you may be painfully aware of how much practice most musicians do. You will also have noticed what a variety of types of practice there are. Worst, from a neighbour's point of view, are probably the scales. For what seems like hours, the single-minded pianist goes up and down their instrument playing tedious, mind-numbing sequences of notes. But on other occasions they play 'the real thing' – actual pieces of music written for performance. Sometimes they stop and repeat bits, but occasionally they play the pieces from beginning to end. If your pianist neighbour has talent, these may be enjoyable to listen to.

Language learning can involve a similar variety of practice types, which have much in common with the musician's equivalents. Similar to the scales are what we call drills – highly repetitive, controlled, tedious and mind-numbing (but for the learner this time, not their neighbour). In fact one applied linguist, Debyser (1974), has made the parallel explicit by using the word scales to refer to a type of repetitive practice that includes the language learner's drills. At the other end of the spectrum is doing 'the real thing', and in the case of language this means using language for those activities language is usually used for – holding conversations, having discussions, writing letters, and so on.

In this chapter we shall focus on these two practice types. There are a number of labels the language teaching world use to refer to them, controlled practice and free production being common ones. But (risking controversy perhaps) we shall stay with the names *scales* and *the real thing* to punch home the idea that they have parallels in other areas of skill learning. Our concentration on just two types should not disguise the fact that between the extremes there are many intermediary stages – forms of practice that are not as controlled as drills, nor as open-ended as free communication. Before reading on, it is worth a moment's thought to consider what such 'in-between' activities might be like.

12.4 Scales (drills)

12.4.1 Five characteristics of scales

What are scales like? As we shall see later, the following five characteristics will help to distinguish them from 'the real thing.' You will notice that nearly all of them are related to the theory of behaviourism, discussed in 3.2.2:

(a) **Repetitive.** Scales depend for their effect on being done lots of times. *How many times can I get my learners to repeat an item in ten minutes?* is the question teachers ask in this respect. This characteristic shows the centrality of drilling in a behaviourist-based approach (like AL) where the importance of repetition was paramount. The search for an answer to the 'How Many Question' may lead you in the direction of pairwork, because in a pair each student can produce more language than when you have to deal with the class as a whole. It might also lead you in the direction of techniques like the substitution table, illustrated below. Those of you who are mathematically inclined might like to work out how many different sentences can be formed from this table:[5]

	city village	he visited	was		beautiful interesting
The	countries places	they stayed in	were	very	remote exciting

(b) **Relative meaninglessness.** As we shall see later, efforts can be made to inject some meaningfulness into scales. But they are in themselves relatively meaningless. This is partly because of their repetitive nature. To make practice meaningful often requires time, to create a context and provide the opportunity for the learners to become engaged in the situation. Individual drills tend to be 'nasty, brutish, short … and meaningless' (to develop Thomas Hobbes' description of the life of man).

(c) **Part practice.** Scales tend to focus on one small area of language (a single sentence pattern, for example), and practise it in isolation. Again, there is the influence of behaviourism here. The word isolative is sometimes used to describe this characteristic; another key word (met in 9.3) was 'incrementalism' – the procedure of gradually building language up bit by bit.

(d) **Indirect.** Very often drills bear little resemblance to the overall behaviour we are trying to develop ('the real thing', sometimes called – rather ghoulishly – the terminal behaviour). Scales are not real piano playing, and you would indeed feel cheated if you went to a piano recital where the pianist came on the stage and played just scales for an hour. Similarly, drills are not what people do when they speak or write to each other. The value of these practice types is that they are felt to contribute indirectly and cumulatively to the terminal behaviour. They are stepping stones.

(e) **Controlled.** Scales usually provide the learner with very little freedom indeed to say what they want to say. There is no room for improvisation.

12.4.2 Meaninglessness and meaningfulness

In 9.5 (entitled *The shift from 'how' to 'what'*) we discussed a movement away from practising the mechanics of grammar, towards an emphasis on message-focus. With this shift came a questioning of the value of meaningless drills, and discussion about how some degree of meaningfulness could be injected into scale-like practice. An applied linguist who discussed this issue at length was Julian Dakin. Here is an exercise abridged from Dakin (1973).

B12.4 Buying books you don't read

In this exercise, the teacher – or language laboratory tape – says the sentences in bold, and the learners produce the sentences in italics. To ensure that you understand how the drill works, invent some more items, giving the actual sentences both teacher and learner would say. Be sure also that you are clear on what is being practised here.

You bought the book. You didn't read it.
I have already bought the book, but I haven't yet read it.

> **You cooked the food. You didn't eat it.**
> *I have already cooked the food, but I haven't yet eaten it.*
> Would you describe this drill as 'meaningful' or 'meaningless'? Why?

The exercise in Box 12.4 is practising formation of the present perfect tense (positive and negative), in conjunction with the adverbs *already* and *yet*, which (unlike some adverbs) can be placed directly before the past participle forms (*bought* and *read*, *cooked* and *eaten*). The exercise is in fact one of Dakin's examples of a meaningless drill. For him the revealing characteristic is that you could do the exercise without actually knowing what the verbs *buy*, *read*, *cook* and *eat* mean, though you would of course have to know how to form the appropriate parts of these verbs (*eaten* etc.).

Dakin is critical of the meaninglessness of many drills developed in the audio-lingual tradition, pointing out that they can be done in totally mechanical fashion, without any regard for meaning. He talks about the *tumtetum effect*, and illustrates this by means of a foolish but revealing parody of a drill using nonsense words. In this, the teacher says the 'sentence' *Tum tumtete tonk te*, which the learner repeats. The teacher then gives some words to replace *tonk*, and the learner produces new 'sentences', like this:

teacher	learner
Tum tumtete tonk te	Tum tumtete tonk te
konk	Tum tumtete konk te
bonk	Tum tumtete bonk te
honk	Tum tumtete honk te

Though meaningless exercises like the one in Box 12.4 are not nearly so common in language teaching today as they were in the heyday of AL, they are still found. Indeed many would argue that they serve a useful purpose, giving learners some basic practice in manipulating structures that have just been introduced to them. But meaninglessness is not just of restricted value. It is also boring, and most teachers today take pains to try to introduce a degree of meaningfulness into their controlled practice. This is not always easy because, as we have already noted, a degree of meaninglessness is in the very nature of drilling, and you are unlikely to be able to make any drill highly meaningful. But there are degrees of meaningfulness, and most teachers today would argue for 'as meaningful as possible.'

But how can 'total *tumtetum*' be avoided? One of Dakin's answers is shown in CW12.5 (*Felicity eats fish*). Another way of creating meaningfulness is by introducing into the exercise an element of problem solving, or interpretation of some information given, or just plain fun. Box 12.5 stays with the area of negatives and illustrates exercises of this sort. Notice that the exercises are very controlled. If they are made more fun than the *tumtetum* one we saw in Box 12.4, this is not achieved by varying the amount or complexity of the language the learner uses.

B12.5 Two ways to practise saying 'no'

Here are two drills. They have in common that they are practising simple negative sentences.

(a) This is adapted from *Now for English* (Johnson 1983), a book, you'll recall, intended for young children. A picture shows six objects – perhaps a train, a bus, a car, a plane, a ship, a bicycle. A pupil volunteer must identify one of these objects by saying what it <u>is not</u>. They might, for example, say *It isn't a train. It isn't a bicycle. It isn't a car. It isn't a ship. It isn't a plane. What is it?* The first pupil to put up their hand and answer *It's a bus* becomes the next 'volunteer.'

(b) This is from *New English File Elementary Online* (https://elt.oup.com/student/englishfile/elementary/?cc=us&selLanguage=en). It is a game of the 'space invaders' sort. The instructions given on the screen are: 'Your mission is to go home to your planet. Hit the words in the correct order. Don't hit DANGER. Don't run out of fuel. Use the stick to control your ship.' In the first example given, the words that appear in different parts of the screen are *reading, DANGER, long, books, like, don't* and *I*. The learner uses their mouse to direct a missile at the words in the right order – in this case *I, don't, like, reading, long, books*. The game is timed, and a score is kept, with penalties every time the word *DANGER* is hit.

In Box 9.11, we came across a quotation from Stevick (1976), part of which dealt with the concept of meaningfulness. He said that 'Meaning depends on what happens inside and between people.' Finding out about your classmates – their habits, way of life, likes, dislikes – has become a major activity type in foreign language teaching. Questionnaires, quizzes and mini-surveys are techniques for doing this. For example, one unit in Kay and Jones (2000) is about relaxation and how people spend their spare time. In one exercise, learners are asked to find out about their classmates' spare-time activities. They ask questions about how many in the class are reading a novel at the moment, how many like reading biographies, how many prefer watching a film to reading a book. Such activities are particularly useful for practising functions like *finding out about*, *expressing likes and dislikes*, or *expressing preferences*. This reminds us that although all the drills we have seen in this section focus on structural areas, there is certainly such a thing as the 'functional drill.' You might like to ponder how you would devise a drill practising *inviting people* and *accepting/declining invitations*. What would your functional drill look like?

12.4.3 Communicative drills

In Johnson (1980a) I argue that 'conveying information' is often (though not always) an essential part of communication. For communication truly to take place, people need to be telling each other things they don't already know. In a language teaching exercise where people give each other already-known information, this essential element is missing. For communication to occur, there needs to be an 'information gap.' According to this line of argument, some communication is viewed as 'bridging an information gap.'

Many language teaching exercises, like the one in Box 12.6, lack an information gap.

B12.6 Telling your partner what they can see

This drill is taken from Broughton (1968). The students work in pairs, one asking and the other replying. Do the exercise alone in your head, working out what would be said for each picture.

| 1 Peter | 2 Janet | 3 Jillian | 4 Tom | 5 Alan |

Ask:

Is	Janet Tom Peter Alan Jillian	standing sitting	by the window? on the stairs? by the door? on the bus? on the scooter?

Answer:

Yes, No,	he she	is isn't

In this exercise both students are looking at the same page. So Student A is asking questions to which they already know the answers, and Student B is supplying answers which they know A already has. However useful the drill may be as structural practice, it is, from a communicative point of view, something of a charade. No information is changing hands. Box 12.7 contains my modified version of this exercise.

B12.7 Telling your partner what they can't see

This is an 'information-gapped' version of the drill above. Can you figure out how it works? Clue: creating an information gap involves use of a sheet of paper. The procedure is described under the box.

Ask your partner a question, and write names under the pictures.

| Who's that | standing

sitting | by the window?
on the stairs?
by the door?
on the bus?
on the scooter? |
| --- | --- | --- |

- -

Give your partner information

1 Peter   2 Janet   3 Jillian   4 Tom   5 Alan

To do this exercise, Student A covers the portion of the page below the dotted line with a piece of paper. Student B covers the top of the page in the same way.

By asking the students to look at different parts of the page (and by supplying one picture without names), an information gap is created. Now Student B does not know what A will ask, and A does not know how B will reply. There is an information gap. Hence communication – viewed as a 'bridging of the information gap' – becomes possible. Student A asks questions like *Who's that sitting by the window?* and B replies *Peter*. Student A writes Peter's name under picture 1. When the exercise is finished, A uncovers the bottom of the page to check that all their answers are right.

Why is the information gap important? One reason is motivational. It must be rather tedious for students constantly to be telling each other things that they already know and can in fact see before their very eyes – a recipe for boredom indeed. But more important is that without an information gap present, crucial communicative processes may not get practised. Consider Student A's role in the Box 12.6 drill. There is no reason at all why they should even listen to, let alone process, what is said to them. They already know the answers to the questions they are asking. In fact, they could very well block their ears while B is replying. The drill would still proceed without problems. Ear-blocking is not an action associated with communicative behaviour.

We must be careful not to claim too much for our modified exercise. Like the one in Box 12.6, it remains a simple drill: it practises one structure which is repeated a number of times. But I call it a 'communicative drill' because, having an information gap, it does at least – in a very restricted way – involve communicative processes. The participants have to listen and take in what they are told. Exercises like this are nowadays very common. There is another example at CW12.6 (*Spending money*).

As the pair of scissors in CW12.6 shows, there are different ways of creating an information gap, other than by asking students to conceal part of the page. A further common technique is to have information on different pages of a book. One student looks at one page, their partner at another. Some publishers have even gone as far as publishing two books, one used by Student A in each pair, and the other by Student B. A good example of this is Watcyn-Jones' (1981) *Pair Work*.

B12.8 How can S2 help?

Here are some situations which could form the basis of information gap exercises, each involving students working in pairs – S1 and S2. Choose one of the situations and create an exercise:

(a) Think first about what sorts of sentences the situation will be good for practising.
(b) Then think of a detailed contextualization for your situation (why, for example, in the first situation, does S1 want to go to Oxford?).

(c) Now decide exactly what information you would need to give S2.

(d) It is also very important to think about what S1 is given. In the last situation, for example, you might decide to give S1 a map of the zoo with the locations of some animals marked, but not others.

(e) Finally, plan the exercise in sufficient detail for you to go into a class and use it. This is likely to include preparing worksheets for the learners.

S1 is staying in London and wants to catch a train to Oxford. They don't know the train times. How can S2 help them?

S1 can't decide whether to go on holiday to Macau or Bali. They want a hotel next to a beach, and there mustn't be an airport too close by. They don't want to spend more than £500 per week. How can S2 help them?

S1 wants to stay at home this evening and watch television. But they don't know what's on. How can S2 help them?

S1 wants to visit the zoo with their parents. They are particularly keen to see the lions, giraffes and seals. They don't know whereabouts in the zoo they are. How can S2 help them?

The notion of a 'communicative drill' does not please everyone. Harmer (1982) for example argued (though he may or may not be still of this view) that the concepts of drilling and communication are incompatible. The essence of communicative teaching is message-focus, he claims, and drills cannot of their nature be message-focused. It is in essence the same sort of argument that (as we saw in 9.9.1) led Prabhu in the direction of his procedural syllabus. But you will also remember from Chapter 9 that language teaching which is entirely message-focused runs the risk of creating fossilized learners. To remind yourself of this issue, go back to Chapter 9 and look for the discussion on how language teachers have sought ways of introducing form-focus into message-focused approaches. The key words to look for are *form-focus*, *fossilization* and *fish and chips*. Communicative drills which practise grammar are one way of providing a focus on form.

12.4.4   Yes, but do scales work?

B12.9 The Big Question

Do scales work? This is, surely, the Big Question.

Think first about your experience as a foreign language learner. Have you found drills to be of any value? Then think in more general terms. Can you learn a musical instrument without doing scales? What about a language without doing drills? If your answer is different for music and language, then what is the difference between learning a language and a musical instrument?

Are there likely to be any bad consequences in learning a language without *ever* doing drills? What about learning a language using *nothing but* drills as practice?

Almost all of the recent discussion in language teaching about the pros and cons of drilling has been within the behaviourism versus cognitivism debate. We have already explored these positions and discussed the connection between drilling and behaviourist theory. We have met the basic assumption of AL that 'foreign language learning is basically a mechanical process of habit formation' (Rivers 1964: 31), and in CW9.1 we encountered Nelson Brooks' view (1960: 142) that 'the single paramount fact about language learning is that it concerns not problem solving, but the formation and performance of habits.' Perhaps you would like to go back to CW9.1 and find that quotation; also to Chapter 3, where we considered the cognitivist case against learning as habit formation. Find the L1 example of the child who repeated a wrong sentence (*Nobody don't like me*) eight times, yet despite such repetition presumably eventually moved on, when ready, to the correct form.[6]

In more recent times, there has been some actual research into the role of practice in learning. CW12.7 (*Practice makes less perfect?*) summarizes a piece of small-scale research done by Ellis. He concludes that, at least in the situation he considers, there is little observable value to practice.

In relation to the research described in CW12.7, Ellis is the first to admit that the amount of research done into the value of practice is small and cannot lead to firm conclusions. There are many questions still unanswered. One relates to Pienemann's notion of learnability. Perhaps practice will have value only if the item being practised is close to the point at which it would be acquired in the 'natural order.' Then there is what Ellis (1994: 621) calls the 'delayed effect hypothesis' – the idea that the value of practice (or indeed instruction in general) cannot be expected to appear for a while. This is an attractive idea. I certainly find with learning a musical instrument that practising some tricky sequence does not pay off for quite a while. In fact the practice sometimes has an immediate bad effect, making me play the sequence worse. Have you ever had a similar experience, where practice seems to lead to at least a temporary diminution of performance? If so, why do you think this should be? Note 7 gives one suggestion.

Is there any real alternative to scales, apart from adopting a Prabhu-like approach? Many applied linguists (including Ellis; see 1994: 643) regard language awareness or consciousness-raising activities as being potentially more effective than scale-like practice. Such activities might be useful as an initial step in learning (recall what Schmidt and Frota say in 6.2 about the value of noticing). But they might also be beneficial at some later stage. I can certainly recall instances in my own foreign language learning experience where focusing in a conscious way on structures I had already come across and used was an extremely valuable procedure. Perhaps you have had similar experiences? It is certainly the case that textbooks nowadays tend to contain many 'drawing attention to structure' exercises geared to make the learners notice aspects of language form. Structural practice is not ignored in such books. But the preference now seems to be for 'understanding and (meaningful) practice' rather than simply providing large quantities of controlled drilling as was the case in the days of AL. Do you approve? Think about what language awareness activities can achieve. And controlled drilling? Can one replace the other, or do you need both? Nitta and Gardner (2005) take a look at a number of contemporary textbooks to find out whether in them consciousness-raising tasks have replaced practice exercises. Though there are differences between the various textbooks, the general conclusion is that practice exercises 'still occupy an essential place in ELT materials' (Nitta and Gardner 2005: 9).

12.5   The real thing

Scales may have their place, but the chances are that your answers to Box 12.9's questions will reveal a feeling that some other type of practice will also be necessary for successful foreign language learning. In this section we consider another practice type. We shall ask three questions about 'real-thing practice': what it is, why it is important, and how we can introduce it into the classroom.

12.5.1   The 'what' question: five characteristics of real-thing practice

---

B12.10 Renting a flat

Read this description of an exercise called *Renting a Flat*:

Learners imagine they are going to study at a university abroad. They are told they want to rent a flat in the university town. They are given seven short advertisements for flats to rent taken from a local newspaper. The adverts briefly describe each flat, including details of rental costs. All the flats have potential advantages and disadvantages: they vary in size and price; some are nearer the university, some farther away; some are on noisy main roads (but with good access to public transport), some in quieter locations (with less good access); some are close to shops, some not; some have gardens, some

---

not; some allow smoking on the premises, some do not; some have *en suite* facilities, some not . . . and so on.

Learners first work alone looking at the advertisements and deciding on their own personal favourite. Then they come together – first in pairs, then in groups of four. They imagine that they want to share the flat, and have to decide on a common choice. Several types of follow-up would then be possible. Once a common choice has been made, learners could be made to phone up the landlord of their chosen flat (another learner in class) and make arrangements to come and view the accommodation. They can also be asked to write a letter home describing to their parents the choice they have made.

Be sure you are clear on how the exercise would work in class. Think about what sorts of things the students will want to say when they do the exercise. Also think about 'class management' issues, like what you would say to introduce the exercise, how you would arrange the learners into groups (of two, then four), how you would find out the choices that have eventually been made, and so on. If you have an hour to spare, you might also like to write the advertisements for this exercise yourself, making sure the various flats have a selection of good and bad features.

But the most important thing: look back to the five characteristics of scales found in 12.4.1. Consider this exercise in relation to each characteristic. What is your conclusion? Is *Renting a Flat* a scale?

No, *Renting a Flat* is not a scale. Your conclusion is likely to have been that it has none of a scale's five main characteristics. This leads us to a characterization of real-thing practice in which the contrast with scales could not be more marked:

(a) **Non-repetitive.** Real-thing exercises do not rely on repetition for their value. In fact, any particular activity of this type is often just done once, or possibly twice. This is not just because their value does not lie in repetition, but also because by their very nature they are time-consuming activities. Think how long it would take to set up and execute *Renting a Flat* in class.

(b) **Meaningful.** *Renting a Flat* has been developed in the expectation that the situation will engage the learners; the result should be discussion that is lively and even earnest. As we noted earlier in this chapter, creating meaningfulness is a time-consuming business, which is one reason for (a) above.

(c) Real-thing practice is **whole practice.** Scales concentrate on small segments of behaviour. In the real thing, the learner 'puts it all together.'

(d) **Direct.** At this stage, we make efforts to practise the terminal behaviour itself – actually using language in simulations of real situations. It is, indeed, the real thing. The word 'simulation' is important in this respect. A lot of real-thing practice involves the learners in pretence: *pretending* that you want to rent a flat, *pretending* you are the director of a company chairing a board meeting, and so on; look back to 9.7 where this same point was made in relation to practising functions. There are similarities between this kind of exercise and the practice given to novice pilots in aircraft simulators. Both attempt to reproduce the conditions of real activities, but in a 'safe' environment – the classroom or the simulating machine.

(e) **Free.** In real-thing practice, the learners are allowed to express their ideas, thoughts and feelings, in line with their wishes and capabilities. The teacher would not normally insist on specific language items being used.

12.5.2   The real thing: the 'why' question

> ## B12.11 Your answer?
>
> Before you read the following paragraphs, think how you would answer these questions: what would the learners lack if there was no 'real-thing' element in their classes? Why is it important?

In much audiolingual teaching, there was no real-thing practice. New structures were introduced and drilled. Then you went on to the next structure. The belief seems to have been that once a structure has been thoroughly drilled, no further exercising will be necessary; the structure will make its way from controlled classroom practice into everyday use without any further effort. For me, one of the major insights of recent years in applied linguistics is the realization that the transfer from controlled classroom practice to free outside use is extremely difficult to achieve. Much work has to be put into it. This has led in recent times to importance being given to real-thing practice. Indeed, if any practice type nowadays has to sing for its supper, it is the scale (pun intended).

There are three reasons why real-thing practice is important. The first is the *need for freedom*. As we saw in 9.7, one of the insights of communicative methodology was the realization that learning a language involves mastering many types of skill, not just grammatical ones. We now realize the importance of risk-taking skills and the development of strategic competence. (Remember strategic competence? It is one of Canale and Swain's categories of competence from 2.5.) Being prepared to take risks is indeed a vital part of language learning. The learner who is not prepared to do this may never open their mouth. One of the risk-taking skills is circumlocution: being able to express an idea when you do not have the real words to do so. You also have to have the confidence to start sentences when you do not know how to finish them. I remember vividly a problem I had learning German, a language in which verbs sometimes come at the end of sentences. I would often start a sentence, but then realize with increasing panic as the sentence went on that I did not know what verb should go at the end. There would be perspiration and silence where the verb should be. 'Communicating with inadequate means' is a skill that every language learner needs to develop. Perhaps you can remember moments in your own experience when you have had to 'communicate with inadequate means'?

Risk-taking skills can only be developed if we loosen the reins that control learners, allowing them the freedom to express themselves as they wish. This means real-thing practice. But, you may cry, if reins are loosened, then the learners will make errors. Is that such a terrible thing? According to behaviourism, of course, errors were to be avoided at all costs. But we now have a more relaxed attitude towards errors. Indeed, they may be seen as useful for the learning process (a general view of learning captured in an expression we met in Box 3.1 that 'we learn through our mistakes'). Certainly a learner who develops a fear of making errors is unlikely to be a good communicator.

The second reason for the importance of this practice type is the *need for meaningfulness*. Earlier in this chapter we looked at attempts to make drills as meaningful as possible. But the point was made that there are indeed limits on the extent to which this can be done. The truth is that if we want a significant degree of meaningfulness, this implies lots of real-thing practice.

B12.12 What you really, really want to say

The *Renting a Flat* simulation in Box 12.10 is an attempt to put learners in a situation where they will have a desire to communicate. Or will they? You could argue that *Renting a Flat* is unlikely to engage the learner very much, because the situation is 'externally imposed' on them by the teacher or textbook. H. Johnson (1992) looks at simulations like this, and explores ways in which the learner may be encouraged to participate more in their construction, in order to increase learners' 'engagement' in the language involved. Perhaps in the case of *Renting a Flat*, before the learners see the advertisements, they could be asked to think about accommodation features particularly important for them, discussing some of the vocabulary useful in describing such features. Are there any other ways in which *Renting a Flat* might be modified to increase learner participation?

A third reason for the importance of the real thing is the *need for fluency practice*. The concepts of <u>fluency</u> and <u>accuracy</u> have been much discussed in recent decades in language teaching (for example in Brumfit's 1984 book, which is subtitled *The Roles of Fluency and Accuracy*). What do these terms mean? You may wish to attempt your own definitions before reading on.

One dictionary (Richards *et al.* 1985) defines accuracy as the 'ability to produce grammatically correct sentences.' Correctness is certainly a central idea, although it is possible to broaden use of the term to apply to different aspects of language use, not just the grammatical. CW12.8 (*Different ways of being wrong*) is all about this.

The word 'fluency' is far more problematical, and is used in a large number of different ways. The aspect of it we shall focus on here is what we shall call 'combinatorial skill.' This is the skill of 'being able to do many things correctly at the same time.' This skill is not easy. Think about it first in terms of a non-language skill – learning a musical instrument. You may be able to play a note completely in tune when it occurs in a scale, when your full attention is concentrated on playing in tune. But when you are performing an actual piece, many things have to be done at the same time. The timing must be right, as well as the dynamics (loudness and softness), and the sound quality. With all these things to attend to, the note in question may slip out of tune. It is the same in a foreign language conversation. Your grammar, your pronunciation, your cohesion (and all the

other skills we saw in CW12.8) may be perfect when doing drills geared to practise each of these in isolation. But getting all these things right when you have to do them together is a quite different matter. To master that skill you need <u>whole practice</u> rather than <u>part practice</u>, and whole practice is real-thing practice.

12.5.3   The real thing: 'how'

Rough Guide to Three Real-thing Activity Types

(1) Role play and simulation

What they are: In role play, learners play characters, often following instructions given on 'role cards.' For example, Learners 1, 2 and 3 might be friends wanting to go on holiday together. They discuss possible destinations, then phone up Learner 4, a travel agent, to make bookings. In a simulation, learners are themselves in an invented situation. The 'Renting a Flat' exercise in Box 12.10 is an example. However, many writers use the terms 'role play' and 'simulation' interchangeably.

  Comment: Wilkins (1973) makes a distinction between the 'language of reporting' and the 'language of doing.' An example of the first is the sentence

---

The manager threw the drunk out of the restaurant. This reports something that happened. An example of the second is *Get out, or I'll call the police*, the words actually used to throw the drunk out. Wilkins makes the point that reporting is easy to set up in class, and most traditional exercises involve it. But (he argues) we need to practise the second as well, and for this we need exercises like role play. See the comments in 12.5.1 about *pretending*.

Reading: For discussion of these techniques in language teaching, see Sturtridge (1981).

A task for you: Question 2 in the 'Issues to think or write about' section at the end of this chapter give you the chance to create a role-play activity.

(2) Communication games

What they are: According to Richards *et al.* (1985: 118), a game in language teaching has the following characteristics. It involves: (a) a particular task or objective; (b) a set of rules; (c) competition between the players; and (d) communication between the players by spoken or written language.

Examples: Many popular games can be used for language teaching – for example, *Twenty Questions* and *Charades*. Board games (and card games) can also be used, usually with some adaptation to make sure that language is introduced. An example is mentioned after this Rough Guide.

Comment: Games of all sorts use the concept of the information gap. An example is the child's game of *Pin the tail on the donkey*. In this, a child is blindfolded and has to pin a cardboard tail onto a picture of a donkey. The child who puts the tail nearest to where it should be is the winner. Blindfolding is a way of creating a physical information gap. The game in CW12.9 is also centred around an information gap.

Reading: For general discussion, including a short classification of games, see Maley (1981). Two collections of games to practise specific grammar points are Rinvolucri (1985) and Ur (1988). Jill Hadfield has also produced a series of books containing communication games for different learner levels (Hadfield 1987, 1990, 1997, 1999).

A task for you: Think about *Charades* or *Pin the tail on the donkey*. What kind of language content could the game be used to practise (what functions, what structures, what lexis)? Try to devise an activity based around one of these games for an appropriately aged group of learners. Prepare it in enough detail to go into the class and use it.

(3) Discussions and debates

Examples: These can be informal affairs involving activities like finding differences between pictures. Social and moral issues (e.g. the danger of global warming) can also be involved. A hoary old favourite is the *Balloon Debate*, where learners represent well-known figures flying together in a hot-air balloon. The balloon is losing height, and people have to be thrown out to keep the balloon safe. Learners argue for the character they represent to remain in the balloon.

Comment: Debates and discussions need careful preparation for success. Learners do not automatically have opinions on all topics, and even if they do, these are not usually expressed without some coaxing. It is sometimes necessary to use stimuli (e.g. visuals), or to start with a survey of opinions round the class – or to use some other means for allowing thoughts to be mustered.

Reading: Ur's (1981) *Discussions that Work* is a classic – an excellent collection of ideas for discussions.

A task for you: Choose a topic for a debate. It could be on a social or moral issue, or it could be the *Balloon Debate*. How might you prepare for the discussion? Think of some ways in which you could spend 10 minutes helping your learners to think what to say and how to say it.

If you would like to take a closer look at a real-thing activity, look at the one in CW12.9 (*Battleships and zoos*), which also gives you the opportunity to construct an activity of your own.

12.6 Activity sequences

12.6.1 The three Ps

In this chapter we have considered two types of classroom activity which we have called *conveying language* and *practising language*. The second of these has been subdivided into *scales* (or *drills*) and *real-thing practice*. How can these activities be sequenced? In what order should they go?

One activity sequence has been accepted by applied linguists and practised by teachers for many decades. The sequence is often referred to as 'the three Ps', standing for *presentation → practice → production*. You will probably be able to make immediate associations between these Ps, and the activities we have been discussing. At the *presentation* stage, the item to be taught is introduced. This is a version of our 'conveying language.' It is then *practised* in drills or scales (the name 'manipulation' is also used for this stage). The *production* stage – our 'real-thing practice' – is likewise known by different names; van Els *et al.* (1984: 264) mention 'transfer', 'comprehension' and 'development', while 'free practice' is also commonly used. One of the language teaching methodologists who did much to popularise discussion of the three stages in recent times is Don Byrne, particularly in *Teaching Oral English* (1986). PPP (as it is called) has various sequences embedded within it. These are mentioned in CW12.10 (*From P to P to P*).

The PPP sequence has not been without its critics. Some describe it pejoratively as a 'transmission model', because it is based on a view of learning in which knowledge is 'transmitted' from teacher to learner (you may wish to remind yourself of what Moskowitz says in 9.8 about 'information transmission'). Transmission models have fallen out of favour in recent years, and the PPP sequence has therefore also lost its place in the sun. But in 1998 Skehan had to admit that PPP is 'probably still the most common teaching approach when judged on a worldwide basis' (1998: 94).

12.6.2 The deep-end strategy

What are the alternatives to PPP? We have already seen one possibility in CW9.7, the *pre-task → task → post-task* sequence (and variations thereof) associated with TBT. Because of the current interest in tasks, this sequence is indeed nowadays quite common. Another possible candidate is offered by Brumfit (1979 and elsewhere). He suggests that the most lasting impact of communicative language teaching is replacement of the traditional PPP sequence with the one shown in Box 12.13.

B12.13 Three Ps: but in which order?

Below is what Brumfit (1979: 183) calls a 'reversal of traditional methodological emphases.' Think of the sequence below in terms of the traditional three Ps. In which order do these come below?

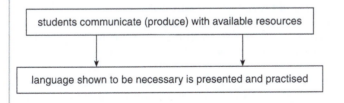

Brumfit's sequence is *production → presentation → practice*. Its starting point is some kind of free-production exercise. So at the beginning of the lesson, the learners might be asked to do a role-play exercise, or play a game, or hold a discussion. This would happen without any linguistic preparation. The teacher would listen to their performance, and on the basis of it would decide what needed to be presented and practised.

There are advantages (and disadvantages as well) to this exciting proposal. One advantage is that the learners really do have the chance to develop strategic competence and to practise the risk-taking skills we discussed earlier in this chapter. At the first stage they really are in a risk-taking situation, being asked to say things they have not been taught how to say. In a paper (Johnson 1980b), I call the procedure the 'deep-end strategy.' Why this name? Because there are two ways to teach someone how to swim. One of them is the behaviourist way of teaching strokes bit by bit, and slowly shaping the behaviour. The other way is to throw learners in at the deep end. Those who survive learn how to swim. Those who don't …!

Here, to finish the chapter, are some connections to ponder. In CW6.3 we presented a view of language teaching which emphasized the processes of declarativization and proceduralization, and introduced two 'pathways', called DECPRO and PRODEC. How does traditional PPP fit into this? Is it DECPRO or PRODEC? And what about the deep-end strategy? Note 8 gives some suggestions.

Notes

1. One major weapon in the fight for memorability is by chance not well represented in the examples given. This is the visual aid. Pictures of all sorts (including videos) can help to make a presentation vivid, thereby contributing to memorability.
2. In 2b the people who undertook the action are not mentioned – 1b has *by Spielberg*, but there is no *by them* in 2b. The passive is often used when the speaker or writer has no particular interest in conveying – or does not know – who did the action.
3. Chapter 2, Note 5 made the point that 'perfect' is an aspect, and that what is commonly called the 'present perfect tense' is really the 'present tense with perfect aspect.' 'Continuous' is similarly an aspect, and we should really talk of the 'present/past tense with continuous aspect.' But referring to the 'present/past continuous tense' is so widespread in the language teaching literature that we will use these names.
4. The 'new structure' in the passage is a modal verb followed by *have*, as in: *she might have had, she could have worked, she can't have been, she must have been …*
5. The horizontal lines in columns 2 and 4 separate the singular from the plural forms. They indicate to the learner that if they choose an item above the line in column 2 (e.g. *city*) they must select the item above the line in column 4 (*was*). Many substitution tables do not have such lines.
6. Young children do in fact indulge in a kind of 'drilling', known as 'crib talk.' Alone in their cribs or cots, they often practise sequences of sounds and words in a drill-like way. This phenomenon has been described by Weir (1962).
7. Perhaps it is because practice makes the conscious mind pay attention to the sequence, and this may have an initial inhibiting effect.
8. Presentation is clearly associated with declarativization, and the other two Ps with proceduralization. So traditional PPP is a DECPRO sequence – you start off giving your learners some 'information' about language (presentation), which you then set about proceduralizing. It is possible to see the deep-end strategy as a version of PRODEC. At the first stage the learners practise using language. After that they are given information which helps them to declarativize it.

Issues to think or write about

1. The concepts of 'fluency' and 'accuracy' are briefly mentioned in 12.5.2. A lot has been written about these two concepts, which play an important part in recent language teaching approaches. Read about these concepts. Then discuss them. Say what they are and how they differ. Why are they both important in language teaching?

2. Imagine that you have just been teaching the functions of *inviting, accepting and declining invitations*, and *making arrangements* with a group of intermediate students. Now you want to do some real-thing practice using a role-play activity (with the learners working in pairs or groups). Think of a situation for practising these functions, and actually prepare the role play. If you have time, work it out in enough detail to go into the class and use it. This may well involve preparing worksheets for the learners.

   An alternative: if you did not do the activity in Box 12.8, now is your chance to do so. It involves creating an information gap exercise.

Further reading

There are a number of book series which provide practical help on teaching techniques for EFL teachers. One is the Cambridge Handbooks for Language Teachers series (edited by S. Thornbury). Sample titles are Ur, P., and Wright, A. 1992 *Five Minute Activities*, and Lindstromberg, S. 2004 *Language Activities for Teenagers*.

Another series is Oxford Basics. One book in the series is Hadfield, J., and Hadfield, C. 2000 *Simple Writing Activities*. These authors have also written *Presenting New Language* (1999) in the same series.

A further series is Resource Books for Teachers (edited by A. Maley for Oxford University Press).

There are also a number of websites which provide plenty of useful ideas about teaching techniques. Included are www.esl-lounge.com; www.eslcafe.com; and the British Council's ELT site, www.teachingenglish.org.uk.

Brumfit, C. J. 1984 *Communicative Methodology in Language Teaching* Cambridge: Cambridge University Press
The notion of fluency is discussed at length in Brumfit's book.
For suggested reading on particular activity types, see the 'Rough Guide' in 12.5.3.

13 Skills

13.1 The four skills

Speaking, writing, listening and reading are the four language skills. Most of the example activities we looked at in the last chapter were in the context of the first of these. Now we shall focus on the other three.

There are two conventional ways of dividing the four skills up. The first is into medium, with listening and speaking occurring in the spoken medium, reading and writing in the written medium. The second division is into the receptive skills of listening and reading, and the productive skills of speaking and writing. This use of the terms 'receptive' and 'productive' is probably self-evident. But beware of the once-used terminology which called the productive skills 'active' and the receptive skills 'passive.' As we shall see in this chapter, listening and reading are in fact highly 'active' processes. You are invited to write the words *speaking*, *listening*, *reading* and *writing* inside the box below, to indicate how they stand in relation to these divisions:[1]

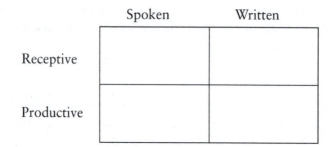

In some approaches to language teaching, the four skills are treated separately. There is a listening comprehension lesson, a speaking lesson, a reading lesson and a writing lesson. There are obvious advantages to doing this. For one thing, our needs analysis is likely to reveal different learner needs for each skill area. Also, each skill poses its own problems, which will sometimes benefit from separate treatment.

But it is important to realize that there are similarities and interconnections between the skills. In this chapter we shall treat listening and reading together, because both involve common processes of *comprehension*. Also, when we look at teaching techniques, we shall often find that listening exercises can be used, with small changes, for the teaching of reading as well, and vice versa. In addition there are processes common to the productive skills, so that techniques for the teaching of speaking can, with modifications, often be used for writing. But there is another set of interconnections to think about. In a later section we shall touch briefly on the idea that to be a good writer, it helps to be a good reader. Understanding your reader, knowing what they are expecting next and anticipating how they will interpret what you write are essential skills for good writing. One might even go so far as to say that teaching good writing involves teaching someone to be a good reader. All this adds up to the fact that although it is sometimes useful to look at the four skills separately, we must not forget ways in which they are similar, and how they interconnect.

This chapter looks at the processes involved in the comprehension and production of language. Understanding these processes will reveal what the foreign language learner needs to be able to do in order to comprehend and produce the language properly. We will also think about how teaching can help the learner master these processes.

13.2   Comprehension

13.2.1   Bottom-up processing

Things have developed a lot in the teaching of comprehension in the past few decades. One of the main agents of change has been psycholinguistics. This branch of linguistics is defined as 'the study of the cognitive processes that support the acquisition and use of language' (de Bot and Kroll 2002: 133). A major concern of this field is to ask what procedures humans follow when they try to understand a piece of speech or writing. The answer to this question has changed rather dramatically in recent decades. This change has had its effect on language teaching, because the procedures people use when they comprehend language are just what we have to ensure that our learners master. To understand these procedures, we need to do a little psycholinguistics.

Sometimes in the following discussion we shall focus on reading, sometimes on listening. But most of what is said applies to both. We shall use the word *text* to apply to pieces of language that are spoken as well as written. As a prelude to discussion, you are invited to read – and then temporarily forget about – the passage given in Box 13.1. We will talk about it in a later section.

B13.1 Reading about a peace march

Read this passage quickly through. What you have read will be discussed later.

A peace march

Taken from Bransford and Johnson (1973, cited in Clark and Clark 1977: 163):

> The view was breathtaking. From the window one could see the crowd below. Everything looked extremely small from such a distance, but the colourful costumes could still be seen. Everyone seemed to be moving in one direction in an orderly fashion and there seemed to be little children as well as adults. The landing was gentle and luckily the atmosphere was such that no special suits had to be worn. At first there was a great deal of activity. Later, when the speeches started, the crowd quietened down. The man with the television camera took many shots of the setting and the crowd. Everyone was very friendly and seemed to be glad when the music started.

Here is the common-sense, layman's view of reading: a text is a collection of words – the little black marks on the page – grouped into phrases, sentences, paragraphs. In order to understand the text, what the reader needs is the linguistic knowledge necessary to decipher the little black marks. According to this view, meaning is something that resides in the text itself. The reader prises the meaning out of the text, like an oyster out of its shell.

Associated with this view of reading (and listening too) is a model of comprehension processing which was a focus of psycholinguistic thought before the 1970s. The procedure described in this model has come to be known as <u>bottom-up</u>. In bottom-up processing, the starting-point is the text itself. The reader attends to individual words and structures in the text, from these gradually building up an interpretation of the whole. Imagine, for example that you read the following sentence (taken from Clark and Clark 1977):

The farmer put the straw on a pile beside his threshing machine.

Processing this in a bottom-up way, you would identify that a farmer is (roughly speaking) a person engaged in agricultural pursuits, and that the word *the* is signifying that some particular farmer is being spoken about. You would then move on to the word *put*, identifying it as describing a past action, of 'placing' or 'setting down.' When you came to the word *straw*, you would consult your 'internal dictionary', which would tell you that the word has at least two meanings – *grain stalk* and *drinking tube*. You would hold these two meanings in your mind until a later stage when you were considering the meaning of the whole sentence. At that point you would doubtless decide that the first meaning was the one intended here. You would continue through this sentence in the same manner, word by word, in a process involving what was traditionally called <u>parsing</u>. The term 'bottom-up' is used because in this process you begin at the 'bottom', with the text itself. Another term used by psychologists for the same process makes this notion even clearer. It is <u>data-driven processing</u>. To consider some more words, like *straw*, with two meanings (and for some practice at parsing), take a look at CW13.1 (*Parse yourself*).

We are going to think about learning and teaching comprehension in a later section (13.2.4). But it is worth having these issues at the back of your mind all the time, and here are two questions to ponder, based on what we have so far discussed. If we view comprehension as a bottom-up process, what does this imply for learning and teaching? What kinds of skills do we have to teach learners to ensure that they can comprehend in a bottom-up way?

13.2.2 Six 'strange occurrences'

How adequate is the bottom-up model of comprehension processing? There are some 'Strange Occurrences' that take place when readers and listeners set to work on texts. We shall explore some of these. They will lead us to conclude that the bottom-up processing model is an incomplete and inaccurate representation of comprehension.

Strange Occurrence 1 is that it is possible to understand every word of a text and still not know what it is about. We have already come across this idea, in 2.4.1, where we discussed the notion of 'rules of use.' When the old Croatian lady said *Where are you going?* to me, I understood her grammar and the signification of every word, but failed to identify their function as a greeting. In this example, cultural knowledge is important. CW13.2 (*The left little finger*) gives another example where the knowledge required is not cultural but specialist.

Strange Occurrence 2 is that it is possible not to understand some parts of a text, yet still know what it is about. Some time ago our dog Bertie chased a sheep on the hill behind our house. I said to him: *Now you know you shouldn't do that. That's naughty. I've told you not to chase sheep. If I catch you doing that again there'll be trouble.* He did not understand many of these words. But he knew I was angry, and he knew why. He understood the underlying message perfectly. In case you are unconvinced by an example of listening involving another species, have a look at the exercise in Box 13.2.

B13.2 Biners injured

This exercise, taken from Grellet (1981: 36), is based on an article that appeared in the *Daily Telegraph*. Some invented words have been inserted, which means that you will not be able to understand every word. The passage shows how it is possible to understand the gist of a text when not all words are understood. What do you think the imaginary words might mean?

Train derailed

Plicks are believed to have caused the dolling of a two-car diesel passenger train yesterday. The train, with 24 biners on board, hit a metal object and

---

> ratteol 100 yards of track before stopping four pars from Middlesbrough. Three people were taken to hospital, one slightly ropped, the others tinding from shock.

Strange Occurrence 3 is that it is possible to understand a message even when there is no evidence for your interpretation in the actual words on the page. Look back to Chapter 2 and find the example of this exchange:

A: There's the doorbell.
B: I'm in the bath.

This small snatch of dialogue has a 'subtext' that reads:

A: There's someone at the door. Can you go and open it?
B: No I can't, because I'm in the bath.

You might say that this exchange is 'about' who will answer the door. Yet answering the door is not in fact mentioned. The word <u>inferencing</u> is commonly used to describe what the reader or listener does here.

What the Strange Occurrences so far suggest is that the black marks on the page (or in the case of listening, the sound waves in the air) play only a part of what we do when we read or listen. It is beginning to be clear that the reader or listener brings a lot of themselves with them to the job of interpreting. *Strange Occurrence 4* illustrates just how far this can go. It is an example of how it is possible to think you have been told something that was not in fact said at all. In 1932 the psychologist Bartlett told some American Indian folk tales to British subjects, asking them immediately to retell the stories in their own words. Coming from a very different culture, these stories would have been very odd indeed to the British listeners, containing many details which would bewilder them. The fascinating result of his experiment was that the listeners changed the stories to fit in with their own expectations. This even involved adding details to make the stories conform to listener expectations. One story, for example, describes how an Indian was wounded in battle. How he was wounded is not stated in the original, but some British listeners add the detail that it was by an arrow. This is because the listeners know that bows and arrows are the means Indians use for fighting. Their embellishments make it clear that the subjects came to the stories with some already-existing set of expectations which played a major part in how they 'understood' the story.

Strange Occurrence 5 is exemplified in the text you read in Box 13.1 (deliberately put earlier so that you would not be alerted to the possibility of any 'Strange Occurrence' in it). You may (or may not!) have noticed a sentence in it that does not relate to the title, or indeed the rest of the passage. It is the sentence about the space landing. In Bransford and Johnson's experiment, people failed to recall that sentence well. It is as if they blotted it out because it did not fit into their expectations, aroused by the title. When Bransford and Johnson changed the title of the passage to 'A Space Trip To An Inhabited Planet', subjects' recall of that same sentence was much better. This example shows that readers are able to ignore something said in a text if it does not fit in well to expectations. It is almost as if they had not read or heard it.

Our final *Strange Occurrence, number 6*, is that different people will take different 'information' out of a text. There can be many reasons for this, and in some circumstances you will perhaps not find this strange at all. You will probably accept, for example, that no two individuals will comprehend a play like Shakespeare's *Hamlet* in quite the same way. But on a more banal level, one major reason for this phenomenon relates to the *reason* why the person is reading or listening. There is an example in CW13.3 (*Catching a train*) that shows how individuals with different reasons for listening will extract different pieces of information from the same message. They are listening *for* different things. Therefore, perhaps, they are listening *to* different things. CW13.3's Edinburgh train example shows how our purpose for listening/reading involves us being *selective* with our attention. We do not pay equal attention to everything we hear or read. As Faerch and Kasper (1986: 265) put it: 'the principle that "all input must be accounted for" applies to computational but not to human information processing.' Computers do it, not humans.

Our purpose is also likely to set limits on how much we actually need to understand. Most purposes are not likely to be highly rigorous, demanding anything like 'total comprehension' (whatever that might be). *Partial* understanding is usually enough. Take the word 'Ayatollah' as an example. The *Cambridge Encyclopedia* (Crystal 1990) defines this as 'a Shiite Muslim religious title … referring to a clergyman who has reached the third level of Shiite higher education, is recognized as a mujtahid, and is over 40.' Most readers from non-Muslim societies will doubtless not know this, and few would be able to come up with such a precise definition. So there is a sense in which they *do not* understand the word. But few of us actually need such a precise definition. We may know that an Ayatollah is a religious leader in Islam, and this restricted knowledge is probably enough to ensure comprehension of the text in which we come across the word. There is, in other words, a level on which we *do* understand the word. Full comprehension is rarely required by a reader or listener, or, for that matter, possessed by the writer or speaker.

In the next section we will consider what our six Strange Occurrences tell us about comprehension. Before reading on, perhaps you will find it useful to make, by way of a summary, a list of the six Occurrences with brief notes explaining in your own words what each one is.

13.2.3 Top-down processing

Taken as a whole, our Strange Occurrences clearly indicate that although the text itself is of course important for comprehension, what the reader or listener brings to the text is also very important. This is why the bottom-up model cannot alone account for comprehension. As early as the 1930s and the work of Bartlett that we have referred to, psychologists were concerned to develop a processing model which would take account of the listener/reader's role in comprehension. The model that emerged involves a type of processing called <u>top-down</u>. This term captures the idea that the starting point is within the mind of the listener/reader and, as with 'bottom up', there is another term psychologists use which clarifies the meaning. It is <u>concept-driven processing</u>.

An important notion in top-down processing is what Bartlett (1932) calls <u>schemata</u> (singular: <u>schema</u>). These may be described as the 'mental frameworks' we hold as individuals, and which we bring with us when we read or listen to a text. In the case of the British listeners to Bartlett's American Indian stories, the schemata are about American Indians, their lives and the weapons they use when they fight. It is from the American Indian schema of some listeners that the arrow makes its way into the story. In this case the result is an error (because the arrow should not be there), but schemata play an important part in comprehension, even from an early stage in the process. Comprehension does *not* follow a totally bottom-up pathway, and we do *not* logically work through all possible interpretations of a text (as a machine might) before deciding what it means. Instead, we take shortcuts. We use background knowledge to select the most likely interpretation, often without even being aware of other possible interpretations. Our agricultural sentence – *The farmer put the straw on a pile beside his threshing machine* – is a good example of this. We saw that the word *straw* has at least two possible meanings, and that in purely bottom-up processing we would note these meanings when we came to the word, only deciding at a later stage which was intended. This is the way an intelligent computer might process the sentence. But the likelihood is that, faced with a sentence like this, we would not even consider the second meaning. Words like *farmer* and *threshing machine* would immediately invoke our 'farmyard schema', and in this the word *straw* has only one meaning. Comprehension is a process of *making sense of a text*, in the most cost-effective (but not necessarily the most thorough) way.

How do bottom-up and top-down processing relate to each other? There have been various models of comprehension which have encompassed both types of processing, including one which was developed by the cognitive psychologist Anderson (1983), whose work we met in 6.4. It is important to realize that all recent models involve *both* types of processing. It may be that in different situations one will be more prominent than the other. Faerch and Kasper (1986: 264), for example, suggest that in highly predictable contexts – where there are plenty of contextual clues available to help work out what is being said – top-down may be used more. In situations where little context is provided, we may need to resort more to bottom-up processing. But overall, both are needed. Even the highly skilled reader/listener will engage in bottom-up processing, and although some of the examples we have given of top-down processing have ended in inaccuracies (British listeners adding possibly wrong information to the Indian stories, for example), this type of processing is also vital. It enables us to interpret texts in realistic time (not going through the various interpretations of each word, for example).

13.2.4 Comprehension skills for learners

What does our discussion about comprehension processes tell us about the different types of knowledge the foreign language learner needs to master? How does the learner need to be equipped if they are to be a good reader/listener? To repeat a point made earlier, it is important to ask such questions because their answers will help us identify what needs learning and teaching. High on the list, and not to be forgotten, is knowledge of the target language. A non-native listener/reader's problems with a text may be due largely to deficiencies in banal but vital areas, associated with bottom-up processing, like vocabulary and grammar. As Eskey (1988: 94, cited in Paran 1996) puts it: 'Good readers know the language. They can decode ... both the lexical units and syntactic structures they encounter in texts.' But knowledge of the target language needs to go beyond the understanding of words and structures in isolation. There are the 'rules of use' which enable you to interpret what is actually being 'said' in a message. And to understand messages, background knowledge is also important. The aspect of this that we have focused on is schemata, though psychologists and applied linguists have introduced various other concepts to refine and develop this notion of background knowledge.[2] Hedge (1985) divides background knowledge into *general knowledge, subject-specific knowledge* and *cultural knowledge*. The learner will need varying quantities of these according to the texts being read or listened to. They will also need *reasons* for listening or reading.

Think now in terms of skills. Identifying the different types of knowledge we have been discussing has led applied linguists to develop lists of the skills that the learner will have to master. Some of these lists are, in Williams' words (1998: 334), 'vague' and 'overlapping.' Some are also very long: Grellet (1981) uses Munby (1978 – a book briefly mentioned in CW11.3) and has a reading-skill list with no fewer than 19 items on it. Some commonly listed skills are clearly related to bottom-up processes, like *word recognition* and *understanding word meaning*. Others equally clearly involve top-down processing, like *applying schemata to texts, predicting* and *inferencing*. Then there are skills associated with understanding of general message. Williams (1998: 333) mentions *identifying main ideas* and *following the development of an argument* in this category. Important characteristics for some of these skills are 'being selective' and 'being partial' – the capacity to focus on some pieces of information and ignore others, particularly in relation to a given purpose for reading/listening. Vague, overlapping and long as some of these lists may be, they are useful attempts to specify learning aims in a precise way.

Does the FL learner need more bottom-up or more top-down practice? As we have seen, both are important, and what the learner requires can often best be assessed by looking at what they have already been given. Many learners suffer from a surfeit of bottom-up. This develops in them the habit of processing word by word, and refusing to progress if one word is not understood. So if they do not know what a *pile* is in our *The farmer put the straw on a pile beside his threshing machine*, they would give up before *threshing machine* was ever reached. Recall just this situation in Box 9.9 where an unknown word brought comprehension to a grinding halt. These learners desperately need training in top-down. But in recent years, top-down listening and reading have been fashionable, and there is the danger of developing a breed of learners who are expert in applying schemata to texts without too much regard for what the texts actually say. This danger is well expressed by Paran (1996), who argues the need for attention to bottom-up skills. The healthy diet needs both.

13.3   Facilitating comprehension

As you read through this section, remember that when the examples given refer directly to the teaching of reading, they are often likely to apply to the teaching of listening too, and vice versa.

13.3.1   Practising bottom-up skills

Traditional comprehension exercises focus on bottom-up processing. At their worst, these can be of the *Cat sat on the mat* variety. The text tells the students that the cat sat on the mat. Then a series of questions ask such things as *Who sat on the mat? What did the cat do? Where did the cat sit?* More imaginative approaches ask questions about a variety of different linguistic levels. There is also room for exercises practising skills in isolation. CW13.4 (*A word recognition exercise*) gives an example. Grellet (1981), in her useful source of ideas on reading comprehension, has a large collection of exercises dealing with specific skills like *deducing the meaning and use of unfamiliar lexical items through understanding word formation*, and *developing word comprehension speed*.

13.3.2   Understanding communicative value and main points

The result of nothing but the *Cat sat on the mat* type of comprehension questions will be learners who are not trained to recognize the communicative functions in a text. One way to do this is by asking which of a series of statements most clearly captures what is being said in a given text. This exercise will be particularly useful if you make sure that all the statements say things that are mentioned in the text. The learner's task is to distinguish important from less important information. Here is a silly example which stays with the cat and mat theme. Imagine a listening passage containing the utterances *Just look at my beautiful mat. It's filthy all over. There's no doubt about it. The cat sat on the mat.* You might give learners the following three statements, asking which most clearly captures what the speaker is saying:

(a) The speaker is expressing their fondness for their mat.
(b) The speaker is blaming the cat for making a mess.
(c) The speaker is stating that no part of the mat is now clean.

The correct answer is (b). But notice that the other two statements, (a) and (c), also express ideas that are there in the 'text.' The speaker *is* fond of the mat, and no part of the mat is now clean. Exercises of this sort are commonly found in textbooks nowadays. Cunningham and Moor (2005b), for example, offer a reading passage (in Module 12) about someone who tries to give up watching TV. One of the exercises has the instruction: 'Read the text quickly. Which sentence best describes the attitude of the writer towards television?' Learners are given a choice of four – (a) to (d).

There are two traditional exercise types which are sometimes branded as old-fashioned, but which can be very useful in this context. The first is translation. This has, according to Cook (1998b: 359), 'been dismissed by almost all twentieth-century theories and methodologies.' But translation is now enjoying a revival, because we have come to realize that being able to translate a passage well involves a clear understanding of the writer's intention. A good translator has to understand functions and speech acts, not just the signification of individual words and sentences. The second traditional exercise is particularly useful for facilitating understanding of the intention of a text as a whole. It is *précis*, or summary writing. As with translation, this has a dusty, old-fashioned air about it. But in order to be able to write a good summary, you have to have understood what the main points of a text are, distinguishing them from other less important points that are also made in it.

If you want to try your hand at précis writing, write a summary of the paragraph above, using no more than 50 words. As you do this, notice the kinds of decisions you are making. Many will be about identifying which points are main and which subsidiary.

13.3.3   Forming or activating schemata

In cases where students do not have background knowledge appropriate for the understanding of a passage, ways of giving it to them need to be found. Here is how one book (Harmer 2004) does it. One of his units is about New Year's resolutions. Before reading the passage, learners are given some information about how the New Year is celebrated in Anglo-Saxon cultures, and this includes information about the custom of making (and breaking!) New Year's resolutions. Learners are asked to think about similarities and differences in the way they celebrate the New Year in their own countries. Another textbook, by Phillips and Phillips (1997: 5), has a useful phrase to describe what happens here. They call it *Background Building*, defined as 'activities to encourage students to access useful "frames" or "scenarios" for the type of text to follow.' Pre-reading or pre-listening exercises like Harmer's are also a common way of activating background knowledge that learners already possess. The next time you are in a library containing FL textbooks which specialize in reading or listening, take some off the shelves. The chances are that they will contain pre-reading/listening activities. There is one book, by Hess (1991), that consists of nothing but 'pre-text' activities. It provides a set of games, discussions and activities involving looking up information that will 'motivate, challenge, and arouse curiosity' (p. ix) before texts are read or heard.

B13.3 Background building in ice

Look back to *The Ice Maiden* passage in 12.2. What areas of background knowledge would you think necessary to enable a group of learners that you know to understand and enjoy this passage? Think in general terms of some ways in which this background knowledge could be provided.

Is there likely to be anything in the learners' own experiences that you could get them to think about as preparation for reading the passage? How could you activate this already-possessed knowledge?

13.3.4   Developing predictive skills

One common pre-reading/listening activity involves asking learners to predict what a text will be about. For example, the reading component in a textbook by Cunningham and Moor (2005c, Module 6) consists of six short articles taken from a newspaper. One of the pre-reading activities gives the headlines together with very short descriptions of each passage. The learners match the headlines with the descriptions. Then they read the articles and find out whether their matchings were correct. One reason why activities like this are useful is because part of the top-down process is to be able to make sensible guesses as to what is coming next in a context. Good readers and listeners can do this. One exercise type which helps develop predictive skills is called <u>cloze</u>. In a cloze test or exercise, learners are given a text with some words missing. Trying to guess what the words are is a form of prediction. In many instances of cloze, single words are deleted at regular intervals (every seventh word, for example). The exercise in Box 13.4 is of a type sometimes called <u>selective cloze</u>. Here words are not omitted at regular intervals, and the omissions have been chosen to make the learner think about the content and organization of the text. The gaps are all of the same length, though what fills them may be one word or a whole chunk of text. In exercises like this, it does not matter if the learner cannot guess the actual words; more important is whether the gist of what is missing can be predicted. Try the exercise yourself. The passage is taken from 1.2, so you can check your version against the original.

B13.4 What's missing?

Learner number one is Lilian Rivera. She lives in Santiago, the capital city of Chile. She has a bachelor's degree in business studies from _____, and she wants to do a master's degree overseas. She has _____ universities in Britain, the United States and Australia, and there is the chance that she may receive some scholarship money. _____ all the universities require her to take an internationally recognized English test before _____, and her score on the test must be very high. It is now January, and _____ is in June. She does not enjoy language learning at all, but her situation explains very well why _____ spent in the (for her) tedious business of _____ her English.

If you would like to develop a feel for how to 'selectively cloze' a passage, why not choose another learner from 1.2, select a few words to blank out, and ask a colleague to fill in the gaps?

Though they are a little tedious to prepare, you can also create 'large text deletion' activities. You may like to try one out with a friend. You need to identify a passage and turn a good portion of it into blanks, one blank for each deleted word. As your friend makes guesses, you check the words in the original, and write them into the blanked version.[3] You could again use *The Ice Maiden* passage from 12.2 to experiment. To make the activity reasonably short, give the first paragraph ('An amazing discovery') in full. Then write a blank for every word in the next two paragraphs ('One metre seventy' and 'Dressed like a man'). Your friend's job is to replace every blank with a word. If you are feeling particularly generous, you could let your friend read very quickly through the original passage before the activity starts. If the activity works with your friend, try it on any students you may be teaching.

We have here been looking at cloze as a teaching technique. In the next chapter (14.3.2), we will come across it again in the context of testing.

13.3.5 Purposeful comprehension

Some, but not all, of reading and listening is for a specific purpose – to find out some specific piece of information, for example. One major difference between the way comprehension used to be practised and how it is practised nowadays is that we now commonly state a clear reason why a passage should be read or listened to; it is purposeful comprehension. We saw an example of a purposeful reading exercise in Box 9.8. We made the point there that purposeful comprehension is important because it teaches the invaluable skill of 'not trying to understand everything.' Then look back at Box 9.9 and remind yourself of the '100 per cent comprehension' school and the dangers it holds.

The exercise exemplified in Box 9.8 is of the type called <u>information transfer</u> (IT).[4] IT exercises work by asking the learner to transfer information from one representation to another – from a passage to a map in the case above. Box 13.5 gives some other examples of IT exercises. Some of these are reading, some listening. But in all cases the exercises could be modified for practice in the other medium.

B13.5 Five information transfer exercises, plus one

For each exercise, say what the transfer is *from* and *to*. For example, in exercise 1 it is from tape to clock faces.

1. An exercise for young children. A picture shows a space ship with an astronaut doing various activities, like eating breakfast, exercising, going to bed. There is a clock beside each picture, but with the hands missing. Learners listen to a tape describing the *Astronaut's Day*. It tells them what the astronaut does and at what time. They use this information to put hands on the clocks (from Scott 1980).
2. Different learners read five different passages, each describing the guilty secret of one character (a headmaster, a novelist, a writer, a journalist and a cartoonist). Learners are given a blank table. It has a column for each character, and rows labelled with a number of emotions – anger, disgust, happiness, etc. Learners decide what emotion the character they are assigned felt in the passage they have read, and put ticks in appropriate boxes. Information is then shared with the rest of the class (Hadfield and Hadfield 1995).
3. Learners listen to a woman talking about her family. The task is to use what the woman says to fill in a partially completed family tree (West 1999).
4. A lady phones up an interior design company for some information. The person she wants to speak to isn't there, so the receptionist has to take a message. Learners have a blank message pad with the headings *Caller's name*, *Company*, *Phone Number*, *Message*. They have to listen to the conversation and fill in the pad (Burke and Brooks 2000).
5. Jordan's (1990) *Academic Writing Course* contains an activity in which students are given a table containing information about six dictionaries intended for learners of English. The information includes such things as the number of words each dictionary covers, the number of illustrations

---

it provides, and so on. Learners are told they have received a letter from a friend asking for advice on which dictionary to buy. The task is to reply with a recommendation. This exercise well illustrates how a receptive (reading) exercise can be linked to a productive (writing) one.

If you would like to try writing your own IT exercise, look at number 2 of the 'Issues to think or write about' section at the end of this chapter.

A particularly imaginative form of IT exercise, pioneered by Geddes and Sturtridge (1979 and 1982), has come to be known as <u>jigsaw</u> listening and reading. In this, the class divides up into groups, with each group listening to or reading a different text. The groups then come together and pool their information, to complete the 'jigsaw.' Exercise 2 in Box 13.5 was of this sort. Another example is found in Hadfield and Hadfield (1995, Unit 6). Learners are shown a series of postcards from John, who is on holiday in Asia. There is also a route map which shows the locations he visits. Learners are each given one postcard, and a main aim of the activity is for learners to combine information on the various postcards and to mark on the route map when John visited which places, as well as retelling the news that John relays.

A small but important point about the order in which you do things in class: perhaps you find yourself saying, 'Yes, purposeful comprehension, which is very selective and partial, is very important. But I want something more. I think learners need to spend time studying texts, even in a bottom-up, form-focused way.' This is a sensible standpoint. But if you want to practise *both* comprehension for a specific purpose *and* detailed textual study, then the order in which you do it is crucial. If you do the detailed analysis first, then your learners will never practise selecting, being partial, ignoring the unwanted. You need to do it the other way round. First, set a specific reason for comprehending, then do the more detailed study of the text.

While on the question of ordering classroom events, there is a common sequence of activities used for the practising of receptive skills. For reading, this sequence is *pre-reading activities* → *while-reading activities* → *post-reading activities*. We have already mentioned a number of possible pre-reading activities, including (in 13.3.3) preparing the learner for reading by forming or activating relevant schemata. Actually setting the while-reading task is also something that will happen at the pre-reading stage. While-reading itself involves undertaking the task as set. Hedge (2000: 210) gives the following examples of while-reading activities: learners may be asked to 'follow the order of ideas in a text, react to the opinions expressed, understand the information it contains, ask themselves questions; make notes; confirm expectations or prior knowledge; or predict the next part of the text from various clues.' Post-reading activities can be very varied, encompassing any follow-up or exploitation of what has been read. The class can go through and check what was done during while-reading. There can be a discussion of some interesting issue raised by the reading, or written work can be set, based on some aspect of what has been read. You came across another pre-, while- and post- sequence in CW9.7, where we considered *pre-task* → *task* → *post-task* in TBT, and in 12.6.2, where this was discussed as an alternative to the traditional PPP sequence.

13.4 Writing

13.4.1 Writing and speech

In the previous section, the point was made that listening comprehension exercises can be turned into reading comprehension, and vice versa, usually without much difficulty. To some extent the same is true for speaking and writing exercises, and for this reason a number of the techniques introduced in Chapter 12 can be adapted for writing practice. For example, nearly all the practice stage exercises, including the information gap ones, can be modified just by asking the students to write down sentences rather than saying them, though since writing is a longer process than speaking, you have to bear in mind how time-consuming some drills will be. You are invited to pick out at random a few of the example exercises introduced in Chapter 12, and think how they could be converted into writing exercises. Choose real-thing activities as well as scales.

The teacher can, then, use speaking exercises for writing practice, and indeed, as Byrne (1988) notes, a major and respectable use of writing is as a reinforcement to what is done in speech practice. Written work also, incidentally, has the great advantage of being visible evidence of effort. A written exercise can be taken home to a parent as proof of work done. Speaking practice often suffers from a lack of documentary evidence.

But writing is more than speech written down. There are many aspects of writing that are different from speech. CW13.5 (*Complaining in speech and writing*) asks you to consider some of these, and Box 13.6 gives a summary of some of the more important ones. This latter box needs treating with care. What the differences between speaking and writing are depends on what kind of speaking and what kind of writing we are considering. A formal spoken lecture will have certain characteristics in common with a written essay, while an informal note to a spouse about what shopping they should buy on the way home will have certain characteristics in common with spoken conversation. Box 13.6 looks at rather formal writing and rather informal speech, and if you vary this, the differences may disappear. For example, it may be true that contracted forms do not appear often in writing an academic essay, but this would not be true about a note to a spouse.

The existence of these differences carries a clear message. When we are teaching speaking, we are *not* at the same time teaching writing. Writing is indeed more than speech written down.

B13.6 Some differences between speaking and writing

a) General

(i) Learned vs taught. Everyone learns to speak. Not everyone learns to write; it has to be taught.
(ii) Writing is more 'organized.' Why?

(a) There is less 'redundancy.' The reader cannot rely on repetitions to clarify. The writer is often not given immediate feedback. In speech, if something is unclear, your interactant immediately tells you, and you can rephrase your message.
(b) Permanence of the written medium and knowledge of scrutiny. When you write something, you know it is there for ever. It is also available for others to scrutinize and 'pick over.' But digital recordings are rapidly changing this situation by making speech potentially permanent.
(c) Writing is often 'fuller.' This is because you are less certain of what knowledge you share with your reader, since their identity is often more vague.

b) Linguistic

(i) Some structural differences: for example, contracted forms are less common in writing (so we may say *didn't* but write *did not*).
(ii) No intonation, stress or gestures to help clarify meaning in writing. We have to find other ways of achieving what these things manage. Note also that there is no punctuation in speech.

c) Functional

Perhaps there is more 'language of reporting' in writing than speech. Certainly a needs analysis of speaking and writing uses would identify different purposes and notions/functions.[5]

13.4.2 Teaching the 'joining-together' skills

Of the differences described in Box 13.6, the one that perhaps has the most implications for teaching is that writing is more organized. Part of what this implies is that attention has to be given to the 'joining-together' skills of cohesion and coherence. We discussed these concepts in 2.4.2. There we noted that a passage is more than a sequence of individual sentences. We spoke of two types of rules of discourse, concerned with grammatical unity (cohesion) and sense unity (coherence). If you need to remind yourself of the difference between these concepts, look back to Box 2.12.

How can we teach cohesion and coherence? Some of the exercises we considered under the receptive skills can be useful here. Cloze activities (the one in Box 13.4, for example) can be extremely useful in drawing the learner's attention to passage organization, particularly if the teacher carefully selects which words to omit from the text so as to focus on organization. Another technique involves giving the learner sentences in isolation, and asking them to join the sentences together. This technique is known as <u>sentence combining</u> (SC). Box 13.7 illustrates two SC exercises.

B13.7 Two versions of sentence combining (SC)

1. One version of SC involves taking a text and dividing it into separate sentences, repeating information where necessary. The learners have to join the sentences together. Try it. You will come across the original sentences a little later in this chapter (at the end of this section):
   - Hedge (1988: 136) gives an example.
   - Hedge asks learners to analyse a given text.
   - Hedge provides a number of statements.
   - The statements describe what is done in a text.
   - *Supporting an argument with an example* is an example of a statement.
   - *Making a general statement* is another example of a statement.
   - Learners write a number beside each statement.
   - The numbers show how a text is organized.

   Now find another passage (in this book or from elsewhere). From it, create a series of sentences as above, suitable for an SC exercise.

2. In another version of SC you give the learners an opening sentence, then a series of choices as to what will follow. Hamp-Lyons and Heasley (1987: 52), for example, have an exercise with the following instruction: 'Read the beginning of the text and choose one sentence from the two which follow it. Keep choosing one sentence from each two, continuing the text as you think the writer might have written it.'

   According to the kind of sentences you offer as a choice, this exercise can be used to practise coherence or cohesion.

SC involves a process of what might be called 'passage assembly', and this process is highly productive as a technique for practising the 'joining-together' skills. You will find more examples in CW13.6 (*Two 'passage assembly' activities*).

The exercises in CW13.6 involve the learner in assembling a passage out of given sentences. A further set of techniques popularly used for teaching joining-together involves 'passage *re*-assembly.' Hedge (1988: 136) gives an example. She asks learners to analyse a given text. She does this by providing a number of statements describing what is done in the text, like *supporting an argument with an example*, and *making a general statement*. Learners write a number beside each statement to show how the text is organized. She then suggests a new opening sentence for the text, and asks how the order would change if the passage started in that way. This is actually quite a natural task. As you may have discovered from your own experience at academic writing, you often find yourself rewriting paragraphs, perhaps to begin in a different way. Different beginnings often require total reorganization of paragraphs – an exercise in cohesion and coherence.

13.4.3   Process writing

Much traditional writing practice focuses attention on helping the learner to say – accurately and appropriately – what they want to say in writing. It is concerned with the content or <u>product</u> of learner writing. An alternative approach which has become popular in recent years looks in detail at the processes writers go through when they produce texts; these are then practised in class. This approach is called <u>process writing</u>.

B13.8 Writing procedures

One book particularly influential in the area of process writing is by White and Arndt (1991). They begin their book by identifying the major procedures involved in producing a piece of written work. A diagram showing the procedures is given below. But before looking at this, think yourself what these procedures might be. What stages do you go through when writing an essay? Begin with the very first stages of planning (long before your first sentence is written) and end at the point where the essay is a finished product.

When you have identified the stages, compare your thoughts with White and Arndt's.

Here are the major writing processes White and Arndt (1991: 4) identify:

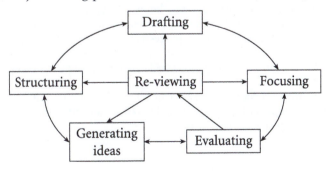

Source: White, R. V., and Arndt, V. 1991 *Process Writing* © Longman Group UK Ltd 1991, Pearson Education Limited

White and Arndt suggest a wealth of techniques for practising these in class. CW13.7 (*How to generate, focus and structure*) gives some examples.

In our treatment of writing we have focused on just some of the skills involved. These have been chosen partly because they are the ones that have most interested applied linguists and teachers in recent years. Another reason is that they are skills particularly associated with writing and may not receive attention in a course with a bias on teaching the spoken language. But do not forget that there really is much more to teaching writing than developing the joining-together skills and the processes of composition that we have covered. Among many other things, a good writer must have a grasp of basic sentence construction, and somehow or other this needs to be taught.

Sometimes (though not always!) in language teaching, what you teach gets learned, and what you do not teach does not get learned. In the late 1970s, when much attention was given to teaching cohesion, one sometimes found the strangest examples of student writing as a result. An essay might contain very many (unnaturally many, in fact) sophisticated 'link expressions', such as *however, moreover, nevertheless, on the other hand*. But between these elegant link expressions might be the most awful English, full of errors. This was the result of teaching the joining-together skills and not much else. Beautiful joints, holding nothing together.

Notes

1. This is how the four skills are categorized:

	Spoken	Written
Receptive	Listening	Reading
Productive	Speaking	Writing

2. As well as schemata, two other concepts, known as <u>scripts</u> and <u>scenarios,</u> are used to describe aspects of background knowledge. If you want to know more about schemata, scripts, scenarios and comprehension processes in general, Brown and Yule's (1983) *Discourse Analysis* is a good read.
3. Computer versions of such games are described in a number of places, including by Higgins and Johns (1984).
4. I discuss information transfer exercises in Paper 15 of Johnson (1982).
5. For a lengthier discussion of speech/writing differences, looked at from a slightly different perspective, see Chapter 6 of Short (1996).

Issues to think or write about

1. Find out all you can about one (or more) of the following concepts discussed in this chapter:

    schemata · · · · · · · · · · inferencing · · · · · · jigsaw listening/reading

    sentence combining · · · · process writing

2. Here's a situation (based on an exercise in Morrow and Johnson 1979) you can use to write your own IT exercise. Imagine Paul White wants to join the Britannia Sports Club. He writes a letter to the club's membership secretary containing information about himself. Your learners pretend to be the secretary, who uses the letter to fill in the application form. Here is the filled-in form:

BRITANNIA SPORTS CLUB: MEMBERSHIP APPLICATION

Surname: <u>White</u> · · · · · · · · · · · · · · · · · · *First Name(s)*: <u>Paul</u>

Date of Birth: <u>14/8/78</u> · · *Nationality*: <u>British</u> · · · · · *Marital Status*: <u>M</u>

Address: <u>15, Welling Close, Portmede, SN4 8QT</u>

Phone: <u>07946-83212</u> · · · · · · · · · · · · · · · · · · *Occupation*: <u>Teacher</u>

To turn this situation into an exercise you need to:

- Write a letter from Paul to the membership secretary containing all this information.
- Take some (but not all) of the information from the form (what you take out is what your learner must put in).
- Write instructions describing the situation and telling your learners what they must do.

If possible, try your completed exercise out on a friend.

Further reading

Clark, H. H., and Clark, E. V. 1977 *Psychology and Language* New York: Harcourt Brace Jovanovich
Though now inevitably dated, this book provides a highly readable account of the areas of psycholinguistics covered in this chapter.

Johnson, K. (ed.) 2005 *Expertise in Second Language Learning and Teaching*
    Basingstoke: Palgrave
Several contributions in this book provide brief state-of-the-art accounts of the skills.
Particularly relevant to this chapter are Goh (on listening), Wallace (on reading), and
Weigle (on writing).

Rost, M. 1990 *Listening in Language Learning* London: Longman
Provides a detailed consideration of listening.

Hadfield, J., and Hadfield, C. 1995 *Reading Games* London: Longman
Provides practical ideas on reading.

Hedge, T. 2005 *Writing 2nd Edition* Oxford: Oxford University Press
Hedge's book covers both the theory and practice of foreign language writing.

14 Tests

14.1 Introduction

It is an unfortunate truth that those who populate the world of foreign language education divide themselves into two camps, which rarely meet except on the verbal battlefield. They are the Teachers and the Testers. When they do meet in battle, the Teachers are inclined to say things like 'Let's learn to teach before we learn to test' and (unkindest cut of all) 'We deal with people, you deal with statistics.' The Testers on the other hand sometimes regard the Teachers as rather a vague lot, well-meaning perhaps, but who tend to be unspecific about their aims and objectives, and on finding out whether they have been met. As a result, Testers and Teachers may sit in different parts of the staff common room. Perhaps the Testers think the Teachers are talking over coffee about whether Maria and Giovanni in Class 1 are dating, while the Teachers may suppose that the Testers are discussing what mark out of ten to give their coffee – for flavour, price and overall quality.

It is natural that individuals with different outlooks and interests should be drawn towards either the teaching or the testing field. But the kinds of stereotypes just mentioned can be dangerous if they lead us to believe that the one field can do without the other. So it is vital for teachers to recognize the necessity for testing, and the potential value of tests for teaching. Testing is important for almost all the stakeholders involved in the education process. The learner wants to know how well they are doing, and wants the 'piece of paper' at the end of the course that will help open professional doors. The teacher wants to know not only how the learner is progressing, but also how they, the teacher, are succeeding in their job. Then there are parents, educational authorities and countless others who have some interest in the learner's progress. This includes the all-important outsiders – the potential employer, or the university administrator (to mention just two), who rely heavily on what tests tell them about learner proficiency levels.

Another reason why testing is important for teaching is to do with the phenomenon known as washback, or backwash. This is the effect that testing has on teaching. For better or worse, tests and exams exert control over what goes on in classrooms. This is because very many language teaching classes are geared more or less directly to the tests or examinations the learners will end up taking.

Teachers must often 'teach to' a test. If the test is a bad one (or the teacher is too narrow in their interpretation of it), the result may be negative washback, where we can say that teaching suffers because of the test coming at the end of the course. But if the test is a good one, and its nature well understood by the teacher, the effect on the teaching may be very positive. There will be positive washback.

So teachers need testers. Perhaps the two groups should even learn to love one another. Sitting together in the staff common room would be a good start.

B14.1 Tests you have known

Think about your own experiences with language tests. Have some that you have taken been better than others? Use your personal experiences as the starting point to think about what makes a good test … and what makes a bad one.

14.2 Types of test

We have already come across one type of test, the aptitude test, in 7.2.2. This, we saw, did not measure any actual performance or level of achievement, but attempted to measure potential – how well a learner might progress if they were to learn a language. Though some of the test types we shall be concerned with in this chapter do have a similarly forward-looking component to them, they mainly focus more on what *has been done*, on what level of achievement or proficiency a learner has reached.

Writers on testing sometimes divide test types into two broad categories, within which sub-categories are recognized. These broad categories are achievement and proficiency tests. Achievement tests are concerned with how well a learner has done in relation to a particular course or programme. They usually come at the end of programmes, and are deliberately based on the content covered in it. Diagnostic tests are also concerned with achievement, or lack thereof. They are often geared to assess the success of some small stretch of teaching, and perhaps to suggest where remedial work will be required. Achievement tests are useful to the teacher as well as the learners; they indicate how well teaching has succeeded, and where improvements need to be made.

Proficiency tests do not relate to any specific content or programme. They are tests of what level has been reached in the language, and stand independent of any course. Their results are statements to the world about what a learner can do. Sometimes proficiency tests may have a particular end user in mind. For example, there may be a proficiency test at the end of a pre-sessional course which states the extent to which a learner is ready for a specific area of use – studying an academic subject in the foreign language. Alternatively, they may be more general statements of level. The well-known Cambridge tests (First Certificate and Proficiency – see 14.8 below) are of this type, and have no specific end user in mind. Indeed, part of their value is that they have come to be generally recognized as statements of overall proficiency that have validity in very many situations. <u>Placement</u> tests are a particular sort of proficiency test. They are given at the beginning of language teaching programmes, to help with decisions as to which classes learners should be put into. Though these tests are generally concerned with proficiency, they can be drawn up with the coming teaching programme in mind. So, to stay with the pre-sessional example, a placement test for such a course would perhaps want to tap the language skill areas that are to be covered on the course. For example, if the learners are to be studying *taking lecture notes* as one component of their course, then the placement test might measure present proficiency in that area.

If you are the sort of person who finds making lists a useful tool to learning, why not make a list of the various test types mentioned here, with very brief notes about each one.

14.3 Approaches to language testing

14.3.1 The psychometric approach

We have seen at various times in this book the way that structural linguistics and behaviourism have had an effect on language education. Testing is no exception, and the approach to testing predominant in the 1960s (particularly associated with Lado 1961) was one which owed much to these traditions. There was an emphasis on the testing of language structure, usually (as in audiolingual language teaching) in decontextualized, sentence-level form. There was also emphasis placed on being scientific (recall Bloomfield's preoccupation with this in 3.2.1). Importance was hence given to objective and accurate measuring, and the word <u>psychometric</u> (meaning 'psychological measuring') is often used to describe this approach. Another expression associated with this form of testing is <u>discrete point</u>. As with behaviourist teaching, individual items are focused on discretely – one at a time, that is.

In psychometric testing, the <u>multiple-choice question</u> has pride of place. You might imagine that it is extremely easy to write good multiple-choice questions. CW14.1 (*How to write bad multiple-choice questions*) shows that this is not always the case. It also illustrates some of the technical terminology associated with the area.

Multiple-choice questions have many advantages. If well constructed, they provide clear-cut right and wrong answers, thus avoiding endless agonizing debates about whether a particular answer is correct or not. They are also very easy to mark, which is particularly important when a large number of test results are required in a short space of time. But they have many disadvantages. Here are some mentioned by Baxter (1997) and Weir (1990):

- The restricted number of choices offered makes it possible to have a reasonable chance of guessing the correct answer. Sometimes, if the questions have been poorly constructed, it may even be possible to arrive at the correct answer without referring to the text;
- We saw in CW14.1 that it is difficult to write good multiple-choice questions. It is sometimes also difficult to invent an adequate number of good questions from a text;
- Multiple-choice items will only test a restricted number of skills. Some grammar points are difficult to test in this way. Think for example about the difference between *some* and *any* (we discussed this in 11.2.2 and again in 12.2). If you write a test item, you will have a correct answer (perhaps it will be *some*), but it may be difficult to think of more than the one obvious distractor (*any*). Other activities, like writing, involve whole areas of skill that it is difficult to imagine being tested by multiple-choice;
- Multiple-choice can lead to harmful washback. A teacher working to the test may decide to base too much classroom work on multiple-choice exercises.

14.3.2 Integrative testing

The reaction against discrete-point testing can be related to the 'sociolinguistic revolution' (discussed in 3.3) that had its effect on language teaching. It was largely the work of John Oller, whose 1979 book launched a strong attack on the psychometric, discrete-point approach.

The starting point for the change was the realization that there were interesting correlations between the results of discrete-point tests and tests which have come to be known as integrative (or holistic). These are tests that deliberately do not attempt to isolate discrete items or skills and test them separately. They are concerned with a learner's performance when using language skills together. The correlations are interesting because integrative tests are relatively easy to construct. What is the point, the argument ran, in struggling to set up discrete-point tests based on small differentiated areas of language competence, when a simply constructed integrative test will do the same job?

The technique that has pride of place in the integrative world is the cloze test. In 13.3.4 we looked at cloze used as an exercise, and the version illustrated in Box 13.4 was a selective cloze exercise. In numerical cloze, words are deleted at regular intervals (perhaps every seventh word will be removed). Try the one in Box 14.2. Notice here how the first few sentences are given, to provide a context. Notice also how the passage is set out. The blanks are numbered, and the answers are to be written on the right. This makes marking easy; the marker holds a piece of paper with the correct answers beside what the learner has written, and writes a tick or cross beside each.

B14.2 A numerical cloze

You will find the original passage in 1.5, and the answers are given for convenience in Note 1.

Classroom 1 is in Abu Dhabi, in the United Arab Emirates, and the language being taught is Arabic. The pupils are children, the sons and daughters of business people and diplomats living in the Emirate. Their native language is English, but this is hard to believe as you listen to what goes on during the school day. From the time they arrive till the time they leave, the pupils are spoken to almost entirely in Arabic. They are greeted by their teacher

(1) _____ *Arabic, their lessons are conducted*	(1) _____
in (2) _____, *teachers speak to them in*	(2) _____
the (3) _____ *and the dinner hall in Arabic,*	(3) _____
(4) _____ *say goodbye to them at*	(4) _____
the (5) _____ *of the day in Arabic.*	(5) _____
When (6) _____ *pupils started at this school,*	(6) _____
they (7) _____ *replied to the teachers in*	(7) _____
English (8) (_____ *is, the teachers spoke Arabic*	(8) _____
and (9) _____ *pupils responded naturally in English),*	(9) _____
but (10) _____ *time this has changed, and now the*	(10) _____

pupils themselves are increasingly using Arabic.

Why not choose another passage from this book and make a numerical cloze test out of it? Try it out on a colleague.

Cloze tests can be marked in one of two ways. In the 'exact' method, the marker insists on the very words that appeared in the original. This makes marking very quick, with no need to agonize about whether a particular answer is correct or not. But the method may not appear very fair, and certainly an educated native speaker would score less than 100 per cent marked like this. The alternative is the 'acceptable' method, where words which did not in fact appear, but are perfectly acceptable, are considered as right. For example, the actual word used for (7) in Box 14.2 is *themselves*. You may well have chosen a word like *always*, which fits the context equally well. By the exact method you would be marked wrong, but by the acceptable method you would be marked right. The acceptable method does of course involve agonizing, and sometimes lengthy, debate among markers about whether something a learner has written is acceptable or not. But the interesting thing is that whichever method is used does not seem to make much difference as far as *ranking* the learners (putting them in order) by result is concerned.

Though cloze tests are usually associated with reading comprehension, they can be used with spoken texts as well. All you need is a transcription of spoken English (a conversation perhaps) to put your blanks into. A book which provides a collection of spoken cloze texts is Garman and Hughes (1983).

Because the words in a numerical cloze are deleted in a mathematical way (every seventh word, for example, may be taken out), these missing words will represent different grammatical categories and types of vocabulary. The passage in Box 14.2 illustrates this well, and you are invited to look quickly through it to identify some of the word categories (nouns, verbs, etc.) that have been deleted. This is one sense in which cloze is 'holistic' and not 'discrete point' – no one area of language is focused on, and different linguistic levels are involved. As we have noted, the findings of Oller and others seemed to suggest that these tests yielded results that were comparable to those of discrete-point tests. How can this be? Maybe there exists some underlying language competence that makes its appearance in both cloze-type tests and discrete-point ones. This view was put forward by Oller as the <u>Unitary Competence Hypothesis</u> (UCH). According to it, all tests, integrative and discrete-point, are tapping the same competence, so whatever kind of test you give will yield similar results. As Baker (1989) puts it: 'all tests, whatever their label, measure this general factor.' The inevitable result of this view was that integrative tests, being so easy to construct, began to take the place of discrete-point ones.

Cloze may have pride of place among the integrative testing techniques, but there are others. Included in Oller's (1976: 156) list are translation, essay and oral interview. Two further ones are worthy of mention. One might be seen as a version of cloze, and is known as the C-test. In this version, the second half of every second word is deleted. This type of test suffers from a face validity problem – a concept that is discussed in more detail in 14.4.1. This means that those who take it may need some convincing that it is valid as a language test. Try the example in CW14.2 (*A C-Test*) and see whether you agree.

If you follow the exact scoring method with a C-test, native speakers are likely to achieve higher marks than with cloze, though your experience with CW14.2 may lead you to realize that the answers are not always obvious or easy. There is research to suggests that C-tests yield valid and reliable results (Klein-Braley and Raatz 1984).

Another integrative technique is dictation. Though this was decried in the 1960s because it was unclear exactly what it was testing, later research showed it to be of value, and in the 1980s it enjoyed a revival. Davis and Rinvolucri's (1988) book full of interesting dictation techniques is evidence of this revival. A potential advantage that it has over cloze is that it includes a listening component. It is also easy to administer. But it is difficult to score. It takes a very long time to mark a dictation, and all kinds of difficult decisions may loom. Is a small misspelling, for example, as serious as completely missing out a word? The potential for heated debate is endless.

Towards the mid-1980s, doubts began to be expressed regarding the UCH. Particularly, the statistics that led to the initial correlations between discrete-point and integrative tests were questioned, and it began to be felt that tests like cloze were not living up to their expectations. Many today continue to see advantages to integrative tests like cloze, particularly in situations when some idea of general proficiency is what is required (as in placement testing, for example). But integrative tests, and the UCH underpinning them, are no longer assumed to have the power once attributed to them.

14.3.3 Communicative testing

Communicative language teaching, which we discussed in 9.7, finds its parallel in communicative language testing. A common basis to both is an interest in the uses to which language is put, and in many so-called communicative tests, learners are asked questions about the function of utterances rather than their grammatical structure. Box 14.3 illustrates.

B14.3 Testing appropriateness

Harrison (1983: 100) provides an example of how some tests try to find out whether a learner can make responses which are appropriate to context. The example comes from the Certificate Examination set by ARELS, the (British) Association of Recognised English Language Schools.

In the test the learner hears a number of utterances (questions or comments), either on tape or said by the examiner. The learner is asked to 'reply in a natural way' after each one. Responses are recorded on tape and assessed for appropriateness. Here are three sample utterances:

1. *Hasn't it been a marvellous summer!*
2. *Do you know if the banks are open on Saturdays?*
3. *I'd love one of those cream cakes, but I really shouldn't. I'm on a strict diet.*

What do you think is the expected answer for each of these three items? An inappropriate answer to item 3 would be *Well don't have it then. Perhaps you should show some self-control.* Explain why. Later in this chapter, in CW14.8, there are more examples of inappropriate answers like this.[2]

A second aspect of communicative testing is the importance it gives to text and task authenticity. As we saw in 12.2, CLT revolted against the kind of dialogue found in Box 12.3 – the one where two people were asking rudely about trains to Millville. Thought was given to ensuring that language was used in a manner appropriate to its context. It was also felt to be important that the language introduced should be useful. A process of needs analysis would ensure that what was taught would be not just authentic, but relevant also. Similar preoccupations made themselves felt in the testing world, and affected not just language, but task selection also. It was part of the spirit of the time to argue that tasks given in tests should be similar to those undertaken in the real world. Morrow, whose 1977 document was important in the development of communicative testing, well represents this spirit.

Take a look at CW14.3 (*Indirect and direct tests*) for another aspect of communicative testing. Yet another characteristic is that communicative tests tend to treat the four skills separately, providing information about a learner's performance in each. This characteristic relates to the process of needs analysis. In 13.1 it was mentioned in passing that a needs analysis may well provide different specifications for each of the four skills. This is because a learner's writing needs, for example, will be different from their speaking needs. Notional/functional teaching claimed that it would produce syllabuses and teaching that was sensitive to these differences in needs. In communicative testing this idea led to language tests which were also sensitive to skill differences. So the questions behind communicative tests are often not general ones like *What is this learner's English like?*, but more specific ones: *What is this learner's spoken English like? What about their reading, listening, writing?* The result is what is known as profile reporting, where learners are given separate scores for each of the four skills, together perhaps with descriptions of skill levels achieved. Good examples are two tests widely used to assess English for the purposes of academic study (already mentioned in Note 2 at the end of Chapter 1). These are the British IELTS test (International English Language Testing System) and the American TOEFL (Test of English as a Foreign Language). As well as an overall mark, scores for each skill are given, and these individual scores may play a part in whether a student is accepted to study at an institution. For example, because writing is an important activity in academic study, a university might insist that Lilian (the Chilean student we met in 1.2) should get a particularly high test score for writing. Notice that behind this procedure of treating the four skills in separation is a view quite contrary to the UCH we considered earlier. The underlying view seems to be a divisible competence hypothesis, suggesting that language competence has separate components that need to be tested separately.

Mention of needs analyses and the different specifications they will yield introduces a further distinction often made by testers, between norm-referenced and criterion-referenced tests. This is discussed in CW14.4 (*Norms and criteria*).

14.4 Concepts of test construction

How do you construct a test? Two characteristics which a good test should possess are validity and reliability, which we shall now look at in turn.

14.4.1 Validity: five types

Heaton (1988: 159) defines validity as 'the extent to which [a test] measures what it is supposed to measure *and nothing else.*' If a test is valid, the outsider who looks at an individual's score knows that it is a true reflection of the individual's skill in the area the test claims to have covered. There are different sorts of validity. <u>Content validity</u> is about what actually goes into the test. To have content validity, a test's content must be seen as representative of the subject area being covered. In an achievement test, for example, the course content must clearly be represented in the test itself. This raises an important issue which all tests must face – the question of <u>sampling</u>. A test cannot of course deal directly with every single item covered on a programme. Such a test would be impossibly long. The test must operate by selecting sample items from the total content (of a programme, for example) and making a statement which in effect says that if a learner knows the sample material, it is a reasonable assumption that they have grasped the entire material. Good sampling is very important. It fails if the test items are regularly perceived as covering just one small area of the total behaviour. If this happens, bad washback will occur, because only that small area will get taught in future. For example, if a test is supposed to cover both speaking and writing, but in fact regularly only deals with written skills, then it will not be long before speaking quietly disappears from the school curriculum training for the test. To achieve content validity, it is important for the tester to draw up a detailed <u>content specification</u> – in effect a list of everything the test will cover. They then need to ensure that this specification is sampled in an even way over time. We shall look at how to draw up content specifications in 14.5.

Heaton's definition of validity specifies that the test should measure what it is supposed to measure, and nothing else. The 'nothing else' can indeed be very hard to eradicate. Imagine, for example, a test of written English which involved learners writing an essay with the title: 'Discuss the idea that a healthy body means a healthy mind (Juvenal's *mens sana in corpore sano*).' The point is that there is much more to writing a good essay on this topic than having good English. In particular it involves the ability to structure an argument. There might well be a case for testing this in an academic context. But if we are dealing with general learners, and are interested mainly in the quality of their English, this test would be inappropriate. A similar point might be made about the *Balloon Debate* we met in 12.5.3. The game may well stimulate classroom discussion. But it would be a poor way of testing, since it involves the ability to persuade, as well as perhaps requiring some knowledge of celebrities. It is possible to investigate content validity through research. One method for this is followed by Alderson and Lukmani (1989). They give testers a list of the skills that are supposed to be being tested in some test items, and ask them to identify which skills are in fact being tested by which item. This is a way of making sure that what the tester thinks is being tested is in fact what the test focuses on.

Content validity involves the judgements of professionals regarding whether a test covers what it should cover. <u>Face validity</u>, on the other hand, is to do with what the world thinks of the test. It relates again to that all important figure in the testing world, the outsider. They must be able to look at a test and, as a layperson perhaps, be convinced that it is a test giving valid information about language use. Indirect tests are naturally the ones that are most likely to be condemned as having poor face validity. Perhaps you might hold the rather unlikely belief, for example, that a good test of pronunciation in a foreign language would be to ask learners to write FL words in phonetic script. But it is doubtful that a layperson would share this view, and they might well condemn the test as the production of 'experts who think they know everything.'

Face validity is a phenomenon that is sometimes highly related to a specific environment. We met an example of this in 9.9.1, though it was concerned with teaching, not testing. In the early days of Prabhu's experiment, we noted that 'the children had severe problems with the lessons; they had never come across classes like that before.' The children changed their view over time, but at first Prabhu's approach clearly had no face validity for them. Recall also the comments about appropriate methodology in 10.4. What is important is not what you do, but how people *perceive* what you are doing.

We have seen that one way in which CLT has had an effect on testing is to give importance to needs analysis, and careful selection of content in relation to terminal needs. Consequently, one important characteristic of communicative tests is that their content relates clearly to what the learner will have to do in the outside world. From this communicative point of view, face validity is (as Heaton 1988 points out) something more than a question of public relations. It is a declaration of the *authenticity* of the test.

Construct validity deals with the relationship between a test and a particular view of language and language learning. As an example of low construct validity, imagine a test which today claimed to measure ability to communicate orally. You know from your reading of earlier chapters that the notion of communicative competence has had a very special and detailed interpretation since the 1970s. If the test ignored that interpretation and consisted of nothing but a series of multiple-choice questions dealing with structural aspects of the language, you might say that it lacked construct validity. The last two types of validity are discussed in CW14.5 (*Empirical and consequential validity*). Now would be a good time to take a look at this.

If you have access to a language test, take a look at it in terms of the various kinds of validity we have discussed. How valid is it? If you do not have easy access to any, you could use one of the Dialang tests. They are mentioned in 14.7, and are available online at https://dialangweb.lancaster.ac.uk.

14.4.2 Reliability

'The reliability of a test', Harrison (1983: 10) says, 'is its consistency. There would be little point in trying to measure people's waists with a piece of elastic. What is needed is a tape measure which stays the same length all the time.'

Reliability has two main sides to it. One is to do with marking, and ensuring that different markers give comparable marks to the same script, as well as that the same markers give the same marks on two different occasions. Testing mythology is full of anecdotes about what effect a good lunch will have on the score a candidate receives, as well as about the effects of time of day (some people – including markers – are more alert in the morning, while others feel most awake in the evening). Second is test/retest reliability. This ensures that the same test will give the same results on two different occasions. This will not happen if, for example, the test is poorly constructed and the instructions can be interpreted in more than one way. It may also not happen if the conditions under which the test is administered are different on the two occasions.

The following paragraphs discuss how you can find out whether a test is reliable in these two ways, and what you can do to make your tests reliable. Before reading on, think how you would answer these questions.

It is a relatively simple matter for you to find out whether you have these two sorts of reliability. Comparing the marks of different markers, as well as giving a marker the same paper to mark on different occasions, will give you information about marking reliability. One way of establishing whether test/retest reliability exists would be to repeat a test with the same group after a period of time (during which no language teaching had taken place). Alternatively, parallel forms of the same test can be given to the same group, in the expectation that they will get the same marks.

How do you create reliability if it does not exist? For marking, it is partly a question of training, to ensure that your markers use clear criteria in a consistent way. As an added safeguard, the system should allow for tests to be marked by more than one marker where this is felt necessary. Professional testing organizations expend a great deal of effort to make sure that both these things happen. CW14.6 (*How to be reliable*) lists some of Hughes's (1989) suggestions in relation to both the forms of reliability we have been describing.

14.4.3   The tension between reliability and validity

Both reliability and validity are important for a test. As S. McDonough (1998a: 188) puts it: 'reliability is essential in a test, because without it one cannot believe the results ... but it is useless unless the test is valid as well, for without validity one does not know what has been tested.' It is relatively easy to achieve reliability at the expense of validity. To make a test reliable, you aim for clear, 'unadventurous' questions where there are no doubts about the correct answers. So for example, a spelling test in which the learner has to underline the correct spelling of a word is likely (if properly constructed) to be reliable. But if this test is put forward as a measure of writing skills in general, including 'high-order' skills such as cohesion, coherence and organizational ability, then it is not likely to be considered valid. This is an extreme example, but at various points in test construction, the tester is likely to find a conflict between reliability and validity. This conflict may be expressed in the form of a question you find yourself asking: 'Do I make this test item clear and unambiguous (suggesting reliability) or more related to what language users actually have to do (suggesting validity)?' It is a little like the conflict between clarity and memorability that we saw in 12.2.

A number of writers suggest that it is better to create a test that is initially valid and then seek ways of making it reliable, rather than creating a reliable test and trying to make it valid. The dog must wag the tail.

14.5   Test production

We have seen that tests operate by sampling from a specification. A first step in test production is therefore to produce a specification. This is a kind of syllabus for a test. Like other types of syllabus, it can take many forms. Heaton (1988: 13) gives two examples which show how test specifications, like teaching syllabuses, reflect different views of language. One example is based on a grammatically oriented course. It simply lists the structures that have been taught, and gives some statement about their relative importance. His second example is also a list, but of functions, not structures, again listed with weightings. Syllabus inventories like the Council of Europe's Threshold Level can be used as the basis for test specification. If you want to know what a test specification is like, take a look at CW14.7 (*A battery for academic French*).

An important ingredient of test specifications (not shown in CW14.7) is a <u>rating scale</u>. This states what levels of performance are expected for various grades or bands to be achieved. We have already mentioned that the practice of profile reporting results in statements in relation to each of the four skills. Statements of levels of performance often need to go even further than this and divide up each skill into component parts. Box 14.4 contains part of a statement of levels of performance for oral skills. It lists some 'categories for rating' – different aspects of speaking which should be assessed. Before looking at it, give a thought to what aspects you consider important to rate for the speaking skill.

B14.4 A rating scale for spoken interaction

Weir (1995) gives an example of a rating scale developed for a test known as TEEP (Test of English for Educational Purposes). This test identifies four levels of performance – 0, 1, 2 and 3. The categories for rating are:

A. Appropriateness
B. Adequacy of vocabulary for purpose
C. Grammatical accuracy
D. Intelligibility

E. Fluency

F. Relevance and adequacy of content

Under each of these categories, four statements are given, characterizing what a learner must do to reach each of the four levels. Below are the statements just for levels 1 and 2, in each category. The statements have been abridged in some cases, and their order has been mixed. For each statement, decide which of the categories above it measures. When you have done this for all categories, you will have two statements per category. Decide which of the two statements is for level 1, which for level 2. For example, if you think the first statement below is about fluency, and characterizes level 2, you would write E2 beside it.[3]

(i)   Misunderstandings may occasionally arise through inappropriateness, particularly of sociocultural convention.

(ii)   Inadequacy of vocabulary restricts topics of interaction to the most basic.

(iii) Responses of limited relevance to the task set.

(iv)   Responses characterized by sociocultural inappropriateness.

(v)   Some grammatical inaccuracies; developing a control of major patterns.

(vi)   Rhythm, intonation and pronunciation require concentrated listening, but only occasional misunderstanding is caused or repetition required.

(vii) Some misunderstandings may arise through lexical inadequacy or inaccuracy … though there are signs of a developing active vocabulary.

(viii) Utterances hesitant and often incomplete … sentences are for the most part disjointed and restricted in length.

(ix)   Understanding is difficult, and achieved often only after frequent repetition.

(x)   Utterances may still be hesitant, but are gaining in coherence, speed and length.

(xi)   Responses for the most part relevant to the task set, though there may be some gaps or redundancy.

(xii) Syntax is fragmented and there are frequent grammatical inaccuracies … confusion of structural elements.

One problem with rating scales like this is that by concentrating on details, they may lead the tester to ignore overall learner performance – a case of not seeing the wood for the trees. One answer is to use (together with, or instead of, the type of rating scale we have seen) an <u>impression scale</u>. This allows the tester to form a general impression of performance, and base marking on that. Guidelines can be given to help the tester structure their impressions.

An issue which rating scales like this raise is the amount of training that is needed to ensure reliability of marking. If you wanted to use the scale given in Box 14.4, for example, you would need to make sure that all markers agreed on their interpretations of all the statements given in relation to all the categories.

Notice in passing how difficult it is to balance different aspects of learner performance. You will find an example in CW14.8 (*A choice between evils*). It gives three learner responses to a test question, each wrong in different ways. The tester's conundrum is to decide the comparative seriousness of their errors. It is a common problem.

14.6   Testing the four skills

We have spent time looking at various components a test must possess. But what do tests actually look like? In this section we shall briefly consider testing in relation to the four skills. Part of the purpose will be to give a flavour of what kind of techniques are used in language testing. Not surprisingly, there will be many overlaps with language teaching techniques – another reason why testers and teachers really should talk to each other.

In 13.1 we noted that there are similarities and differences between the four skills, suggesting that there will be similarities and differences in the techniques used to teach them. So it is also with testing. Here is a 'Rough Guide' to the testing of the four skills:

B14.5 Rough Guide to Testing the Four Skills

Testing receptive skills

Issues

Receptive skills are easier to test in an objective way; problems of the sort found in CW14.8 can, for example, be avoided. But they are more difficult to test in a direct way. This is because listening and reading are naturally covert activities (an idea discussed in 8.3), and there is usually no visible or audible outcome from them. A difference between listening and reading is that speech is transient. Unless a transcript is provided, the learner cannot go backwards and forwards over the text to search for a piece of information. If you provide a transcript, you will not be testing the ability to process listened-to language quickly.

Techniques

Information transfer: Look back to Box 13.5, which contains a collection of IT exercises. Think about how each of them could be used for the testing of first reading, then listening.

 Note taking: This has the advantage of being direct (and therefore having face validity, as well as leading to possible beneficial washback). The learner can be given skeleton notes (with some blanks in it) of a 'lecture' which they

---

listen to on tape. The task is to fill in the blanks. Note taking can be used for reading too.

Matching: Learners may, for example, read or listen to a passage describing a picture. Four slightly different pictures might be shown. Learners have to decide which one is being described.

Passage assembly (or reassembly): This is a teaching technique we looked at in CW13.6. It can be used for testing reading. For example, exercise 2 in CW13.6 (with sentences on one piece of paper in jumbled order, rather than on separate cards) can be used as a test item.

Testing speaking

Issues

This poses many problems. It can be a very time-consuming business – a nightmare with a big test where thousands of learners have to be tested quickly. Also there are the many different levels on which performance has to be assessed. As we saw earlier (in Box 14.4), marking schemes which recognize different levels are needed. In addition, there are difficulties involved in marking objectively with face-to-face contact. Hughes (1989: 113) puts it this way:

> it is obvious that scorers should not be influenced by such features as candidates' pleasantness, prettiness, or the cut of their dress. The truth is that these are hard to exclude from one's judgement – but an effort has to be made!

Techniques

Oral interview: This is where the examiner asks the learner questions about themselves, and perhaps also about a passage or picture sequence given in advance. This is a traditional technique.

Role play and simulation: These techniques are now also popular (see 12.5.3 for discussion of these in relation to teaching). The learner can be given a role card just before the test, asking them to act a role. The tester can also play a character in the role play. Here is an example of an instruction (from Carroll and Hall 1985: 51):

> You are at Amsterdam (Schipol) Airport having just missed the 1320 flight to Brussels where a friend, Mr Raymond, has arranged to meet you. You now want to do two things – make arrangements for a later flight and contact Mr Raymond in Brussels. Please explain your situation at the Information Desk.

Imitation: This was one of the French proficiency tests given in the large good language learner study (Naiman *et al.* 1978) that we saw in 8.3. The tester says a series of sentences to the learner, each longer than the one before. The learner repeats each sentence. The idea is that the longer the sentence the learner can repeat without error, the higher their level. A very indirect test, with little face validity. But it has the advantage of being quick to administer, and might be used in a situation where rough and fast decisions are needed (for example, as a placement test for a course which has to begin almost immediately).

Testing writing

Issues

As with speaking, there are many different levels that have to be taken into account, including spelling, vocabulary use, grammar, treatment of content, stylistic appropriacy and organizational skill. Also as with speaking, there are plenty of side-issues to distract the marker. A notorious one is handwriting. Though there may be circumstances in which handwriting should be assessed, it is peculiarly common for a marker to find that poor handwriting unjustly leads to a judgement about poor content.

The kind of banding system which we saw in Box 14.4 should be drawn up for writing as well as speech (though the aspects of performance being judged will of course be different). In one writing test discussed by Hughes (1989: 95), the following aspects are specified: communicative quality, organization, argumentation, linguistic accuracy and linguistic appropriacy.

As with speech, there is no reason why this 'analytic' way of marking should not be supported by a more 'impressionistic' judgement, where markers allow themselves to express an overall 'feeling' for learners' achievement.

Techniques

Passage assembly: Many of the techniques already discussed are suitable for the testing of writing (including, yet again, the ubiquitous information transfer exercise). So passage assembly, an item mentioned above under 'Testing Reading', is relevant for writing also.

Picture stimulus: Heaton (1988: 142) illustrates how a picture can be the basis for a writing test. His example shows a map of an accident 'black spot.' Various features indicate why accidents happen there – for example, there is a bus stop just by a crossroads, so cars sometimes overtake stationary buses very close to the crossroads. Learners are asked to write a letter to a local newspaper describing the dangers of the 'black spot.'

14.7 Online testing

Testing, like teaching, is rapidly adapting to the Internet Age. One of the major testing resources available online is the Dialang scheme, developed by a large number of institutions throughout Europe, with the support of the European Commission. The scheme provides tests of listening, writing, reading, structures and vocabulary for 14 European languages. The aim of the tests is not to provide learners with 'pieces of paper' (certificates of proficiency), but just to give them information about what stage they have reached in a language, as well as feedback and advice. Dialang's web address was given in 14.4.1. The website provides detailed information about the scheme, and allows you to download tests. If you have knowledge of any of the languages they cover, why not try a test on yourself? Those who have never experienced a language test first-hand will find it a salutary experience!

Cambridge English also have a series of tests online, at www.cambridgeenglish.org/test-your-english. There are plenty of others, which you can find by using a search engine and entering 'online language tests.'

14.8   Some important tests

One of the major British examining boards is UCLES, the University of Cambridge Local Examination Syndicate, and they administer a number of tests which have come to be accepted worldwide. Of their range, the two best known are the First Certificate in English (FCE) and the more advanced Certificate of Proficiency in English (CPE). This latter is in some countries of the world regarded as an important qualification for non-native teachers of English to possess. A test specifically geared for non-native teachers is the UCLES Cambridge Examination in English for Language Teachers (CEELT). ARELS also has a much-used range of tests, particularly their three-level Examinations in Spoken English and Comprehension.

In the United States there is a set of levels for speaking proficiency known as the ACTFL Proficiency Guidelines. There are four levels, which deal with a number of languages.

For testing suitability for academic study, the two best-known tests have already been mentioned. They are the British Council's IELTS and the American TOEFL. Very many institutions of tertiary education in the English-speaking world have entry qualifications regarding English language proficiency that are stated in terms of scores on the IELTS and TOEFL tests.

Notes

1. The deleted words are: (1) in; (2) Arabic; (3) playground; (4) and; (5) end; (6) the; (7) themselves; (8) that; (9) the.
2. In British English the expected answers might be along the following lines:

   (1) Yes, it really has. Absolutely wonderful.
   (2) No, most banks are closed on a Saturday.
   (3) Oh go on! You can start your diet again tomorrow.

3. The expected matchings are:

(i)	= A2	(ii)	= B1	(iii)	= F1	(iv)	= A1
(v)	= C2	(vi)	= D2	(vii)	= B2	(viii)	= E1
(ix)	= D1	(x)	= E2	(xi)	= F2	(xii)	= C1

Issues to think or write about

1. Section 14.5 mentions using an 'impression scale' for marking. A lot of institutions and teachers still use this as their main method of marking. For example, when marking a piece of written work, they will read it through, gaining an impression of its quality as they go along. At the end, their culminative impression leads to a mark. What are the advantages and disadvantages of this way of marking, as opposed to using a more controlled and systematic method?

2. CW14.1 provides some examples of poor multiple-choice questions for a given passage. Write some (say 5 or 6) good multiple-choice questions for the same passage.

    If you wish to try your hand at writing a numerical cloze test (and did not do this in Box 14.2), use the same passage in 14.5 to produce one of these.

    Try your test(s) out on a colleague.

Further reading

Heaton, J. B. 1990 *Classroom Testing* London: Longman
Accessible discussion which will be useful for language teachers.

Hughes, A. 1989 *Testing for Language Teachers* Cambridge: Cambridge University Press
Looks at practical issues of test construction, but also covers more theoretical areas such as validity, reliability and washback.

Alderson, J. C., Clapham, C., and Wall, D. 1995 *Language Test Construction and Evaluation* Cambridge: Cambridge University Press
Useful for those wanting to develop their own tests. It contains a useful collection of test specifications for actual tests.

Bachman, L. F. 1990 *Fundamental Considerations in Language Testing* Oxford: Oxford University Press
Chapter 5 provides a complete framework for test specification.

Underhill, N. 1987 *Testing Spoken Language: A Handbook of Oral Testing Techniques* Cambridge: Cambridge University Press
A thorough treatment of oral testing techniques.

15 When all has been said
Preparing and managing lessons

15.1 Introduction

We have talked about learning, about teaching, about syllabuses, methods and much more besides. All (well, quite a lot) has been said, and hopefully, you have gained useful knowledge. But even when all has been said, there is still a lot more involved in becoming a language teacher. There are many practical skills to be mastered. This final chapter is about some of these.

This book cannot offer detailed teacher training. The most it can do is to try to give you a sense of what skills are involved in preparing and managing lessons. Because this chapter is about practicalities, it contains plenty of activities – many more than in other parts of the book. It is also a chapter full of questions. Do not be put off by their number. The intention is certainly not to daunt you with the complexity of what good language teaching involves – indeed, many of the skills described here come easily to novice teachers. The modest aim is to make you aware of what these skills are, and to stimulate you to think about them.

15.2 Lesson planning

15.2.1 Making a lesson plan

Lesson planning (LP), you may think, is a rather simple, low-level process that does not deserve much attention in a book like this. In fact, it really is a rather high-level activity which involves knowing about, and knowing how to do, many things. To plan a good lesson, you need to know a lot about your students and the context in which you are learning – the theme of Chapter 10. You also have to know about syllabuses, what the aims of the course you are teaching are, and how it is organized. That's Chapter 11. Then you have to know something about methods and techniques – the concerns of Chapters 9 and 12 – and also about skill teaching (Chapter 13). Since LP also involves thinking about classroom logistics, as well as evaluation, Chapters 14 and 15 are relevant too. Indeed, much of what has been dealt with in Part 3 of the book comes into LP.

Here are some initial questions to think about in relation to LP:

B15.1 LP: some initial thoughts

What is a lesson plan? What kind of information should it contain? What do lesson plans look like?

   Imagine that you are the Director of Studies in a language institute. The Principal asks you to draw up a 'skeleton' lesson plan template for use by all teachers in the institute. The template must be no more that one side of paper and it should consist of nothing more than headings, plus spaces for the teachers to fill in details in relation to specific lessons. One of the headings, for example, might be *Materials*. Here teachers can say what section of what textbook they will use for their lesson, whether there will be any specially prepared handouts, and so on. What else would your template include? Spend some time preparing it. Then, if possible, compare it with a colleague's. Use your two templates as a launch pad for discussion on how to answer the *What* questions above.

What is a lesson plan? According to Woodward (2001: 1), the planning process includes 'considering the students, thinking of the content, materials and activities that could go into a … lesson, jotting these down, having a quiet ponder, cutting things out of magazines.' Woodward's list is not intended as a complete one, and you may wish to add to it, given your ruminations in Box 15.1. Later in this section you will be asked to consider the areas to be covered in a lesson plan in more detail.

   Lesson plans vary enormously from teacher to teacher in terms of length and complexity. Harmer (2001) talks about a 'planning continuum.' At one end are the teachers who make 'formal plans' providing a full map of the lesson. At the other end of the continuum are teachers who plan no more than a 'jungle path', giving only the vaguest idea of what will happen in class. Between the two comes the 'corridor plan' which provides the main shape of the lesson, but not much detail. Differences in the degree of planning a teacher will undertake reflect differences in personal teaching style, and perhaps also differing views about the nature of language learning and teaching. But another important factor is degree of teaching experience. Before reading on, perhaps you would like to speculate whether experienced teachers are more likely to provide more detailed plans than novices, or vice versa.

   Maybe, you might think, experienced teachers well understand the necessity for detailed planning and (as perhaps more senior members of their institution than the novices) are likely to plan more. On the other hand, experienced teachers *need* to plan less, simply because they have done it more often. The reality is that novice teachers are in fact likely to spend more time planning, and to do it in more detail. For one thing, elaborate plans will provide them with a sense of security so they can face their first lessons with confidence. Woodward (2001: 4) remembers back to her novice days and how she sometimes spent all evening preparing one lesson. Now, with 20 years' experience behind her, she says: 'I can plan a lesson in about ten minutes … I'm not alone in this. One experienced colleague writes nothing down but says he does a lot of thinking in the bath in the morning.' Nearer the jungle path than the corridor plan. You may like to find out how some teachers that you know plan their lessons. Are they of the jungle path, corridor or formal plan school? Perhaps you can find out from them how many of the headings you identified in Box 15.1 concern them? If you work in an institution where subjects other than languages are taught, it might be interesting to see how non-language teachers plan their lessons. Certainly, any differences you note in how teachers plan will be interesting. In particular, is there any relationship between the amount that they plan and their degree of experience? As well as talking to teachers, you could also ask one if you could observe their lesson and afterwards write a lesson plan based on what you observed.

B15.2 To plan or not to plan

Since experienced teachers do not always see the need to plan in detail, the question arises: how important is planning? This is something you might ask the teachers you talk to, and it is certainly something you should ask yourself. If you think it is important, try to come up with a list of reasons why. This issue is discussed immediately below.

But it is possible to over-plan. Think then also of some limits on the value of planning. Should all parts of all lessons be planned? If not, why not? And – a very important question this – for what reasons might you decide to deviate from a lesson plan? This issue is discussed a little later in the chapter.

Even experienced teachers whose plans are nearer jungle path than corridor plan are likely to acknowledge that LP should take place. Woodward (2001: 181) gives a list of reasons. One is the sense of security mentioned earlier. She also notes that when learners can see that a plan is being followed, it gives them confidence that what is happening in class is thought-out and purposeful. Above all, what plans do is provide a framework. They 'help us shape the space, time and learning we share with students' (Woodward 2001: 1).

In Box 15.1 you were asked to think about what is involved in LP. We shall now consider the factors in more detail, and it is at this point that the complexity of the process becomes evident. Take a look at the table below. On the left some areas important in LP are listed (in no particular order). More detailed descriptions are on the right, but in jumbled order. There are alternative ways of doing the first stage of this activity. If you wish you can match the labels and the descriptions by writing down numbers and letters. So if you think that *Class members* is about whether you use a textbook or worksheets (it isn't, of course!), then you write (1)(e). But since many of the labels on the left are self-explanatory, you may feel it a waste of time to match all labels and descriptions in this way. If so, as an alternative, look at just the labels and say what each refers to. If you are not sure in a particular case, then look for the corresponding description on the right.

(1)	Class members	(a)	What you hope to achieve in the lesson
(2)	Teacher preparation	(b)	How long each stage of the lesson will take
(3)	Topics	(c)	What are the main stages of the lesson? What activities are involved in each?
(4)	Resources	(d)	All about your students
(5)	Evaluation	(e)	Will you use a textbook? Worksheets?
(6)	Teaching sequences	(f)	What subject areas will your lesson cover? A contemporary social issue? An aspect of your learners' personal lives?
(7)	Language content	(g)	Will learners be talking to each other (S → S), or to the teacher (S → T)? Will the learners work alone, in pairs, groups, or as a class?
(8)	Lesson shape	(h)	Will the focus (overall and at each stage) be on speaking, listening, reading or writing?
(9)	Reviewing	(i)	What language items will be covered? New structures? New functions? New lexis?
(10)	Troubleshooting	(j)	What do you expect your learners to find challenging in the lesson?
(11)	Fluency vs accuracy	(k)	Will you do any revision of work from the last lesson? Will you go over what you have taught at the end of the present lesson?
(12)	Aims	(l)	What do you need to do before the lesson? Write worksheets?
(13)	Follow-up	(m)	What exactly will happen during each of your activities? Exactly who is doing exactly what, exactly when? (Exactly why is of course also an important question!)
(14)	Timing	(n)	How will you find out whether your learners have mastered what you taught?
(15)	Variety and grading	(o)	Is there a good variety of activities in the lesson? Is there gradation throughout, from easy to difficult?
(16)	Learner difficulties	(p)	What do you expect the learners to know or be able to do by the end of the lesson?
(17)	Activity mechanics	(q)	What needs to be explained? What will you say?
(18)	Skills	(r)	Is your overall approach PPP, deep-end or something else?
(19)	Explanations	(s)	What can go wrong? How will you handle it?
(20)	Interaction types	(t)	What will you ask your learners to do after the lesson? Any homework?
(21)	Intended learning outcomes	(u)	Which parts of the lesson will focus on fluency, and which on accuracy?

The descriptions of the first four labels on the list (*Class members*, *Teacher preparation*, *Topics* and *Resources*) are particularly short. Try to elaborate them a bit. What specifically would you want to know about the class members? What other sorts of teacher preparation might there be? Think of more examples of possible topics. What other resources are available to language teachers?

Now another task: the labels on the left are not organized at all. Some are to do with the *shape* of the lesson. Others are to do with the lesson's *content*. Still others deal with the *mechanics* of the lesson (practical issues to do with how things are managed). Not all of the labels fit into these three categories. Find just two for each category – two labels to do with *shape*, two for *content* and two for *mechanics*.

When I started to devise the table above, I began with very many more than 21 labels, revealing just how complex a process LP is. With all these things to think about, where do you start? We are about to discuss this. As preparation, look once again at the labels in the table. Which of them would you think about first when planning your lesson? Which of them would come later? Try to get a feel of how you might go about the process of lesson planning.

According to some educationalists (Tyler 1950, for example), there is a 'logical' way to plan a lesson. You start by specifying objectives. Then you select learning activities and organize these into a sequence. Finally you specify evaluation procedures. But research reported by Taylor (1970) and Clark and Yinger (1987) shows that experienced teachers do not in fact follow this sequence. Studies in the general educational field (for example Clark and Yinger 1979; Yinger 1977; Zahorik 1975) suggest that experienced teachers tend to make 'the activity' the unit of organization for their lesson plans. This means that their starting point in planning is the question: 'what are the main activities I will do during my lesson?' As Woodward (2001: 185) puts it: many teachers 'first concentrate on materials and activities, crafting useful, interesting lessons without thinking too much about goals first.' Was the activity a starting point you identified in relation to the table earlier?

Should inexperienced teachers – teachers in training – copy the more experienced in this respect? Perhaps it is acceptable for experienced teachers not to start with objectives because they carry syllabuses around in their heads, developed through years of experience. Like many of the procedures and short cuts used by the experienced, they are possibly not best practice for the novice. What do you think?

Whatever the starting point for lesson planning, it is unlikely to be a linear process, moving serenely from one stage to the next. You will probably find yourself moving backwards and forwards a lot. Here's an example: you might decide you will think about the content of your lesson before you turn your attention to timing – how long each part of the lesson will take. But when you come to look at timing you may decide there is too much content in your lesson for the time available. So you go back and modify your aims. These new modified aims may then make you reconsider the timing question yet again, spending more time than planned on one activity, and less on another. And so it goes on, backwards and forwards. It is right that it should go on thus.

Earlier we discussed the value of lesson plans, and Woodward's view that they 'help us shape … space, time and learning.' But she also makes the point that plans are 'not legally binding. We don't have to stick to them come hell or high water.' The sensible teacher will deviate from their lesson plan whenever what Allwright (1984) calls a 'learning opportunity' presents itself. A learner may ask a question which the teacher deems worthy of a lengthy answer even though it leads away from the lesson plan. Or a topic may come up which, the teacher immediately notices, particularly interests the learners. They might decide to pursue it, again even though it does not follow the lesson plan. Some of these opportunities will be what Harmer (2001: 319) calls *magic moments* – golden opportunities to teach something, too good to miss. There is an example of a magic moment of sorts in one of Chapter 12's Companion Website entries, though it occurs at the beginning of the lesson rather than part way into it. Try to find this example (hint: it is to do with righteous indignation).[1] CW15.1 (*En casa de herrero, cuchillo de palo*) contains another magic moment. These examples show that teachers need to be opportunistic as well as organized.

15.2.2 From jungle path to formal plan: an activity

As we have seen, teachers vary considerably in the detail their lesson plans contain – from jungle path to formal plan. We have also seen that experienced teachers tend towards the jungle path end of the spectrum, because much of what would be contained in a formal plan is in their head and does not need to be specified in detail each time they plan.

The activity which finishes this section is a lengthy one. It invites you to think in detail about the procedures you will use in a lesson. The activity is based on a short set of materials written especially for this chapter. They are set out below. You are asked to imagine you have decided to use these materials (their title is *Climate Change*) to teach an appropriate group of students. But how exactly will you use them? As you will see, there are some instructions given in the materials, but they are rather short and vague (as instructions in textbooks often are), so it will not always be immediately obvious how the exercises should be done. First read through the *Climate Change* materials and think about how you might use them in class. After them are some specific questions to ask yourself.

Climate Change

1. Listening and reading

Everyone knows that the world's climate is changing. But why? And what will the consequences be? Listen to what Alan James, a meteorologist, says in this interview.

Interviewer:	So, Alan, what exactly is causing climate change?
Alan:	Remember first of all that the world's climate has always changed naturally. Over the past few millions of years there have been several ice ages, for example. But there seem to be particular reasons for change today. These are partly to do with greenhouse gases.
Interviewer:	And what is a greenhouse gas?
Alan:	It's one that traps heat in the atmosphere, and so causes global warming. Carbon dioxide is a greenhouse gas. If greenhouse gases increase, the temperature of the planet will rise.
Interviewer:	What will happen then?
Alan:	Naturally if the temperature rises then the desert areas will get bigger. The Sahara for example will grow significantly in size.
Interviewer:	And what about the colder regions of the earth?
Alan:	There is a real danger to the ice cap. If the ice cap melts then sea levels throughout the world will rise. That will cause widespread flooding.
Interviewer:	And what about world weather patterns?
Alan:	If we continue to produce greenhouse gases, then the weather will become more extreme – stronger winds, wilder storms, longer periods of drought.
Interviewer:	And what can be done about this?
Alan:	Well if we do nothing, the world will face huge problems, that's for sure. We need international agreements to cut down on the production of greenhouse gases. It's the only answer.

2. IF and THEN

a) Using information from the interview, draw lines in the table from IF to THEN.

IF	**THEN**
greenhouse gases increase	widespread flooding
planet's temperature rises	earth's temperature rises
ice cap melts	huge global problems
we continue to produce greenhouse gases	Sahara grows
we do nothing	stronger winds

b) Work in pairs. Ask questions like this: *What will happen if greenhouse gases increase?* Reply *The earth's temperature will rise.*

c) Make sentences: *If greenhouse gases increase, the earth's temperature will rise.*

How it works

If is sometimes followed by a present tense, even though we are talking about the future:

If greenhouse gases increase, ...
If the planet's temperature rises, ...

will often appears in the other half of the sentence:

... the earth's temperature will rise.
... the Sahara will grow.

Sentences like this using *if* are sometimes called the 'first conditional.' It is used to describe something that is possible, or likely to happen.

3. What will happen?

Finish these sentences:

1. If you give me your phone number,
2. If I lose my purse,
3. If John is late for school,
4. If it rains this afternoon,
5. If Helen's car breaks down,
6. If   , I'll buy a new one.
7. If   , I'll go to bed.
8. If   , I'll eat at home.
9. If   , I'll go there tomorrow.
10. If   , I'll buy you a sandwich.

4. An energetic week

You have a week's holiday. Here are some things to do. Decide which activity you will do each day. Work in pairs. Find out what your partner will do each day:

What are you doing on Monday?
I'll go sailing if there is a good wind.

Day	Activity 1	Activity 2
Mon	Sailing (there must be a good wind)	Rowing (will the water be too rough?)
Tues	Tennis (can someone lend you a racket?)	Badminton (but can you find a partner?)
Wed	Yoga (is there a class that day?)	Salsa dancing (are you feeling energetic enough?)
Thurs	Swimming (but is the water too cold?)	Horse riding (does the school open on Thursdays?)
Fri	Having a long rest!	

Now for the questions to ask yourself:

General

- The lesson covers the 'first conditional.' What are the main points your learners need to know about the first conditional? What difficulties do you think they might have with the form? In your experience, have you come across any common errors in the use of this conditional? How might you handle these?
- The first conditional is introduced 'formally' in the box entitled *How it works*. But maybe you feel you should say something about it before then. Or not? If yes, what would you say? And when?

In the 'Issues to think or write about' section at the end of this chapter, you are given the chance to find out about how the entire conditional system works in English. This includes 'second' and 'third' conditionals as well as the 'first conditional' covered here.[2]

1. Listening and reading

- What might you do to introduce the topic of 'climate change' and to stimulate your class to think about it? Any pre-reading/listening activities? Any visuals that might help?
- The text has some quite difficult vocabulary in it. Identify some of the words learners might have difficulty with. Can you do anything to help them with vocabulary problems?
- How will you handle the reading and listening? Would the learners read first, then listen, or vice versa?

2. IF and THEN

- Perhaps you should draw the lines (from IF to THEN) in the table on your own copy, just to make sure it is clear what the answers are and that there are no unforeseen difficulties. Perhaps indeed you should do all the exercises yourself in advance. Unexpected difficulties in teaching are so common that they can be regarded as expected!
- How will you handle 'IF and THEN'? What will your instructions to the learners be? What *exactly* will you say? Do you predict the learners will have any difficulties knowing what they must do? If so, how would you handle these difficulties?
- In (c), will the learners say their sentences to a partner, to themselves or to the teacher? Do you, for each part of the exercise, need to check the learners' answers? If so, how will you do it?
- How much time will you spend on the listening/reading and on Exercise 2?

How it works

- Earlier you were asked to think about what you would need to tell your learners about the first conditional. Does the box here do the job well? Will you need to add to/modify it in any way?
- Exactly what are you going to do with the box? Who will do the talking, you or the learners?
- Do you think your learners will have problems understanding the explanation in the box? What kind of problems? How will you handle them?
- How much time do you plan to spend on the box?

3. What will happen?

- How will you manage these exercises? Will the learners work alone, in pairs, in groups? Will you go over the answers? How? Is there any interest to the class in finding out what kinds of answers were given (in terms of content, not grammar)?
- The exercise asks learners to invent their own sentences. They may need some help to understand what is required of them, as well as with actually doing it. What help can you give?
- Do you feel the section provides enough practice? If not, what might you add?
- All the sentences here begin with the *if* clause. Perhaps you will want to give practice putting the *if* clause second (*I'll call you tomorrow if you give me your phone number* as well as *If you give me your phone number I'll call you tomorrow*). How would you manage that?
- Are there any other linguistic points you need to be aware of that might come up?
- How much time will you spend on each of these 'What will happen' activities in class?

4. An energetic week

- How exactly will learners do this exercise? Working in pairs? What instructions would you need to give them to set the exercise up? Should learners write down the answers they are given?
- Is it clear what *if* sentences will come out of the exercise? Do the exercise yourself to be sure in your own mind what is required (*I'll go sailing if there is a good wind*). Unexpected problems to expect? Think particularly of the verbs associated with the activities – *go* sailing, *play* tennis, *do* yoga, etc. Do you need to draw attention to these before doing the exercise? How?
- How much time will you spend on each of these 'An energetic week' activities in class?

- Can you think of ways of developing this exercise once learners have chosen their activities? Are there any possibilities for learners to compare answers or for a class survey? ('Mini-surveys' are briefly discussed in 12.4.2.)
- All the exercises in these materials are relatively controlled. Can you think of any activity to practise the first conditional in a freer way?

Teaching really is a complex skill, isn't it?

15.3   Error correction

15.3.1   Different attitudes, different error types: some 'revision'

Another important skill that teachers have to master is how to correct learner errors. We have already discussed errors at various points in this book, enough perhaps to make you realize that there are a number of different views about them and their significance for language learning and teaching. The aim of this section is to go over ('revise', if you like) what has already been said.

Certainly the question 'what part do errors play in learning?' has received different answers in line with different learning theories. In the behaviourist tradition we looked at in 3.2.2, the belief was that practice makes perfect, or at least permanent. Errors therefore had to be avoided because if they are repeated they become difficult or impossible to eradicate. Indeed, Nelson Brooks (1960: 58 – we described him in CW9.1 as 'an evangelical advocate of AL') goes so far as to relate errors to sins: 'like sin, error is to be avoided and its influence overcome', he says, adding just a touch of humanity at the end: 'but its presence is to be expected.' In later, more cognitive views of learning, errors might be seen as hypotheses about how the language works, and hence regarded as useful to the learning process. We have also argued, in another part of the book, that an important skill for learners to master is to continue producing language even though they know they are making errors. Learning to live with your own errors can, we argued, be fostered by 'real-thing practice.' Look back and find where that point was made.

Along with these different attitudes towards errors come, as you would expect, different views about the value of error correction (EC). So in AL – the approach associated with behaviourism – we find a lot of EC. At the opposite extreme are views regarding acquisition, like Krashen's. As we saw in 5.2.1, there is not much EC in the L1 learning situation, so it will be largely avoided in any FL approach based on making parallels between L1 and FL acquisition. EC is of its nature a highly form-focused activity, and is indeed one of the two central characteristics (discussed in 5.1.2) that Krashen associated with learning as opposed to acquisition.

We have also looked (in 4.3) at a general categorization of errors into *intralingual* and *interlingual* (including so-called developmental errors). An interlingual error we considered there was the sentence *Did she wanted to go to the cinema yesterday?* Find this example and remind yourself what we said about where this error 'comes from.' To take this issue up again: one reason why a learner may produce this sentence is that they have a wrong hypothesis about how English works. They think this is how you ask a question in English. You might say that their interlanguage (a word you met in 8.3) is faulty at this point. But there is another possibility. Perhaps they know very well that the correct form is *Did she want?* But in the middle of a conversation, when they are concentrating on *what* they are saying (not *how* they are saying it), the incorrect form slips out. In Johnson (1988) I use Corder's (1981) terms *error* and *mistake* – terms that we have so far been using interchangeably – to distinguish these two possibilities. If a learner gets something wrong because they have incorrect interlanguage knowledge, we can say that they make an <u>error</u>. <u>Mistakes,</u> on the other hand, are to do with the notions of *processing ability* and *procedural knowledge* discussed in 6.3. They occur in the 'hurly-burly' of conversation where there are many things to get right at the same time (recall the discussion of *combinatorial skill* in 12.5.2?). The learner knows the right form, but produces the wrong one. You could say that in this situation they fail to 'perform their competence' (the phrase is taken from Ellis 1985). Look back to Box 3.6 and you will find plenty of examples of what we there called 'performance-related slips.' One of the characteristics of these slips/mistakes is that learners can probably correct themselves after the event, when the hurly-burly of conversation is over. When we come to consider ways of correcting learners, we shall see why the error/mistake distinction can be important.[3]

15.3.2 Error correction: the *Should* and *When* Questions

In one of the few papers devoted to the topic of EC, Hendrickson (1978) asks five important questions: should learner errors be corrected?; when should they be corrected?; which ones should be corrected?; how should they be corrected?; and who should do the correction? – *should, when, which, how* and *who*. Before you read about these questions, think what possible answers there might be to each one. Think also of the pros and cons associated with your possible answers.

We have already seen that the *Should* Question will receive different answers according to your views about language learning and teaching. It is interesting to note that learners themselves often seem to crave huge amounts of EC. Chaudron (1988, who also based his discussion around the same five questions) cites a number of studies showing this, including Cathcart and Olsen (1976), whose survey of 149 learners reveals that they wanted all their errors to be corrected. Many teachers, including myself, will be able to think of situations where learners have asked to be corrected, even in situations where the focus is clearly on message and fluency rather than form and accuracy. But in spite of what learners say they want, many teachers have different EC habits according to whether accuracy or fluency is the focus. As Hendrickson (1978) puts it in his discussion of the *When* Question, where 'instructional focus is on form, corrections occur more frequently.' The clear disadvantage of too much EC when attention is on fluency is that it disrupts the flow of speech – the very thing that you are trying to practise. EC can be a real conversation-stopper.

This does not necessarily mean that errors should go uncorrected in fluency practice. They can be noted down (or tape-recorded) and corrected after the event.[4]

15.3.3 Deciding what to correct: the *Which* Question

Which errors? Unless your learners are of a very high level, it will often be either impossible or undesirable to correct all their errors – EC really is a medicine where an overdose can kill. So some means of selection needs to be used. Before reading on, think about what criteria you could use to prioritize which types of error to correct.

One possibility is to focus on particular sorts of errors on different occasions (verb forms one day, pronunciation errors on another, for example). Hendrickson's view is that three sorts of errors should receive priority: ones that impair communication, those that stigmatize the learner, and particularly frequent ones. A distinction which is often made in relation to impairing communication is Burt and Kiparsky's (1972) between *global* and *local* errors. Global errors affect the whole sentence structure and often lead to lack of understanding. Local errors come in specific parts of sentences and often do not significantly hinder communication. As regards stigmatizing, look back to the discussion in 5.4.2 about the *Fish-and-Chips Syndrome*. We said that the utterance *Give to me fish and chips* might result in a plate of food, but would not create a good impression on hearers. As we put it there – 'it might succeed communicatively (and digestively) but it would fail integratively.' Frequency of errors is often an important consideration for teachers, who are likely to become irritated when a learner repeats an error which has been dealt with time and time again in class.

Mention of teacher irritation raises the point that what makes an error serious depends a lot on who you ask. Take a look at CW15.2 (*Dizzys from wine*) which is all about error gravity.

15.3.4 The *How* Question

Now for the all-important *How* Question. Correcting an error may at first sight seem straightforward. But when you begin to analyse what is involved, it becomes quite complex. Two of the central features of error correction episodes are (a) indicating that an error was committed, and (b) correcting the error. Before you read on, list some of the ways in which (a) and (b) may be done.

We discussed the sentence **Did she wanted to go to the cinema yesterday?* a few pages back. Imagine that Maria, a learner in your class, made this error (or mistake? – recall our earlier discussion). Below are some possible teacher reactions, listed (a) to (i). Put into words what the teacher is doing each time. Do these reactions expand the list of techniques you have just been thinking about?

(a) *Did she wanted*? (with strong emphasis on *wanted*)
(b) Did she ...? (gesticulating to the learner to supply the missing word)
(c) No, the verb's wrong.

(d) *Wanted?*

(e) No, *did she want.*

(f) I see, Maria. And did she want to go to the cinema yesterday? What was the answer?

(g) *Did* has to be followed by the infinitive of the verb. Not *wanted* but *want.*

(h) Can you see what's wrong with what you said?

(i) Can anyone see what's wrong with what Maria said?

Below are descriptions of these ways of indicating and correcting errors. Match these descriptions with the teacher reactions above. You will find the matchings in Note 5.

Indicating that an error was committed

1 You can repeat the part of the sentence containing the error emphasizing the incorrect word.

2 Some teachers develop signs to indicate an error – clicking their fingers, making some facial gesture. You can even develop different signs for different types of error. Gower *et al.* (2005) for example suggest 'finger correction' where different finger positions indicate different types of error.

3 You can repeat the wrong word with question intonation.

4 You can identify the error by saying what part of speech it involved.

Indicating the correct version

5 You can encourage the learner to correct the error themselves rather than giving the correct answer.

6 You can continue the interaction, finding a way of repeating the sentence using the correct form.

7 You can ask the class to help.

8 You can give an explanation using metalanguage (look back to 12.2 to remind yourself what this term means).

9 You can simply give the correct version.

Indicating and correcting errors are just two of the features involved in error correction. Allwright's (1975) list has nine features on it (though of course not all will be present in every EC episode). His features are:

• indication that an error was committed;

• identification of the type of error;

• location of the error;

• mention of who made the error;

• selection of a remedy;

• provision of a correct model;

• the furnishing of an opportunity for a new attempt;

- indication of improvement;
- offering of praise.

The importance of some of these depends on whether the learner has made an error or a mistake. Imagine for example that a learner insists on saying *He go*, even though they are continually told by the teacher that the correct form is *He goes*. Perhaps the learners are also quite able to correct themselves after the event, and this will strongly suggest that they are making a mistake rather than an error. There is no point in treating a mistake as if it were an error. Giving the *He go* learner a lengthy explanation about how the simple present tense is formed is a waste of time. They know this already. Their problem is that in the hurly-burly of rapid talk, they get it wrong. What they need is not Allwright's 'provision of a correct model', but his 'furnishing of an opportunity for a new attempt.' In Johnson (1988) I argue that if a learner is to eradicate mistakes, the 'new attempt' must be under the same 'hurly-burly conditions.' Practising the form in a drill, where the learner's attention is fully focused on nothing but the mistake, will do no good – they will say *He goes* every time, because there is no hurly-burly to confuse the issue. What this learner needs is practice in what 12.5.2 calls 'combinatorial skill.'

So far we have been concentrating on correction of spoken language. There are different techniques available for EC of written work than for speaking. Many teachers develop systems of <u>marking codes</u> to indicate the presence of different sorts of error. Here are some of the marking codes suggested in Hedge (2005):

Editing code

WF	wrong form	WF	The harder you work the <u>best</u> will be your achievements.
WW	wrong word		...patient, funny, and <u>kindly</u> WW
T	wrong tense		In the last few weeks you <u>didn't have</u> much fun
Λ	something is missing		You arrived in Brighton Λ1st July.
Sp	wrong spelling		<u>con</u>fortable sp
WO	wrong word order		You haven't seen [yet] London
P	wrong punctuation		Look out. P
V	wrong verb form		The Titanic <u>sunk</u> very quickly.
//	new paragraph needed		
φ	not necessary		John came in and ⊘he⊘ sat down.
‿	You don't need a new sentence. Join up the ideas.		
?	I don't understand what you're trying to say.		
〰	This isn't quite right. It needs clearer expression. Usually the teacher provides an alternative.		
[ ]	This part needs to be re-arranged or reworded.		
!!	You really should know what's wrong here because —we've just done it in class		

Using codes like this is a convenient way of giving learners information on where they have gone wrong. The word <u>reconstruction</u> is sometimes used to describe this procedure. But in terms of one of Allwright's features, reconstruction is only partially satisfactory. The feature is *provision of a correct model*. For this, a technique known as <u>reformulation</u> (discussed by Levenston 1978, Cohen 1983 and Allwright *et al.* 1984) is particularly useful. Its basis is that the teacher (a native speaker if there is one to hand) rewrites a student's essay, as far as possible preserving the intended meaning. Reformulation is different from reconstruction. In the latter errors are simply corrected. The result will be sentences free from gross malformations, but ones which may not remotely resemble sentences a competent user of the language would produce to express the same content. What reformulation offers, and reconstruction partially fails to offer, is a true model of how to express things in the foreign language.

B15.3 More on useless cats

Look back at the 'Cats' essay you saw in Box 2.2.

(a) Try using Hedge's coding system on the essay. Since we did not give Hedge's entire list of marking codes, there will be errors in the essay that are not covered by these codes. Invent new codes to cover these errors.

(b) Now try reformulating the essay. Rewrite it to express the meanings that you think the writer intended (which are not always that easy to discern!). You can change the sentences as much as you want to make the meaning clear.

(c) If you want to see the difference between reformulation and reconstruction, rewrite the essay yet again. This time, make all the changes suggested by the codes you used in (a) above, but make no other changes. The result will be an error-free piece of writing, but probably one that is quite different from your reformulated version.

15.3.5 Who should correct? The *Who* Question

Who should correct learner errors? Possible candidates are the teacher, the learner who made the error (self-correction), and other learners in the class (<u>peer correction</u>). Before reading on, think about the advantages and disadvantages of these three candidates.

It is most often the teacher who does the correcting, though many teachers sing the praises of self-correction and would accept that getting the learners to identify and correct their own errors is the ideal. One reason why teachers sometimes fail to foster self-correction is that they come in with the correct version before the learner has a chance to self-correct. This can be because the teacher wants to avoid an embarrassing long silence while the learner searches for what to say. But sometimes braving the embarrassing silence is rewarded with the learner identifying and correcting the error for themselves. Take a look at CW15.3 (*Towards error recognition*). It shows a suggestion from Brumfit (1977) of a sequence of stages for written EC, moving learners gradually towards recognition of their own errors. His final stage is peer correction, a useful and common technique in groupwork. Some of the advantages and disadvantages of peer correction are mentioned in Note 6.

15.4   Grouping learners in class

15.4.1   Three ways of grouping

Sometimes language school principals have been known to stroll nonchalantly down the corridors of their school, casually glancing through the glass doors into various classrooms to see how things are going. If you ever take that stroll, you may be struck by the various ways in which learners are grouped. Sometimes the class is working as a whole, with the teacher conducting things from the front in the 'traditional' way. In other classes the learners may be in groups of different sizes – pairs, threes or fours, for example. In yet other classes, learners may be working quietly alone. What are the pros and cons of these various ways? Think about this before reading on.

Below is a short list of advantages and disadvantages associated with each. Consider which method the statements relate to. If you wish, you can write a 1 (whole class), 2 (groups), or 3 (alone) beside each statement. For example, if you think that working alone helps learners to develop a sense of belonging to a large unit which remains constant over time, then write 3 beside the first statement (this is not of course the right answer!):

- Learners can develop a sense of belonging to a large unit which remains constant over time.
- Learners have much more chance to talk.
- There can only be a small amount of talk time for each learner.
- It is possible for a few dominant individuals to control what happens, with less dominant ones not joining in at all.
- Learners can develop independence of mind and individual working habits.
- Learners are not able to benefit from the help of their peers.
- The teacher has relatively little control over what happens. Things can get very noisy and out-of-hand.
- Learners feel more comfortable and uninhibited because they are interacting with peers, not the teacher.
- Learners may start to talk in their L1 rather than using the FL.
- Learners can work at their own pace, faster or slower than others, as they wish.
- It is particularly easy for the teacher to keep control over what is happening.

15.4.2 Class layouts

Different ways of grouping students naturally suggest different 'desk patterns.' In the traditional classroom, the teacher sits in the front, centre. The learners are in serried ranks in front of them. Even if they wanted to move the desks, as we noted in 10.4, in some situations this would be impossible because they would be bolted to the floor (not conducive to relaxed learner-to-learner interaction). Nowadays greater efforts are made to allow flexibility of classroom layouts. Below are diagrams of four possible class layouts, one for pairwork, one for groupwork and two for whole-class activity. Decide which is which (x = a learner, 'T' is the teacher and the rectangles are desks/tables).

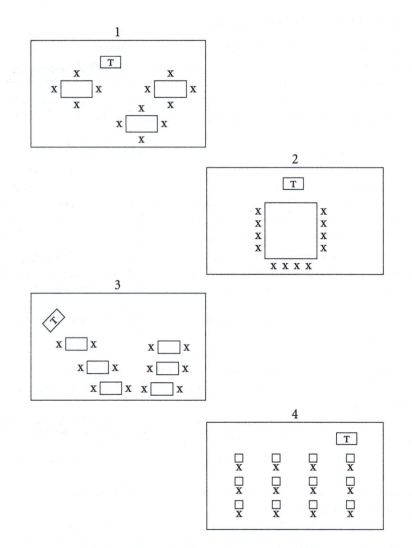

Note that the teacher's position differs in these layouts. Do you prefer one teacher position to another? Why? What about the two whole-class layouts; is one preferable to the other, and if so, why? These are just four of a number of possible layouts for whole-class, group and pairwork. Think of some more, and consider the pros and cons of each.

15.4.3 Groupings and different activity types

When is it appropriate to use the different learner groupings we have been considering – whole class, pairwork, groupwork, working alone? Which type of grouping would you use for the following situations? Why?

- You want your learners to do a simulation involving four business people working for the same company, planning an advertising campaign for a new product they are about to launch.
- You want to do a role-play activity in which one learner (a customer) phones up another (a travel agent) and books a holiday.
- You want to explain to your learners how simple past tense questions are formed in English. After that you plan to do some quick practice, selecting learners and asking them to form simple past questions.
- You want your learners to write a composition based on notes they have been given.
- You want your learners to discuss a social issue, putting forward different points of view.
- You want to do an information gap exercise in which Student A has some information and has to convey it to Student B.
- The class have been doing a task together in groups. You now want to compare the thoughts of the various groups and try to reach some conclusions.

Try to generalize out of these example situations, to make some general statements about when the various groupings are appropriate.

As you can see from the situations above, you will sometimes use more than one way of grouping at different stages of the same activity. This will help to give your lesson variety and flexibility. Imagine for example that you have a problem-solving task for your students – a rather open-ended one with various possible answers. Perhaps you will set up the activity with the class as a whole, telling them what needs to be done. Then you might ask the class to work in pairs. After they have considered the problem for a while, you could get the pairs to come together into larger groups to compare and combine their solutions. You might then finish off the activity with whole-class discussion.

15.4.4 Forming groups

How do you decide which learners to put together in a group? Think of some possible criteria. Here is an imaginary conversation on the topic between four imaginary teachers:

T1:   It's all to do with social dynamics. I like to put students who are friendly together. The easiest way of doing this (with adults at least) is to ask them to form their own groups. This way you can be almost sure that friends will end up together. And more important even than putting friends together is keeping learners who don't like each other apart. That's crucial.

T2:   The trouble with putting friends together is that they are likely to talk in their own language. They may have great fun but they won't do much work. Often I find that I have to *separate* friends rather than putting them together.

T1:   So what criterion do you use?

T2:   Well, I like to consider their level of language. I usually put students of roughly the same level together. This means that (at least in theory) no one dominates because they are better than the others. Also, learners will work at roughly the same pace if they are at the same level. No one student will be holding the group up or hurrying it along.

T3:   I consider level of language as well, but this leads me in quite a different direction. I like to put students at different levels together. That way, the weaker students have someone to help them along. It also means that the groups end up roughly similar, each with a mix of good and bad students together.

T4:   Well, I'm different from all of you. I don't think you can really seriously manipulate groups, even if you think you can. I use a variety of criteria, but they really add up to making the choice random. For example, I sometimes put students together according to size – the tallest together, for example. Or according to the alphabetic order of their names. Or even according to what colour shoes they are wearing.

T3:   That's silly.

T4:   *(a little hurt)* No it isn't.

T3:   Yes it is.

T4:   Isn't.

T2:   But how can you use a variety of criteria? You only need to put the class into groups once. They can stay in the groups for all the lessons. This gives them a sense of belonging with a particular group.

T4:   Oh no. I try to have different groups each lesson. This leads to variety, and the chance to work with different people. It means that each lesson pupils meet different personalities, different views, different talents.

T3:   Well, I still think that basing it on shoe colour is silly.

Can you think of any other pros and cons of the different criteria the four teachers discuss? Can you think of other criteria? Perhaps you can ask some real teachers (unlike the imaginary ones in the conversation) how they like to group students, following what criteria.

15.5 And in the end...

I concluded earlier editions of this book by saying how aware I was of how many important topics had not been covered. I have that feeling again, though I know very well that this book cannot be (and is not intended as) a full training course. But here, at the very end, is a small selection of issues to do with FL classrooms that you, as teachers, are probably already thinking about. Nothing but a few questions, and one or two things to read:

Selecting what textbook to use with your students

What sorts of things would you look for? The unit of organization used would be one of them (Chapter 11 should be useful here). You need to understand how the book is organized (Box 11.4 deals with this). And what methods does the book use (Chapters 9, 12 and 13)? You need to think also about how well suited the materials are to your teaching context (the topic of Chapter 10). What else would you look for? Something to read: Cunningsworth, A. 1997 *Choosing Your Coursebook* London: Macmillan Heinemann.

Dealing with large classes

In some contexts language teachers have to work with classes of 50 learners or more (even over 100 sometimes). What sorts of activities can you use in such situations? Is it feasible to deal with high numbers by using groupwork? How can you keep control of such large classes? And how will you manage to mark the written work of so many learners (a very practical, but highly important topic, this!)? Something to read: Hayes, D. 1997 'Helping teachers to cope with large classes' *ELT Journal* 51/2: 106–16. And Hess, N. 2001 *Teaching Large Multilevel Classes* Cambridge: Cambridge University Press. There is also a useful bibliography on the topic (which is, however, not easy to get hold of): Coleman, H. 1989 *Learning and Teaching in Large Classes: A Bibliography* Leeds and Lancaster: Lancaster–Leeds Language Learning in Large Classes Research Project.

Keeping discipline

This is a problem that all teachers meet, but there are particular issues in relation to language teaching because you often want your classes to be full of speaking practice (sometimes described by teachers of other subjects as 'noise'), and full of movement (learners changing groups etc.). You need to think about what the ideal well-disciplined language class would be like (probably rather different from the well-disciplined geography class). Then you need to develop strategies for dealing with classroom incidents. These might include personality clashes between learners, dealing with uncooperative students – and what else? Wragg (1981) and Widdowson (1987) are worth consulting.

Giving instructions

What you say to the learners when you set up a classroom activity may well determine how successful it is. Many a splendid activity has been ruined by poor instructions. Chapters 12 and 13 contain material for thought here, and indeed the issue comes up in the large-scale activity earlier in this chapter (15.2.2). You might like to choose some other activity from one of these chapters and think exactly what you would need to say to your class to set it up. Take a look at the 'Renting a Flat' activity in Box 12.10, for example. You are asked there to think about 'management' details. Maybe now you could think about what your exact instructions would be. Something to read: Swift, S. *Giving and Checking Instructions*. Available at www.eslbase.com/teaching/giving-checking-instructions.

Notes

1. The example is in CW12.3.
2. As Swan (2005a) points out, it is useful to teach learners the first, second and third conditionals. But there are other types of conditional sentences which also need teaching.
3. The distinction poses us with a terminological problem. A word is needed that will describe both errors and mistakes. There are words like 'malformation' which will do this, but they are a little clumsy, and for this reason 'error' will continue to be used in this meaning. When 'error' is not being used in this general sense, but as something distinct from a mistake, this will be made clear in the context.
4. Don't forget also the possibility of 'handling errors in advance' – predicting what errors your learners might make and going over them before the fluency practice takes place (for example in the pre-task stage we talked about in CW9.7). This is sometimes referred to as *feedforward*, instead of the more normal *feedback*.

5. The matchings are: (a)1; (b)2; (c)4; (d)3; (e)9; (f)6; (g)8; (h)5; (i)7.
6. A danger is that the correction will not be a proper one. A real error may be missed or wrongly corrected. It may even happen that a correct form is thought to be wrong and corrected. Some learners do not like peer correction because it shows that the classmate who is correcting them has superior knowledge to them. They may lose face. An advantage of peer correction is that it does not involve the teacher. Some learners like this because they feel ashamed or threatened if it is the teacher who does the correction.

Issues to think or write about

1. The *Climate Change* materials in 15.2.2 talk about the 'first conditional.' Find out all you can about conditional sentences in English, including the so-called second and third conditionals.

2. Now that you have reached the end of the book, why not write a short summary of it? Restrict yourself to fifty words per chapter, focusing on the main points. If you wish, you can also add an evaluative element to your comments. What has interested you most in what you have read? What least? What is missing from the book? What does it include that you wish weren't there?

Further reading

Richards, J. C., and Renandya, W. A. (eds) 2002 *Methodology in Language Teaching* Cambridge: Cambridge University Press
This has a number of chapters dealing with issues raised in this chapter. Section 2 covers lesson planning and classroom management, and Section 3 looks at classroom dynamics.

Woodward, T. 2001 *Planning Lessons and Courses* Cambridge: Cambridge University Press
A book devoted to lesson planning written by an experienced practitioner.

Edge, J. 1989 *Mistakes and Correction* London: Longman
Provides practical guidance in error correction.

Dörnyei, Z., and Murphey, T. 2003 *Group Dynamics in the Language Classroom* Cambridge: Cambridge University Press
Comprehensive discussion of the theory and practice of group dynamics in language teaching.

Prodromou, L., and Clandfield, L. 2007 *Dealing with Difficulties* Peaslake, Surrey: Delta Publishing
This ELT-related book deals with a number of the issues raised in 15.5, and more besides.

'And so, my friends, I cease.'

Beaumont and Fletcher,
The Knight of the Burning Pestle

References

Abercrombie, D. 1949 'Teaching pronunciation' *English Language Teaching Journal* III/1: 1–11. Reprinted in Abercrombie, D. *Studies in Phonetics and Linguistics* Oxford: Oxford University Press, 1965, 28–40

Al-Bulushi, A. 2010 *Task-Based Computer-Mediated Negotiation in an EFL Context: The Ins and Outs of Online Negotiation of Meaning Using Language Learning Tasks* Saarbrücken: VDM Verlag Dr. Müller

Alderson, J. C., Clapham, C., and Wall, D. 1995 *Language Test Construction and Evaluation* Cambridge: Cambridge University Press

Alderson, J. C., and Lukmani, Y. 1989 'Cognition and levels of comprehension as embodied in test questions' *Reading in a Foreign Language* 5/2: 253–70

Alexander, L. G. 1968 *Look, Listen and Learn: Teacher's Book 1* Harlow: Longman

Alexander, L. G., Allen, W. S., Close, R. A., and O'Neill, R. J. 1975 *English Grammatical Structure* Harlow: Longman

Allwright, R. L. 1975 'Problems in the study of language teachers' treatment of learner error'. In Burt, M. K., and Dulay, H. C. (eds) *New Directions in Second Language Learning, Teaching and Bilingual Education* Washington, DC: TESOL, 96–109

Allwright, R. L. 1984 'Why don't learners learn what teachers teach? The interaction hypothesis'. In Singleton, D. M., and Little, D. G. (eds) *Language Learning in Formal and Informal Contexts* Dublin: International Review of Applied Linguistics, 3–18

Allwright, R. L. 1991 *The Death of the Method* (Working Paper 10). The Exploratory Practice Center, The University of Lancaster, England

Allwright, R. L., and Bailey, K. M. 1991 *Focus on the Language Classroom* Cambridge: Cambridge University Press

Allwright, R. L., Woodley, M.-P., and Allwright, J. M. 1984 'Investigating reformulation as a practical strategy for the teaching of academic writing.' Paper presented at the BAAL Annual General Meeting, September 1984

Anderson, J. R. 1982 'Acquisition of cognitive skill' *Psychological Review* 89/4: 369–406

Anderson, J. R. 1983 *The Architecture of Cognition* Cambridge, MA: Harvard University Press

Arnold, J. 1999 'Visualization: language learning with the mind's eye'. In Arnold, J. (ed.) *Affect in Language Learning* Cambridge: Cambridge University Press, 260–78

Austin, J. L. 1962 *How to Do Things with Words* Oxford: Oxford University Press

Bachman, L. F. 1990 *Fundamental Considerations in Language Testing* Oxford: Oxford University Press

Bagarić, V., and Djigunović, J. M. 2007 'Defining communicative competence' *Metodika* 8: 94–103

Bailey, K. M. 1996 'The best laid plans: teachers' in-class decisions to depart from their lesson plans'. In Bailey, K. M., and Nunan, D. (eds) 1996 *Voices from the Language Classroom* Cambridge: Cambridge University Press, 15–40

Bailey, N., Madden C., and Krashen, S. D. 1974 'Is there a "natural sequence" in adult second language learning?' *Language Learning* 21: 235–43

Baker, D. 1989 *Language Testing: A Critical Survey and Practical Guide* London: Edward Arnold

Ballard, K. 2001 *The Frameworks of English* Basingstoke: Palgrave

Bartlett, F. C. 1932 *Remembering* Cambridge: Cambridge University Press

Batstone, R. 1996 'Key concepts in ELT: noticing' *English Language Teaching Journal* 50/3: 273

Baxter, A. 1997 *Evaluating Your Students* London: Richmond Publishing

Beretta, A., and Davies, A. 1985 'Evaluation of the Bangalore project' *English Language Teaching Journal* 39/2: 121–7

Berko, J. 1958 'The child's learning of English morphology' *Word* 14: 159–77

Bialystok, E. 1990 *Communication Strategies: A Psychological Analysis of Second-Language Use* Oxford: Basil Blackwell

Bloom, B. S. (ed.) 1956 *Taxonomy of Educational Objectives: The Classification of Educational Goals* New York: David Mckay Co Inc

Bloomfield, L. 1933 *Language* New York: Holt

Boas, F. (ed.) 1911 *Handbook of American Indian Languages: Part 1* Bulletin 40, Bureau of American Ethnology, Smithsonian Institution, Washington, DC

Borg, S. 2001 'The research journal: a tool for promoting and understanding researcher development' *Language Teaching Research* 5/21: 56–177

de Bot, K., and Kroll, J. F. 2002 'Psycholinguistics'. In Schmitt, N. (ed.) *An Introduction to Applied Linguistics* London: Edward Arnold, 133–49

Bransford, J. D., and Johnson, M. K. 1973 'Considerations of some problems of comprehension'. In Chase, W. G. (ed.) *Visual Information Processing* New York: Academic Press, 383–438

Breen, M. P. 1983 'Prepared comments to Johnson, K. Syllabus design: possible future trends'. In Johnson, K., and Porter, D. (eds) *Perspectives in Communicative Language Teaching* London: Academic Press, 58–66

Brindley, G. 1989 'The role of needs analysis in adult ESL programme design'. In Johnson, R. K. (ed.) *The Second Language Curriculum* Cambridge: Cambridge University Press, 63–78

Brinton, D. M., Snow, M. A., and Wesche, M. 2003 *Content-based Second Language Instruction* Michigan Classics Edition, Ann Arbor, MI: University of Michigan Press

Brooks, N. 1960 *Language and Language Learning: Theory and Practice* New York: Harcourt, Brace and World, Inc

Broughton, G. 1968 *Success with English* Harmondsworth: Penguin

Brown, G., and Yule, G. 1983 *Discourse Analysis* Cambridge: Cambridge University Press

Brown, H. D. 1973 'Some limitations of C-L/CLL models of language teaching' *TESOL Quarterly* 11: 365–72

Brown, H. D. 2006 *Principles of Language Learning and Teaching* 5th edn Englewood Cliffs, NJ: Prentice-Hall

Brown, R. 1973 *A First Language: The Early Stages* Cambridge, MA: Harvard University Press

Brown, R., and Hanlon, C. 1970 'Derivational complexity and order of acquisition in child speech'. In Hayes, J. (ed.) *Cognition and the Development of Language* New York: Wiley and Sons, 1–53

Brumfit, C. J. 1977 'Correcting written work' *Modern English Teacher* 5/3: 22–3

Brumfit, C. J. 1979 '"Communicative" language teaching: an educational perspective'. In Brumfit, C. J., and Johnson, K. (eds) *The Communicative Approach to Language Teaching* Oxford: Oxford University Press, 183–91

Brumfit, C. J. 1984 *Communicative Methodology in Language Teaching: The Roles of Fluency and Accuracy* Cambridge: Cambridge University Press

Brumfit, C. J., and Johnson, K. (eds) 1979 *The Communicative Approach to Language Teaching* Oxford: Oxford University Press

Budner, S. 1962 'Intolerance of ambiguity as a personality variable' *Journal of Personality* 39: 29–50

Burke, K., and Brooks, J. 2000 *Wavelength Intermediate* Harlow: Longman

Burstall, C., Jamieson, M., Cohen, S., and Hargreaves, M. 1974 *Primary French in the Balance* Slough: NFER

Burt, M. K., and Kiparsky, C. 1972 *The Gooficon: A Repair Manual for English* Rowley, MA: Newbury House

Butler, S. 1999 'A view on standards in South-East Asia' *World Englishes* 18/2: 187–98

Bygate, M. 1996 'Effects of task repetition: appraising learners' performances on tasks'. In Willis, J. and Willis, D. (eds) *Challenge and Change in Language Teaching* London: Heinemann, 136–46

Bygate, M. 2001 'Effects of task repetition on the structure and control of oral language'. In Bygate, M., Skehan, P., and Swain, M. (eds) *Researching Pedagogical Tasks: Second Language Learning, Teaching and Testing* Harlow: Pearson Education, 23–48

Byrne, D. 1986 *Teaching Oral English* 2nd edn Harlow: Longman

Byrne, D. 1988 *Teaching Writing Skills* 2nd edn Harlow: Longman

Canale, M., and Swain, M. 1980 'Theoretical bases of communicative approaches to second language teaching and testing' *Applied Linguistics* 1: 1–47

Cancino, H., Rosansky, E., and Schumann, J. 1978 'The acquisition of English negatives and interrogatives by native Spanish speakers'. In Hatch, E. (ed.) *Second Language Acquisition* Rowley, MA: Newbury House, 207–230

Carroll, J. B. 1965 'The prediction of success in foreign language training'. In Glaser, R. (ed.) *Training, Research and Education* New York: Wiley, 87–136

Carroll, J. B. 1966 'The contributions of psychological theory and educational research to the teaching of foreign languages'. In Valdman, A. (ed.) 1966 *Trends in Language Teaching* New York: McGraw-Hill, 93–106

Carroll, J. B. 1967 'Research problems concerning the teaching of foreign or second languages to younger children'. In Stern, H. H. (ed.) *Foreign Languages in Primary Education* Oxford: Oxford University Press, 94–109

Carroll, J. B. 1973 'Implications of aptitude test research and psycholinguistic theory for foreign-language teaching' *Linguistics* 112: 5–13

Carroll, J. B., and Hall, P. J. 1985 *Make Your Own Language Tests: A Practical Guide to Writing Language Performance Tests* Oxford: Pergamon Press

Carroll, J. B., and Sapon, S. 1959 *Modern Language Aptitude Test* New York: Psychological Corporation

Carter, R., and Nunan, D. (eds) 2001 *The Cambridge Guide to Teaching English to Speakers of Other Languages* Cambridge: Cambridge University Press

Cathcart, R., and Olsen, W.-B. 1976 'Teachers' and students' preferences for correction of classroom errors'. In Fanselow, J., and Crymes, R. (eds) *On TESOL '76* Washington, DC: TESOL, 41–53

Chastain, 1969 'Prediction of success in audio-lingual and cognitive classes' *Language Learning* 19: 27–39

Chaudron, C. 1988 *Second Language Classrooms* Cambridge: Cambridge University Press

Chen, S. Q. 1990 'A study of communication strategies in interlanguage production by Chinese EFL learners' *Language Learning* 40/2: 155–87

Cheng, P. W. 1985 'Restructuring versus automaticity: alternative accounts of skill acquisition' *Psychological Review* 92: 214–23

Chomsky, N. 1957 *Syntactic Structures* The Hague: Mouton

Chomsky, N. 1959 'Review of Skinner, B. F. *Verbal Behaviour*' *Language* 35: 26–58

Chomsky, N. 1965 *Aspects of the Theory of Syntax* Cambridge, MA: MIT Press

Chomsky, N. 1966 'Linguistic theory'. Reprinted in Lester, M. (ed.) *Readings in Applied Transformational Grammar* New York: Holt, Rinehart and Winston 1970, 51–60

Chomsky, N. 1987 'The nature, use and acquisition of language'. Lecture delivered to the Open University

Chomsky, N. 1988 *Language and Problems of Knowledge* Cambridge, MA: MIT Press

Cioffari, V. 1962 'The influence of the language institute program – past, present, and future' *Modern Language Journal* XLV: 65

Clark, C. M., and Yinger, R. J. 1979 *Three Studies of Teacher Planning* Research Series No. 55 East Lansing, MI: Institute for Research on Teaching, Michigan State University

Clark, C. M., and Yinger, R. J. 1987 'Teacher planning'. In Calderhead, J. (ed.) *Exploring Teachers' Thinking* London: Cassell, 84–103

Clark, H. H., and Clark, E. V. 1977 *Psychology and Language* New York: Harcourt Brace Jovanovich

Clarke, D. 1991 'The negotiated syllabus: what is it and how is it likely to work?' *Applied Linguistics* 12: 13–28

Clyne, M. 1991 *Community Languages: The Australian Experience* Cambridge: Cambridge University Press

Cobuild 1992 *English Usage* London: Harper Collins

Cohen, A. D. 1983 'Reformulating second-language compositions: a potential source of input for the learner' *Education Resources Information Center* 228: 866

Coleman, H. 1989 *Learning and Teaching in Large Classes: A Bibliography* Leeds and Lancaster: Lancaster–Leeds Language Learning in Large Classes Research Project

Cook, G. 1998a 'Pragmatics'. In Johnson, K., and Johnson, H. (eds) *Encyclopedic Dictionary of Applied Linguistics* Oxford: Blackwell Publishers, 249

Cook, G. 1998b 'Translation in language teaching'. In Johnson, K., and Johnson, H. (eds) *Encyclopedic Dictionary of Applied Linguistics* Oxford: Blackwell Publishers, 359–60

Cook, G., and Seidlhofer, B. (eds) *Principle and Practice in Applied Linguistics* Oxford: Oxford University Press

Corder, S. P. 1967 'The significance of learners' errors' *International Review of Applied Linguistics* 9: 149–59

Corder, S. P. 1981 *Error Analysis and Interlanguage* Oxford: Oxford University Press

Coulavin, A. 1983 'Excuses, excuses' *Practical English Teaching* 4/2: 31

Crace, A., and Wileman, R. 2002 *Language to Go: Intermediate* Harlow: Longman

Cross, T. G. 1977 'Mothers' speech adjustments: the contribution of selected child listener variables'. In Snow, C. E., and Ferguson, C. A. (eds) *Talking to Children* Cambridge: Cambridge University Press, 151–88

Crossman, E. R. F. W. 1959 'A theory of the acquisition of speed-skill' *Ergonomics* 2

Crystal, D. 2003 *English as a Global Language* 2nd edn Cambridge: Cambridge University Press

Crystal, D. (ed.) 1990 *The Cambridge Encyclopedia* Cambridge: Cambridge University Press

Cummins, J. 1980 'The cross-lingual dimension of language proficiency: implications for bilingual education and the optimal age issue' *TESOL Quarterly* 14: 175–87

Cunningham, S., and Moor, P. 2005a *New Cutting Edge Elementary* Harlow: Longman

Cunningham, S., and Moor, P. 2005b *New Cutting Edge Upper Intermediate* Harlow: Longman

Cunningham, S., and Moor, P. 2005c *New Cutting Edge Intermediate* Harlow: Longman

Cunningsworth, A. 1997 *Choosing Your Coursebook* London: Macmillan Heinemann

Dakin, J. 1973 *The Language Laboratory and Language Learning* Harlow: Longman

Daneman, M., and Carpenter, P. A. 1980 'Individual differences in working memory and reading' *Journal of Verbal Learning and Verbal Behaviour* 19: 450–66

Davis, P., and Rinvolucri, M. 1988 *Dictation: New Methods, New Possibilities* Cambridge: Cambridge University Press

Debyser, F. 1974 'Simulation et réalité dans l'enseignement des langues vivantes' Études 105

Diller, K. W. 1971 *Generative Grammar, Structural Linguistics and Language Teaching* Rowley, MA: Newbury House

Dobson, L., Pugh, A. K., and Howatt, A. P. R. 1981 'Language teaching'. In *Language Learning and Language Teaching* (Block 3 of 'Language in Use' course) Milton Keynes: Open University

Dörnyei, Z. 2005 *The Psychology of the Language Learner: Individual Differences in Second Language Acquisition* London: Lawrence Erlbaum Associates

Dörnyei, Z., and Csizér, K. 1998 'Ten commandments for motivating language learners: results of an empirical study' *Language Teaching Research* 2: 203–30

Dörnyei, Z., and Murphey, T. 2003 *Group Dynamics in the Language Classroom* Cambridge: Cambridge University Press

Dörnyei, Z., and Skehan, P. 2003 'Individual differences in second language learning'. In Doughty, C. J., and Long, M. H. (eds) *The Handbook of Second Language Acquisition* Oxford: Blackwell Publishers, 589–630

Doughty, C. J., and Long, M. (eds) 2003 *The Handbook of Second Language Acquisition* Oxford: Blackwell Publishers

Dudeney, G. 2007 *The Internet and the Language Classroom* 2nd edn Cambridge: Cambridge University Press

Dudley-Evans, T., and St John, M. J. 1998 *Developments in English for Specific Purposes* Cambridge: Cambridge University Press

Dulay, H., and Burt, M. 1973 'Should we teach children syntax?' *Language Learning* 23/2: 245–58

Dulay, H., and Burt, M. 1974 'Natural sequences in child second language acquisition' *Language Learning* 24/1: 37–53

Edge, J. 1989 *Mistakes and Correction* Harlow: Longman

Edge, J. 2006 (ed.) *(Re-)Locating TESOL in an Age of Empire* London: Palgrave Macmillan

Edwards, J. 1994 *Multilingualism* London: Routledge

van Ek, J. A. 1973 'The "Threshold Level" in a unit/credit system'. In Trim, J. L. M., Richterich, R., van Ek, J. A., and Wilkins, D. A. *Systems Development in Adult Language Learning* Strasbourg: Council of Europe, 89–128

van Ek, J. A. 1975 *The Threshold Level* Strasbourg: Council of Europe

van Ek, J. A. 1978 *The Threshold Level for Schools* Harlow: Longman

Ellis, G., and Sinclair, B. 1989 *Learning to Learn English* Cambridge: Cambridge University Press

Ellis, R. 1984 'Can syntax be taught? A study of the effects of formal instruction on the acquisition of Wh- questions by children' *Applied Linguistics* 5: 138–55

Ellis, R. 1985 *Understanding Second Language Acquisition* Oxford: Oxford University Press

Ellis, R. 1994 *The Study of Second Language Acquisition* Oxford: Oxford University Press

Ellis, R. 1997 *Second Language Acquisition* Oxford: Oxford University Press

Ellis, R. 2005 *Planning and Task Performance in a Second Language* Amsterdam: Benjamins

van Els, T., Bongaerts, T., Extra, G., van Os, C., and Janssen-van Dieten, A.-M. 1984 *Applied Linguistics and the Learning and Teaching of Foreign Languages* London: Edward Arnold

Ervin-Tripp, S. 1974 'Is second language learning like the first?' *TESOL Quarterly* 8/2: 111–27

Eskey, D. 1988 'Holding in the bottom: an interactive approach to the language problems of second language learners'. In Carrell, P., Devine, J., and Eskey, D. (eds) *Interactive Approaches to Second Language Reading* Cambridge: Cambridge University Press

Evans, V., and Green, M. 2006 *Cognitive Linguistics: An Introduction* Edinburgh: Edinburgh University Press

Faerch, C., and Kasper, G. 1986 'The role of comprehension in second-language learning' *Applied Linguistics* 7: 257–74

Fennell, J. L. I. 1961 *The Penguin Russian Course* Harmondsworth: Penguin Books

Fitts, P. M., and Posner, M. I. 1967 *Human Performance* Belmont, CA: Brooks Cole

Fullan, M. G., and Stiegelbauer, S. 1991 *The New Meaning of Educational Change* London: Cassell

Gallaway C., and Richards, B. (eds) 1994 *Input and Interaction in Language Acquisition* Cambridge: Cambridge University Press

Gardner, R. C. 1985 *Social Psychology and Second Language Learning: The Role of Attitudes and Motivation* London: Edward Arnold

Gardner, R. C., and Lambert, W. E. 1972 *Attitudes and Motivation in Second-Language Learning* Rowley, MA: Newbury House

Garfinkel, H. 1967 *Studies in Ethnomethodology* Englewood Cliffs, NJ: Prentice Hall

Garman, M., and Hughes, A. 1983 *English Cloze Exercises* Oxford: Blackwell

Garnett, W. 1992 'A back-to-the drawing-board oboe' *Double Reed News* 19: 22–5

Gass, S., and Varonis, E. 1994 'Input, interaction and second language production' *Studies in Second Language Acquisition* 16: 283–302

Gass, S. M. 2003 'Input and interaction'. In Doughty, C., and Long, M. H. (eds) *Handbook of Second Language Acquisition* New York: Basil Blackwell, 224–55

Gattegno, C. 1972 *Teaching Foreign Languages in Schools: The Silent Way* New York: Educational Solutions Inc.

Geddes, M., and Sturtridge, G. 1979 *Listening Links* London: Heinemann

Geddes, M., and Sturtridge, G. 1982 *Reading Links* London: Heinemann

Genesee, F. 1976 'The role of intelligence in second language learning' *Language Learning* 26/2: 267–80

George, H. V. 1963 'A verb-form frequency count' *English Language Teaching* 18: 1

Gillette, B. 1987 'Two successful language learners: an introspective report'. In Faerch, C., and Kasper, G. (eds) *Introspection in Second Language Research* Clevedon, Avon: Multilingual Matters, 267–79

Gimson, A. C., and Cruttenden, A. 2001 *Gimson's Pronunciation of English* 6th edn (revised by A. Cruttenden) London: Edward Arnold

Goh, C. 1998 'Strategic processing and metacognition in second language listening', Unpublished PhD thesis, Lancaster University

Gower, R., Phillips, D., and Walters, S. 2005 *Teaching Practice Handbook* Basingstoke: Macmillan

Graddol, D. 2007 *English Next* London: British Council

Green, P. S. 1975 (ed.) *The Language Laboratory in School* Edinburgh: Oliver and Boyd

Greenbaum, S., and Whitcut, J. 1989 *Longman Guide to English Usage* Harlow: Longman

Grellet, F. 1981 *Developing Reading Skills* Cambridge: Cambridge University Press

Grigorenko, E., Sternberg, R., and Ehrman, M. E. 2000 'A theory based approach to the measurement of foreign language learning ability: the Canal-F theory and test' *Modern Language Journal* 84/3: 390–405

Guiora, A. Z., Brannon, R. C. L., and Dull, C. Y. 1972 'Empathy and second language learning' *Language Learning* 22: 111–30

Hadfield, J. 1987 *Elementary Communication Games* London: Nelson

Hadfield, J. 1990 *Intermediate Communication Games* London: Nelson

Hadfield, J. 1997 *Advanced Communication Games* Addison Wesley

Hadfield, J. 1999 *Beginners' Communication Games* Harlow: Longman

Hadfield, J., and Hadfield, C. 1995 *Reading Games* Harlow: Longman

Hadfield, J., and Hadfield, C. 1999 *Presenting New Language* Oxford: Oxford University Press

Hadfield, J., and Hadfield, C. 2000 *Simple Writing Activities* Oxford: Oxford University Press

Halliday, M. A. K. 1975 *Learning How to Mean* London: Edward Arnold

Hamp-Lyons, L., and Heasley, B. 1987 *Study Writing* Cambridge: Cambridge University Press

Harley, B. 1989 'Functional grammar in French immersion: a classroom experiment' *Applied Linguistics* 10: 331–59

Harmer, J. 1982 'What is communicative?' *English Language Teaching Journal* 36/3: 164–8

Harmer, J. 2001 *The Practice of English Language Teaching* 3rd edn London: Pearson Education

Harmer, J. 2004 *Just: Reading and Writing* London: Marshall Cavendish

Harrison, A. 1983 *A Language Testing Handbook* Basingstoke: Macmillan Publishers

Hawkins, R. 1998 'Learning strategies'. In Johnson, K., and Johnson, H. (eds) *Encyclopedic Dictionary of Applied Linguistics* Oxford: Blackwell Publishers, 195–7

Hayes, D. 1997 'Helping teachers to cope with large classes' *ELT Journal* 51/2: 106–16

Heaton, J. B. 1988 *Writing English Language Tests* Harlow: Longman

Heaton, J. B. 1990 *Classroom Testing* Harlow: Longman

Hedge, T. 1985 *Using Readers in Language Teaching* London: Macmillan

Hedge, T. 1988 *Writing* 1st edn Oxford: Oxford University Press

Hedge, T. 2000 *Teaching and Learning in the Language Classroom* Oxford: Oxford University Press

Hedge, T. 2005 *Writing* 2nd edn Oxford: Oxford University Press

Hendrickson, J. M. 1978 'Error correction in foreign language teaching: recent theory, research and practice' *Modern Language Journal* 62: 387–98

Hergenhahn, B. R., and Olson, M. H. 2005 *An Introduction to Theories of Learning* 7th edn London: Pearson Education

Hermann, G. 1980 'Attitudes and success in children's learning of English as a second language: the motivational vs. resultative hypothesis' *English Language Teaching Journal* 34: 247–54

Hess, N. 1991 *Headstarts* Harlow: Longman

Hess, N. 2001 *Teaching Large Multilevel Classes* Cambridge: Cambridge University Press

Higgins, J., and Johns, T. 1984 *Computers in Language Learning* London: Collins

Hogan, R. 1969 'Development of an empathy scale' *Journal of Consulting and Clinical Psychology* 33: 307–16

Holder, P. (ed.) 1966 *Franz Boas's Introduction to Handbook of American Indian Languages and J. W. Powell's Indian Linguistic Families of America North of Mexico* Lincoln, NE: University of Nebraska Press

Holding, D. H. 1965 *Principles of Training* Oxford: Pergamon Press

Holliday, A. 1994 *Appropriate Methodology and Social Context* Cambridge: Cambridge University Press

Holliday, A. 2005 *The Struggle to Teach English as an International Language* Oxford: Oxford University Press

Howatt, A. P. R. 1984 *A History of English Language Teaching* Oxford: Oxford University Press

Howatt, A. P. R., with Widdowson, H. G. 2004 *A History of English Language Teaching* 2nd edn Oxford: Oxford University Press

Hughes, A. 1989 *Testing for Language Teachers* Cambridge: Cambridge University Press

Hughes, A., and Lascaratou, C. 1982 'Competing criteria for error gravity' *ELT Journal* 36: 175–82

Hughes, A., and Trudgill, P. 1996 *English Accents and Dialects* London: Edward Arnold

Hutchinson, T., and Waters, A. 1987 *English for Specific Purposes* Cambridge: Cambridge University Press

Hymes, D. 1970 'On communicative competence'. In Gumperz, J. J., and Hymes, D. (eds) *Directions in Sociolinguistics* New York: Holt, Rinehart and Winston

Jakobovits, L. A. 1970 *Foreign Language Learning: A Psycholinguistic Analysis of the Issues* Rowley, MA: Newbury House

James, C. 1980 *Contrastive Analysis* Harlow: Longman

Jarvis, H. 2015 'From PPP and CALL/MALL to a praxis of task-based teaching and Mobile Assisted Language Use' *TESL-EJ* 19/1

Jarvis, H., and Achilleos, M. 2013 'From Computer Assisted Language Learning (CALL) to Mobile Assisted Language Use (MALU)'. *TESL-EJ* 16/4

Jarvis, H., and Krashen, S. 2014 'Is CALL obsolete? Language acquisition and language learning revisited in a digital age' *TESL-EJ* 17/4

Jaworski, A. 1998 'Language planning'. In Johnson, K., and Johnson, H. (eds) *Encyclopedic Dictionary of Applied Linguistics* Oxford: Blackwell Publishers, 185–7

Jenkins, J. 2000 *The Phonology of English as an International Language* Oxford: Oxford University Press

Johnson, H. 1992 'Defossilizing' *ELT Journal* 46/2: 180–9

Johnson, K. 1977 'Teaching appropriateness and coherence in academic writing'. Reprinted in Johnson, K. *Communicative Syllabus Design and Methodology* Oxford: Pergamon Institute of English 1982, 176–82

Johnson, K. 1980a 'Making drills communicative'. Reprinted in Johnson, K. *Communicative Syllabus Design and Methodology* Oxford: Pergamon Institute of English 1982, 156–62

Johnson, K. 1980b 'The "deep end" strategy in communicative language teaching'. Reprinted in Johnson, K. *Communicative Syllabus Design and Methodology* Oxford: Pergamon Institute of English 1982, 192–200

Johnson, K. 1981 'Writing'. In Johnson, K., and Morrow, K. (eds) *Communication in the Classroom* Harlow: Longman, 93–107

Johnson, K. 1982 *Communicative Syllabus Design and Methodology* Oxford: Pergamon Institute of English

Johnson, K. 1983 *Now for English* London: Thomas Nelson

Johnson, K. 1988 'Mistake correction' *ELT Journal* 42: 89–96

Johnson, K. 1995 'Methods as plausible fictions' *CRILE Working Paper, No. 23*, Centre for Research in Language Education, Lancaster University

Johnson, K. 1996 *Language Teaching and Skill Learning* Oxford: Blackwell

Johnson, K. (ed.) 2005 *Expertise in Second Language Learning and Teaching* Basingstoke: Palgrave

Johnson, K., and Morrow, K. E. 1979 *Approaches* Cambridge: Cambridge University Press

Jordan, R. R. 1990 *Academic Writing Course* London: Collins

Jordan, R. R. 1997 *English for Academic Purposes* Cambridge: Cambridge University Press

Kachru, B. B. 1983 *The Indianization of English: The English Language in India* Oxford: Oxford University Press

Kachru, B. B. 1985 'Standards, codification and sociolinguistic realism: the English language in the outer circle'. In Quirk, R., and Widdowson, H. G. (eds) *English in the World: Teaching and Learning the Language and Literatures* Cambridge: Cambridge University Press, 11–30

Kaplan, R. B. 1966 'Cultural thought patterns in inter-cultural education' *Language Learning* 16: 1–20

Kay, S., and Jones, V. 2000 *Inside Out* Oxford: Macmillan Heinemann

Keenan, E. L., and Ochs, E. 1979 'Becoming a competent speaker of Malagasy'. In Shopen, T. *Languages and Their Speakers* Philadelphia, PA: University of Pennsylvania Press, 113–239

Kelly, L. G. 1969 *25 Centuries of Language Teaching* Rowley, MA: Newbury House

Kirkpatrick, A. 2011 'English as an Asian lingua franca and the multilingual model of ELT' *Language Teaching* 44/2: 212–24

Klein-Braley, C., and Raatz, U. 1984 'A survey of research on the C-Test' *Language Testing* 1: 134–46

Kormos, J., and Dörnyei, Z. 2004 'The interaction of linguistic and motivational variables in second language task performance' Zeitschrift für Interkulturellen Fremdsprachenunterricht 9/2. Available at www.zoltandornyei.co.uk/uploads/2004-kormos-dornyei-zif.pdf, accessed on 3 October 2016

Kramsch, C., and Sullivan, P. 1996 'Appropriate pedagogy' *ELT Journal* 50/3: 199–212

Krashen, S. 1985 *The Input Hypothesis: Issues and Implications* London: Longman

Krashen, S. D. 1982 *Principles and Practice in Second Language Acquisition* Oxford: Pergamon Institute of English

Krashen, S. D., and Terrell, T. D. 1983 *The Natural Approach* London: Prentice Hall Europe

Krzeszowski, T. P. 1990 *Contrasting Languages: The Scope of Contrastive Linguistics* Berlin: Mouton de Gruyter

Kumaravadivelu, B. 2006 *Understanding Language Teaching: From Method to Postmethod* Mahwah, NJ: Lawrence Erlbaum Associates

Lado, R. 1957 *Linguistics across Cultures: Applied Linguistics for Language Teachers* Ann Arbor, MI: University of Michigan

Lado, R. 1961 *Language Testing* Harlow: Longman

Lambert, W. E., and Tucker, G. R. 1972 *Bilingual Education of Children: The St. Lambert Experiment* Rowley, MA: Newbury House

Larsen-Freeman, D., and Long, M. 1991 *An Introduction to Second Language Acquisition Research* Harlow: Longman

Lee, W. 1968 'Thoughts on contrastive linguistics in the context of language teaching'. In Alatis, J. (ed.) *Report on the Nineteenth Annual Round Table Meeting on Linguistics and Language Studies, Georgetown University* Washington, DC: Georgetown University Press

Lenneberg, E. 1967 *Biological Foundations of Language* New York: Wiley

Lennon, P. 1989 'Introspection and intentionality in advanced second-language acquisition' *Language Learning* 39: 375–95

Levenston, E. A. 1978 'Error analysis of free composition: the theory and the practice' *Indian Journal of Applied Linguistics* 4/1: 1–11

Levine, A., Reves, T., and Leaver, B. L. 1996 'Relationship between language learning strategies and Israeli vs. Russian cultural-educational factors'. In Oxford, R. L. (ed.) *Language Learning Strategies around the World: Crosscultural Perspectives* National Foreign Language Resource Center, Manoa: University of Hawaii Press, 35–46

Levy, M. 1997 *CALL: Context and Conceptualisation* Oxford: Oxford University Press

Lewis, E. G., and Massad, C. E. 1975 *The Teaching of English as a Foreign Language in Ten Countries* New York: Wiley

Lightbown, P. M. 1987 'Classroom language as input to second language acquisition'. In Pfaff, C. W. (ed.) *First and Second Language Acquisition Processes* Rowley, MA: Newbury House

Lightbown, P. M., and Spada, N. 2006 *How Languages Are Learned* 3rd edn Oxford: Oxford University Press

Lindstromberg, S. 2004 *Language Activities for Teenagers* Cambridge: Cambridge University Press

Long, M. H. 1983 'Native speaker/non-native speaker conversation and the negotiation of comprehensible input' *Applied Linguistics* 4: 126–41

Long, M. H. 1985 'A role for instruction in second language acquisition: task-based language training'. In Hyltenstam, K., and Pienemann, M. (eds) *Modelling and Assessing Second Language Acquisition* Clevedon, Avon: Multilingual Matters, 77–100

Long, M. H., and Porter, P. 1985 'Group work, interlanguage talk and second language acquisition' *TESOL Quarterly* 19: 207–28

Lukmani, Y. 1972 'Motivation to learn and language proficiency' *Language Learning* 22: 261–73

Lyons, J. 1970 *Chomsky* London: Fontana/Collins

McCarthy, M. 1990 *Vocabulary* Oxford: Oxford University Press

McDonough, J. 1998 'Learner training'. In Johnson, K., and Johnson, H. (eds) *Encyclopedic Dictionary of Applied Linguistics* Oxford: Blackwell Publishers, 193–5

McDonough, S. H. 1981 *Psychology in Foreign Language Teaching* London: Allen and Unwin

McDonough, S. H. 1998a 'Language testing'. In Johnson, K., and Johnson, H. (eds) *Encyclopedic Dictionary of Applied Linguistics* Oxford: Blackwell Publishers, 187–92

McDonough, S. H. 1998b 'English for specific purposes'. In Johnson, K., and Johnson, H. (eds) *Encyclopedic Dictionary of Applied Linguistics* Oxford: Blackwell Publishers, 105–10

McKay, S. L. 2002 *Teaching English as an International Language* Oxford: Oxford University Press

Mackey, W. F. 1965 *Language Teaching Analysis* Harlow: Longman

Mackey, W. F. 1970 'A typology of bilingual education' *Foreign Language Annals* 3: 596–608

McLaughlin, B. 1987 *Theories of Second-Language Learning* London: Edward Arnold

McLaughlin, B. 1990 'Restructuring' *Applied Linguistics* 11/2: 113–128

McLaughlin, B., Rossman, R., and McLeod, B. 1983 'Second-language learning: an information-processing perspective' *Language Learning* 33: 135–58

McNeill, D. 1970 *The Acquisition of Language* New York: Harper and Row

Maley, A. 1981 'Games and problem solving'. In Johnson, K., and Morrow, K. (eds) *Communication in the Classroom* Harlow: Longman, 137–48

Markee, N. 1997 *Managing Curricular Innovation* London: Allen and Unwin

Meddings, L. 2003 'A Dogme lesson idea' *Humanising Language Teaching* 5/6. Available at www.hltmag.co.uk/nov03/less1.htm, accessed on 5 October 2016

Meddings, L., and Thornbury, S. 2003 'What Dogme feels like' *Humanising Language Teaching* 5/6. Available at www.hltmag.co.uk/nov03/sart1.htm, accessed on 5 October 2016

Medgyes, P. 1994 *The Non-Native Teacher* London: Macmillan

Mehrabian, A. 1970 'The development and validation of measures of affiliative tendency and sensitivity to rejection' *Educational and Psychological Measurement* 30: 417–28

Messick, S. 1970 'The criterion problem in the evaluation of instruction: assessing possible, not just intended, outcomes'. In Wittrock, M. C., and Wiley, D. E. (eds) *The Evaluation of Instruction: Issues and Problems* New York: Holt, Rinehart and Winston

Messick, S. 1989 'Validity'. In Linn, R. L. (ed.) *Educational Measurement* 3rd edn New York: Macmillan, 13–103

Miller, G. A. 1974 'Psychology, language and levels of communication'. In Silverstein, A. (ed.) *Human Communication* New York: John Wiley

Mitchell, R., and Miles, F. 1998 *Second Language Learning Theories* London: Edward Arnold

Montgomery, C., and Eisenstein, M. 1985 'Real reality revisited: and experimental communicative course in ESL' *TESOL Quarterly* 19: 317–33

Morrow, K. E. 1977 *Techniques of Evaluation for a Notional Syllabus* London: Royal Society of Arts

Morrow, K. E., and Johnson, K. 1979 *Communicate 1 and 2* Cambridge: Cambridge University Press

Moskowitz, G. 1978 *Caring and Sharing in the Foreign Language Class* Rowley, MA: Newbury House

Munby, J. 1978 *Communicative Syllabus Design* Cambridge: Cambridge University Press

Murphy, R. 1990 *Essential Grammar in Use* Cambridge: Cambridge University Press

Naiman, N., Fröhlich, H., Stern, H., and Todesco, A. 1978 *The Good Language Learner* Research in Education Series, 7 Toronto: Ontario Institute for Studies in Education

Nemser, W. 1971 'Approximative systems of foreign language learners' *International Review of Applied Linguistics* 9: 115–23

Neves, D. M., and Anderson, J. R. 1981 'Knowledge compilation: mechanisms for the automization of cognitive skills'. In Anderson, J. R. (ed.) *Cognitive Skills and Their Acquisition* Hillside, NJ: Lawrence Erlbaum Associates, 57–84

Newmark, L. 1963 'Grammatical theory and the teaching of English as a foreign language'. In Lester, M. (ed.) *Readings in Applied Transformational Grammar* New York: Holt, Rinehart and Winston, 210–18

Newmark, L. 1966 'How not to interfere with language learning'. Reprinted in Brumfit, C. J., and Johnson, K. (eds) *The Communicative Approach to Language Teaching* Oxford: Oxford University Press, 160–6

Newmark, L., and Reibel, D. A. 1968 'Necessity and sufficiency in language learning' *International Review of Applied Linguistics* 6/2: 145–64

Newport, E. L., Gleitman, H., and Gleitman, L. R. 1977 'Mother, I'd rather do it myself: some effects and non-effects of maternal speech style'. In Snow, C. E., and Ferguson, C. A. (eds) *Talking to Children* Cambridge: Cambridge University Press, 109–50

Nisbet, J., and Shucksmith, J. 1986 *Learning Strategies* London: Routledge

Nitta, R., and Gardner, S. 2005 'Consciousness-raising and practice in ELT coursebooks' *ELT Journal* 59/1: 3–13

Odlin, T. 1990 *Language Transfer* Cambridge: Cambridge University Press

Oller, J. W. 1976 'A program for language testing research'. In Brown, H. D. (ed.) Papers in Second Language Acquisition. Language Learning, Special Edition No. 4, 141–66

Oller, J. W. 1979 *Language Tests at School* Harlow: Longman

O'Malley, J. M., and Chamot, A. U. 1990 *Learning Strategies in Second Language Acquisition* Cambridge: Cambridge University Press

Oxenden, C., and Latham-Koenig, C. 1999 *English File: Intermediate* Oxford: Oxford University Press

Oxford, R. 1990 *Language Learning Strategies: What Every Teacher Should Know* Rowley, MA: Newbury House

Oxford, R. (ed.) 1996 *Language Learning Strategies around the World: Cross-cultural Perspectives* Honolulu: University of Hawaii Press

Palfreman, J. 1983 'A Child's Guide to Languages' *Horizon* BBC Television

Palmer, H., and Palmer, D. 1925 *English through Actions* Reprinted edition Harlow: Longman Green, 1959

Palmer, H. E. 1922 *English Intonation with Systematic Exercises* Cambridge: Heffer

Paran, A. 1996 'Reading in EFL: facts and fictions' *ELT Journal* 50/1: 25–34

Parasher, S. V. 1994 'Indian English: certain grammatical, lexical and stylistic features'. In Angithotri, R. K., and Khanna, A. L. (eds) *Second Language Acquisition: Socio-cultural and Linguistic Aspects of English in India* New Delhi: Sage Publications, 145–64

Parrot, M. 2000 *Grammar for English Language Teachers* Cambridge: Cambridge University Press

Parry, T. S., and Stansfield, C. 1990 *Language Aptitude Reconsidered* Englewood Cliffs, NJ: Prentice-Hall Regents

Pennycook, A. 1994 *The Cultural Politics of English as an International Language* Harlow: Longman

Phillips, D., and Sheerin, S. 1990 *Signature* London: Nelson

Phillips, J. 1973 'Syntax and vocabulary of mothers' speech to young children: age and sex comparisons' *Child Development* 44: 182–5

Phillips, T., and Phillips, A. 1997 *Key Skills for FCE* New York: Prentice Hall Phoenix ELT

Phillipson, R. 1992 *Linguistic Imperialism* Oxford: Oxford University Press

Pica, T. 1987 'Second language acquisition, social interaction, and the classroom' *Applied Linguistics* 8: 3–21

Pica, T., Young, R., and Doughty, C. 1987 'The impact of interaction on comprehension' *TESOL Quarterly* 21: 737–58

Pickett, G. D. 1978 *The Foreign Language Learning Process* London: British Council

Pienemann, M. 1985 'Learnability and syllabus construction'. In Hyltenstam, K., and Pienemann, M. (eds) *Modelling and Assessing Second Language Acquisition* Clevedon, Avon: Multilingual Matters

Pimsleur, P. 1968 *Language Aptitude Battery* New York: Harcourt Brace and World

Pimsleur, P., Sundland, D. M., and McIntyre, R. D. 1964 'Under-achievement in foreign language learning' *International Review of Applied Linguistics* 2/2: 113–50

Politzer, R. L. 1961 *Teaching French: An Introduction to Applied Linguistics* Boston, MA: Ginn & Co.

Prabhu, N. S. 1987 *Second Language Pedagogy: A Perspective* Oxford: Oxford University Press

Prabhu, N. S. 1990 'There is no best method – why?' *TESOL Quarterly* 24/2: 161–76

Pritchard, D. F. 1952 'An investigation into the relationship of personality traits and ability in modern language' *British Journal of Educational Psychology* 22: 157–8

Prodromou, L., and Clandfield, L. 2007 *Dealing with Difficulties* Peaslake, Surrey: Delta Publishing

Rao, R. 1978 'The caste of English'. In Narasimhaiah, C. D. (ed.) *Awakened Conscience: Studies in Commonwealth Literature* Delhi: Sterling, 420–2

Read, C., and Matthews, A. 1991 *Tandem Plus* London: Nelson

Reynolds, M. 1994 *Groupwork in Education and Training* London: Kogan Page

Richards, J., Platt, J., and Weber, H. 1985 *Longman Dictionary of Applied Linguistics* Harlow: Longman

Richards, J. C. 1971 'A non-contrastive approach to error analysis'. Reprinted in Richards, J. C. (ed.) *Error Analysis* Harlow: Longman 1974, 172–188

Richards, J. C. (ed.) 1974 *Error Analysis* Harlow: Longman

Richards, J. C. 1985 'The secret life of methods'. In Richards, J. C. *The Context of Language Teaching* Cambridge: Cambridge University Press, 32–45

Richards, J. C., and Renandya, W. A. (eds) 2002 *Methodology in Language Teaching* Cambridge: Cambridge University Press

Richards, J. C., and Rodgers, T. S. 2001 *Approaches and Methods in Language Teaching* 2nd edn Cambridge: Cambridge University Press

Richterich, R. 1972 'Definition of language needs and types of adults'. In Trim, J. L. M., Richterich, R., van Ek, J. A., and Wilkins, D. A. *Systems Development in Adult Language Learning* Strasbourg: Council of Europe, 29–88

Rinvolucri, M. 1985 *Grammar Games* Cambridge: Cambridge University Press

Rivers, W. M. 1964 *The Psychologist and the Foreign Language Teacher* Chicago: University of Chicago Press

Robb, T. N. 1996 'E-mail keypals for language fluency' Available at www.cc.kyoto-su.ac. jp/~trobb/keypals.html, accessed on 3 October 2016

Roberts, J. T. 1998 'Humanistic approaches'. In Johnson, K., and Johnson, H. (eds) *Encyclopedic Dictionary of Applied Linguistics* Oxford: Blackwell Publishers, 158–61

Rogers, J. 1982 '"The world for sick proper"' *ELT Journal* 36/3: 144–51

Rogers, M. 1994 'German word order: a role for developmental and linguistic factors in L2 pedagogy'. In Bygate, M., Tonkyn, A., and Williams, E. (eds) *Grammar and the Language Teacher* New York: Prentice Hall, 132–59

Rossiter, M. J. 2003 'The effects of affective strategy training in the ESL classroom' *TESL-EJ* 7/2

Rost, M. 1990 *Listening in Language Learning* Harlow: Longman

Rubin, J. 1975 'What the good language learner can teach us' *TESOL Quarterly* 9: 41–51

Rutherford, W., and Sharwood Smith, M. 1985 'Consciousness-raising and universal grammar' *Applied Linguistics* 6: 274–82

Samuda, V. 2001 'Guiding relationships between form and meaning during task performance: the role of the teacher'. In Bygate, M., Skehan, P., and Swain, M. (eds) *Researching Pedagogic Tasks: Second Language Learning, Teaching and Testing* London: Pearson Education, 119–40

Scherer, G. A. C., and Wertheimer, M. 1964 *A Psycholinguistic Experiment in Foreign Language Teaching* New York: McGraw Hill

Schmidt, R. 1983 'Interaction, acculturation and the acquisition of communicative competence'. In Wolfson, N., and Judd, E. (eds) *Sociolinguistics and Second Language Acquisition* Rowley, MA: Newbury House, 137–174

Schmidt, R. 1990 'The role of consciousness in second language learning' *Applied Linguistics* 11: 129–58

Schmidt, R., and Frota, S. 1986 'Developing basic conversational ability in a second language: a case study of an adult learner of Portugese'. In Day, R. (ed.) *Talking to Learn: Conversation in Second Language Acquisition* Rowley, MA: Newbury House

Schoenfeld, A. H. 1985 *Mathematical Problem Solving* Orlando, FL: Academic Press

Schumann, J. 1978 *The Pidginization Process: A Model for Second Language Acquisition* Rowley, MA: Newbury House

Scott, W. 1980 *Are You Listening?* Oxford: Oxford University Press

Seidlhofer, B. 2001 'Closing a conceptual gap: the case for a description of English as a lingua franca' *International Journal of Applied Linguistics* 11/2: 133–58

Selinker, L. 1972 'Interlanguage' *International Review of Applied Linguistics* 10: 209–31

Selinker, L., and Lamendella, J. 1978 'Two perspectives on fossilization in interlanguage learning' *Interlanguage Studies Bulletin* 3: 143–91

Shamim, F. 1996 'In or out of the action zone: location as a feature of interaction in large ESL classes in Pakistan'. In Bailey, K. M., and Nunan, D. (eds) *Voices from the Language Classroom* Cambridge: Cambridge University Press

Shapira, R. G. 1978 'The non-learning of English: a case study of an adult'. In Hatch, E. (ed.) *Second Language Acquisition* Rowley, MA: Newbury House

Shiffrin, R. M., and Dumais, S. T. 1981 'The development of automatism'. In Anderson, J. R. (ed.) *Cognitive Skills and Their Acquisition* Hillside, NJ: Lawrence Erlbaum Associates, 111–40

Short, M. 1996 *Exploring the Language of Poems, Plays and Prose* Harlow: Longman

Sinclair, J., and Coulthard, M. 1975 *Towards an Analysis of Discourse* Oxford: Oxford University Press

Sinclair, J. M., and Renouf, A. 1988 'A lexical syllabus for language learning'. In Carter, R., and McCarthy, M. (eds) *Vocabulary and Language Teaching* Harlow: Longman, 141–60

Skehan, P. 1989 *Individual Differences in Second-Language Learning* London: Edward Arnold

Skehan, P. 1998 *A Cognitive Approach to Language Learning* Oxford: Oxford University Press

Skehan, P. 2002 'Theorising and updating aptitude'. In Robinson, P. (ed.) *Individual Differences and Instructed Language Learning* Amsterdam: Benjamins, 69–93

Skehan, P., and Foster, P. 1997 'Task type and task processing conditions as influences on foreign language performance' *Language Teaching Research* 1: 185–211

Skinner, B. F. 1957 *Verbal Behaviour* New York: Appleton Crofts

Smith, D. M. 1972 'Some implications for the social status of pidgin languages'. In Smith, D. M., and Shuy, R. W. (ed.) *Sociolinguistics in Cross-Cultural Analysis* Washington, DC: Georgetown University Press

Smith, N., and Tsimpli, I.-M. 1995 *The Mind of a Savant* Oxford: Blackwell Publishers

Smith, N., Tsimpli, I.-M., and Ouhalla, J. 1993 'Learning the impossible: the acquisition of possible and impossible languages by a polyglot *savant*' *Lingua* 91: 279–347

Snow, C. E. 1972 'Mothers' speech to children learning language' *Child Development* 43: 549–65

Snow, C. E., and Ferguson, C. A. (eds) 1977 *Talking to Children: Language Input and Acquisition* Cambridge: Cambridge University Press

Sparks, R. L., and Ganschow, L. 2001 'Aptitude for learning a foreign language' *Annual Review of Applied Linguistics* 21: 90–111

Spolsky, B. 1969 'Attitudinal aspects of second language learning' *Language Learning* 19: 271–85

Spolsky, B. 1989 *Conditions for Second Language Learning* Oxford: Oxford University Press

Spolsky, B., Green, J. B., and Read, J. 1974 'A model for the description, analysis and perhaps evaluation of bilingual education' *Navajo Reading Study Progress Report No. 23* Albuquerque, NM: University of New Mexico

Sridhar, S. N. 1996 'Towards a syntax of South Asian English: defining the lectal range'. In Baumgardner, R. J. (ed.) *South Asian English* Chicago: University of Illinois Press, 55–69

Stern, H. H. 1975 'What can we learn from the good language learner?' *Canadian Modern Language Review* 31: 304–18

Stern, H. H. 1983 *Fundamental Concepts of Language Teaching* Oxford: Oxford University Press

Stevick, E. 1976 *Memory, Meaning and Method* Rowley, MA: Newbury House

Stevick, E. 1989 *Success with Foreign Languages* New York: Prentice Hall

Strevens, P. 1971 'Alternatives to daffodils'. In *Science and Technology in a Second Language* CILT Reports and Papers 7 London: Centre for Information on Language Teaching and Research

Sturtridge, G. 1981 'Role-play and simulations'. In Johnson, K., and Morrow, K. (eds) *Communication in the Classroom* Harlow: Longman, 126–30

Swain, M. 1995 'Three functions of output in second language learning'. In Cook, G., and Seidlhofer, B. (eds) *Principle and Practice in Applied Linguistics* Oxford: Oxford University Press, 125–44

Swales, J. 1990 *Genre Analysis* Cambridge: Cambridge University Press

Swan, M. 1994 'Design criteria for pedagogic language rules'. In Bygate, M., Tonkyn, A., and Williams, E. (eds) *Grammar and the Language Teacher* London: Prentice Hall, 45–55

Swan, M. 2005a *Grammar* Oxford: Oxford University Press

Swan, M. 2005b *Practical English Usage* Oxford: Oxford University Press

Swan, M., and Walter, C. 1990 *The New Cambridge English Course Student's Book 2* Cambridge: Cambridge University Press

Swift, S. 'Giving and checking instructions' An ELT Notebook blog. Available at http://eltnotebook.blogspot.co.uk/2006/11/giving-and-checking-instructions.html, accessed on 3 October 2016

Tarone, E. 1977 'Conscious communication strategies in interlanguage'. In Brown, H. D., Yorio, C. A., and Crymes, R. C. (eds) *On TESOL '77* Washington, DC: TESOL

Taylor, B. P. 1975 'The use of overgeneralization and transfer learning strategies by elementary and intermediate students of ESL' *Language Learning* 25: 73–107

Taylor, P. H. 1970 *How Teachers Plan Their Courses* Slough: NFER

Thomas, J. 1983 'Cross-cultural pragmatic failure' *Applied Linguistics* 4/2: 91–111

Thornbury, S. 1997a *About Language: Tasks for Teachers of English* Cambridge: Cambridge University Press

Thornbury, S. 1997b 'Reformulation and reconstruction: tasks that promote "noticing"' *ELT Journal* 51/4: 326–35

Thornbury, S. 2000 'A Dogma for EFL'. Available at http://nebula.wsimg.com/fa3dc7052 1483b645f4b932209f9db17?AccessKeyId=186A535D1BA4FC995A73&disposition =0&alloworigin=1, accessed on 5 October 2016

Trim, J. L. M., Richterich, R., van Ek, J. A., and Wilkins, D. A. 1980 *Systems Development in Adult Language Learning* Oxford: Pergamon Institute of English

Tyler, R. W. 1950 *Basic Principles of Curriculum and Instruction* Chicago: Chicago University Press

Underhill, N. 1987 *Testing Spoken Language: A Handbook of Oral Testing Techniques* Cambridge: Cambridge University Press

Ur, P. 1981 *Discussions that Work* Cambridge: Cambridge University Press

Ur, P. 1988 *Grammar Practice Activities* Cambridge: Cambridge University Press

Ur, P. 1996 *A Course in Language Teaching* Cambridge: Cambridge University Press

Ur, P., and Wright, A. 1992 *Five Minute Activities* Cambridge: Cambridge University Press

Vigil, N. A., and Oller, J. W. 1976 'Rule fossilization: a tentative model' *Language Learning* 26/2: 281–95

Wardhaugh, R. 1970 'The contrastive analysis hypothesis' *TESOL Quarterly* 4: 123–30

Watcyn-Jones, P. 1981 *Pair Work: Activities for Effective Communication* Harmondsworth: Penguin

Waters, M., and Waters, A. 1995 *Study Tasks in English* Cambridge: Cambridge University Press

Weir, C. J. 1990 *Communicative Language Testing* London: Prentice Hall

Weir, C. J. 1995 *Understanding and Developing Language Tests* New York: Phoenix ELT

Weir, R. H. 1962 *Language in the Crib* The Hague: Mouton

Wertheimer, M. 1945 *Productive Thinking* New York: Harper and Row

Wesche, M. B., and Skehan, P. 2002 'Communicative, task-based, and content-based language instruction'. In Kaplan, R. B. (ed.) *Oxford Handbook of Applied Linguistics* Oxford: Oxford University Press, 207–28

West, C. 1999 *Listen Here! Intermediate Listening Activities* Jersey: Georgian Press

White, L. 1991 'Adverb placement in second language acquisition: some effects of positive and negative evidence in the classroom' *Second Language Research* 7: 133–61

White, R. V. 1979 *Functional English* London: Nelson

White, R. V. 1988 *The ELT Curriculum* Oxford: Basil Blackwell

White, R. V., and Arndt, V. 1991 *Process Writing* Harlow: Longman

Widdowson, H. G. 1972 'The teaching of English as communication' *English Language Teaching Journal* 27/1: 15–19

Widdowson, H. G. 1980 'Models and fictions' *Applied Linguistics* 1/2: 165–70

Widdowson, H. G. 1987 'The roles of teacher and learner' *ELT Journal* 41/2: 83–8

Widdowson, H. G. 1996 *Linguistics* Oxford: Oxford University Press

Widdowson, H. G. 2003 'English as an international language'. In Widdowson, H. G. *Defining Issues in English Language Teaching* Oxford: Oxford University Press, 45–59

Widin, J. 2010 *Illegitimate Practices: Global English Language Education* Clevedon, Avon: Multilingual Matters

Wilkins, D. A. 1972 *Linguistics in Language Teaching* London: Edward Arnold

Wilkins, D. A. 1973 'An investigation into the linguistic and situational common core in a unit/credit system'. In Trim, J. L. M., Richterich, R., van Ek, J. A., and Wilkins, D. A. *Systems Development in Adult Language Learning* Strasbourg: Council of Europe, 129–43

Williams, E. 1998 'Teaching reading'. In Johnson, K., and Johnson, H. (eds) *Encyclopedic Dictionary of Applied Linguistics* Oxford: Blackwell Publishers, 330–5

Willis, J. 1996 *A Framework for Task-based Learning* Harlow: Longman

Windeatt, S., Hardisty, D., and Eastment, D. 2000 *The Internet* Oxford: Oxford University Press

Witkin, H. A., Dyk., R., Faterson, H. F., Goodenough, D. R., and Karp, S. A. 1962 *Psychological Differentiation* New York: Wiley

Woodward, T. 2001 *Planning Lessons and Courses* Cambridge: Cambridge University Press

Wragg, E. C. 1981 *Class Management and Control* London: Macmillan Education

Wright, S. 2004 *Language Policy and Language Planning: From Nationalism to Globalisation* Basingstoke: Palgrave Macmillan

Yinger, R. J. 1977 'A study of teacher planning: description and theory development using ethnographic and information processing methods'. Unpublished doctoral dissertation, Michigan State University

Yoko, I. 2003 'Word recognition exercises: an application of a bottom-up reading model in ELT' *The Language Teacher*, February. Available at http://jalt-publications.org/old_tlt/articles/2003/02/ichiyama, accessed on 3 October 2016

Zahorik, J. A. 1975 'Teachers' planning models' *Educational Leadership* 33: 134–9

Index